Acknowledgements

Professional

This book has taken more than twenty years of author preparation and three years to write. Besides my immediate family, many people have influenced and encouraged its writing along the way.

Thanks to the many Bible scholars, theologians, and teachers, some who are well-known and some who are not, who have contributed to the development of this work. I thank you for believing in this project enough to share your biblical insight and permissions to reprint your material.

Your willingness to share is a testament to the common understanding among Christians, despite our different church affiliations. This document ultimately highlights the areas of our Christian unity!

Thanks to all my original Booksurge points of contact for the first edition and to Citi of Books Publishing company for your help in producing a new edition. You all have truly been a Godsend.

Author, Jennifer B. Price

Illustrations

❐ **World Missions Collection Clip Art Graphics**
Thanks to the World Missions Collection Clip Art Graphics for granting me permission to use clip art from their Volume 1 and Volume 2 collections and providing me the high-quality digital images to use in this work.

- **Page #'s**: 1-6, 1-11, 1-15, 1-23, 1-28, 2-11, 2-15, 2-24, 3-3, 5-24, 6-4, 6-13, 6-25, 7-9, J_Tab-3, , 10-5, 12-16

❐ **The Bible in Pictures**
Thanks to the Administrator of the creationism.org website for making the Bible in Pictures and Dore' Bible Illustrations woodcut drawings available to the public, and for providing high quality digital images for use in this work.

- **Page #'s**: 9-24, 10-7, 11-16, 12-23, 12-24

❐ **Public Domain Clip Art–Breadsite.org**

- **Page #'s:** 7-19, 7-22

Contents

FOREWORD BY DR. JEFFREY L. SEIF

KNOW HIS WORD BIBLE STUDY

1ST QUARTER

Inductive Chronological Bible Study
for Youth and Adults

Old Testament:
Genesis, Job, Exodus, Leviticus, Numbers,
Deuteronomy and Half of Joshua

JENNIFER B. PRICE

CITIOFBOOKS, INC.
3736 Eubank NE Suite A1
Albuquerque, NM 87111-3579
www.citiofbooks.com
Hotline: 1 (877) 389-2759
Fax: 1 (505) 930-7244

Ordering Information:

Quantity sales. Special discounts are available on quantity purchases by corporations, associations, and others. For details, contact the publisher at the address above.

Printed in the United States of America.

ISBN-13:	Softcover	979-8-89391-024-7
	eBook	979-8-89391-025-4

Library of Congress Control Number: 2024906332

The author conceived the idea for producing a workbook for youth study on the Word of God in 1999. The four-book manuscript was begun in 2003. The completed first draft was produced Dec. 2005 to Dec. 2006, adding the dimension of formatting the study as an all-in-one teacher and student manual. After extensive editing, the first edition publication began in 2008 and was completed in 2012. This 2024 publication is a second edition.

Acknowledgements

Family

I thank my husband, Robert,

and our four children—Chris, Joe, Candi and Alex—

for their patience and understanding during the writing

of this book. My achievements are yours, too!

Your loving wife and mother,

Jennifer

Special thanks to my mother Lillian and my sister Janis who have supported me in all my adventures. Thank you for your love and prayers.

Contents

Contents

Daily Lesson Study Pages

Appendices

Contents

Intro to Bible Books

Maps

Contents

Charts

Contents

Charts continued

Contents

Charts continued

Foreword

I came to know Jennifer Price when she studied under me at Grace School of Ministry, Houston, Texas. Immediately, she struck me as an energetic and highly engaged student. Her love for the Lord was immediately apparent, as was her seemingly boundless enthusiasm.

When she handed in projects, I noted how she applied her energetic spirit to the task, with the net result that her papers were full of information.

With these experiences behind me, I opened her draft of ***Now is the Time for God's Children to Know His Word.*** I wasn't just taken back by the sheer size of the work—sizable though it is. I was struck by her detail in the volume's content. The integration of charts and narrative guarantees that the text will live up to its title: "...Know[ing] His Word."

If you want your kids to know it, let Jennifer show it!

As is the case with biblical studies generally, readers may well find themselves at a place where they do not agree with everything. You will however agree that Jennifer Price has labored to help your kids know God's Word. She has done this with verve, with vitality and with a sense of purpose that is in high demand but short supply in the church today.

Knowing her as I do on this basis and others, I am pleased to commend her volume.

Dr. Jeffrey L. Seif—May 12, 2007

Dr. Seif is an alumnus of Moody Bible Institute; Trinity College; Southern Methodist University (Masters, Doctorate); Perkins School of Theology; and the Graduate Theological Foundation.

He has appeared on the 700 Club, has over 100 TV appearances on subjects dealing with the Jewish origin of the Christian faith, and has written several books and Bible study curriculums detailing Jewish-Christian Studies.

For seventeen years, Dr. Seif served as professor of Bible and Ministry, as well as chair of the Language, Extension Studies, and Jewish Studies Departments at Christ for the Nations Institute (Dallas, Texas).

Dr. Jeffrey Seif succeeded Zola at the teaching helm of Zola Levitt Ministries, assuming duties as the ministry's principal spokesperson.

Commendation: Biblical Studies

I met Jennifer Price several years ago when she presented her Bible Study book on the Holy Spirit in a workshop. She is a passionate writer and prolific lecturer who uses time wisely and yet shares a wealth of information within a specific time limit.

In her current four-book curriculum, ***Know His Word Bible Study***, readers will become more knowledgeable in Biblical Studies. Each book is carefully designed in quarters to be read in 52 weeks.

The way the curriculum is organized, every age group can benefit from this work. ***Know His Word Bible Study*** can be used by families, Sunday Schools, leaders of Biblical Studies, Bible Institutes, colleges, pastors, missionaries, and members from the youngest to mature adult.

I highly recommend Jennifer's works. I also recommend her as an excellent lecturer who leaves her audience in awe and wonderment as to how she has the time to study, research and write so thoroughly being a wife and mother of four.

In my seventy years in ministry, from all my studies I find ***Know His Word Bible Study*** to be one-of-a-kind. I do believe Jennifer's proficiency in sharing the Word will prepare others for leadership in ministry.

If you try her books, you will like them!

Dr. Earline O. Allen, D. Min.—Nov. 19, 2012

Dr. Allen is an alumnus of Southern Bible Seminary, Birmingham, AL (Bachelor of the Bible and Bachelor of Theology); Mid-America Bible College, Oklahoma City, OK (B.S. in Christian Education); Mt. Hope Bible College, Houston, TX (Master of Religious Education); Houston Graduate School of Theology, Houston, TX (Doctor of Ministry).

Dr. Allen was the Founder and Dean of Greater Emmanuel Bible Institute (Houston, TX). For over 35 years she led the training of ministry students in receiving Evangelical Training Association (ETA) certifications and in preparatory coursework for Ministerial and Missionary licensing.

She was a Certified Teacher, Lecturer, Licensed Missionary; Recipient of outstanding Leadership in Ministry Award; Recorded Vocalist; COGIC Scholar; and former COGIC Dean-Convention Workshop, Member of Licensing and Ordination Board, and of Business & Professional Women.

Author of several books including: The Wheat, the Rope, and the Rain; The History of the Church of God in Christ in Texas; Christian songbooks with over 450 songs from the early 1900s.

In December 2014, Dr. Earline Opal Allen went home to be with the Lord.

Author's Introduction

Author's Introduction

Bible Study Purpose

Know His Word Bible Study is the second in a series of three Bible study workbooks designed for youth and adults. The purpose of these Bible studies is to facilitate students in gaining a foundational understanding of God's Holy Spirit, Word, and the Power in the Blood of Jesus. Such knowledge can help believers experience victorious, abundant living on earth.

First John 5:8 identifies three things that bear witness to Jesus being the Son of God in the earth. This author believes these three things are worthy of focused study and comprehension by youth, as well as adults.

> *And there are three that bear witness in earth, the spirit, and the water and the blood: and these three agree in one.*
>
> *[Ephesians 5:26 explains "water" symbolizes the Word of God.]*

- ❐ The first Bible study written by the author—***Know His Spirit Bible Study*** *[original title–Now is the Time for God's Children to Know His Holy Spirit]*—helps youth and adults learn what being filled with God's Holy Spirit means. It highlights the purpose, promises and spiritual power accessible to believers.

- ❐ The second Bible study—***Know His Word Bible Study*** *[original title Now is the Time for God's Children to Know His Word]*—is a set of four workbooks divided into 1st, 2nd, 3rd, and 4th quarter sections, designed to help youth and adults in their study of the entire Word of God. By using the King James Bible, the easy-to-understand New Living Translation One Year Chronological Bible, and using the scripture insight provided in this Bible study curriculum, the student will gain a solid foundation in understanding God's Word, which they should build on the rest of their lives.

- ❐ The third Bible study—***Know His Blood Bible Study***—provides insight on the powerful benefits available for victorious living through understanding the spiritual power in Jesus' blood.

For more information, go to www.knowbiblestudies.com.

Author's Introduction

Rationale for Bible Study Workbooks Written with Youth in Mind

The Bible clearly warns that the activities on earth will continue to increase in ungodliness as we hurry to the end of this present age. In these latter days of the earth, Christian parents will be challenged in their ability to raise Godly children who can withstand satan's deceitful tactics (1 Timothy 4:1–16 and 2 Timothy 3:1–7).

The Good News of the Gospel is that God, through Jesus Christ, has poured out His spirit for the benefit of all flesh in these latter days. Youth can be equipped with everything they need to live righteous in an ungodly world, stand firm in Christian faith in perilous times, and be mighty witnesses for Christ, helping to bring in God's last days' harvest of souls (Acts 1:8; 2:17–21).

The author believes this ***Know His Word Bible Study*** series is one of the tools parents can use to help their youth become "strong in the Lord and the power of his might," as they gain an understanding of the deeper things in God's Word but on their level (Ephesians 6:10–18).

Read the "Youth Bible Reading Age Guidance."

Disclaimer on What You Will Know at the End of this Study

God Wants YOU to Understand His Word, but...

- ❒ **You can NEVER understand God's Word in a "final" sense.** This is because our infinite God is speaking to finite humankind through His Word. God has an eternal view of things that is bigger than anything man can understand fully in our temporary bodies with our limited minds.
- ❒ **Even when your HEAD does not understand what you read in the Bible, your SPIRIT will still be blessed by reading it.** When you pray and ask God to open up your understanding as you read, then God's Word, which is alive, will perform a sanctifying process in your spirit and soul. This will happen when you read from a standpoint of trusting in God as your loving Father, Savior and Helper.
- ❒ **Settle in your mind that you will spend a lifetime of study in God's Word, so your participation in this study is simply a beginning.** Through this study you can establish a good foundational understanding of God's whole Word. But you will need to build upon what you learn at the end of this study, through a lifetime study of God's amazing Word.

Youth Bible Reading Age Guidance

The Holy Bible contains content that addresses all aspects of human behavior, which could be viewed as including the good, the bad, and the ugly. **As a result, parents/guardians need to make the final decision on what age is appropriate for their youth to read the entire Bible.**

The author of ***Know His Word Bible Study*** highly recommends that regardless of the youth participant's age, **parents/guardians should read along with their youth, or at a minimum engage in regular conversations with their reader. This is to provide clarification and guidance as needed.**

The movie industry created a rating system for movie content. The rating system provides parents/guardians with some advance understanding of the type of content the movie contains. This facilitates parents/guardians in deciding if a movie is appropriate for their youth to view, with or without them being present.

Some movies also provide brief word descriptors to categorize content that is rated higher than the "G" rating which is deemed suitable for general audiences. Examples of these descriptors are "strong violence, language, sexual content, nudity, disturbing material."

This author asked a few parents how they would rate the overall Bible content if using the movie industry rating system. While it was difficult for anyone to agree on a rating for the entire Bible, the general feedback was that they would rate some content as being G (for general audiences), some content PG (needing parental guidance), some content PG-13 (inappropriate for children under 13), and a few passages as being R (anyone under 17 requires a parent or adult guardian).

With the above in mind, herein is a list of some passages that parents and guardians should be aware of, which will help them decide the age their youth should read the entire Bible. Alternately, parents/guardians could have their youth skip reading these passages until they are older, or they could engage in a discussion before the youth does the reading to prepare their hearts and minds. This will also ensure that the takeaway messages the parents want their youth to learn are communicated.

Youth Bible Reading Age Guidance

Content for Parent/Guardian Youth Bible Reading Age Assessment

While the Bible provides God's guidance on what is righteous behavior, it also records wrong behavior performed even by those who are endeavoring to live for Him. Then God progressively reveals corrective action. If youth do not understand this, they may misinterpret the actions of wrong behavior as being approved by God, simply because it is written in the Bible. **This is why parent/guardian guidance is needed for youth readers, and ideally, they should read along with them.**

The below passages are identified because of how clear the Bible content is written on those difficult topics, which may cause youth to need assistance in understanding what they should learn from them. **This list may not be exhaustive from the viewpoint of every parent, but these are the ones the author feels most significant to highlight.**

Note: Some Bible versions use the most discrete and poetic expressions possible for difficult topics. Two such Bible examples are the King James Version (KJV) and Tree of Life Version (TLV)[1].

This second edition of *Know His Word Bible Study* has also been updated to use more discrete expressions. This allows parents/guardians to have the greatest latitude in discussing delicate topics with their youth.

Bible Passage	Page Number	Content Descriptor
Know His Word Bible Study–1st Quarter		
Genesis 19:4-8	1-22, 1-23, 1-25	sexual
Genesis 19:30-38	1-22, 1-23, 1-25	sexual
Know His Word Bible Study–2nd Quarter		
Judges 4:21	13-18	strong violence
Judges 19:22-30	14-14	disturbing material
Song of Solomon/Songs	23-6 to 23-9	sexual
Know His Word Bible Study–3rd Quarter		
Lamentations 2:20-21	35-6	disturbing material
Lamentations 5:11	35-6	disturbing material
Know His Word Bible Study–4th Quarter		
Revelation 17:4-6	52b-30, 52b-31	disturbing material

[1]Appendix C

Challenges in Understanding the Bible[2]

The Bible is God's Word to humankind on what He wants us to know about Him (who created us), about having the right relationship with Him, and about living a great life according to His wisdom and design plans.

- The Bible was written over a 1,600-year period with over 40 writers, who were from different locations with different languages and cultures. But God is the one, true author, who watched over its continuity of thought. God has ensured the Bible says what He wants it to say (2 Timothy 3:16).

There are challenges to the modern understanding of the Bible as God intended. These challenges are described in two books the author highly recommends for further reading to gain a thorough understanding of them[2]:

- *How Can I Understand the Bible?* by Discovery House Publishers
- *Interpreting the Scriptures: A Textbook on How to Interpret the Bible*, by Kevin J. Conner and Ken Malmin

Challenges to Understanding the Bible include:

- **Language challenge** (Bible written in three languages that no longer exist)
- **Cultural challenge** (Way of life in Bible times different than modern)
- **Geographical challenge** (Bible lands and locations different than modern)
- **Historical challenge** (Some historical events difficult to verify today)
- **Understanding the Bible Text in Proper Context challenge**
    - **Context of Immediate Setting** (original meaning when written)
    - **Context of Plain and Normal Meaning of Words**
      Most wording in the Bible is not symbolic of "deeper" thoughts, but it means just what it says.
    - **Context of the Bible as a Whole**
        - **Context of a Verse Is the Passage**
          Must read sentences before and after a verse that logically go along with the verse to properly understand the verse's meaning. Do not interpret one verse alone.
        - **Context of the Passage Is the Book**
          Must read with an understanding of the Bible book writer's overall purpose for writing.

[2]Appendix C

Challenges in Understanding the Bible[2]

- **Context of the Book Is the Testament**
  Must read with the understanding:
    - Old Testament focuses on ethnic groups of Israel and Gentiles, and God's requirement for man to keep His Law given to Israel through the prophet Moses—"God's Law."
    - New Testament focuses on the Church and God's provision for humankind's salvation through faith in God's Son Jesus Christ—"God's Grace."
- **Context of the Testament Is the Whole Bible**
  The 39 books of the Old Testament and 27 books of New Testament are all chapters in one unified book that progressively expresses God's unified thought to man.

- **Context of Foundational Truths of Sound Doctrine**
    - **Law and Grace**
      Old Testament Law versus New Testament Grace
    - **Justification and Sanctification**
        - Justification is when God declares as righteous all who trust in His Son Jesus Christ for their salvation.
        - Sanctification refers to God's progressive work to transform his children's lives into the right reflection of his character (holiness). This takes a person's lifetime.
    - **Jews, Gentiles and the Church** (1 Corinthians 10:32)
        - **God chose the Jews (Israel)**
            - These are the biological descendants of Abraham, Isaac, and Jacob whom God chose to be in a special covenant relationship with him. They were chosen to be blessed by God and to be a blessing to all nations of the earth.
            - Through Israel, the world received the Law of Moses, the Prophets and Oracles of God, and the Messiah, who is Jesus Christ, the Son of God and Savior of the world.

[2]Appendix C

- **God identifies the Gentiles.**
  - These are people of all nations of the earth who are not Jews (Israelites) biologically.
  - When referred to in a spiritual sense (meaning not biologically), Gentiles are not in covenant relationship with God.
- **God chose the Church.**
  - These are people from all nations of the earth who are in special covenant relationship with God by their faith in Jesus Christ (Jews and Gentiles).
  - Church people are "called out" from the world by their own profession of faith in Christ to live as God's righteous children on earth.
  - In a spiritual sense, the Church represents the "true Israel" of God.

- **Two Phases of Jesus Christ's Return**
  The Bible speaks of Jesus Christ (Israel's Messiah) returning to earth. However, His return will occur in two phases. Often the scriptures speak of these two phases in the same passages. It takes careful reading of the text to understand which phase is being described.
  - **Phase 1 (Rapture of the Church)**
    Jesus Christ returns for the Church, who is caught up to meet Him in the air (known as "the rapture"). In this phase, Jesus comes in the clouds, but does not return to live and rule on the earth. According to the scriptures, this phase could occur any time (1 Thessalonians 4:16–17).
  - **Phase 2 (Second Coming of Christ)**
    Jesus Christ returns to live and rule on the earth. He is accompanied by the resurrected Church and the holy angels. This "second coming" of Jesus Christ to the earth occurs at the end of a great period of apocalyptic events on the earth (Revelation 19:11–21 through 20:1–6).

[2]Appendix C

Help with Challenges in Understanding the Bible

Know His Word Bible Study helps with the challenges of understanding the Bible in several ways, such as the language and context challenges.

Know His Word Bible Study Helps with the Language Challenge

- To address the language challenge perfectly, Bible readers would need to study the Bible in its original languages. However, these ancient languages are not readily accessible and would take many years and diligent scholarly pursuit to learn and understand.
- Outside of doing such, this study recommends the reader use a version of the Bible that has language they can read and understand. For example, the New Living Translation (NLT) One Year Chronological Bible is easy to read and understand by youth as well as adults.
- Please know that the author of *Know His Word Bible Study* sometimes includes the King James Version (KJV) of a passage in the daily study lessons. This is primarily due to the author's familiarity with the King James Version of a passage and the value she places on that version of the scriptures. The reader can then view the passage in both the NLT and KJV as a part of their study process.

Know His Word Bible Study Helps with the Context Challenge

- To address the context challenge, Bible readers will benefit the most from studying the entire Bible in the order events occurred. This is the best way to understand why and to whom the text was written.
- *Know His Word Bible Study* along with a Study Bible helps with the Context Challenge. This is because this Bible Study contains charts, maps, and resource material to help with understanding context. A good study Bible, such as the New Living Translation One-Year Chronological Bible, also contains helpful study notes, and at the same time presents the text in the order events occurred as best understood by those translators. It also includes notes that give insight on the differences in the understanding of Bible scholars on the order of events.
- By reading through the Bible, you will also discover the foundational truths of sound doctrine, but this process is rough until you finish the entire Bible. Know His Word Bible Study helps this process with its daily study lessons that highlight many truths as they unfold before your eyes.

Help with Challenges in Understanding the Bible

Know His Word Bible Study Helps with Cultural, Geographical and Historical Challenges

- *Know His Word Bible Study* includes introductions to Bible books and many helpful study notes to educate the reader on the background of the text, background on the writer, and background on geographical locations. Maps and helpful pictures are also included to help the reader visualize the Bible lands and cultures.
- Most of all, as you read through the Bible from beginning to end in time-ordered sequence, you will gain an understanding of it in the proper context and setting. This type of study will give you a solid foundation for building up your future and continued study of Bible passages.

Know His Word Bible Study Helps with Understanding the Bible so Readers Can Apply Its Wisdom to Their Everyday Lives

The practical goal of studying the Bible is to understand it well enough to apply its wisdom for the benefit of our everyday lives. This is best done by the Bible student who has read the entire Bible well enough to get a solid foundation of understanding all it has to offer.

Optimally, the author recommends students read through the Bible at least three times close together, such as in a three-to-six-year period.

- 1st Reading — To learn what is in the Bible.
- 2nd Reading — To become more comfortable with what is in the Bible.
- 3rd Reading — To study the Bible, with the goal of understanding it from an overall view of its content.

Youth Should Read Bible History along with World History

For youth who are reading through the Bible, they should time their second or third reading to occur around the time the subject of world history is taught to them in school.

This is because events in the Bible reflect real events in history, which are not adequately understood unless Bible history is factored into the learning of world history. These are not two different histories, but simply two different views of the same history.

After the three readings, youth will be specially blessed in all their future Bible readings, which will be greatly benefited by their insight on God's movement in history past, current events and His future plans.

Principle #1:

God wants His children to read and understand His Holy Word the right way, so He has provided help for us to do so.

The help comes...

- Directly from God's Holy Spirit (John 16:7–13; 1 Corinthian 2:9–16; 1 John 2:20, 27).
- From Spirit-filled teachers who have been specially gifted by God to teach His Word (Ephesians 4:11–16; 1 Corinthian 12:28).

The author has allowed the Holy Spirit to guide her in scripture interpretations and in the use of other Spirit-filled teachers' works for interpretative assistance for this particular work. You, the reader, are also encouraged to pray and ask the Holy Spirit to guide you in understanding and confirming God's truths for yourself.

Principle #2:

The literal method of interpreting the Scriptures has been used by the Know His Word author and is encouraged for use by students (John 8:31–32; Deuteronomy 30:11–14; Romans 10:6–8). The below explanation of this method is from the book *Interpreting the Scriptures: A Textbook on How to Interpret the Bible* by Kevin J. Conner and Ken Malmin, p.15–16 (excerpt reprinted by permission):

> ***Definition: The literal method assumes that the words of Scripture in their plain evident meaning are reliable; that God intended His revelation to be understood by all who believe; that the words of Scripture communicate what God wants man to know; and that God based the communication of truth on the regular laws governing communication, thereby intending for it to be interpreted by those same laws. This is not to deny the Holy Spirit's involvement in both the production and the interpretation of the Bible.***
>
> - ***The literal sense does not exclude the figurative.***
>   *The figurative meaning of words is not opposed to the literal sense. This is because figurative language is a part of normal communication; it is also encompassed by the literal system of interpretation. Thus, the literal includes the figurative.*
> - ***The literal method does not exclude the spiritual meaning.***
>   *The Bible is a spiritual book conveying spiritual truth and therefore must be spiritually interpreted. This can be done by accepting as sufficient the illuminated literal meaning of the words.*

[3]Appendix C

- ***The literal interpretation does not exclude application.***
  The task of literal interpretation is first to discern the meaning of God's Word, and then, upon that basis, to apply it. A general rule of the literal method is: "There is one interpretation, but many applications."

- ***The literal method does not exclude depth of meaning.***
  In that God is the virtual Author of Scripture, some truths therein are patent, outward, and certain figures of speech, such as types, symbols, and allegories, do have hidden meaning. However, this meaning is solidly based on the earthly sense of the words and necessitates that interpretation remain within the proper boundaries of truths plainly revealed in God's Word.

Principle #3:

Scripture must be compared with other scripture in order to get *"a more complete and accurate picture"* **of God's thoughts and plans on a topic and in order to properly interpret Biblical prophecy** (Isaiah 28:9–10; 2 Peter 1:20).

As the "Virtual Author" of the Bible, God did not reveal His whole counsel on any topic to just one of the Biblical writers. Therefore, the Bible interpreter must compare Scripture with Scripture.

Principle #4:

Interpret in light of possible time Intervals (Examples: Isaiah 61:1–3 with Luke 4:17–21; Joel 2:28–32 with Acts 2:16–21 and with Matthew 24:29 and Revelation 8:12).

Below is an excerpt from Dr. Paul Benware's book *Understanding End Times Prophecy—A Comprehensive Approach*," p. 29–30.

> *When the prophets proclaimed God's message, they frequently were unaware that there was going to be an interval of time between prophetic fulfillments. When a prophet placed several events side by side in his message, they did not necessarily mean that fulfillment would occur at the same time or that one fulfillment would immediately follow the other.*

References[2]:

1. *Interpreting the Scriptures: A Textbook on How to Interpret the Bible,* by K. Conner and K. Malmin; City Bible Publishing; 1983; p. 15–16.
2. *Understanding End Times Prophecy–A Comprehensive Approach,* by Paul N. Benware; Moody Publishers; 2006; Chapter 1, p. 21–33.

[3]Appendix C

Author's Notes

Family Bible Study Tips: Author's Note

The Most Fun Way to Read through the Bible Is as a Family!

The most fun way to read through the Bible is for the whole family to do it together. In the year 2003, the Holy Spirit led me to invite my whole family to do this very thing. Participants included my immediate family (elementary school, middle school, high school, college and two adults), along with my mother and sister.

What a challenging but enjoyable year it was. The challenge was centered on the use of a one-year chronological scripture listing I received in an email from a friend. With the list in hand, some of us used the King James Version, while some used the New International Version of the Bible. In addition, everyone was on their own in finding Bible helps to understand the readings and the chronological sequence.

The enjoyment came from having a unique conversation piece all year long. As we read through the Bible together, we chose to use what we read to handle tough life issues and to engage in biblical debates.

At the year's end, none of us could remember every line and every word of what we read, but our spirits were greatly enriched because of this family adventure in reading through the Bible.

In 2004, I read the New Living Translation One-Year Chronological Bible. Its chronological sequence closely followed what I agreed with from my own research the previous year when using the email listing of scriptures. I then purchased this Bible for my family to read together, which some completed in 2005.

Family Bible Study Tips

When reading as a family, what worked best for us was allowing each person to read on their own and then coming together for a combined discussion on the readings. You may want to try this also. If a child is young, someone may need to read to them. We were amazed at how the Holy Spirit helped our discussions.

Know His Word Bible Study was written because of what I learned would be helpful for Bible readers to gain a good foundation of understanding what they read. It will work for individual, family, or Church group studies.

Individual Reading Tips

For the individual reader, try the following to get started:

- **Morning Reading:** Set aside 15 to 20 minutes in the morning to read the daily Bible reading assignments. Read before you begin with the day's activities.
- **Night Reading:** Set aside 15 to 20 minutes before going to bed to review the daily study lessons in this Bible Study. This will serve as a review and reinforcement of key points from each day's Bible reading.

Tips for Teaching Youth to Read, Study and Apply the Bible (God's Word) to Their Everyday Lives

Helpful Tips for Parents

I. Bible Reading Tips (Personal Reading / Study Time) 2 Tim. 3:15–16

1. Youth use a Bible version with language they can understand, and King James Version (KJV)
2. Help youth identify consistent time to read/study the Bible.
3. Encourage use of Bible study helps for inductive study on youth level.

II. Bible Study Tips (Parent/Teacher Help Youth to Understand) Deut. 6:6–7; Isaiah 54:13

1. Youth need a Teacher:
   - Holy Spirit has a role (Rom. 8:14)
   - Parent has a role (Prov. 6:20–22)
   - Teacher has a role (Eph. 4:11–15)
2. Ask your youth what stood out to them from the reading.
3. Make Bible study a part of your everyday conversation, not just some laborious task (e.g., while in the car, at the bus-stop, watching movie, etc).

III. Bible Application Tips (Youth Living and Praying God's Word) Prov. 20:11, Mark 10:14–15

1. Allow youth to talk honestly about what they read in the Bible compared to what they see in life.
2. Allow Word of God to help change or confirm youth and family's daily actions.
3. Pray for youth to read and do God's Word; Teach them to pray God's Word.

Seven Helpful Tips for Students

1. Pray for Understanding
2. Read for Understanding
   - First, read the Bible Scriptures
   - Second, use study material
   - Read over the material:
     - Next: Write your own answers to questions
     - Last: Review answer sheets provided
3. Ask Parents for Help
   - They may not know answers immediately, but God will guide them.
4. Ask Spirit-filled Teachers for Help
   - Ask church or Christian school teachers.
   - Look over answers from study material.
5. Use Reading Club Methods
   - Discuss Bible Study with a partner who is reading same material as you
   - Treat like a Book Reading Club
6. Pray for the Holy Spirit to Guide You
   - In what you learn.
   - In how you respond to what you learn.
7. Pray God's Word Over Your Life
   - When you pray God's Word, your prayer allows God to transform your life to reflect His right living

Church School Bible Study Tips: Author's Note

With twenty years of dedicated study of God's Word behind me, spanning from my childhood to middle age years, I was led by the Holy Spirit into a three-year fresh reading of the entire Bible, but this time, the Spirit led me to read through the Bible chronologically, meaning in the order events occurred.

- 2003: My family read through the Bible together using a chronological listing I received in an email. For this I used the King James Bible.
- 2004: I read New Living Translation One-Year Chronological Bible.
- 2005: I attended a year-long Bible institute that was taught by a Jewish-Christian professor. Under his teaching, my understanding of Bible and Church history was broadened.
- 2006: With the backing of my home church's Pastor and Sunday School Superintendent, I led our youth Sunday school department in reading through the Bible. The Sunday school purchased forty-five NLT One-Year Chronological Bibles, which were distributed to middle school, high school and college students and their class teachers.

  For this pilot program, I provided the first draft of the daily study lessons each week (mid-Dec. 2005 to mid-Dec. 2006), which was patterned after all I had learned from three years of intensified study. The below tips are based on lessons learned from conducting this free **Know His Word Bible Study** program in 2006 at my home church.

Church School Bible Study Tips

- Meet with parents of potential youth participants to explain the reading plan (see Student Letter of Committed Participation).
- Get student commitment letters signed by parents and students.
- Students who participate in reading through the Bible need to attend the Church school sessions to discuss the lessons.
- Any tests given at the end of each quarter must be simple and leave students with a feeling of positive accomplishment.
- Hold a Parent-Teacher-Student Meeting in mid-session to encourage students to maintain their commitment. A "pep-rally!
- During the following times students may get weary in reading: weekends, spring break, summer breaks, vacations, holidays. If youth get behind it is difficult to make up the reading, so encourage them to keep reading during breaks.
- When youth establish a daily reading discipline, they will be more likely to continue reading their Bibles daily from this experience forward.

Student Letter of Committed Participation

Students who participate in reading through the Bible will be given an awesome opportunity, which includes an awesome responsibility.

❒ **Awesome Opportunity–Read through the entire Bible using an easy-to-understand language and format.**

- Student will be guided by Spirit-filled teacher and Know His Word Bible Study daily lessons, to bring out key points that help make readings relevant to student's everyday life, while also providing a sound foundational exposure to what is in the Bible.
- Student should also discover how individual reading time will strengthen their personal relationship with Bible author, God.

❒ **Awesome Responsibility–Students must commit to…**

- **Keep up with Bibles.** Most Church schools will only provide them once. If Bible is lost, student will have to purchase or use another.
- **Dedicate a minimum of fifteen minutes daily to Bible reading** and strive to dedicate additional minutes for study sheets.
- **Attend most, if not all, the Sunday school or designated group study sessions**.
- **With the permission of parents** (and doctor if you are under medical care), **prayerfully consider fasting from one food item during the study session**, as a reminder and commitment to God to love His word more than that food item. The food you give up is to be prayerfully determined / led by the Holy Spirit, who will help you to be successful in your study time of sacrifice.
- **If you get weary or behind, commit to talk with your parent, Sunday School Superintendent or Ministry leader and God about it, and endeavor to get back on track somehow.** Strive to complete your goal. You can do it, with God's help!
- **Talk with parents about your plans to commit to God. Ask if they will approve and then pray for you, encourage you, and help you achieve this goal.** Your Youth Ministry Leader will be a committed participant and your prayer partner. **Student and parent sign below if student can commit.**

I, ______________________, commit to read through the entire Bible on this date _____________. With my parent's permission I give up _____________ food item (e.g. chocolate, chips, soda).

Parent signature of approval and support: ____________________

How to Use This Bible Study

Know His Word Bible Study is designed to help students read and study the Bible in a 52-week curriculum. As a teacher and student manual all-in-one, this Bible Study can be completed by an individual student, in a family study setting, by a church study group, or in a school setting.

Use the following techniques to maximize study results

- **Review:** All introductory material preceding the lesson study pages at least once, to gain insight on Bible background and study approaches.
- **Read:** "Reading Assignment" **at top of the daily** lesson study pages. Optional: Use the One-Year Chronological New Living Translation (NLT) Bible for easy access to the daily reading assignment text.
- **Complete:** Daily lesson study pages.
- **Compare:** First develop your answers to lesson exercise questions, and then compare with those provided in the Appendix. Trust the Holy Spirit to teach you and guide you into all truth. This is not an exercise in "getting the answers right," but a study to get to know God's Word for yourself. Allow the Holy Spirit to speak to you as you read and think about the questions (John 14:26; 15:26–27, 16:13).
- **Enhance:** Use the King James Bible Authorized Version, a Bible dictionary, and review the additional study material provided for each lesson and/or week.

Bible Study Organization

Know His Word Bible Study is organized in fifty-two weeks (Week 1–Week 52) with seven lessons each week. It is further divided in four quarter books covering three months of study material as follows:

- 1st–3rd Quarter cover the Old Testament
- 4th Quarter covers the New Testament

Study pages include Bible book introductions, daily lesson study pages, maps, and additional reference material that explain the timeline of events and background for the people, places, and/or locations of events.

Daily lessons are presented in three sections, although on some days lesson content for some sections is combined.

- **I. Lesson Exercise**
  This section includes notes and questions from the daily reading.
- **II. Find Jesus in the Lesson**
  This section gives insight on how passages from the reading point to Jesus Christ. Christ is revealed in the Bible from beginning to end.
- **III. Closing Thoughts**
  This section offers additional insight into lessons on selected topics.

Bible Book Abbreviations

Timescale

This workbook uses BC and AD to keep with the long-time tradition of recognizing the birth of Jesus Christ as the central figure for defining time.

- **BC stands for "Before Christ."**
  - **BCE** stands for "Before the Common Era"; it covers the same time as BC.
- **AD** stands for the Latin phrase *Anno Domini*, which means "in the year of the Lord" or "since Christ was born." Time is calculated from Christ's birth.
  - **CE** stands for Common Era, which covers the same period as AD.

Scripture References

Most Scripture passages are taken from the Holy Bible, New Living Translation (NLT) version, unless otherwise stated. Scriptures marked KJV are taken from the Holy Bible, King James Version.

Bible Book Abbreviations below in parentheses are frequently used.

Old Testament					
Genesis	(Gen.)	Lamentations	(Lam.)	Romans	(Rom.)
Exodus	(Ex.)	Ezekiel	(Eze.)	1 Corinthians	(1 Cor.)
Leviticus	(Lev.)	Daniel	(Dan.)	2 Corinthians	(2 Cor.)
Numbers	(Num.)	Hosea	(Hos.)	Galatians	(Gal.)
Deuteronomy	(Deut.)	Joel		Ephesians	(Eph.)
Joshua	(Josh.)	Amos		Philippians	(Phil.)
Judges		Obadiah	(Obad.)	Colossians	(Col.)
Ruth		Jonah		1 Thessalonians	(1 Thess.)
1 Samuel	(1 Sam.)	Micah		2 Thessalonians	(2 Thess.)
2 Samuel	(2 Sam.)	Nahum		1 Timothy	(1 Tim.)
1 Kings		Habakkuk	(Hab.)	2 Timothy	(2 Tim.)
2 Kings		Zephaniah	(Zeph.)	Titus	
1 Chronicles	(1 Chron.)	Haggai	(Hag.)	Philemon	(Phil.)
2 Chronicles	(2 Chron.)	Zechariah	(Zech.)	Hebrews	(Heb.)
Ezra		Malachi	(Mal.)	James	
Job				1 Peter	(1 Pet.)
Psalms	(Ps.)	New Testament		2 Peter	(2 Pet.)
Proverbs	(Prov.)	Matthew	(Matt.)	1 John	
Ecclesiastes	(Eccl.)	Mark		2 John	
Song of Songs	(Song.)	Luke		3 John	
Isaiah	(Isa.)	John		Jude	
Jeremiah	(Jer.)	Acts		Revelation	(Rev.)

Calendar Notes: Jewish, Julian and Gregorian Calendars[4]

Jewish (Hebrew) Calendar Notes:

- God's Biblical calendar in Scripture has a 30-day month and a 360-day year. (cf. Gen. 1:14; 7:11, 24; 8:3, 4)
- The Jewish calendar is said to be calculated from the creation of the world. It is based on a twelve-month lunar calendar with an extra month occasionally added. The months are alternately thirty and twenty-nine days long. Seven times during every nineteen-year period, an extra twenty-nine-day month is inserted.
- The first month on the Jewish calendar is Nisan (derived from Babylonian name), the start of Passover. *The pre-exilic name for Nisan is Abib.
- The Jewish New Year (Rosh Hashanah) occurs in Tishri, the seventh month. This is when the year number is increased.

Julian Calendar Notes:

- Roman Julius Caesar instituted a calendar consisting of a solar year of twelve months with 365 days, and an extra day added every fourth year. Errors in previous calendars had become obvious as the seasons were significantly misaligned from the months. After accepting the suggestions of an astronomer, Julius Caesar ordered Romans to adopt his new calendar.

Gregorian Calendar Notes:

- Under the leadership of Pope Gregory XIII, the Gregorian calendar was designed to correct the errors of the Julian calendar. It is used by most of the world.

Comparison Table: Jewish and Gregorian Calendars

Jewish	Gregorian	Jewish	Gregorian
1. Nisan *(Abib*)*	Mar – Apr	7. Tishri *(Elthanim)*	Sep - Oct
2. Iyar *(Zif)*	Apr - May	8. Cheshvan *(Bul)*	Oct - Nov
3. Sivan	May - Jun	9. Kislev	Nov - Dec
4. Tammuz	Jun - Jul	10. Tevet	Dec - Jan
5. Av *(Ab)*	Jul - Aug	11. Shevat	Jan - Feb
6. Elul	Aug - Sep	12. Adar I *(leap years only)*	Feb – Mar (in leap years)
		12. Adar *(month 13 in leap years)*	Feb - Mar

[4]Appendix C:

Bible Facts

How We Got the Bible

Ten Key Points

1. The Bible is inspired by God (2 Timothy 3:16-17; 2 Peter 1:20-21).

2. The Bible is made up of 66 different books that were written over 1600 years (from approximately 1500 BC to AD 100) by more than 40 kings, prophets, leaders, and followers of Jesus. The Old Testament has 39 books (written approximately 1500-400 BC). The New Testament has 27 books (written approximately AD 45-100). The Hebrew Bible has the same text as the English Bible's Old Testament, but divides and arranges it differently.

3. The Old Testament was written mainly in Hebrew, with some Aramaic. The New Testament was written in Greek.

4. The books of the Bible were collected and arranged and recognized as inspired sacred authority by councils of rabbis and councils of church leaders based on careful guidelines.

5. Before the printing press was invented, the Bible was copied by hand. The Bible was copied very accurately, in many cases by special scribes who developed intricate methods of counting words and letters to insure that no errors had been made.

6. The Bible was the first book ever printed on the printing press with moveable type (Gutenberg Press, 1455, Latin Bible).

7. There is much evidence that the Bible we have today is remarkably true to the original writings. Of the thousands of copies made by hand before AD 1500, more than 5,300 Greek manuscripts from the New Testament alone still exist today. The text of the Bible is better preserved than the writings of Caesar, Plato, or Aristotle.

8. The discovery of the Dead Sea Scrolls confirmed the astonishing reliability of some of the copies of the Old Testament made over the years. Although some spelling variations exist, no variation affects basic Bible doctrines.

9. As the Bible was carried to other countries, it was translated into the common language of the people by scholars who wanted others to know God's Word. Today there are still 2,000 groups with no Bible in their own language.

10. By AD 200, the Bible was translated into seven languages; by AD 500, 13 languages; by AD 900, 17 languages; by AD 1400, 28 languages; by 1800, 57 languages; by 1900, 537 languages; by 1980, 1,100 languages. Source: *The World Christian Encyclopedia.*

Bible Facts: Evidence for Integrity of the Bible[1]

The Bible is God's Holy Word, written by holy men, inspired by God's Holy Spirit for the benefit of all humankind (John 16:13; 2Tim. 3:16; 2Pet. 1:20–21).

The Bible:

- Has **66** books written over 1,600 years (from approx. 1500 BC to AD 100)
- Has more than 40 authors from every walk of life, including: kings, prophets, military leaders, peasants, philosophers, fishermen, tax collectors, poets, musicians, statesmen, scholars, shepherds and followers of Jesus Christ.
- Was written in different places such as: the wilderness, palaces, behind prison walls, while traveling, exiled on an isle.
- Was written in times of war and sacrifice and times of peace and prosperity.
- Was written on three continents: Asia, Africa and Europe.
- Was written in three ancient languages: Hebrew, Aramaic, and Greek.
- Has continuity of symbols, names, and doctrine, defying human ability over such a long period of time written under so many different conditions.

There are archeological and historical confirmations for events, locations, and persons described within the Bible. Here are three notable resources:

- Bible: ***Archeological Study Bible*** published by Zondervan Corporation.
- Pamphlets: ***Archeology and the Bible: Old Testament and New Testament*** published by Rose Publishing, Inc.
- Reputable history books: ***Antiquities of the Jews and Wars of the Jews*** by ancient Jewish (non–Christian) historian Flavius Josephus.

Although none of the original scriptural manuscripts exist, the oldest copies, including the latest discoveries from the Dead Sea Scrolls— discovered between 1947 and 1956 with manuscripts dating from 250 BC— **confirm scriptural accuracy:**

- Reference: Rose Publishing, Inc.'s pamphlet *How We Got the Bible.*
- Reference *The Dead Sea Scrolls Bible: The Oldest Known Bible Translated for the First Time into English* by Abegg, Jr., Flint, and Ulrich.
- Find detailed evidence for integrity of the scriptures from Josh McDowell's book *The New Evidence that Demands a Verdict*

Similarities between Protestant, Hebrew and Roman Catholic Bibles:

- Protestant Bible has 66 books: 39 in Old and 27 in New Testament
- Hebrew Bible (Jewish) contains all the same books as Protestant Old Testament, except books are organized differently
- Roman Catholic Bible includes same Old Testament books as Hebrew and Protestant Bibles, but also adds Apocrypha ("hidden") books. These additional books are accepted by Roman Catholic Church as a second canon (deutero-canonical), but they are not accepted by Protestants
- New Testament books are the same in Roman Catholic Bible, Protestant New Testament Bible, and Complete Jewish Bible (translated by Stern)
- Reference: Rose Publishing, Inc.'s Pamphlet *Bible Translations Comparison—Compare Twenty Popular Versions of the Bible*

[1]Appendix C

Bible Facts: Bible Canon[1]

"Every Scripture is God-breathed (given by His inspiration) and profitable for instruction, for reproof and conviction of sin, for correction of error and discipline in obedience, [and] for training in righteousness (in holy living, in conformity to God's will in thought, purpose, and action)."   2 Timothy 3:16, Amp

"Above all, you must realize that no prophecy in Scripture ever came from the prophet's own understanding, or from human initiative. No, those prophets were moved by the Holy Spirit, and they spoke from God." 2 Peter 1:20, 21, NLT

The Bible provides insight on its origin and integrity as God's Word:

- **Examples of Scripture Proclamations to Divine Inspiration**
  Ex 32:16; **Lev** 1:1; **Num** 1:1; **Deut** 31:24-26; **Neh** 13:1; **Jer** 1:11; **Ezra** 1:1, 5:1;**Zech** 7:12; **Eph** 2:20; **Heb** 1:1-2, 2:3; **1 Tim** 5:18 with **Luke** 10:7 and **Deut** 25:4

- **Christ's Witness to Old Testament as Sacred Scripture**
  Luke 24:44; **John** 10:31–36; **Luke** 11:51; **Matthew** 23:35

- **New Testament Witness to Old Testament as Sacred Scripture**
  Matt. 21:42; 22:29; 26:54, 56; **Luke** 24; **John** 5:39; 7:38; 10:35; **Acts** 17:2, 11; 18:28; **Rom.** 1:2; 4:3; 9:17; 10:11; 11:2; 15:4; 16:26; **1 Corinthians** 15:3,4; **Galatians** 3:8; 3:22; 4:30; **1 Timothy** 5:18; **2 Timothy** 3:16; **2 Peter** 1:20, 21; 3:16

- **New Testament Explains How God's Children Can Know His Word** **John** 10:3–5, 16, 27; 16:13–15; **Rom.** 8:14; **1 Cor.** 2:12–16

As explained in the above scriptures, Old Testament prophets, priests, and scribes and New Testament apostles and Church fathers were all guided by God's Holy Spirit in identifying which writings should be bound together as God's Authoritative Word—His sacred Scripture. The same Spirit that moved men to write the "God-breathed" Word of God also revealed to other men how to clearly recognize those writings.

Measuring Rod = Standard = Canon

Josh McDowell's book *Evidence that Demands a Verdict* provides a detailed history of the construction of the Bible, for both Old and New Testaments. It is interesting to note that Origen, who was one of the early Church fathers, used the word **"canon"** to describe the list of books that became the officially accepted make-up of the Bible. It became necessary for the Church leaders to publish the official list because there were other letters and writings, which in some cases contained helpful historical information from that timeframe, but they were not accepted as canonical. This is because of the inconsistent, inaccurate or fanciful text observed within the writings or because of a concern with their authors/sources.

[1]Appendix C

Bible Facts: Bible Canon[1]

The word "canon" is derived from the word "reed," which in English is "cane" and in Greek "kanon." Since the reed in ancient times was used as a measuring rod, the word "canon" began to represent a measuring "standard."

The idea of the "Bible canon" has to do with recognition of God's authoritative Word. God's Authoritative Word was to be used by His children as the standard for defining, measuring, and evaluating their faith in Him and faith walk with Him.

Some writings from the Old Testament timeframe were not included in the Bible canon. Some of these writings are known as the Apocrypha, which means "hidden books." The Catholic Church includes these books as a part of their Bible. They consider these books "deutero-canonical," which means "second canon." Some apocrypha book titles or content include names of important Bible figures. However, using a "reputable" name alone was not enough to qualify a book for inclusion in the Bible canon, for the reasons explained above.

Likewise, some writings from the New Testament timeframe were not included in the Bible canon. These writings are referred to by some as the "Lost Gospels." Similar to the Old Testament apocrypha, some of the titles on these documents have powerful names, such as names of the Apostles. But as explained before, the Spirit of God led His children from the very beginning as to which documents were to be included.

Below is a list of some excellent reading materials to help in understanding how we got the Bible. The pamphlets are reasonably priced, colorful, and easy to read. The books are also easy to understand, while providing more details on these topics.

Pamphlets:

From Rose Publishing, Inc.–easy to order from Hendrickson Rose

- ***How We Got the Bible***: Timeline of Key Events in History of the Bible
- ***The Gospels: "Lost" and Found:*** Were other "Gospels" included in the New Testament then later rejected? Are the Gospels reliable?
- ***Bible Translations Comparison:*** Compares 20 popular versions

Books:

- ***The New Evidence That Demands A Verdict by Josh McDowell***; 1999; Thomas Nelson Publishers
    - Evidence I and II—Fully Updated in One Volume to Answer Questions Challenging Christians in the Twenty-First Century.
- ***The Dead Sea Scrolls Bible*—Translated and with Commentary by Martin Abegg Jr., Peter Flint and Eugene Ulrich**; 1999; HarperCollins Publishers.

[1]Appendix C

Comparison Chart: Old Testament Books in Hebrew (Jewish), Protestant and Catholic Bibles[2]

HEBREW BIBLE / TANAK (Jewish Bible)	OLD TESTAMENT (Protestant Bible)	OLD TESTAMENT (Roman, Greek)
I. Law (Torah)		
Genesis (B'resheet)	Genesis	Genesis
Exodus (Sh'mot)	Exodus	Exodus
Leviticus (Vayikra)	Leviticus	Leviticus
Numbers (B'midbar)	Numbers	Numbers
Deuteronomy (D'varim)	Deuteronomy	Deuteronomy
	Joshua	Joshua
II. Prophets (Nevi'im)	Judges	Judges
A. Early Prophets	Ruth	Ruth
Joshua (Y'hoshua)	1 Samuel	1 Samuel
Judges (Shoftim)	2 Samuel	2 Samuel
1 Samuel (Sh'mu'el Alef)	1 Kings	1 Kings
2 Samuel (Sh'mu'el Bet)	2 Kings	2 Kings
1 Kings (M'lakim Alef)	1 Chronicles	1 Chronicles
2 Kings (M'lakim Bet)	2 Chronicles	2 Chronicles
	Ezra	Ezra
B. Latter Prophets	Nehemiah	Nehemiah
Isaiah (Yesha'yahu)	Esther	*Tobit*
Jeremiah (Yirmeyahu)	Job	*Judith*
Ezekiel (Yechezk'el)	Psalms	Esther &*Additions*
The Twelve (Shneim-'Asar):	Proverbs	Job
Hosea (Hoshea)	Ecclesiastes	Psalms
Joel (Yo'el)	Song of Solomon	Proverbs
Amos ('Amos)	Isaiah	Ecclesiastes
Obadiah ('Ovadyah)	Jeremiah	Song of Solomon
Jonah (Yonah)	Lamentations	*Wisdom of Solomon*
Micah (Mikhah)	Ezekiel	*Ecclesiasticus (Sirach)*
Nahum (Nachum)	Daniel	Isaiah
Habakkuk (Havakuk)	Hosea	Jeremiah
Zephaniah (Tz'fanyah)	Joel	Lamentations
Haggai (Hagai)	Amos	*Baruch and Letter of Jeremiah*
Zechariah (Z'kharyah)	Obadiah	Ezekiel
Malachi (Mal'akhi)	Jonah	Daniel and *Additions*:
	Micah	*Susanna*
III. Writings (Ketuvim)	Nahum	*Song of the Young Men*
Psalms (Tehillim)	Habakkuk	*Bel and the Dragon*
Proverbs (Mishlei)	Zephaniah	Hosea
Job (Iyov)	Haggai	Joel
Song of Songs	Zechariah	Amos
(Shir-HaShirim)	Malachi	Obadiah
Ruth (Rut)		Jonah
Lamentations (Eikhah)		Micah
Ecclesiastes (Kohelet)		Nahum
Esther (Esther)		Habakkuk
Daniel (Dani'el)		Zephaniah
Ezra ('Ezra)		Haggai
Nehemiah (Nechemyah)		Zechariah
1 Chronicles		Malachi
(Divrei-HaYamin Alef)		*1 Maccabees*
2 Chronicles		*2 Maccabees*
(Divrei-HaYamin Bet)		

- Book names in *italics* are the **deuteron-canonical books** included in Roman Catholic Bible; also referred to as Apocrypha books by some.
- **Apocrypha means "hidden" and deutero-canonical means "second canon".** The Hebrew Canon and Protestant Bibles do not recognize these additional books as canon or proto-canonical.

Additional Apocryphal Books in some lists:
- *1, 2, 3 and 4 Esdras*
- *Psalm 151*
- *The Song of the Three Holy Children*
- *The Prayer of Manasses*
- *3, 4 Maccabees*

[2]Appendix C

Old Testament Quotations in New Testament by Hulitt Gloer[3]

Holman Bible Dictionary Excerpt - reprinted by permission

The Influence of Old Testament is Seen Throughout New Testament

New Testament writers included approximately 250 direct Old Testament quotations, and if one includes indirect or partial quotations, the number jumps to more than 1,000. It is clear that the writers of the New Testament were concerned with demonstrating the continuity between the Old Testament Scriptures and the faith they proclaimed. They were convinced that in Jesus the Old Testament promises had been fulfilled.

The Uses of Old Testament Quotations

New Testament writers used Old Testament quotes for at least 4 reasons:

1) **to demonstrate that Jesus is the *fulfillment* of God's purposes and of the prophetic witness of the Old Testament Scriptures** (Romans 1:2; Matthew 4:14; Matt. 12:17–21; Matthew 21:4–5)
2) **as a source for *ethical instruction* and *edification* of the church** (Romans 13:8–10; 2 Corinthians 13:1)
3) **to interpret contemporary events** (Romans 9–11; Romans 15:8–12)
4) **to prove a point on the assumption that the Scripture is God's Word** (1 Corinthians 10:26, 14:21, 15:55)

Some Old Testament quotations are used in their *literal historical sense* and, therefore, have the same meaning in the New Testament as they had in the Old Testament.

The quotation of Psalms 78:24 in John 6:31 is a good example of such usage.

Some quotations reflect a typical approach to interpreting the Old Testament in first-century Judaism known as *Midrash*.

Midrash is an exposition of a text that aims to bring out its contemporary relevance. Old Testament text is quoted and explained to make it apply to or be meaningful for the current situation. The use of Gen. 15:6 in Rom. 4:3–25 and the use of Psalms 78:24 in John 6:31–58 reflect such an approach.

Some Old Testament texts are interpreted *typologically*.

In this approach, the New Testament writer sees a correspondence between persons, events, or things in the Old Testament and persons, events, or things in their contemporary setting. The correspondence with the past is not found in the written text, but within the historical event. Underlying typology is the conviction that certain events in the past history of Israel as recorded in earlier Scriptures revealed God's ways and purposes with persons in a typical way. Matthew's use of Hosea 11:1 (Hosea 2:15) suggests the Gospel writer saw a correspondence between Jesus' journey into Egypt and the Egyptian sojourn of the people of Israel.

[3]Appendix C

Old Testament Quotations in New Testament by Hulitt Gloer[3]

Holman Bible Dictionary Excerpt - reprinted by permission

Jesus re-capitulated or re-experienced the sacred history of Israel. The redemptive purposes of God demonstrated in Exodus (reflected by the prophet Hosea) were being demonstrated in Jesus' life.

In some cases, the understanding and application of the Old Testament quotation is dependent on an awareness of the quotation's wider context in the Old Testament.

The use of the quotation is intended to call the reader's attention to the wider Old Testament context or theme and might be referred to as a "*pointer quotation*." In first-century Judaism where large portions of Scripture were known by heart, it was customary to quote only the beginning of a passage even if its continuation was to be kept in mind. A good example of this use may be seen in Romans 1–3. Paul had discussed both the faithfulness of God and the sinfulness of humanity. In Romans 3:4 Paul quoted Psalms 51:4 to support his first point. He continued his argument with a further reference to human wickedness, which is, in fact, the subject of Psalms 51:5; but he did not feel the need to quote the verse, since it was already suggested to those familiar with the biblical text.

Finally, there is a limited *allegorical* use of the Old Testament text in which the text is seen as a kind of code having two meanings

—the literal, superficial level of meaning, and a deeper, underlying meaning such as in Galatians 4:22–31.

Despite similarities with contemporary Jewish use(s) of the Old Testament, the New Testament writers interpreted the Old Testament in a radically new way.

New Testament writers did not deliberately use a different exegetical method. They wrote from a different theological perspective. The writers of the New Testament were convinced that the true meaning of the Old Testament is Jesus Christ and that He alone provides the means of understanding it.

True interpretation of the Old Testament is achieved by reading Old Testament passages or incidents in light of the advent of Christ.

While many of the Old Testament texts quoted in the New Testament had already been accepted as messianic (for example, Psalms 110:1) or could in light of Jesus' actual life claim to be messianic (Psalms 22:1; Isaiah 53:1), for the early Christians, all Scripture was to be interpreted by the fact of Christ because it is to Him that the Old Testament Scripture points (John 5:39).

In summary, the New Testament writer quoted or alluded to the Old Testament in order to demonstrate how God's purposes have been fulfilled and are being fulfilled in Jesus.

[3]Appendix C

Bible Construction

Testament Means Covenant[4]

Q1: What is a "testament" as used in Bible testaments?

The word "testament" is a derivation of the Latin word *testamentum.* This word was first used in Jerome's Latin Vulgate Bible to translate the Hebrew word *b'rith*, which means covenant. The Greek equivalent of *b'rith* is *diatheke,* which also means covenant. Testament is used to describe the two main divisions of the Bible: Old and New Testament, which really mean Old and New Covenant.

It should be understood then that the Bible is generally to be looked at as a covenant between God and man.

Saint Jerome, whose name in Latin was Eusebius Hieronymus, lived in the fourth century from AD ~347 to 420. He was a Church father and doctor of the Church, as well as a revered Biblical scholar. His most important work was translation of the Bible into Latin, called the Latin Vulgate, which means "common translation." Over twenty-three years of labor, Saint Jerome used the Hebrew Old Testament and Greek New Testament to develop the new Bible. This Latin Vulgate Bible became the standard text for Roman Catholics for a long time, until the Bible began to be translated in modern languages.

Q2: Why are there an Old Testament and a New Testament?

The Old Testament represents an Old Covenant between God and man; The New Testament represents a New Covenant between God and man.

Covenant means a binding agreement or contract between two partners. In the Bible, God's covenants are primarily His way of creating a relationship between Himself and humankind. Covenant relationships include the shedding of blood to "spiritually sign" covenant agreements and a "physical sign" or seal of the covenant. There are partner obligations, along with blessings for keeping covenant and curses for breaking covenant agreements.

- **Old Testament or Old Covenant between God and man was limited in that, it was:** (Gen. 12:1–3; Ex. 20:5–6; Ex. 24:1–11)
    - Based on the shed blood of animals
    - Based on keeping over 600 laws and commandments
- **New Testament or New Covenant between God and man is unlimited in that, it is:** (Matt. 26:26–28; Heb. 9 and 10)
    - Based on the shed blood of Jesus Christ, who was fully God and fully man
    - Based on humankind accepting Jesus Christ as Lord and Savior of their lives

[4]Appendix C

Bible Construction Timeline[5]

Approx. Date	Key Construction Events	Notes
1450–400 BC	Hebrew Bible is written	Mainly in Ancient Hebrew, with a portion in Aramaic (written on scrolls)
250–100 BC	Septuagint (by 72 Jewish scholars in Alexandria, Egypt)	Ancient Greek translation of Hebrew Bible (scrolls)
200 BC	Hebrew Bible was arranged by subject	Historical books (Law), Prophetic books (Prophets), Poetic books or Writings (Psalms); (scrolls)
AD 45–100	New Testament is written	Ancient Greek (scrolls and papyrus)
AD 200	Bible is already translated into seven languages	Many language translations continued from this point
AD 300	New Testament books in open circulation	Roman Emperor Constantine legalizes Christianity in 313 A.D.
AD 397	Standard of 27 New Testament books confirmed by Church Fathers Council of Carthage	Official Church confirmation recognizes three centuries of use by followers of Christ
AD 382–420	St. Jerome translates Bible into Latin = Latin Vulgate	First use of "Old Testament" and "New Testament" terms
AD 300–1400	Bible copied on fine quality animal skin	Vellum / codex copies
AD 500–900	Special Jewish scribes called "Masoretes" carefully made copies of Hebrew Bible	Hebrew Bible = Old Testament
AD 1382	First English Bible: Wycliffe	Named after John Wycliffe
AD 1455	World's first printing press; Gutenberg Bible is first book ever printed	Printing press invented by German/ Johann Gutenberg
1516	New Testament updated using ancient languages/copies	By Erasmus, Greek scholar
1525–1536	Tyndale and Coverdale English Bible translations	First complete Bibles printed in English
1560–1599	Geneva Bible, entire Bible from ancient Hebrew & Greek	Chapters & Verses, legible type, notes, maps, italics
1611	King James Version or Authorized Version, still used today = most popular Bible	King James I of England commissioned 54 scholars to develop this version
1629–1947	Older copies of Hebrew Bible found (i.e. Old Testament)	1947 discovery of Dead Sea Scrolls
1855–present	Modern Bible Versions (from ancient manuscript copies)	No originals of Bible text exist, only ancient copies

[5]Appendix C

Bible Bookcase
Genesis
Exodus
Leviticus
Numbers
Deuteronomy
LAW
Joshua
Judges
Ruth
1 Samuel
2 Samuel
1 Kings
2 Kings
1 Chronicles
2 Chronicles
Ezra
Nehemiah
Esther
HISTORY
Job
Psalms
Proverbs
Ecclesiastes
Song of Solomon
POETRY
Isaiah
Jeremiah
Lamentations
Ezekiel
Daniel
MAJOR PROPHETS
Hosea
Joel
Amos
Obadiah
Jonah
Micah
Nahum
Habakkuk
Zephaniah
Haggai
Zechariah
Malachi
MINOR PROPHETS
Matthew
Mark
Luke
John
GOSPELS
Acts
HISTORY
Romans
1 Corinthians
2 Corinthians
Galatians
Ephesians
Philippians
Colossians
1 Thessalonians
2 Thessalonians
EPISTLES TO CHURCHES
1 Timothy
2 Timothy
Titus
Philemon
EPISTLES TO FRIENDS
Hebrews
James
1 Peter
2 Peter
1 John
2 John
3 John
Jude
Revelation
GENERAL EPISTLES
© 2008 RW Research, Inc. Rose Publishing, Inc.
Reprinted by permission

Bible Book Summaries– Old Testament

Bible Books Summaries – Old Testament

- **Law Books – 5**
- History Books – 12
- Poetry and Wisdom Books – 5
- Major Prophets – 5
- Minor Prophets - 12

Law – 5 Books

Book	Key Word(s)	Summary
Genesis	Beginnings	God begins everything. Humankind sins and is separated from God. God begins a ♦ covenant relationship with Abraham. The children of Abraham, Isaac and Jacob become God's chosen people the Israelites. God promises to send the Israelites a special person and give them a special land.
Exodus	* Redemption	The Israelites exit from slavery in Egypt by the mighty power of God. God uses Moses to lead them to the Promised Land. God makes a covenant with the redeemed Israelites, giving them the Ten Commandments and Laws of Moses.
Leviticus	Holy Living	Levites are one of the twelve tribes of Israel. God uses the Levites to lead the Israelites in true worship and holy living.
Numbers	Wanderings	The Israelites wander in the wilderness for 40 years because they did not believe God could give them the Promised Land. They were numbered two times in this book. The first time was before their wanderings. The second time was after the unbelievers died in the wilderness.
Deuteronomy	Second Law	God makes a second covenant agreement with the grown-up children of the Israelites who left Egypt, giving them the Laws of Moses a second time.

♦ Covenant means a binding agreement or contract between two partners. In the Bible, God's covenants are primarily his way of creating a relationship between Himself and humankind. Covenant relationships include the shedding of blood to "spiritually sign" covenant agreements and a "physical sign" or seal of the covenant. There are partner obligations, along with blessings for keeping covenant and curses for breaking covenant agreements.

* Redemption, Redeemed, and Redeemer all come from the word "redeem", which means "to save, to deliver, to set free."

Bible Books Summaries – Old Testament

- Law Books - 5
- **History Books – 12**
- Poetry and Wisdom Books – 5
- Major Prophets – 5
- Minor Prophets - 12

History Books - 12

Book	Key Word(s)	Summary
Joshua	Victory	God helps Joshua lead the Israelites in victorious battles, until they conquer and settle into the Promised Land.
Judges	Defeat	After Joshua dies, the Israelites stop serving God. Israel's enemies begin to defeat and hurt them. When they remember to ask God for help, God sends Judges to deliver them.
Ruth	*Kinsman Redeemer	Ruth is a Moabite woman who stays with her Israelite Mother-in-law Naomi after both their husbands die. Ruth's devotion to Naomi and Naomi's God is admired by one of Naomi's rich kinsman. This * Kinsman Redeemer marries Ruth who becomes the Great-Grandmother of King David and an ancestor of Jesus Christ.
1 Samuel	King	Samuel is the last Judge and first prophet for the Israelites. When Samuel becomes old, the Israelites ask for a King to rule over them like the other nations. Saul is the first King and David is second.
2 Samuel	David	Under King David the Israelite nation became powerful, conquering all the Promised Land. God makes a covenant with David to establish his house and his kingdom forever.
1 Kings	Division	David's son Solomon begins as a strong King of Israel. But Solomon's many wives turn his heart away from God. The Israelites became a divided Kingdom when Solomon's son is King. Ten tribes make up the northern kingdom called Israel. Two tribes make up the southern kingdom called Judah.

* A Kinsman is a blood relative. A Kinsman Redeemer is a relative who saves, delivers or sets free a member of their family. Naomi and Ruth needed help from poverty and from having no way to increase their family. Their Kinsman Redeemer met both needs.

History Books – 12 continued

Book	Key Word(s)	Summary
2 Kings	Captivity	God wanted the Israelites to lead other nations in following His ways. But the Israelites followed the wrong ways of other nations instead. After 209 years of warning, God let the Assyrian nation defeat and capture the northern kingdom, Israel. 145 years later, God let Babylon defeat and capture the southern kingdom Judah. The Israelites are also called the Jews.
1 Chronicles	True Worship	King David established the true worship of God among the Israelites. Musical instruments, Psalms and 24-hour Worship help the Israelites bring God's presence in their midst.
2 Chronicles	Temple Worship	King Solomon builds a magnificent temple in the city of Jerusalem, for worshipping God. God blesses Solomon and Israel with great wisdom and riches. After the Kingdom was divided, the good Kings of Judah lead revivals of true worship. After the last good King dies, Babylon captures Judah and destroys the Temple.
Ezra	Spiritual Restoration	After 70 years of living in Babylon, some of the Jews return to the Promised Land to rebuild their nation and temple. The priest Ezra is a spiritual leader who teaches the people the laws of Moses, so they can restore their covenant relationship with God.
Nehemiah	Government Restoration	Nehemiah becomes the Governor of the Jews who returned to the Promised Land. Under his leadership the people become well organized. They rebuild the walls of Jerusalem in 52 days.
Esther	Deliverance	Esther wins a beauty contest to become the new Queen for the King of Persia. She did not tell the King she was a Jew. After 3 days of fasting and prayer, Queen Esther wisely asks the King to deliver all the Jews from the evil plot against them.

- Law Books – 5
- History Books – 12
- **Poetry and Wisdom Books – 5**
- Major Prophets – 5
- Minor Prophets - 12

Poetry and Wisdom Books - 5

Book	Key Word(s)	Summary
Job	Sovereign	God describes Job as a perfect and upright man. But God allows Job to go through great suffering by the works of satan, so he can prove a point to satan. By this story, we learn that God is sovereign, which means God can allow things to happen that we do not always understand.
Psalms	Praise the Lord	Psalms are praises to God that can be read or sung with tunes played on musical instruments. Half the Psalms were written by King David. The others were written by choir leaders, other Kings, one by Moses and unknown authors. Topics include praise, worship, laments, prayers for deliverance, and thanksgiving.
Proverbs	Wisdom	Proverbs are a collection of wise sayings that give guidance for everyday living. By following the practical wisdom in Proverbs, a person can have health, success, and happiness in life. Many proverbs were written by King Solomon.
Ecclesiastes	Meaningless (Vanity)	In Ecclesiastes, the Teacher (Preacher) describes the meaningless (vanity) or emptiness of a person's life when they pursue happiness "under the sun", by human methods. In the end, true happiness is only obtained from God (who is above the sun). Many think that King Solomon wrote Ecclesiastes as a part of the lessons he learned from researching happiness through wisdom and foolishness.
Song of Solomon (Song of Songs)	Love better than wine	Song of Solomon is the wonderful, ultimate song Solomon wrote that describe the beauty of love between a man and woman.

- Law Books – 5
- History Books – 12
- Poetry and Wisdom Books – 5
- **Major Prophets – 5**
- Minor Prophets - 12

Major Prophets – 5

Book	Key Word(s)	Summary
Isaiah	Salvation of the Lord	Isaiah's name means "salvation of the Lord". In this book, the plan of salvation for the Israelites and all of humankind is presented, which includes having hope in the coming Messiah. Messiah is another name for the "special person" God promised would come since the book of Genesis.
Jeremiah	New Covenant	God used Jeremiah to give Judah their final warning of coming destruction because of their continuous sin. He also gave instructions on what the nation was to do after the destruction, which resulted in a 70-year exile in Babylon. Jeremiah also prophesied of the future time when God would make a new covenant with Israel and Judah, when he would restore their relationship because of His everlasting love for the united nation.
Lamentations	Deep Sorrow	When Judah was captured, its capital city Jerusalem, also called Zion, was destroyed. Jeremiah is thought to be the weeping author of this book who describes his deep sorrow at the fall of Jerusalem (or Zion). He pleads for God's mercy on Zion's future.
Ezekiel	God's Glory	Ezekiel was a priest and prophet who was taken away captive to Babylon. In Babylon he saw visions of God's glory. He watched God's glory reveal the sins of Judah, then depart the temple leaving Jerusalem open for destruction. He saw visions of God's glory returning in the future to a new temple and new Holy Land. Ezekiel spoke prophecies concerning the reunited Israelite nation and on the future of other nations.
Daniel	Kingdoms	God shows Daniel visions that describe the rise and fall of all the kingdoms of the world. Daniel's final vision is of the Kingdom of God being established on earth.

* Prophecies are God's words spoken by a prophet, who is God's messenger. In the Old Testament, prophecies were often predictions about events to happen in the future. Prophets can preach words of warning, instruction and comfort.

- Law Books – 5
- History Books – 12
- Poetry and Wisdom Books – 5
- Major Prophets – 5
- **Minor Prophets - 12**

Minor Prophets - 12

Book	Key Word(s)	Summary
Hosea	God's Loyal Love	God uses Hosea to demonstrate his loyal love for Israel. Hosea's wife is unfaithful and gets in trouble. Hosea helps her get out of trouble and restores her as his wife. Hosea's wife is like Israel who gets in trouble because of her unfaithfulness to God. After Israel gets in trouble, God promises to restore the nation to following him.
Joel	Day of the Lord	Joel warns about the coming of a great and terrible day of the Lord. In that day God's judgment will destroy land and people because of continuous sins. Joel's prophecies describe destruction that has already happened and more destruction that is yet to happen in the future.
Amos	Judgment	God uses Amos to announce his coming judgment on the nations surrounding Israel, and in Israel. Amos, who is a shepherd turned prophet, describes the sins that have brought on God's judgments. In the end, Amos announces that God will one day restore Israel back to his favor.
Obadiah	Edom's Doom	Obadiah spoke prophecies about the coming destruction of Edom, which is a nation near Israel. The people of Edom are descendants of Esau who was Jacob's (Israel's) brother. Because Edom helps in the destruction of Israel, God punishes them.
Jonah	Nineveh's Mercy	Nineveh is the capital city of Assyria, which is the nation that eventually destroyed Israel. God tells the reluctant Israelite prophet Jonah to tell Nineveh they should repent, or God will destroy them. Nineveh listens to Jonah, repents, and obtains God's mercy.
Micah	Judgment and Restoration	Micah warns Judah and Israel about the coming destruction because of the nations' sins. But Micah also spoke prophecies that in the last days, the worship of God will be established on earth. Israel and Judah will become one nation again and be the center for the worship of God, with God's special person (Messiah, King) as ruler.

Minor Prophets – 12 continued

Book	Key Word(s)	Summary
Nahum	Nineveh's Destruction	About 100 years after God shows mercy to Nineveh (after Jonah's preaching), God uses Nahum to announce Nineveh's coming destruction. As capital city of the nation Assyria, God's judgment on Nineveh was in punishment for Assyria's destruction of the northern kingdom Israel.
Habakkuk	The "just" shall live by their faith	Habakkuk struggles with God's way of bringing judgment on his chosen people the Israelites. Habakkuk understands that they should be punished because of their sins against God. He does not understand why God uses nations who have sinned worse than Israel to execute this punishment. God assures Habakkuk that all who do wrong will be punished, and those who do justly will live good lives because of their faith in God.
Zephaniah	The Day of the Lord is Near	Zephaniah speaks the Word of the Lord in Judah during the time of King Josiah. He warns that the day of God's anger is near because of continuous sins. After the destruction, the Israelite nation will be restored. One day God, as Israel's King, will change Israel from being a "shame" to becoming a "praise" among all the peoples of the earth.
Haggai	Rebuild the Temple	The seventy (70) years of exile in Babylon are over. Many Jews returned to their homeland to live. To help rebuild the nation, they must rebuild the Temple of God to reestablish centralized worship. Haggai speaks strong words from God encouraging the people to finish building the Temple.
Zechariah	Future visions	Zechariah has visions of the future, including visions of a restored Israel, visions of nations joined to Israel to serve God, and visions of events connected with the first and second comings of the King. Along with Haggai, Zechariah's words encourage the Jews who returned from exile, to rebuild the Temple and prepare for future blessings from God.
Malachi	Messenger	Malachi is believed to be the last Old Testament prophet, before 400 silent years with no word from God, after which time Jesus Christ is born. The Israelites had not only returned to their homeland, but they returned to their old sinful ways. Malachi warns the people because more destruction is coming. Then Malachi spoke prophecies about a future messenger of God who will come to correct things.

Intro to–
Inductive
Chronological
Bible Study

Intro to Chronological Bible Study: Old Testament

Definition of "Chronological":

Arranged in the order in which events happened; according to date.

Studying the Bible inductively means you engage with scripture in an interactive manner to learn how to interpret scripture for yourself.

Studying the Bible chronologically means to study the information within the Bible in the order events actually occurred.

In regular Bibles, the books are organized by category or type of book. You can see the categories in the chart "Bible Bookcase." As a result, the books are not organized based on when Bible events occurred.

To get a picture of how the Old Testament Books would be organized if they were arranged chronologically, review:

- "Chronological Layout of Old Testament Books"
- "Chronological Summary of the Old Testament"

Optional: Use One-Year Chronological New Living Translation Bible[7]

To understand the time order when events occurred in the Bible, the One-Year Chronological Bible New Living Translation (NLT) has gone one step further than reordering entire books of the Bible to be arranged in chronological order.

- This Bible has reordered all the text from within the Bible books in chronological order. This means events from across different Bible books now lay next to each other according to the time every event occurred. This is based on the thinking of many Bible scholars.
- For example, the life and times of King David are described in 1 and 2 Samuel. The psalms he wrote that go along with those events are in the book of Psalms. The One-Year Chronological NLT Bible places the psalm that goes along with an event next to that event within the text.
- Another example is how the same events in the life of Jesus Christ that occur in different Gospels are placed next to each other in this chronological Bible. By putting events together in this way, it makes understanding the Bible as one continuous Word of God much easier.

Because of the easy to read and understand language in the One-Year Chronological New Living Translation Bible, and the interlinking of stories together from different books based on the time order events occurred, the author's daughter calls this Bible, "The Storybook Bible." It IS easy to read, and it is the whole Bible with God's true story!

Daily reading assignments in this ***Know His Word Bible Study*** are based on the ***NLT One Year Chronological Bible***. As an option, you can use this NLT Bible along with this study for quick access to the readings.

Disclaimer: This study is not associated with the Chronological Study Bibles for NLT or any other versions.

[7]Appendix C

Chronological Layout of Old Testament Books

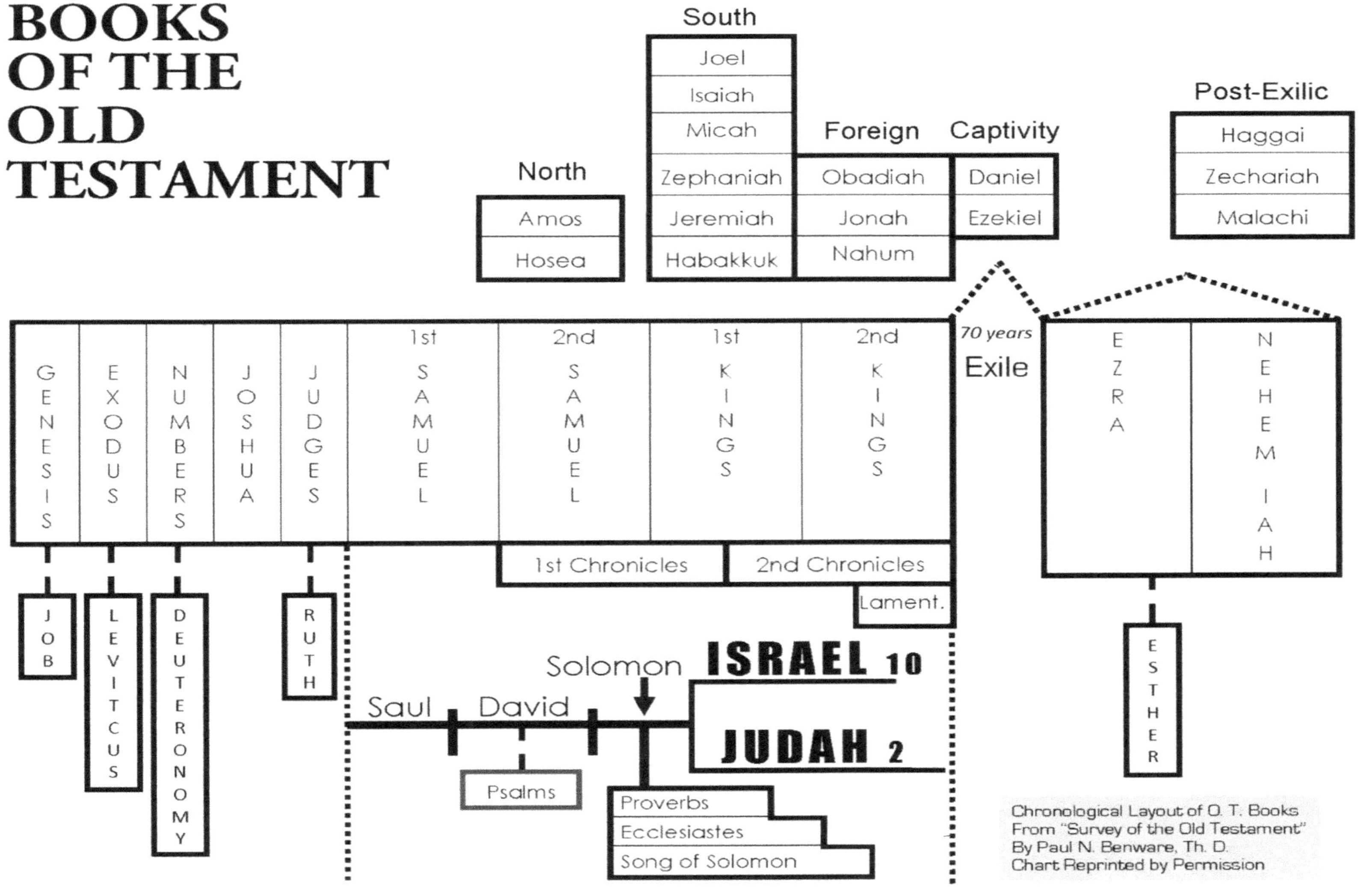

Chronological Summary of the Old Testament

Chronological Summary of the Old Testament

- Chronological Bible study means reading Bible events based on timing (i.e. date order) events occurred.
- The below Bible books are considered the eleven foundational books of the Old Testament by Dr. Paul Benware
- Review chart *"Books of the Old Testament"* to visualize how all the other Bible books lay out in relation to the eleven foundational books. Exact date of some books (e.g. Job, Joel, Esther) are not known. The chart represents a popular chronological order.
- See "Old Testament Book Summaries" for a summary of the content information on all O.T. books.

				KEY		
	Era	**Event and Time**	**Book**	**Words**	**Chapter**	**Comments**
Formative Year's	Mankind	Abraham Born 2166 B.C	Genesis	Beginnings	12	God begins all creation and begins dealing with all mankind; then God begins dealing with Abraham and his descendants.
	Israel	Israelites Formed 1400 B.C.	Exodus	Redemption	12, 20	God forms the Israelite nation from Abraham, Isaac and Jacob's descendants; God gives Israel laws to keep *(led by Moses)* and the land of Canaan *(Promised Land)* to occupy *(led by Joshua)*. After Moses and Joshua's death, God intended to lead Israel with help of priests' instructions on the law.
			Numbers	Wandering	14	
			Joshua	Victory	6	
Theocracy	Israel's Theocracy Years	Joshua Dies 1390 B.C.	Judges	Defeat	2	"Theocracy" means ruled / governed by God. Israel, who should have been ruled by God during this era, was ruled by sin instead.
Monarchial	Israel's Monarchial Years	King David's Reign 1000 B.C.	1 Samuel	King	8	Israel demanded a King to rule over them to be like other nations.
			2 Samuel	David	7	David was greatest King *(Monarch)* of Israel. After his son Solomon's rule, Israel was divided into Northern and Southern Kingdoms because of sins.
		Divided Kingdom 930 B.C.	1 Kings	Division	12	
			2 Kings	Captivity	17, 25	Northern Kingdom *(Israel)* was taken captive & destroyed by Assyria. Southern Kingdom *(Judah)* was taken captive & preserved in exile by Babylon.
Exile	Israel's Exile Years	Exiled 605–535 B.C.				70 Years of Exile in Babylon *(ref. Ezekiel, Daniel)*
Post –Exilic Years	Israel's Post-Exile Years	Restored 535–430 B.C.	Ezra	Spiritual Restoration	6, 9	Judah returned to Promised Land and re-built a second Temple to restore worship of True God
			Nehemiah	Political Restoration		Political and Governmental order was also restored

Comparison Chart:
Chronology of Old Testament 17 Prophetic Books
Five Major Prophets and Twelve Minor Prophets[10]

Paul N. Benware Survey of the Old Testament		Tim LaHaye Prophecy Study Bible		The One Year Chronological New Living Translation	
Prophet	Approx. Date (BC)	Prophet	Approx. Date (BC)	Prophet	Approx. Date (BC)
Obadiah	845	Obadiah	Same dates as in *Survey of the Old Testament* by Paul Beware		
Joel	830	Joel		*Joel*	*400 BC or 830 BC*
Jonah	780	Jonah		Jonah	Same dates as in *Survey of the Old Testament* by Paul Benware
Amos	760	Amos		Amos	
Hosea	750	Hosea		Hosea	
Isaiah	740	Isaiah		Isaiah	
Micah	735	Micah		Micah	
Nahum	650	Nahum		Nahum	
Zephaniah	635	Zephaniah		Zephaniah	
Jeremiah	626	Jeremiah		Jeremiah	
Habakkuk	609	Habakkuk		Habakkuk	
Daniel	605	Daniel		Daniel	
Ezekiel	593	Ezekiel		Ezekiel	
Lamentations	586	Lam.		Lamentations	
				Obadiah	586
Haggai	520	Haggai	Same dates as Benware	Haggai	Same dates as Benware
Zechariah	520	Zechariah		Zechariah	
Malachi	430	Malachi		Malachi	
				Joel	400

<u>General Chronological Flow of Old Testament Books</u>

Law Books (Formative years) ➪ Theocracy era books ➪

United Kingdom books ➪ Divided Kingdom books ➪

Exile books ➪ Post Exile books

[10]Appendix C

Apologetics: Bible and Christian

***

A Defense of the Word of God and the Faith generated by that Word!

***

But sanctify the Lord God in your hearts: and be ready always
to give an answer to every man that asketh you
a reason of the hope that is in you
with meekness and fear:

1 Peter 3:15
King James Version

Apologetics

The word "apologetics" is derived from the ancient Greek word *apologia,* which described the response a defendant or lawyer would give to accusations lodged against the defendant in a court case. This response was not an apology as understood by the modern sense of the word. Instead, it was a "defense" intended to refute the accusation.[1]

Bible and Christian Apologetics

There are questions concerning the integrity of the Word of God as presented in the Holy Bible, along with questions regarding the Christian faith and faith walk generated through the study of this Word.

This section provides an overview of the solid apologetics or defense for the integrity of the Bible being the Word of God, the Messianic messaging found throughout the Bible, and for the Christian faith founded upon both.

For a more detailed discussion on these topics, review the referenced material. In the meantime, Enjoy!

Contents:

[1]Appendix C

King James Version and non-KJV

"We believe the Bible to be the inspired and only infallible written Word of God."

The above phrase is the first line in the Statement of Faith for some Christian Churches. Today, the validity of this statement is under attack.

- The Authorized King James Version (KJV) of the Bible has been a popular Bible for English speaking people since its publication.
- More than 50 Non-KJV English Bible Versions have been published since the KJV. These Bibles are very helpful in using language that is more understandable to the modern reader.
- When some content of the KJV Bible is compared with some non-KJV Bibles – specifically a comparison of select passages in the non-KJV passage with its corresponding passage in the KJV – the reader discovers that there are some differences which could be perceived as conveying different meanings.
- Sometimes the explanation for the differences is shown using brackets or footnotes. The reasons provided for the translation differences range...
    - From explaining that the oldest known source documents used to develop the Bible translations did not contain the passage
    - To questioning whether the passage is truly God's Word because of the possible effect of the translator's human bias.
- For God's Word to be "inspired" and "infallible," there should not be multiple meanings that portray multiple doctrines in multiple Bibles.
- Of note, there is a detailed scholarly perspective on comparing the KJV with non-KJV Bible translations in the book "Look What's Missing" by David W. Daniels.
- According to Daniels, the King James Version (KJV) Bible is not just another translation. Based on his arguments in that book, KJV should be considered "the inspired and only infallible written Word of God."

Reference[2]:

David W. Daniels, **Look What's Missing** (Chick Publications, 2017)

[2]Appendix C

King James Version and non-KJV

God magnifies His Word above His name and promised to preserve His Word for us.

…" for thou hast magnified thy word above all thy name."
Psalm 138:2

"The words of the Lord are pure words…
Thou shall preserve them from this generation forever."
Psalm 12:6-7

The above passages reveal that God gives the highest honor to His Word, and He wants every generation to know and understand His Word.

When the Authorized KJV Bible was developed, it was translated by scholars who were intentional in developing the most accurate translation, from the ancient sources available, into the common language of the English-speaking people at the time of its publication in the 17th century.

- Non-KJV Bible Versions are helpful to the modern reader in understanding some of the words in the KJV that are no longer used today. Additionally, Bible scholars have supplied many helpful resources for understanding the Bible using non-KJV Bible versions.
- With all the above in mind, the author of the "Know His Word Bible Study" series—who was raised using the King James Version Bible, and who greatly values its divine inspiration has learned to also appreciate the benefits of some of the non-KJV translations.
- By the leading of God's Holy Spirit, Jennifer B. Price utilizes the scriptural foundation of the KJV Bible for all Bible Study, and then utilizes other Bible versions as tools to facilitate the studies, trusting the Holy Spirit to guide in providing a right understanding.
- As an example, "Know His Word Bible Study" uses the daily readings from the "New Living Translation One Year Chronological Bible," and provides explanations based on conducting the study using the KJV Bible as the authoritative guide to understanding the scriptures.

Pray:

God's Holy Spirit will open your understanding and guide you into ALL truth. Psalm 119:18, John 16:13, 1 Corinthians 2:10-12, John 16:13

"For as many as are led by the Spirit of God,
they are the sons of God."
Romans 8:14

The Messiah Jesus saw Himself throughout the text of the Hebrew Bible (Old Testament)...

> *Then he said to them, "Oh, how foolish you are, and how slow of heart to believe all that the prophets have declared! Was it not necessary that the Messiah should suffer these things and then enter into his glory?"*
>
> *Then beginning with Moses and all the prophets, he interpreted to them the things about himself in all the scriptures. Luke 24:25–27*

Modern scholars are increasingly denying that the Old Testament is messianic. These modern scholars contest saying the Old Testament texts were not originally written as direct predictions of the Messiah.

> But in modern times a section of the world of scholarship imbued with and motivated by the spirit of scientific investigation, apart from divine revelation, calls in question, more or less, the authority of the Scriptures and their message (*Messiah: His Historical Appearance*, p. vii).
>
> There is a growing movement by evangelicals to move away from interpreting the Hebrew Bible as a messianic book. They are constraining biblical interpretation to have only a historical context, confined to fulfillment in the prophet's own time (*Messianic Hope,* p.1, 3).

In his book, *The Messianic Hope,* Michael Rydelnik, who is a Messianic Jew (Jewish Christian) and professor of Jewish studies, identifies the reasons why understanding the Hebrew Bible (Old Testament) as messianic is important (p. 8). He explains...

- It is the best way of understanding the Bible as a whole; through seeing the Old Testament as predicting the coming of the Messiah and the New Testament as revealing Him to be Jesus of Nazareth.
- It makes it possible to identify Jesus as the Promised One who Moses wrote about in the law and of whom the prophets wrote (John 1:41, 45).
- It enables the followers of Jesus to have confidence in the Bible as God's inspired Word.

Rydelnik further provides a clear and compelling scholarly case for why the entire Old Testament is messianic, along with his powerful testimony.

Know His Word Bible Study has been written with the concepts and context of the Messianic Bible being God's divine design.

References[3]:

- Cooper, David L., **Messiah: His Historical Appearance** (Biblical Research Society, 1958)
- Rydelnik, Michael, **The Messianic Hope: Is the Hebrew Bible Really Messianic?** (Nashville, TN: B&H Publishing Group, 2010)

[3]Appendix C

Christian and Christendom

"Christian" and "Christendom" as used in *Know His Word Bible Study* mean...

Christian:

- **By Faith**
  - Believe in the Trinity or Triune God => 3 Divine Persons => 1 God
    - God the Father — 1 Corinthians 8:6, Ephesians 4:4–6
    - God the Son — John 1:1–5,14,10:30; Heb. 1:6–8
    - God the Holy Spirit — Acts 5:3–4, 2 Corinthians 3:17
  - Believe Jesus Christ died and rose up from the dead for all; Confess the living Jesus as Lord and Savior of one's personal life.
    - Born Again — John 3:3–8
    - Saved — Romans 10:9–10
    - New Creation in Christ — 1 Corinthians 5:17
- **By Relationship**
  - Child of God — John 1:12
  - Beloved of the Father — Col. 3:12
  - Saved by the Son — John 3:16–17
  - Guided by Holy Spirit — Romans 8:14
  - Follower of God as His dear child, walking in love as Christ also has loved you — Ephesians 5:1–2

My old self has been crucified with Christ. It is no longer I who live, but Christ lives in me. So I live in this earthly body by trusting in the Son of God, who loved me and gave himself for me. Galatians 2:20

Christendom:

> *Generally, refers to the worldwide community of those who adhere to the Christian faith, with religious practices and doctrine gleaned from the teachings of the Bible. Spread throughout the world, Christendom consists of people from many nations and of various ethnicities.[4]*

References[4]:

- Geisler, Dr. Norman, Essential Doctrine Made Easy, Key Christian Beliefs, Rose Publishing, Inc., 2007
- The Trinity, What is the Trinity and What do Christians Believe?, Rose Publishing, Inc., 1999
- *What is Christendom?, Got Questions.org, 2013

[4]Appendix C

At God's appointed time in history, God the Son became human to provide the way of salvation for all humans according to God's will. Through divine conception, God the Son was born Jesus, the Christ, fully God and fully human.

While modern teachings increasingly challenge the validity of the Christian claim to Jesus' divinity, the Bible and early Church teachings on this subject are definitive. Reference *Reinventing Jesus: How Contemporary Skeptics Miss the Real Jesus and Mislead Popular Culture*[5] and the many references cited in the book for detailed discussion points.

Some of the scriptures and teachings declaring Jesus' divinity include:

- **From Judaism**
  - For New Testament Jews to worship Jesus as Lord, He had to be God. This is because of the Jew's strict belief in the monotheistic (one) God as recited in the Shema prayer which begins "Listen, Israel: The Lord is our God, the Lord is one" (Deuteronomy 6:4).
  - Consider the below passages from the Gospels and Larger New Testament which record the testimonies and declarations of the Jewish disciples of Jesus.
- **From the Gospels**
  - Jesus Christ is the Son of God is declared by His disciples:
    - Matthew 1:20–23
    - Mark 1:1
    - Luke 1:35
    - John 1:1–3, 14–18 and John 20:28
  - Jesus Christ is God is affirmed by Jesus' actions and words:
    - Mark 2:1–12;
    - Mark 14:53–64 with Psalm 110:1 and Daniel 7:13–14;
    - John 8:56–59 and John 10:30
- **From the Larger New Testament**
  - Son of God is God is explained by Apostle Paul and in Hebrews:
    - Acts 9:1–5
    - Romans 10:9–13 with Deuteronomy 21:23 and Galatians 3:13
    - Philippians 2:6–11 (Exodus 20:4–5 with Philippians 2:10; and Isaiah 45:23)
    - Hebrews 1:6–14

[5]Appendix C

In less than 150 years after Jesus' life on earth, non-Christian writers recorded their observations of how Christians worshipped Jesus as God.

- **From Second Century non-Christian writings**
  - ~112 A.D. Pliny the Younger, who was governor of a secluded Roman province in Asia Minor, executed Christians because of their worship of Christ as if worshiping a god.
  - ~170 A.D., Greek satirist Lucian of Samosata criticized Christians for their worship of Jesus as God although He had been crucified.
  - ~177 A.D., Roman philosopher Celsus criticized Christians for their worship of Jesus as God, who he perceived was just a man.

The early Church Fathers declared Jesus' divinity as learned from Jesus' disciples confirmed by their personal experiences in defending the faith.

- **From the early Church Fathers' writings**
  - ~90s – 150 A.D. Apostolic Church Fathers—Men who were taught directly by Jesus' disciples. These include the writings of Ignatius of Antioch and Polycarp.
  - ~100–240 A.D. Apologist Church Fathers—Men who wrote to defend the Gospel against heresies. These included the writings of Polycarp and Tertullian.
  - ~300 – 400 A.D. Nicene Church Fathers—Men who participated in writing the 325 A.D. Nicene Creed, such as Augustine of Hippo.
    - Nicene Creed declares Jesus Christ is "very God of very God"

      We believe in one God, the Father Almighty, Maker of all things visible and invisible.

      And in one Lord Jesus Christ, the Son of God, begotten of the Father [the only-begotten; that is, of the essence of the Father, God of God], Light of Light, very God of very God, begotten, not made, being of one substance with the Father;

      By whom all things were made [both in heaven and on earth]; Who for us men, and for our salvation, came down and was incarnate and was made man; He suffered, and the third day he rose again, ascended into heaven; From thence he shall come to judge the quick and the dead.

      And in the Holy Ghost.

<u>**References[5]:**</u>

- Komoszewski, Sawyer, and Wallace, **Reinventing Jesus—How Contemporary Skeptics Miss the Real Jesus and Mislead Popular Culture** (Kregel Publications, 2006)
- Bible Study Tools.com, history

[5]Appendix C

There are different types of Bible Studies. This means there are different ways to study the abundance of information contained in the Bible. For example, **Know His Word Bible Study** is an inductive and chronological study. This study guides the reader in understanding the entire Bible content based on the order events occurred.

Another way to study the entire Bible is by studying topics. The most thorough way to study topics is to review what the entire Bible says about that particular topic. This allows the reader to follow along with how God progressively reveals His whole guiding thoughts on the topic, from its beginning introduction to its final ending revelation.

Systematic Theology is the way Bible scholars have studied the entire Bible and systematically organized the major topics, as God has revealed information on them, from the book of Genesis to the book of Revelation.

The major topics of focused study ("ology") in Systematic Theology, as defined by Bible scholars, are called Doctrines.

Below is a table of doctrinal topics that can be found in different Systematic Theology books. The actual list in a book is determined by the author's area of focus. This list is simply a representation of typical topics.

Systematic Theology Typical Doctrinal Topics

Topic "ology"	Topic "Doctrine" Description
Bibliology	The Doctrine of the Bible (Word of God)
Theology	The Doctrine of God (Trinity, God the Father)
Christology	The Doctrine of Christ (God the Son)
Pneumatology	The Doctrine of the Holy Spirit (God the Holy Spirit)
Angelology	The Doctrine of angels (angels and fallen spirits)
Anthropology	The Doctrine of man
Hamartiology	The Doctrine of sin
Soteriology	The Doctrine of salvation
Misthology	The Doctrine of rewards
Ecclesiology	The Doctrine of the Church
Eschatology	The Doctrine of last things

Dr. Arnold G. Fruchtenbaum[6] authored the book "Israelology: The Missing Link in Systematic Theology." Dr. Fruchtenbaum presents a strong discussion on how God's use of the nation of Israel —past, present, and future— is key to understanding doctrines in Systematic Theology.

Know His Word Bible Study author also views Israelology as a vital part of Systematic Theology, especially when considering the words of the Apostle Paul regarding the nation of Israel in Romans Chapter 11.

Based on Romans 11, which overviews God's use of the nation of Israel—past, present, and future—, and the systematic Bible research on this topic by Dr. Fruchtenbaum, Israelology should be included in addition to Ecclesiology, which is the Doctrine of the Church.

Topic "ology"	Topic "Doctrine" Description
Bibliology	The Doctrine of the Bible (Word of God)
Theology	The Doctrine of God (Trinity, God the Father)
Christology	The Doctrine of Christ (God the Son)
Pneumatology	The Doctrine of the Holy Spirit (God the Holy Spirit)
Angelology	The Doctrine of angels (angels and fallen spirits)
Anthropology	The Doctrine of man
Hamartiology	The Doctrine of sin
Soteriology	The Doctrine of salvation
Misthology	The Doctrine of rewards
Israelology	The Doctrine of Israel (nation of Israel in past, present)
Ecclesiology	The Doctrine of the Church
Israelology	The Doctrine of Israel (nation of Israel in future)
Eschatology	The Doctrine of last things

Romans 11: 7, 25-26a

"So this is the situation: Most of the people of Israel have not found the favor of God they are looking for so earnestly. A few have—the ones God has chosen—but the hearts of the rest were hardened.

I want you to understand this mystery, dear brothers and sisters, so that you will not feel proud about yourselves. Some of the people of Israel have hard hearts, but this will last only until the full number of Gentiles comes to Christ. And so all Israel will be saved."

[6]Appendix C

Charts in the **Introductory** sections of this study describe and provide scholarly support for the author's interpretive approach of Holy Scripture:

*** Author's Introduction ***	
Contextual	Help with Challenges in Understanding the Bible
Literal; Prophetic	Principles for Interpreting Bible Scriptures/Prophecy
*** Bible Facts ***	
Holistic	Old Testament Quotations in the New Testament
*** Apologetics: Bible and Christian ***	
Doctrinally Inerrant	King James Version and non-KJV
Messianic; Jesus is The Messiah	Messianic Bible
Trinitarian; Ecclesiastic	Christian and Christendom
Jesus is Son of God, Word of God, and God	Jesus' Divinity, Israelology, Vital Part of Systematic Theology
*** Weeks…Intro Pages***	
Progressive Revelation	Messiah, Our Savior—Revealed from the Beginning
Recognize God's Chosen	Jewish Scholars Used as Resources
Scholarly Affirmable Hermeneutics; Exegesis	Find Jesus in the Lesson: Old and New Testaments

Interpreter's Tools	**Scriptural Guidance**
• **Holy Word**	2 Timothy 3:16–17
• **Holy Spirit**	1 Corinthians 2:11–14
• **Spirit-Led Inductive Study**	2 Timothy 2:15
• **Spirit-Inspired Teachings**	Ephesians 4:11–16

Interpreter's Beliefs	**Jesus' Example**
• **Scripture is God's Word**	John 10: 34–35
– All Scripture—OT+NT— is God's Word	
– God is the primary author	
• **Scripture is Authoritative**	John 10:34–35, Mark 12:24
– Inerrant in everything it asserts	
– Cannot be annulled through unbelief	
• **Scripture is Divinely Inspired**	Matthew 5:18; 2 Peter 1:19–21
– Plenary Verbal Inspiration	
– Spiritually alive / life / light	
• **Scripture is Scripture's Interpreter**	Luke 24:25, 44–45; Rev. 19:10

- Explanations for assertions in Scripture are in other areas of Scripture
- Scripture, as a whole, points to Jesus who IS the Word of God.

> *Any question relating to Jesus of Nazareth is a historical subject and must be studied according to the canons of historical criticism and the laws of evidence. Just as microbes and germs are studied through the microscope and the heavens are explored by the spectroscope and telescope, all questions concerning Jesus of Nazareth must fundamentally be studied from the standpoint of genuine evidence and by historical methods.*
>
> *Every question relating to Jesus of Nazareth, of whom one reads in the Scriptures, harks back to Him as He was when He was here nineteen hundred years ago and must be studied in the light of all Scripture—the Old Testament which foretells His Advent, the New Testament which records His life and labors—and also in the light of all extra-Biblical evidence available* (Cooper, **Messiah: His Historical Appearance**, 1958).

Dr. Cooper's declaration above concerning the verifiable historicity of Jesus also applies to the whole of scripture. Extra-Biblical evidence confirming Bible events, places and people, including affirmations for Jesus as a historical figure, exist in plentiful supply to use for satisfying the scientific investigator's evidential quest. The below references can be used to identify many references. For example...

- McDowell, in his book "Evidence," describes thirteen non-Christian, non-Biblical ancient sources that witness to Jesus being a historical figure; and to the foundations of Christian beliefs based on His life, such as belief in His resurrection. This is in addition to numerous extra-Biblical ancient Christian sources (**The New Evidence**, Part Two, Chapter 5, pp.119–136).
- **NIV Archaeological Study Bible** includes 500+ insightful articles and full color photographs of discoveries of all kinds (p. xiii), that serve as reliable verifications for events, people, and places named throughout the Bible text.
- Urquhart's book gives specific examples of how modern discoveries counter arguments from "higher criticism" scholars against the Christian "ordinary view" of *Verbal Inspiration* of Scripture (**Inspiration and Accuracy**, Book III).

Know His Word Bible Study Includes Extra-Biblical Evidence

To expose readers to some of the extra-Biblical evidence that exists, and to encourage new generations of Bible-focused researchers and explorers, this Bible Study includes the following in each of the four Quarter books:

- Excerpts from Ancient Jewish Historian—Josephus and Jewish Writings
- Excerpts from Archaeological Discoveries
- Chronological Notes to facilitate independent extra-Biblical research

<u>**References[7]:**</u>

- David L. Cooper, **Messiah: His Historical Appearance**, 1958 (Los Angeles, CA: Biblical Research Society)
- Josh McDowell, **The New Evidence That Demands A Verdict**, 1999, (Nashville, TN: Thomas Nelson Publishers)
- NIV **Archaeological Study Bible**, 2005, (Grand Rapids, MI: Zondervan)
- John Urquhart, **The Inspiration and Accuracy of the Holy Scriptures** (1895), Kessinger Publishing's Rare Reprint

[7]Appendix C

After Jesus' resurrection from the dead, He spoke the words below to two disciples who were walking on a road to the village of Emmaus.

And beginning at Moses and all the prophets, he expounded unto them ***in all the scriptures*** *the things concerning himself…*

…that all things must be fulfilled, which were ***written in the law of Moses, and in the prophets, and in the psalms****, concerning me.*
Luke 24:27, 44

"Scriptures" Background:

There is a debate among Bible scholars on which version(s) of the scriptures Jesus used, meaning which version(s) did He read and quote from, as recorded in the New Testament Gospels.

Specifically, did Jesus use the scriptures from the original Hebrew/Aramaic writings, which is the content contained in the Bible Old Testament; Or did Jesus also use the Septuagint, which is described as a Greek translation of the Old Testament Hebrew/Aramaic writings.

The New Testament uses the term "scriptures" and does not specify a translation version for the Old Testament content. When Jesus is recorded as quoting from the scriptures, the text differs slightly from the way the referenced passage is worded in the Old Testament. See the example. Some scholars explain that these differences represent Jesus verbalizing a Greek translation of the Hebrew/Aramaic scriptures. However, the entire New Testament was written in ancient koine Greek which was the common language spoken by people during the life and times of Jesus. Jesus most likely understood the Hebrew, Aramaic, and Greek languages because of his Jewish heritage and the Greek culture of His times.

Example: Luke 4:18-19 which references Isaiah 61:1-2a

Isaiah 61:1-2a KJV	Luke 4:18-19 KJV
The Spirit of the Lord GOD is upon me; because the LORD hath anointed me to preach good tidings unto the meek;	The Spirit of the Lord is upon me, because he hath anointed me to preach the gospel to the poor;
he hath sent me to bind up the brokenhearted,	he hath sent me to heal the brokenhearted,
to proclaim liberty to the captives,	to preach deliverance to the captives,
and the opening of the prison to them that are bound;	and recovering of sight to the blind, to set at liberty them that are bruised,
To proclaim the acceptable year of the LORD,	To preach the acceptable year of the Lord.

Scholarly Debate Simplified:

The concern with the Septuagint, along with its associated Apocrypha, is that the content includes text and books that were not accepted as Bible canon (protocanonical). This means they were not accepted as the authoritative Word of God. For this reason, they were purposely not included in the Authorized Version of the Bible (King James Version).

The Bible scholars' debates on this topic are identified by the *Know His Word Bible Study* author as "Septuagint Frequently Asked Questions (FAQs)."

Septuagint FAQ's:

- Is the Septuagint authoritative scripture?
- Was the Septuagint developed before Jesus was born?
- Did Jesus read the Septuagint?
- Did Jesus quote scriptures from the Septuagint?

Septuagint Brief Background:

The name **Septuagint**, also referred to as **LXX**, comes from the Latin word "septuaginta" which means "seventy." The Septuagint supposedly contains the original Hebrew/Aramaic scriptures *(meaning the scriptures contained within the Bible Old Testament)* translated into the ancient koine Greek language. Some historical writings explain that the Septuagint was developed by 72 Jewish elders—made up of 6 elders from each of the twelve tribes of Israel, who knew the Hebrew/Aramaic and Greek languages—for the purpose of providing a version of the scriptures that could be understood by Greek-speaking Jews. Bible scholars debate the date of the Septuagint, and they do not agree if it was available before or after the birth of Jesus Christ. In addition, Bible scholars debate the translation accuracy of the Septuagint's content, which leads to the question of whether Christians should regard it as representing the authoritative Word of God. The Apocrypha is a collection of books written in the four centuries between the Old and New Testaments that first appeared within the Septuagint.

This Author's Research Results:

Because the entire New Testament was written in the common Greek language, it is not obvious to this author if Jesus' quotation of the scriptures, that are recorded in their Greek form, is a result of His ever using a Greek translation of the Old Testament or not. However, based on review of Jewish and non-Jewish sources, it is the *Know His Word Bible Study* author's position that the Bible canon/protocanonical books are the only Authoritative Words of God.

References for Further Study[8]:

- Josephus, **Appendix Dissertation IV**, **The Complete Works of Josephus**
- Edersheim, **Life and Times of Jesus the Messiah, Unabridged**, p. 15–22
- Daniels, **Did Jesus Use the Septuagint?**
- McDonald, Sanders, **The Canon Debate**
- Evans, **Scriptures of Jesus and His Earliest Followers,** p. 191-194, 2002

[8]Appendix C

Early Church Father St. Augustine stated in principle the dictum[9]...

The Old Testament is the
New Testament concealed and
the New Testament
is the Old Testament revealed!

Therefore, to gain a clearer understanding
of the New Testament,
it is best to read the entire Old Testament.

Use Know His Word Bible Study books—
1st Quarter, 2nd Quarter, and 3rd Quarter—
to help in your reading, studying, and
understanding the Old Testament.

This will prepare you for understanding
the information
provided in the New Testament!

[9]Appendix C

Know His Word Bible Study

Old Testament: Weekly Study Intro Pages

Contents:

Tips on How to Use This Bible Study

Use the following techniques to maximize study results

- **Review:** All introductory material preceding the lesson study pages at least once, to gain insight on Bible background and study approaches.
- **Read:** "Reading Assignment" at top of the daily lesson study pages. Optional: Use the One-Year Chronological New Living Translation (NLT) Bible for easy access to the daily reading assignment text.
- **Complete:** Daily lesson study pages.
- **Compare:** First develop your answers to lesson exercise questions, and then compare with those provided in the Appendix. Trust the Holy Spirit to teach you and guide you into all truth. This is not an exercise in "getting the answers right," but a study to get to know God's Word for yourself. Allow the Holy Spirit to speak to you as you read and think about the questions (John 14:26; 15:26–27, 16:13).
- **Enhance:** Use the King James Bible Authorized Version and review the additional study material provided for each lesson and/or week.

Bible Study Organization

Know His Word Bible Study is organized in fifty-two weeks (Week 1–Week 52) with seven lessons each week. It is further divided in four quarter books covering three months of study material as follows:

- 1st–3rd Quarter cover the Old Testament
- 4th Quarter covers the New Testament

Study pages include Bible book introductions, daily lesson study pages, maps, and additional reference material that explain the timeline of events and background for the people, places, and/or locations of events.

Daily lessons are presented in three sections, although on some days lesson content for some sections is combined.

- **I. Lesson Exercise**
  This section includes notes and questions from the daily reading.
- **II. Find Jesus in the Lesson**
  This section gives insight on how passages from the reading point to Jesus Christ. Christ is revealed in the Bible from beginning to end.

III. Closing Thoughts
This section offers additional insight into lessons on selected topics.

Establish a Set Study Plan for each day

- Try reading the daily Bible scriptures in the morning
- Or Listen to an audio of the scriptures when exercising or car riding
- Try completing daily Bible Study lessons in evening

Overview of the Old Testament[1]

The Old Testament is the story of God's magnificent, loving creation of and dealings with humankind. Ultimately, it portrays the great spiritual victories and defeats of men and the amazing faithfulness and grace of God in His relationship with men.

The Old Testament primarily describes this story with a focus on the nation of Israel. Israel is unique and distinct from all the nations of the earth because God entered into a special covenant relationship with them. Israel was specially commissioned by God to bring glory to Himself and to be a resource through whom God would provide salvation for all people.

In Dr. Paul Benware's book, *Survey of the Old Testament*[1], he explains that the Old Testament is divided into two distinct parts, each covering several thousand years of history. Part I begins with "God's Dealings with Humankind"; Part II focuses on "God's Dealings with Israel".

A basic overview of the Old Testament and its presentation of these two distinct parts is discovered from understanding eleven foundational Old Testament books. The following text is an adaptation of this overview from Dr. Benware's book, and is used by permission.

Refer to chart "Chronological Summary of the Old Testament."

Part I. God's Dealings with Humankind

Approximate Dates: Unknown–2100 BC

The first distinct part is Genesis 1–11. It is a record of Gods dealings with humankind generally. During those years, there was no special group such as Israel or the church. God's dealings were with individuals.

❑ **Humankind's Formative Years** **Approx. Dates: Unknown**

Since we do not know the exact date of the universe's creation, we cannot say with certainly, as some do, that **Genesis 1–11** covers two thousand years...

- ❋ Much is not recorded about these early years of man, but four important events are included
  - The Creation Account
  - The Fall of Man
  - The Great Flood of Noah's Day
  - The Division of humankind at the Tower of Babel
- ❋ These events are briefly recorded so that we understand where this material universe came from, where sin and evil came from, and why the world of humankind is so fragmented.

[1]Appendix C

Overview of the Old Testament[1]

Part II. God's Dealings with Israel

Approximate Dates: 2100–400 BC

The second distinct part of the Old Testament covers about 2,000 years. This part begins with **Genesis 12** and includes all the rest of the Old Testament. This part can further be broken down into Israel's Formative, Theocracy, Monarchial, Exile and Post-Exile Years.

❑ Israel's Formative Years Approx, Dates: 2100–1400 B.C.

- Genesis 12 is the cornerstone chapter of the Bible. It is here that God selects a man by the name of Abraham and enters into an eternal, unconditional covenant with him and his descendants.

- God made many promises to Abraham *[Abrahamic Covenant]*. These promises included personal blessings to Abraham and his descendants [through his son Isaac and grandson Jacob, who became known as Israel] and blessings that would include all the rest of humankind.

- **Genesis 12–50** records how God began to populate this new nation. When Genesis ends, the nation has grown to about 75 people… But during the 275 years between Genesis and Exodus, a population explosion took place. By the Exodus, the nation's population had grown to more than two million.

- In the book of **Exodus**, God gives Israel a code of laws to live by, to make them a legitimate and great nation. These laws became known as the Mosaic Law because they were given by God through Moses to the nation of Israel.

- In fulfillment of the Abrahamic Covenant, God promised to give Israel the Promised Land as he used Moses to instruct them to take this land from the wicked Canaanite nation. However, the book of **Numbers** records a terrible moment in Israel's history. The first-generation exodus adult Israelites refused to believe and obey God by going in to fight the Canaanites. This kept them from possessing the land. Therefore, instead of living in the Promised Land, Israel wandered in the wilderness region for a total of forty years.

- When that period of discipline was over, God chose Joshua to lead the nation of Israel into conquering the Promised Land after Moses was dead. This period of warfare, under Joshua, took from five to seven years and is described in the book of **Joshua**.

- After Joshua led Israel in breaking all the strongholds of power of the Canaanite people, it was now the task of each individual tribe of Israel to complete the conquest of the land [continuing after Joshua's death].

[1]Appendix C

Overview of the Old Testament[1]

❑ **Israel's Theocracy Years   Approx. Dates: 1400–1100 BC**

❋ When Joshua died, Israel entered a new era in its national life. God did not replace Joshua with a new leader for His people. It was God's intention that the newly formed nation be a theocracy *[God ruling]* with no single human leader. But the theocracy turned out to be a failure because Israel would not obey God's laws *[Mosaic Law]*.

❋ During the more than three hundred years of the theocracy, the book of **Judges** describes how judges had to be raised up again and again in crisis situations. The judges would deliver Israel from her enemies and bring in a time of obedience and peace. But those times eventually gave way once again to sin, unbelief, and idolatry (idolatry is the worship of idol gods in place of worshipping the true and living God). After three centuries of repeated failure, Israel demanded a human king.

Theocracy means ruled by God

Monarchial means ruled by a King

❑ **Israel's Monarchial Years   Approx. Dates: 1100–586 BC**

The United Kingdom

❋ Although Israel's request for a king was repudiation [rejection and rebellion] of God's rulership, God allowed Saul to become Israel's first king. With Saul's coronation Israel entered a third era in her history—the period of monarchy.

❋ The next four foundational books—**1 Samuel, 2 Samuel, 1 Kings and 2 Kings**—record the next 450 years of Israel's history. 1 and 2 Samuel tell stories of Israel's first king, Saul, and Israel's greatest king, David.

❋ God made a marvelous covenant with King David *[Davidic Covenant]*, much of which is fulfilled in David's "great son," the Lord Jesus Christ!

❋ David's' son Solomon reigned after the death of David and was the third and last king to rule over all of Israel's twelve tribes. Because of Solomon's sinful ways, God judged the family of David by dividing the nation into two kingdoms. However, the division did not take place until after Solomon died and his son Rehoboam became king.

[1]Appendix C

❑ **Israel's Monarchial Years cont'd Approx. Dates: 1100–586 BC**

The Divided Kingdom

❋ The Northern Kingdom, Israel, consisted of ten tribes.

❋ The Southern Kingdom, Judah, was made up of two tribes ruled by the family of David.

❋ For two centuries these two kingdoms coexisted, sometimes as friends and other times as foes.

❋ But the time of the divided kingdom came to an end when, because of sin and idolatry, the Northern Kingdom was destroyed by the nation of Assyria. Prior to its destruction, representatives from all ten tribes had migrated to the south to become part of the Southern Kingdom, Judah.

❋ The Southern Kingdom existed for more than one hundred years more. It lasted longer because it was blessed with the presence of some godly kings. But, like the North, the Southern Kingdom went into idolatry.

Exile means forced to leave homeland; taken captive and deported to live in another land

❑ **Israel's Exile Years** **Approx. Dates: 606–536 BC**

❋ This time God used the nation of Babylon as His rod of discipline. Many people from the Southern Kingdom, including Daniel and Ezekiel, were deported from Judah to live in exile in Babylonia. Counting the time the first set of captives was taken to Babylon until the end of Judah's exile totaled seventy years.

❋ During the years of their exile in Babylon, the Israelites remained an intact nation inside a nation as they were able to live and prosper among their captors. God preserved the nation, and the homeland God gave the nation, until the end of the seventy-year exile period. Then, God orchestrated Israel's return to their Promised Land.

[1]Appendix C

Overview of the Old Testament[1]

❒ Israel's Post-Exile Years Approx. Dates: 536–400 BC

- Finally, in fulfillment of His promise, God restored many of the people to their own land. The final period in the Old Testament history of Israel is recorded in **Ezra** and **Nehemiah**. This 150-year period focuses on both the political and spiritual restoration of Judah and on several great men who were used in that restoration.

- With the end of the Jewish history timeframe covered by Nehemiah, the story of the Old Testament ends. Some four hundred years would go by before scripture would pick up the story again. The years of silence would be broken by an angelic messenger, Gabriel, who would announce the birth of John the Baptist and the birth of Jesus the Anointed Messiah, "great son" of David.

- God had not forgotten or gone back on His covenant promises to Abraham and his descendants through Isaac and Jacob (Israel).

- This is a brief overview of the basic story of the Old Testament, as outlined from considering the story as revealed in the eleven foundational books.

- The remaining twenty-eight books of the Old Testament complete the story surrounding each of the periods described above. To get Dr. Paul Benware's view of where these books fit chronologically around the twelve foundational books, reference the chart "Books of the Old Testament—Chronological Layout of O.T. Books."

✞

Summary of the Old Testament Books

Read summaries of all thirty-nine Old Testament books in the Bible book summaries section.

Details of the Old Testament

Now you are ready to jump into the details by reading the entire Bible and using this "Know His Word" Bible study to help you understand what you read.

Enjoy!

[1]Appendix C

Hebrew Bible / Old Testament[2]

Judaism's sacred scriptures are called the Tanakh. Books in the Tanakh were mainly written in Hebrew, so it is also referred to as the Hebrew Bible.

Tanakh = Hebrew Bible

The three divisions that make up the Hebrew Bible are:

1.	**Law (Torah)**	First five books of Bible written by Moses
2.	**Prophets (Nevi'im)**	Early and Latter prophets
3.	**Writings (Ketuvim)**	(Psalms) Poetry, 5 Scroll books, Post-exile records

The word TaNaKh stands for these three divisions: Torah **(T)**, Nevi'im **(N)**, Ketuvim **(K)**. The Tanakh is also sometimes referred to by the name of the first division of the Hebrew Bible, which is the Written Torah.

Written Torah ~ TaNaKH = Hebrew Bible

The largest part of the Christian Bible is the Hebrew Bible which is called the Old Testament. The Hebrew Bible and Christian Old Testament for the Protestant Bible have the same content, except they are arranged in a different order. Some of the books in the Hebrew Bible are combined into one document—1 and 2 Samuel are one book, 1 and 2 Kings are one book, 1 and 2 Chronicles are one book, Ezra and Nehemiah are one book. The book of The Twelve consists of the twelve minor prophets.

Reference the chart on page 6 "Comparison Chart: Old Testament Books in Hebrew (Jewish), Protestant and Catholic Bibles" to see how the twenty-four books of the Hebrew Bible compare with the thirty-nine books of the Protestant Old Testament.

Written Torah ~ TaNaKh = Hebrew Bible = Old Testament

While the Hebrew Bible continues as the sacred scriptures for Judaism, they are not "old" for the Jewish community.

The Christian church refers to its Hebrew Bible as the Old Testament because of passages such as Jer. 31:31–33, 2 Cor. 3:14–15 and Heb. 8:7, 3.

- The title "New Testament" primarily takes its origin from Jeremiah 31:31 in which the prophet foretold how God would establish a "new covenant". This expression is translated in the Greek as "new dispensation" or "new testament."
- The title "Old Testament" for the Hebrew Bible is based on expressions used by New Testament writers for passages attributed to Moses (2 Corinthians 3:14–15 and Hebrews 8:7,13).
- **The Christian faith sees the new covenant promises from the Old Testament fulfilled in the mystery of Christ Jesus, God's Anointed Messiah, also a son of the Jewish people.** (Reference 1 Corinthians 11:25, Hebrews 9:15–28)
- **Christendom owes a great debt of gratitude to the Jewish people** for the great reverential and sacrificial role they played in recording and preserving the Holy Scriptures throughout the ages, for the Old and New Testaments (reference Deuteronomy 4:2; Romans 3:1–2).

[2]Appendix C:

Hebrew Bible / Old Testament[2]

Judeo-Christian Faith

The Christian faith is referred to as a Judeo-Christian faith.

This expression is directly related to the fact that Judaism and Christianity share the same foundation of faith from the Hebrew Bible.

Both acknowledge Abraham as the father of their faith.

Both acknowledge the special role of the Jewish people (also known as Hebrews and Israelites) as the chosen people of God.

By faith in Jesus Christ, Jews and Gentiles are made one habitation of God through the Spirit. (Eph. 2:11–22).

Consider these passages from the Old and New Testaments that emphasize the sacredness of the scriptures as the divinely inspired Holy Word of God:

- ***"Do not add to or subtract from these commands I am giving you. Just obey the commands of the LORD your God that I am giving you." Deut. 4:2***
- ***"So be careful to obey all the commands I give you. You must not add anything to them or subtract anything from them." Deut. 12:32***
- ***"God promised this Good News long ago through his prophets in the holy Scriptures."*** *Romans 1:2*
- ***"Then what's the advantage of being a Jew? Is there any value in the ceremony of circumcision? Yes, there are great benefits! First of all, the Jews were entrusted with the whole revelation of God."*** *Rom. 3:1–2*
- ***"All Scripture is inspired by God and is useful to teach us what is true and to make us realize what is wrong in our lives. It corrects us when we are wrong and teaches us to do what is right. God uses it to prepare and equip his people to do every good work."*** *2 Timothy 3:16–17*
- ***"And I solemnly declare to everyone who hears the words of prophecy written in this book: If anyone adds anything to what is written here, God will add to that person the plagues described in this book. And if anyone removes any of the words from this book of prophecy, God will remove that person's share in the tree of life and in the holy city that are described in this book."*** *Revelation 22:18–19*

[2]Appendix C:

Glossary of Some Hebrew Words[3]

Hebrew-English Word	Meaning
• Adonai	a title of reverence for God, Lord, My Lord
• Avraham	Abraham, father of many
• B'rit Chadashah	New Covenant = New Testament
• Chametz	Leavened bread (bread of slavery)
• Eretz Yisrael	Land inheritance of Israel
• Goel	Kinsman Redeemer
• Karet	To be "cut off" because of sin
• Kohen	Priest (also Cohen), to serve
• Kohen Gadol	High Priest (also Kohen Ha-Gadol)
• Matzah / Matzo	Unleavened bread (bread of freedom)
• Messiah	The Anointed One, Hebrew name for Christ
• Mitzvah, Mitzvot	Command, Commandment
• Mishnah	1st part of Talmud; edited record of early Oral Jewish interpretations of the Torah
• Pesach	Passover
• Rosh Hashanah	Jewish New Year
• Ruach Ha-Kodesh	The Holy Spirit (The Holy Ghost)
• Shabbat (Sabbath)	Seventh day of rest (rest from work)
• Shalom	Peace
• Shavuot	Festival of Harvest (Weeks, Pentecost)
• Shema	To hear, Hebrew prayer basis Deut. 6:4
• Sukkot	Booths (Festival of Booths / Tabernacles)
• Talmid	Disciple, student
• Talmud	Writings with ancient Rabbi scholars' interpretation and explanations on how to carry out the commandments of the Torah
• Tanakh	Hebrew Bible (Torah + Prophets + Writings)
• Torah	First five books of Hebrew Bible, Law books
• Yaakov	Jacob, heel, to follow, one who supplants
• Yeshua	Hebrew name for Jesus (Iesous / Salvation)
• Yitzchak	Isaac (he will laugh, laughter)
• Yom Kippur	Day of Atonement

[3]Appendix C:

The Messiah, Our Savior—Revealed from the Beginning

The inset of the Hebrew-English New Covenant—Prophecy Edition, published by the Hope of Israel Publications begins as follows:

The LORD raised up the nation of Israel, and through the Jewish people, gave the world these three great blessings:

1. The Holy **Scriptures**
2. The Way of **Salvation**
3. The Messiah, our **Savior**[4]

Christians believe the "Holy Scriptures" are God's Word, which reveal God's "Way of Salvation" through "The Messiah, our Savior."

As the experiences related in the Holy Scriptures were taking place and then written about, the full understanding of the role of the Messiah in providing salvation was revealed progressively to the Jewish people.

An Analogy

Consider how newborn babies cannot read a novel following their birth. However, over the course of many years, they learn speech, the alphabet, how to read words and then books. Finally, one day they can read and grasp the more complex concepts communicated in a novel. But they only do this with the assistance of a parent/teacher, one who can open up the student's understanding of what they are reading.

An Explanation

In a similar light, Father God knew humankind could not grasp His complete Way of Salvation from the beginning of time. So, God revealed His plan progressively over the course of many generations. With the help of spiritual teachers/scholars, who have carefully studied the Old and New Testaments, God's Way of Salvation is explained. The primary key to understanding God's Salvation is understanding the Messiah, our Savior.

The Messiah, Our Savior—Revealed from the Beginning

Before the Messiah's full salvation plan was manifested, God established temporary processes in the Old Testament, which served to prepare humankind for the full plan to be revealed in the New Testament. The plan is introduced in stages from the beginning in Genesis and is revealed progressively throughout the Bible until completed in Revelation.

With this in mind. Know His Word author has endeavored to share insight on God's plan of salvation through the Messiah. This begins in Genesis, the first book of the Bible. In the sections entitled "Find Jesus in the Lesson," notes are included to help you see the Messiah and God's way of salvation more clearly, as it is unfolds progressively. **This is because I believe New Testament Jesus Christ is the Messiah, our Savior.**

[4]Appendix C:

Jewish Scholars Used as Resources[5] for Find Jesus in the Lesson

Section II. of *Know His Word* daily study pages is "**Find Jesus in the Lesson.**" The type of information included in that section is described in a chart that follows. Below introduces three authors of Messianic Jewish resources used.

Messianic Jews are Jewish persons who believe Jesus [*Yeshua* in Hebrew] is the Jewish Messiah. They came to this conclusion after diligent study of ancient Hebrew language, the Hebrew Bible, writings by Jewish Rabbis (teachers/scholars) and by studying the New Testament.

- **Alfred Edersheim (***1825–1889)*

  Born in early 1800s in Vienna, Austria to Jewish parents, Edersheim was well educated both in secular subjects of the day and in Talmudic traditions of his family's Jewish faith. As a young man he converted to Christianity, as he came to believe Jesus Christ is the Jewish Messiah. He went on to become a Presbyterian minister and eventually a vicar in the Church of England.

  His unique position as a scholar trained in both Jewish and Christian traditions, including all the Biblical languages, and his extensive knowledge and understanding of the culture and religious beliefs in early first century Roman-ruled Judea, make him quite an authority on all things Biblical.

  In Appendix 9 of his book *The Life and Times of Jesus the Messiah*, Edersheim lists passages in the Old Testament applied to the Messiah or Messianic times in the most ancient Jewish writings. They amount in all to 456: 75 from the Torah, 243 from the Prophets, 138 from the Writings. They are supported by more than 558 separate quotations from Rabbinic writings.

- **Rachmiel Frydland** *(1919–1985)*

  Frydland was raised in an orthodox Jewish home in a village in Poland. At age nine he began study of the Talmud. Later he enrolled in a Rabbinical *Yeshiva* in Warsaw with the goal of becoming a Rabbi. Puzzled by the identity of the Messiah in Daniel 9:24-26, he accepted *Yeshua* [Jesus] as Messiah. By God's grace he survived the great persecution of WW II, living on the edge of death under Nazi rule.

  Frydland was truly a humble scholar and teacher who lived to proclaim the Messiahship of *Yeshua* in many countries and languages. He shared his knowledge of rabbinics and Yeshua in books, articles, and messages.

- **David H. Stern** *(1935–2022)*

  Raised in the Jewish religion by Jewish parents, Stern came to faith in the Jewish Messiah, *Yeshua* [Jesus] when he was thirty-seven years old. Stern's major work is the *Complete Jewish Bible*, which is his English translation of the Old and New Testaments.

  Stern's background includes a Master of Divinity degree from Fuller Theological Seminary, graduate work at the University of Judaism, and a Ph.D. in economics from Princeton University. He taught the first course in 'Judaism and Christianity' at Fuller Theological Seminary and was a professor at UCLA.

  An Israel-based Messianic Jewish theologian, Stern lived in Jerusalem and was active in Israel's Messianic Jewish community.

[5]Appendix C:

Find Jesus in the Lesson: Old and New Testaments

[Jesus said]
Don't misunderstand why I have come. I did not come to abolish the law of Moses or the writings of the prophets. No, I came to accomplish their purpose. I tell you the truth, until heaven and earth disappear, not even the smallest detail of God's law will disappear until its purpose is achieved.
Matthew 5:17–18

Then Jesus took them through the writings of Moses and all the prophets, explaining from all the Scriptures the things concerning himself…

Then he said, "When I was with you before, I told you that everything written about me in the law of Moses and the prophets and in the Psalms must be fulfilled."

Then he opened their minds to understand the Scriptures.
Luke 24:27, 44–45

After His resurrection, Jesus opened the minds of His disciples to understand the Scriptures in the Hebrew Bible that contain things concerning Him and how He fulfills them. Today, we too need Jesus, through the work of the Holy Spirit, to help us understand all Scriptures in the light of Him (John 16:13–15; 1 Corinthian 2:9–16; 2 Corinthian 3:14–15).

This Bible study includes a daily look at how Holy Scriptures from Genesis to Revelation point to Jesus Christ. Identifying passages related to Him in the New Testament may be easy to understand for most readers. However, understanding references to Jesus in the Old Testament as Jesus proclaims is more challenging.

What follows is an explanation of how this author selected the passages for the daily study sheet's section "Find Jesus in the Lesson," along with data from within Christendom that supports the use of this text. However, the author does not expect all readers to agree with all selected texts and the rationale for them.

It is the author's hope at a minimum to familiarize readers with some Bible scholars' understanding of passages throughout the Bible that are interpreted as pointing to Christ. See References for more detailed personal or group study (2 Timothy 2:15).

References[6]:

- Alfred Edersheim, *The Life and Times of Jesus the Messiah*, Anson D. F. Randolph and Company
- Rachmiel Frydland, *What the Rabbis Know About the Messiah—A Study of Genealogy and Prophecy,* Messianic Publishing Company
- David H. Stern, *Complete Jewish Bible*, Jewish New Testament Publications
- Michael Rydelnik, The Messianic Hope: Is the Hebrew Bible Really Messianic? (Nashville, TN; B&H Publishing Group, 2010)
- G.K. Beale, Handbook on the New Testament Use of the Old Testament (Grand Rapids, MI: Baker Academic, 2012)
- *Hebrew-English New Covenant—Prophecy Edition*, Hope of Israel Publications; 324 Messianic Prophecies

[6]Appendix C

- Beale and Carson Editors, *Commentary on the New Testament Use of the Old Testament* (Grand Rapids, MI: Baker Academic, 2007)
- Discovery Series, *Questions Skeptics Ask About Messianic Prophecy*, Managing Editor: David Sper, 1997 RBC Ministries
- "100 Prophecies Fulfilled by Jesus," *Rose Book of Bible Charts, Maps and Time Lines* (Torrance, CA: Rose Publishing, Inc. RW Research, Inc., 2005), p. 81—86; also can be purchased as a pamphlet.
- Prophecies of the Messiah in the Hebrew Bible, Jews For Jesus Website.

"Find Jesus in the Lesson" Text Selection Categories

The information provided in this section of the daily study pages falls into one or more of the below categories.

Hermeneutic and exegetic interpretation of the New Testament's use of Old Testament passages uses direct quotes, allusions, and an awareness of a quotation's wide context in the Old Testament.

Key references for interpretative methods are: *The Messianic Hope: Is the Hebrew Bible Really Messianic?* (Rydelnik) and *Handbook on the New Testament Use of the Old Testament* (Beale)[6].

1. **Messianic Prophecies Category**

   Jesus of Nazareth is presented as fulfilling Messianic prophecies. These are Old Testament Bible prophecies about the "Anointed One", which means Messiah in Hebrew (Christ in Greek). He is the "deliverer" or "savior" of the Jewish people and all the people of the world. These prophecies, which are divinely inspired predictions about the future, were written centuries before Jesus, the Christ, was born.

2. **Typology Category**

   Scriptures speak of interpretations such as typology, where a "type" is a representation of one thing by another. For example, in Hebrews 11:19 Isaac is presented as a type (figure) of Christ. Typology basically refers to persons mentioned in the ancient text who are presented as evoking things to come. However, the idea of typology does not take away from the historical context of the original text. Instead, it presumes an additional deeper meaning that can be drawn from the historical text.

3. **Unity of God's Salvation Plan and the Idea of Fulfillment Category**

   The basic theological understanding that God's plan of salvation, which is fulfilled (culminates) in Christ (Ephesians 1:3–14), is a unity from Genesis to Revelation, but it is revealed progressively over time.

4. **Continuity of Jesus' Family Tree and National Israel Category**

   The continuous, consistent thread of passages describing the family tree of Jesus and National Israel between the Old and New Testament are highlighted Also, Jesus Christ's use of scriptures, people, places or events from the Old Testament, which affirm continuity from the Old to the New Testament, are highlighted.

[6]Appendix C

The Book of Genesis

✞

In the beginning

God created the heavens and the earth.

Genesis 1:1

Preparatory Study Material

Contents

Topic

Various Views on Origins[1]

Reprinted by permission, "Survey of Old Testament" by Paul Benware

Various views have been proposed to answer the question of the origin of the earth and universe.[1]

Great amounts of material have been written in defending and promoting each view. It is impossible to reproduce the argument of the various positions. A brief summary is given of these views, recognizing the fact that within each perspective there may be many different variations.

Evolution

The word evolution simply means "change," "development," or "progress." When applied to earth's origins, it stands for the view that the world and that which is in it began and developed by means of natural processes.

Starting with simple, single-celled organisms, new species of more complex and intricate forms have developed over a period of billions of years. Mutations, natural selection, and vast amounts of time are the basic elements of this view.

A personal Creator God is not needed in this theory...

Theistic Evolution

This view attempts to bring together the basic components of the theory of evolution with the Creator God of the Bible. The basic idea is that God created life but used the process of evolution to bring about the earth and the universe as we observe it today.

This view holds that Adam's body was simply that of an animal that was the result of millions of years of evolutionary development. It proposes that several hundred thousand years ago, God placed an eternal soul into this apelike biped. This act is that which sets animals and man apart.

In trying to combine these views, "theistic evolution" is seen by some as compromising the teaching of Scripture on such subjects as God's direct creation of man, the nature of man, and the origin of sin and death.

Creationism

Creationism believes that almighty God supernaturally created the heavens and the earth by specific acts. Creation was made out of nothing and was instantaneous. God did not use an evolutionary process to bring things into existence.

Within creationism there are several basic viewpoints.

- **The Day-Age View**
- **The Ruin-Reconstruction View**
- **The Literal Day View**

[1]Appendix C

Various Views on Origins[1]

Reprinted by permission, "Survey of Old Testament" by Paul Benware

The Day-Age View (Old Earth)**

This view generally holds that the days of creation in Genesis 1 were not literal twenty-four-hour days, but rather long periods of time. Thus, the earth is old, but man created on the sixth day is relatively young.

Some have held that the days of Genesis 1 are literal twenty-four-hour days, but that there are great amounts of time separating the days.

The Ruin-Reconstruction View (Gap Theory)***

This view, also known as the Gap Theory, proposes a large gap in time between an original creation (found in Genesis 1:1) and a re-creation (found in Genesis 1:3–31). The basic idea is that in the dateless past, God created a heaven and an earth that were perfect. But then satan fell into sin, and with him many other angelic beings also fell. Sin, therefore, entered the universe, and God destroyed the original earth, leaving it "waste and void." After vast amounts of time, God re-created the heavens and the earth.

The days of Genesis 1 are literal twenty-four-hour days, but they describe the re-creation and not the original creation.

The Literal Day View (Young Earth)****

This view holds that the days of creation in Genesis 1 are literal twenty-four-hour days and that they are the days of the original creation. The heavens and the earth that we observe today, though marred by sin, are those created in Genesis 1.

This view also believes in a young earth, meaning that the earth is tens of thousands of years old, not millions or billions of years old.

References:

- ***Original Article "Various Views on Origins"**
  Paul N. Benware, *Survey of the Old Testament* (Chicago, First published in the USA by Moody Publishers, 1988, 1993, Angus Hudson Ltd/Tim Dowley and Peter Wyart trading as Three's Company, 2003), p. 30–31
- ****The Day-Age View** (Old Earth)
  Davis A. Young, *Christianity and the Age of the Earth* (Grand Rapids: Zondervan, 1982).
- *****The Ruin-Reconstruction View** (Gap Theory)
  Arthur Custance, *Without Form and Void* (Brockville, Ont.: 1970).
- ******Young Earth View** (Young Earth)
  John Whitcomb, *The Early Earth*, rev. ed. (Grand Rapids: Baker, 1986); Henry Morris, *Scientific Creationism* (San Diego; Creation-Life, 1981).

[1]Appendix C

Scientific Support for Biblical Creation Story

One of the hottest scientific debate topics is the subject:

"Creation versus Evolution"

- Was the universe and humankind created by an eternal, all-wise God as introduced in Genesis and other books of the Bible?
- Is there scientific proof of the Bible's creation story?

There is scientific support for the biblical creation story.

The following identifies scriptures and scientific resources that can be referenced for further study.

What the Bible says concerning the Creator and Creation

God used WISDOM to design creation!

"The LORD formed me *[sound wisdom and understanding]* ***from the beginning, before he created anything else.***

I was appointed in ages past, at the very first, before the earth began."

Proverbs 8:22–23

Select Old Testament Creation Passages	Select New Testament Creation Passages
- Genesis Chapters 1, 2, 3, 6, 7, 8	- John 1:1–3, 10–14
- Job Chapters 38 and 39	- Romans 1:20–25
- Psalm 104	- Colossians 1:15–18
- Psalm 148	- 2 Peter 2:4–5
- Proverbs 8:22–31	- 2 Peter 3:3–6
- Isaiah 45:12,18	- Revelation 12:9
- Ezekiel 28:11–17	- Revelation 20:1–2

Scientific Support for Biblical Creation Story

II. Scientists and Scientific Support for Biblical Creation Claims

- **Creationism website** provides access to a host of scientists and scientific data that is easily accessible, supporting Biblical creation and scientific principles set forth by the Bible. Their website includes resources that are free, and youth friendly in addition to highly technical material. (creationism.org)
- **Institute of Creation Research (ICR)** has the mission of equipping believers with evidence of the Bible's accuracy and authority through their research, educational programs and media resources. (icr.org)
- **Creation Science Movement (CSM)** was founded in 1932 and is the oldest creationist movement in the world. Another excellent resource of scientists and scientific data in support of the Bible's accuracy. (csm.org.uk)
- **Creation Research Society (CRS)** is a professional organization of trained scientists and interested laypersons that provides scientific backing for special creation. CRS began in 1963 with ten members but now includes hundreds, including international members. (creationresearch.org)
- **Biblical Creation Society (BCS)** is a Christian society that advances and defends the Biblical teaching on creation, from a coherent Biblical and scientific standpoint. This organization has been standing for creation since 1976. (biblicalcreation.org)
- **Mario Sieglie articles in Good News Magazine:** "God, Science and the Bible," "A Planet Perfect for Life," "Our Amazing Spaceship Earth," "The Intelligent Design Revolution" (ucg.org)

III. Archaeological Finds Support Biblical Names, Places, and Events

- *Archaeological Study Bible* by Zondervan Publishing, 2005
- Articles on **"The Bible and Archaeology"** written for **Good News and Beyond Today Magazine** (ucg.org)

Genesis: The Book of Beginnings

❑ Genesis Is the Book of the Beginnings of All Things...

- In **Genesis**
  - Creation of the heavens and earth are begun

- In **Genesis**
  - God authorizes the first Man (Adam) and his wife (Eve) to rule over creation

- In **Genesis**
  - God's adversary the devil, that old serpent, is introduced as liar, deceiver and enemy to Adam, Eve and all humankind

- In **Genesis**
  - Humankind loses Paradise and access to the Tree of Life

- In **Genesis**
  - Man's first sin, humankind's wicked activity such as murder, and the roots of evil in Babylon, are begun

- In **Genesis**,
  - God's plan to restore humankind and creation to His original design plans for them is begun

And so on...

✞

❑ ...Except for the Beginning of God

According to Genesis 1:1, God was (existed, lived) before the beginning of creation. This is because God is an eternal being, with no beginning or end. The eternal God created everything, including time!

As Dr. Myles Munroe says, "God started start."

Before the mountains were brought forth,
or ever thou hadst formed the earth and the world,
even from everlasting to everlasting, thou art God.
Psalm 90:2 KJV

Overview of Creation Story in Genesis 1:3–28, 2:1–3

(based from Amplified Bible)

❑ **Day 1: God creates light.**

First divine command, ***"Let there be light."***

- God then divides the light from the darkness, and calls the light "Day" and the darkness "Night."

❑ **Day 2: God creates the heavens.**

Second divine command, ***"Let there be an expanse..."***

- God then divides the waters that were above this expanse from the waters that were below it, and he calls the expanse "Heaven."

❑ **Day 3: God creates dry land and sea.**

Third divine command***, "Let the waters under the heavens be collected into one place, and let the dry land appear."***

- God then names the dry land, "Earth" and the waters, "Seas."

Fourth divine command, ***"Let the earth bring forth vegetation, plants yielding seed, and fruit bearing trees, in which was their seeds."***

❑ **Day 4: God creates lights in the heavens.**

Fifth divine command, ***"Let there be lights in the expanse of the heavens."***

- These lights were made to separate day from night, and to be signs, and to mark seasons, days and years.

- These lights consisted of "two great lights." The greater light (the sun) was to rule the day, and the lesser light (the moon) to rule the night. God also made the stars. He set all in the expanse of the heavens to give light upon the earth.

❑ **Day 5: God creates sea creatures and birds.**

Sixth divine command, *"Let the waters bring forth abundantly and swarm with living creatures, and let birds fly over the earth in the open expanse of the heavens."*

- God tells these creatures "to be fruitful and multiply."

❑ **Day 6: God creates land animals, including humans beings.**

Seventh divine command, *"Let the earth bring forth living creatures."*

- He makes wild beasts, livestock and reptiles.

Then "*God created man in His own image, in the image and likeness of God He created him; male and female He created them*" *(mankind or humankind).*

- God tells them "to be fruitful, and multiply, and fill the earth, and subdue it."
- God gives both humans and animals plants to eat.
- God describes His creation as "very good."

❑ **Day 7: Day of rest.**

This day God, satisfied that the completed heavens and earth were very good (suitable and pleasant), rests from His work. God blesses and sanctifies the seventh day.

From **Genesis 1,** we learn of God's magnificent creative handiwork:

- In the beginning, God created **The Universe**
- In the beginning, God created **Earth, the Perfect Home for Humankind**
- And finally in the beginning, God created **Humankind, in God's Image, the Children of God**

Genesis: The Book of Beginnings

The Universe

The Universe can be defined as “all matter and energy, including the earth, the galaxies, and the contents of intergalactic space, regarded as a whole.”[2]

Genesis Chapter 1 refers to part of the universe (stars, planets, and galaxies) as the “expanse of the heavens.” God set the sun, moon, and stars in strategic positions within the expanse of the heavens, to establish the earth’s seasons, days, and years for the benefit of earth’s inhabitants.

✞

Earth, the Perfect Home for Humankind

Like a parent who diligently prepares everything for the birth of their beloved child (such as safety, shelter, food, etc.),

God prepared the earth’s environment to be perfect—

For the creation and continuance of humankind

The earth is designed to be comfortably habitable for humankind, as God created a perfect shelter for His multitude of children to be born. The earth was also fully loaded with an eternal pantry worth of food for all living creatures, as the first food was designed with the ability to reproduce more food continuously. This is true as:

- At God’s command vegetation, plants, and fruit-bearing trees were created containing seeds designed to reproduce more of their kind continuously.
- At God’s command the waters brought forth living creatures that He commanded to be fruitful and multiply continuously.
- At God’s command the skies brought forth living creatures that God commanded to be fruitful and multiply continuously.

It takes many scientific fields of study to attempt to understand the awesome design of the universe, earth, physical laws, humans, all living creatures, and the delicate interdependent workings of all creation, which ultimately benefits humankind’s existence.

Here is a list of some of these scientific fields of study:

Actuarial Science, Agricultural Sciences, Agronomy and Soil Sciences, Allopathic Medicine, Analytical Chemistry, Anatomy, Animal Behavior, Animal Sciences, Anthropology, Applied Physics, Aquaculture, Astronomy, Astrophysics, Atmospheric Sciences,

Bacteriology, Biological and Biomedical Sciences, Biophysics, Botany and Plant Sciences,

Cardiovascular Sciences, Cell Biology, Clinical Laboratory Sciences, Cognitive Sciences, Conservation Biology, Dentistry,

Ecology, Environmental Sciences, Epidemiology, Geodetic Sciences, Geology, Geophysics, Geosciences,

Horticulture, Human Development, Human Genetics, Hydrology, Kinesiology and Movement Studies,

Marine Biology, Marine Sciences, Materials Sciences, Medical Microbiology, Medical Physics, Medical/Surgical Nursing, Meteorology,

Natural Resources, Neuroscience, Oceanography, Oncology, Optical Sciences, Pathology, Physics, Physiology, Planetary and Space Sciences, Plant Molecular Biology, Plant Pathology, Plant Physiology, Plasma Physics, Podiatric Medicine,

Toxicology, Veterinary Medicine, Veterinary Sciences, Virology, Vision Sciences, Zoology

---

Yes, all of creation was intelligently and lovingly designed by God!

Humankind, in God's Image, the Children of God

God does everything with purpose in mind. So all His creation, especially humankind, was designed with a specific and very good purpose built within (Isaiah 14:24; Psalm 33:11; Isaiah 55:10–11; Hebrews 6:16–17).

God created humankind in His image. This basically means God made (purposed) humankind to express His image. Like loving parents have children whom they know will look like them, and then they teach/influence them to think and act like them, so God created, made, and instructed humankind to be like Him.

For example...

- **God is a spirit, so He created people to be a spirit-being like Him** (Genesis 1:26–27; John 4:24, Psalms 82:1, 6).

- **God is love, so He made people to love and have fellowship with Him and with each other.**

    - This is why God had humankind on His mind before the world was even created. This is why humankind is the crowning glory of God's creation. This is why God prepared the way for humankind to be restored to right relationship with Him before they were ever created or sinned. And this is why humankind best relates to God through the characteristic of a "love" relationship (Deut. 6:5; Psalms 8:3–9; Mark 12:29–30; Ephesians 1:4–6; Hebrews 2:5–18).

    - Because of this "love" nature, God gave humankind the ability to reproduce more of itself, in a loving manner. This is why God made a male-man and a female-man and told them to commit to one another in a love relationship called marriage (Genesis 1:27–28; 2:18–25; Matthew 19:4–91 John 4:8, 16).

    - This is why God instructs humankind to relate to each other from an overall stance of respect, that has its roots in God's pure, undefiled loving character (Mark 12:30; John 13:34–35; 1 John 1:7; 2:8–11, 1 Corinthians 13:13).

- **God is Creator, so He made people creative.**

    - God gave humans the ability and commandment / instruction to increase in number and fill up the earth (Genesis 1:28).

- **God is Ruler, so He gave people ruling qualities.**

    - God gave the male-man and female-man authority and the commandment / instruction to exercise dominion over the earth, its living creatures and its resources. This means together the male and female were to be the earth's master, responsible for wisely governing over it (Genesis 1:26).

- **Although humankind was created to be a spirit-being like God, God further designed the human spirit to live in a body and become a living soul in order to express God's image on the earth (Genesis 1:26; 2:7, 21–22).**
    - With the human spirit, humankind could relate to God; with the body they could relate to things in the earth; and with the soul they could intellectually process what was learned from God and from earth experiences.
    - The original plan was that humankind would make decisions that were in keeping with the nature of God because humankind had the same nature as God.
    - Like God, humankind rules the visible earth through his physical actions that are generated out of his spirit and soul (heart, mind, intellect) that are unseen.
    - The "seen" activity of humankind is dictated by the "unseen" realm of humankind, in a similar manner that the "unseen" God interacts with the "seen" world (Romans 1:18–21).

- **Sadly, man's original sin destroyed God's original designs for humankind, but God designed a path for restoration in the beginning.**
    - Now you are ready to begin reading the entire Bible.
        - You will learn...
            - The tragic story of humankind's fall from relationship with God, and
            - The magnificent story of God's faithful execution of His plans to restore humankind to relationship with Him

Excerpt from *Dispensational Truth* by Rev. Clarence Larkin[2]

There is no contradiction between the first and second chapters of Genesis as to the creation of man[kind]. The first chapter (Gen. 1:26-28) gives the **FACT** of his creation, the second, the **MANNER OF IT.** Gen. 2:7. One is supplementary to the other.

In chapter one God is spoken of as **"ELOHIM,"** the Creator; in chapter two, He is called **"JEHOVAH"** (The Lord) because He there enters into covenant relations with man.

> At first the name **"Jehovah"** is joined with **"Elohim"** to remove all doubt as to the identity of the Being designated by the compound word.
>
> Now while **either** of these names would suit some passages, in others one would be more suitable than the other.
>
> This accounts for the discriminating use of these two names by the sacred writers and is an answer to those critics who claim that the Scriptures are a clumsy compilation of incongruous and diverse documents which they call Elohistic and Jehovistic.

In Gen. 2:7 we are told that "The **LORD God** formed (Yatsar, fashioned) man of the dust of the ground, and breathed into his nostrils the **'Breath of Life;'** and man became a living soul."

> This may mean that the Lord God-fashioned man out of the "dust of the ground" as a sculptor fashions the statue out of clay, and then breathed into the earthy form the "Breath of Life."

However it was done, we know the work was threefold:

1. The formation of the **"BODY"**—"And the Lord God **formed man of the dust of the ground."**

2. The gift of the **"SPIRIT"**—"And breathed into his nostrils the **'Breath of Life'."** By this is not meant the "Holy Spirit," but the "Spirit" of the "natural man"—that part of man that must be indwelt by the Holy Spirit before he can be born again. It is the "God Conscious" nature of man.

3. The **SOULISH** part of man—"And man became a 'Living Soul'." This is the seat of the "Self-Conscious" nature, of memory, the affections, etc.

The two principal parts of man are the **BODY** and the **SPIRIT,** but as the functions of these are separate, one being physical and the other spiritual, a third part had to be supplied called the **SOUL,** intermediate between them, and through which they may communicate.

Thus man became a "Threefold Being." I Thess. 5:23. Heb. 4:12.

[2]Appendix C

In Adam, as originally created, the Soul was such a perfect medium of communication between the Body and the Spirit that there was no conflict between them. The three blended together in one harmonious whole.

> When man fell the soul became the "battlefield" of the Body and the Spirit, and the conflict began that Paul so graphically describes in Rom. 7:7-24.

Eve was not fashioned in the same way as Adam. She was "made" sometime later. Adam had not found among all the creatures God had made a suitable companion, and God saw that it was not good for him to be alone, so he proceeded to make him an "helpmeet."

> To this end "The Lord God caused a **'deep sleep'** to fall upon Adam and he slept; and He took one of his **'RIBS,'** and closed up the flesh instead thereof; and the **'RIB,'** which the Lord God had taken from man, made (builded) He a **WOMAN,** and brought her unto the man.
>
> And Adam said, This is now bone of my bones, and flesh of my flesh; she shall be called **WOMAN,** because she was taken **OUT OF MAN."** Gen. 2:21-23.

While Adam and Eve were not both fashioned in the same way, they were not evolved from some lower creature, but were direct creations of God, "**male** and **female** created He them." Gen. 1:27.

> The reason why Eve was not fashioned separately from Adam, but was taken out of Adam's side, was to show that in their relation to each other as man and wife they were to be **ONE FLESH.**

That is their interests and sympathies, etc., were to be one, and physically they were to be counterparts of each other. Adam and Eve in their physical relation to each other are a type of Christ and the Church.

> When Eve was presented to Adam he said—"This is now **bone of my bones,** and **flesh of my flesh;"** and the Apostle Paul in speaking of the Church says—"we are **members of His BODY,** and of His **FLESH,** and of His **BONES.**
>
> For this cause shall a man leave his father and mother, and shall be joined unto his wife, and they **two** shall be one flesh. This is a great **'mystery;'** but I speak concerning Christ and the Church." Ephesians 5:30-32

Reference[2]:

Dispensational Truth by Rev. Clarence Larkin. Used by permission of Rev. Clarence Larkin Est., P.O. Box 334, Glenside, PA 19036, U.S.A.

[2]Appendix C

The journey of reading the Bible from Genesis to Revelation

- Beginning the journey does not have to be considered long or hard. For example, you can complete the initial journey of reading through the entire Bible in just one year. With the help of this *Know His Word Bible Study*, you will gain a good foundational understanding of what you have read.
- But the full journey is a lifetime long one. This is because it takes time to digest the wonders of all God has done for YOU, because He Loves You!!!

- **Begin the journey of a restored right relationship with God – Right Now!**
    - The initial step to having a restored right relationship with God is an easy one for you. This is because God has done all the hard part. All you need is faith in God's plans for your restoration (also known as salvation).

For God so loved the world,
that he gave his only begotten Son,
that whosoever believeth in him should not perish,
but have everlasting life.
***John 3:16* KJV**

- To be restored to a right relationship with God, all you need to do is believe in the work His Son Jesus Christ did on your behalf, so that you can be forgiven of all your sins and be justified in the eyes of God.
- So, right now, if you believe in your heart that God raised Jesus from the dead, and if you go tell someone that you accept the living Jesus Christ as the Lord and Savior of your life, then you are immediately restored to a right relationship with God (Romans 10:9–10).
- Now ask your new Savior Jesus Christ, to help you understand the magnificent Word of God, as you prepare to read it from the standpoint of being the beloved child of God. Do this in the form of a prayer from within your heart.

Week 1

Old Testament Begins

Featured Book: Genesis,
and a few passages from 1 Chronicles Chapter 1

Contents:

Peek at the Week

Lesson	Key Events	Find Jesus
1.1	God Creates Everything	Jesus' Role in Creation
1.2	God decides to destroy humankind	Jesus' Family Tree from Adam
1.3	God's Covenant with Noah and his family	Jesus' Family Tree from Noah
1.4	From separated Nations to Abram	Jesus is the Final King of Peace
1.5	God's Covenant with Abraham	Jesus and Israel's Return to the Promised Land
1.6	Lot's Plight	Moabite in Jesus' Family Tree
1.7	Isaac	Isaac's Sacrifice a "Type" of Jesus' Sacrifice

Chronological Notes

*Timetable	Key Events
Undated	God Created the Heavens and Earth
Undated	Adam and Eve Sin
Undated	God Sends the Flood
Undated	Noah's Sons Re-Populate Earth, Languages Separate People
2166 (or 2000) BC	Abram's Birth *(Abraham)*
2091 (or 1925) BC	Abram's Call
2080 (or 1914) BC	Ishmael's Birth
2066 (or 1900) BC	Isaac's Birth
2026 (or 1860) BC	Isaac Marries Rebekah

**All dates are approximate, with uncertainties from Bible scholars leading to early and late dates for some events, such as timing of the exodus.*[1]

[1]Appendix C

Key Word	Key Chapters
Beginnings	12

Intro to Genesis

Title

"Genesis" means "Beginnings." This key word describes the book's theme.

Summary

Genesis shows the good, bad, and ugly of the "beginnings" of all things in quick start fashion:

- In the beginning, God executes a good plan, putting humankind in a good position in life.
- Then, the first man (Adam) and first woman (Eve) fall for the deceptive trick of the crafty serpent, transitioning humankind into a bad position of death.
- This bad position is confirmed as brother kills brother, multiplying into a pattern of wickedness in the earth. This becomes so ugly in God's eyes...
- ...God decides to destroy every living thing He has created.

But Noah finds grace (favor) in God's sight. When God sends a worldwide flood to destroy all living things, Noah's family is preserved in an ark of safety, along with their animal companions. Humankind begins again from the descendants born to Noah's three sons and their wives.

Sin, still present in the heart of humankind after the flood, is evident as seen in the wrong attitudes that led to construction of the Tower of Babel. Eventually one descendant of Noah's son Shem stands out from the crowd. God chooses Abraham, who chooses to follow Him as the one true and living God. **Through Abraham, an opportunity to restore the good that God originally planned for humankind begins.**

❑ **Timetable:** *All dates approximate with early and late dates to account for uncertainties recorded by Bible scholars, such as timing of the exodus.**

Key Events	*Date
• God Created the Heavens and Earth	Undated
• Adam and Eve Sin	Undated
• God Sends the Flood	Undated
• Noah's Sons and Wives Populate Earth	Undated
• Abram's Birth *(Abraham)*	2166 (or 2000) BC
• Abram's Call	2091 (or 1925) BC
• Isaac's Birth	2066 (or 1900) BC
• Isaac Marries Rebekah	2026 (or 1860) BC
• Jacob's Birth	2006 (or 1840) BC
• Joseph at Seventeen years old	1898 (or 1732) BC
• Jacob and Family of Israel Move to Egypt	1876 (or 1710) BC
• Jacob Blesses His Sons	1859 (or 1692) BC

- ❑ **Author: Most Likely Moses**

  Moses was a writer:

  God is the author of the entire Bible, as all scripture was written as inspired by Him (2 Timothy 3:16). God used select men to write down His message for all humankind's benefit. The Holy Spirit of God guided these men to write God's Word as God intended (2 Peter 1:20-21).

  From ancient times, the authorship of Genesis has been attributed to Moses, as with all the first five books of the Bible (Pentateuch). Here are some scriptures that support Moses' authorship: Exodus 17:14; 24:4–7; 34:27; Leviticus 4:1; 6:1, 8; Numbers 1:1, 19; Deuteronomy 17:18–20; 30:10; 1 Kings 2:3; 2 Chronicles 23:18; 34:14; Nehemiah 8:1; Matthew 8:4; 19:7–8; Mark 7:10; 12:26; Luke 16:29, 31; 24:44; John 1:45; 5:46; 7:19

  Some modern scholars believe there were other authors who helped either write or compile the Pentateuch and at different times in Israel's history. To review a detailed discussion on these points of view, as well as strong arguments in support of Moses' authorship and the date of writing, read: "Chapters VII and VIII" in ***Prophecy and History in Relation to the Messiah*** by Alfred Edersheim. For a brief overview on this topic, review "Transition: Book of Genesis" in the ***Chronological Study Bible, p. 3.***[2]

- ❑ **Date of writing: ~1405 BC**

  Many Bible scholars believe Moses wrote the first five books of the Bible during the time he led the children of Israel (Abraham's descendants) in the wilderness. You will be introduced to Moses in the book of Exodus.

- ❑ **Major Events in Genesis:**

Creation of Heavens, Earth and Humankind (Chapters 1–11)		**Creation of God's Chosen People (Chapters 12–50)**	
Creation	**(1–2)**	**Abraham**	**(12–23)**
Fall	**(3–5)**	**Isaac**	**(24–26)**
Flood	**(6–9)**	**Jacob => Israel**	**(27–36)**
Nations	**(10–11)**	**Joseph**	**(37–50)**

Historical Locations: Genesis events occur in Middle East area of the world

See Maps on Events in Genesis

Middle East: Then (Ancient Times)	Middle East: Now (Modern Times)
Egypt	Egypt
Sinai Peninsula	Suez
Canaan (Israel)	Israel, Jordan, Palestine, Lebanon
Mesopotamia	Syria
Assyria, Babylonia, Sumer (Ur)	Iraq (Baghdad)
Hittites	Turkey
Media, Persia, Susa	Iran
Arabian Desert	Saudi Arabia
Cush	Sudan, Ethiopia

[2]Appendix C

First Man > Adam

Reading Assignment: Genesis 1:1–3:24

Lesson 1.1

I. Lesson Exercise

God Creates Man and Woman

God takes the empty, formless, dark earth and a) gives it light, b) gives it form, and c) fills it with good things. Like a loving parent who prepares for the birth of their child, God first puts everything in place to satisfy humankind's every need. Then, God creates the first man Adam, followed some time later by the first woman Eve.

Made In God's Image…

In Genesis 1:26–28, we read how humankind, both male and female, were created in God's image. In John 4:24, Jesus explained that "God is a Spirit." From these two passages we understand that humankind is a "spirit" being like God.

… Male

In Genesis 2:7, we read of two more steps God performed to finish creating the first male of humankind. Next God formed the male's body from the dust of the ground. Then God breathed into the body His breath of life. The man became a living person. Now he could think, walk, communicate spiritually with God; and use his five senses to understand the world. Man could see, hear, smell, talk and feel.

… Female

After giving the man Adam an awesome place to stay, an important job to do, and a simple command to obey, then God gave him the ideal companion to be his wife and share his wonderful life. From Genesis 2:21–22, we learn that God shaped the first female's body from a rib taken out of Adam, whom God had put in a deep sleep.

Because the first female was taken out of a man, Adam called her "woman," which means "female human being". From the womb of the female of humankind, more humans would be born. Adam named her Eve because she would be the mother of all people (Gen. 3:20).

1) In Gen. 1:28, when God blessed the male and female, what purpose did He give both of them for their general earthly activity? __________

2) After Adam and Eve sinned, how did their earthly roles change because of God's punishment? (Gen. 3:16–19) ________________

First Woman > Eve

The Serpent in Genesis Revealed

In the last book of the Bible, the ancient serpent introduced in Genesis is mentioned. From Revelation 12:9, the true identity behind the talking serpent in Genesis is revealed. He is the devil, also known as satan, God's adversary. From Rev 12:9 we learn that in the beginning of time, the devil deceived Eve. But in the end of time, the devil will be successful in deceiving the whole world.

Where Is the Garden of Eden?

Where in the world is the Garden of Eden?

After Adam and Eve sinned, God banished them from the Garden of Eden forever. Eden was guarded by two mighty angels with a flaming sword, to prevent them from reentering and eating from the tree of life in their new sinful state (Gen 3:22–24).

Since their expulsion, the Garden of Eden has never been seen again, but Bible scholars try to guess its location.

Although the exact location of the Garden of Eden is unknown, Genesis 2:10-14 describes four rivers that flow out of Eden.

Two of these rivers, Tigris and Euphrates, are located in modern Iraq, which in Bible times was the land of Asshur.

Look for these rivers on the maps "Middle East: Then (BC) and Middle East: Now."

II. Find Jesus in the Lesson: Jesus' Role in Creation

Throughout the Bible there are scriptures that talk about different parts of the creation story. Read New Testament scripture Colossians 1:15–17 to discover the role Jesus Christ played in creation.

3) What did Christ do in creation? (Col. 1:15–17) ____________________

Jesus, the Promised Conquering "Offspring" of Eve

In Gen. 3:15, God tells the serpent that the woman's offspring (descendant) will strike (bruise, crush) the head of the serpent. Some Bible scholars explain this passage is a prophecy (foretelling) from God introducing the Messiah He would send. Messiah would conquer the devil, which is God and humankind's adversary that worked through the serpent to deceive Eve.

God's promise also gives insight that the offspring would be born of a woman. Bible scholars believe Gen. 3:15 points to the future virgin birth of Messiah.

- **In the book, *What the Rabbis Know About the Messiah*, Rachmiel Frydland refers to the writings of Rabbi David Kimchi, one of the greatest Jewish commentators from the 12th–13th century**. The Rabbi recognized Gen. 3:15 as a prophecy about Messiah's redemption of humankind.[3] Frydland believes the Jewish Messiah is Jesus Christ.
- **In the Hebrew-English New Covenant Bible, another ancient rabbinical source cites Genesis 3:15 as being a Messianic prophecy.** It records a quote by Rabbi Tanchuma on behalf of Rabbi Samuel from Midrash Rabbah 23.[4] The writers of the Hebrew-English New Covenant Bible believe the Jewish Messiah is Jesus Christ.
- **In Appendix 9 of the book, *The Life and Times of Jesus the Messiah*, the author Alfred Edersheim also cites ancient Jewish scholars who identify Genesis 3:15 as a Messianic passage.**[5] Edersheim was a nineteenth-century Messianic Jewish Bible scholar.

Jesus Christ fulfills this promise, by…

- **Being born of Virgin Mary:** Matt. 1:18–25; Gal. 4:4; Heb. 2:14–15; 1 John 3:8
- **And conquering the devil:** Rev. 12:7–17

Prior to the "Intro to Genesis–Preparatory Study Material" section, there are several charts describing Jewish and Christian sources used to identify Messianic prophecies throughout *Know His Word Bible Study*.

Review the charts…

- **Hebrew Bible/Old Testament**
- **The Messiah, Our Savior—Revealed from the Beginning**
- **Jewish Scholars Used as Resources for Find Jesus in the Lesson**
- **Find Jesus in the Lesson: Old and New Testaments**

[3,4,5]Appendix C

III. Closing Thoughts

They Learned the Hard, Deathly Way:

- God told Adam he would "surely die" if he ate fruit from the tree of the knowledge of good and evil. (Gen. 2:16)
- Satan told Eve she and Adam would not die if they disobeyed God, but they would become like God knowing good and evil. (Gen. 3:4)
- Sadly, Adam and Eve learned the hard way that God was right.

Adam and Eve did not experience immediate **physical death** (this came later).

But, they experienced immediate separation from the relationship they had with God, which was **spiritual death**.

Also, their nature immediately changed from one of purity to one of wickedness (**moral death**), which spread to their descendants- all humankind. (Romans 5:12)

From Blessed to Cursed:

- Adam had to do hard labor to eat,
- Eve had to do hard labor to have children,
- And hatred and murder became members of the family.

What a tragic contrast to the paradise existence they first enjoyed. What is worse, God said Eve's descendants and the serpent's descendants would continue to be enemies.

Yet, God gave a promise of hope in Gen. 3:15 in the form of the first prophecy about the Messiah, humankind's Savior and Deliverer.

God Gave a Promise of Hope in Genesis 3:15

Power in the Blood!

> **Reading Assignment:**
> **Genesis 4:1–5:32**
> **1 Chronicles 1:1–4**
> **Genesis 6:1–22**

Lesson 1.2

I. Lesson Exercise

Power in the Blood

The need to present the shed blood of special sacrificed animals for properly approaching God will be described in detail in the book of Leviticus.

But it appears God taught the first family about this from the beginning.

Animals' Skin, Animals' Blood

After Adam and Eve sinned in the Garden of Eden, they clothed themselves with fig leaves in an attempt to cover up their nakedness and shame before God (Gen. 3:7).

"The Lord God made clothing from animal skins for Adam and his wife" Genesis 3:21

Genesis 3:21 gives insight on how fig leaves were not sufficient to make guilty persons presentable before God. So God made Adam and Eve acceptable coverings out of animal skins. With the animals being slain to obtain their skin, their blood was shed.

In the book of Leviticus, we will read how this shed blood of animals is significant in preparing an acceptable covering for man to use in approaching God. Therefore, Gen 3:21 also provides the first insight that God must have instructed the first family on the way to approach Him with their new sinful nature.

Lamb Offerings, Lamb's Blood

The second insight that God had instructed the first family on the proper way to approach Him is seen in the story about the gifts (offerings) Cain and Abel brought to God (Genesis 4:1–7). Cain, a farmer, brought God a gift from the produce of his farm. Abel, a shepherd, offered God the choicest lambs from the best of his flock. God's rejection of Cain's offering and acceptance of Abel's offering reveals again God's patient teaching of the first family on the right way to approach Him.

Blood of Righteous Abel Speaks to God after His Murder

But the Lord said, "What have you done? Listen—your brother's blood cries out to me from the ground!" Gen. 4:10

Next, the first family—Adam the first man, Eve the first woman, and their first two sons, Cain and Abel – experience the first physical death, from a horrible family murder.

Cain, while jealous of his younger brother Abel for presenting an acceptable gift to God, murdered his own brother.

Although Cain silenced his brother's human voice, the scriptures explain that Abel's righteous blood, which was wrongfully spilled upon the ground, spoke to God, and it still speaks to us today.

It was by faith Abel brought a more acceptable offering to God than Cain did. God accepted Abel's offering to show that he was a righteous man. Although Abel is long dead, he still speaks to us because of his faith. Hebrews 11:4

Humankind Begins to Increase and Organize

4) From Gen. 4:17–22, write the "firsts" that are mentioned:
   a) Cain founded a _______________ (vs 17)
   b) Jabal became the first ____________________ (vs 20)
   c) Jubal became the first __________, inventing the ___________ and _____________ (vs 21)
   d) Tubal-cain was first to work with ___________, making instruments of ___________ and __________ (vs 22)

Men Begin to Worship the Lord

5) During whose lifetime did people begin to worship the Lord? (Gen. 4:16) ___________________

6) How did Enoch suddenly disappear? (Gen. 5:24) ________________
   Note: Hebrews 11:5 says of Enoch ***"But before he was taken up, he was approved as pleasing to God."*** Wow, imagine that!

God decides to destroy all humankind except for one family

The rapidly growing population became very evil. The human race was further poisoned by wrongful relations between the sons of God *(some scholars believe these to be fallen angels based on Job 1:6 and Jude 1:6)* and human women, which led to the birth of giants, who are also referred to as "heroes of old." But there was one man, Noah, who was righteous and blameless before God (Gen 6:8–9). This is important because through Noah and his family, the human race gets a second chance.

7) What did God decide to do to all living creatures and how? (Gen. 6:11–12, 17) ____

II. Find Jesus in the Lesson

Jesus' Family Tree from Adam

Luke Chapter 3 lists the genealogy, meaning family tree, of Jesus Christ, tracing His family all the way back to Adam. In fact Luke 3:36–38, 1 Chronicles 1:1–4 and Genesis 5:3–29, all list the same family tree members from Adam to Noah, although these books were written hundreds of years apart by different authors.

III. Closing Thoughts

Today's lesson closes with God's plan of great destruction which would…

"completely wipe out this human race…
and destroy all the animals and birds, too" *(Gen. 6:7).*

Because of humankind's evil heart God was sorry he made them. Consider how humankind's sinfulness affected the physical earth and animals, causing them to be cursed, too.

Thank God for Noah, whose righteousness provided a hope for humankind and the earth. The future of the world would ride in a great, big boat, called an ark.

God gave Noah specific instructions for building this "ark of safety" to house his family and select pairs of animals. They would repopulate earth after world-wide destruction by the Great Flood.

Lesson 1.3

Reading Assignment:
Genesis 7:1–10:5
1 Chronicles 1:5–7
Genesis 10:6–20
1 Chronicles 1:8–16
Genesis 10:21–30
1 Chronicles 1:17–23
Genesis 10:31–32

I. Lesson Exercise

Male and Female Required

God instructs Noah to take seven pairs (pair being one male and one female) of animals on the ark, that God approved for use in eating and offering as blood sacrifices, in properly approaching Him.

Noah was also to take one pair (male and female) of all the other animals.

8) Why did God specify the pairs had to be male and female? (Gen. 7:2–3) ______________________

9) Who were the four pairs of people saved in the ark? (Gen. 7:13)______________________

The Rainbow Is God's Sign

God Makes a Covenant with Noah

After the forty days and forty nights of the great, destroying flood waters, the passengers on the ark had to wait until the flood waters retreated before leaving the ark. Five months later, Noah, his family and the animals got off the boat.

Again, we read how the blood of animals God approved of for use in sacrifices, was presented to Him in an acceptable offering (Gen. 8:20–21). Noah's actions pleased God, so that God made a promise and a covenant agreement with Noah and his sons.

10) What did God promise never to do again? (Gen. 8:21–22)

____

11) What "sign" did God give to Noah and his sons as evidence of this eternal covenant promise with Noah and all living creatures? (Gen. 9:12–13) ______________________

Blessings, Instruction and a Curse

The **blessings and instruction God gave to Noah and his sons** in Gen. 9:1–2 is almost identical to that given to Adam and Eve in Gen. 1:28.

Sometime after God blessed and instructed them to fill and dominate the earth, Noah's son Ham responds in a shameful manner to finding his Father drunk and naked in his tent. Because of his reaction, **Noah pronounced a curse on Ham's son Canaan** (Gen. 9:20–25).

This curse is significant because the fulfilling of this curse will be a main topic of Bible discussion, especially of the Old Testament.

Noah's blessing on his two sons Japheth and Shem (a father's blessing), and his curse on Ham's son are powerful because God honors them (Gen. 9:25–26).

It is important to note that Noah's curse only applied to Ham's son Canaan (Gen. 9:24–25). God had already blessed Ham along with his brothers (Gen. 9:1).

Table of Nations

Genesis Chapter 10 is sometimes called the Table of Nations. The three sons of Noah and their wives begin to have children. They quickly multiply and form nations that eventually spread out over the earth in groups by languages, occupations and family tree.

Look at the Map "(16) Table of Nations" to see where the descendants of Japheth, Ham and Shem migrated to populate the earth.

⇒ **Japheth's offspring**—became seafaring peoples in various lands. This was the smallest group in Gen. 10, but Noah's blessing ensured that their territory would be enlarged. They would share in the prosperity of Shem's offspring.

⇒ **Ham's offspring**—grew the largest, the fastest. This family tree indicates they populated territory in modern day Africa, Middle East and Iraq countries. Ham's offspring develop into powerful warring nations, such as the Philistines, Amorites, Hittites, Jebusites, who will fight diligently against the descendants of Shem. Cities such as Babylon and Assyria will play significant roles in warfare stories of the future. Sodom and Gomorrah will be discussed soon.

⇒ **Shem's offspring**—produced the most important Bible heroes of all.

It is interesting how Bible names tell a story about an important event once you know the meaning of the names. Keep this in mind as you read through the Bible.

12) In Genesis 10:25, what does Shem's great, great grandson's name "Peleg" mean?
    a) ____

    What historical event does Peleg's name describe?
    b) ____

II. Find Jesus in the Lesson

Jesus' Family Tree from Noah's Son Shem

"Then Noah said,
"May Shem be blessed by the LORD my God
... and may he live in the tents of Shem."
Gen. 9:26–27

In the book *What the Rabbis Know About the Messiah,* Rachmiel Frydland explained that in the Jewish Talmud—which is a book with ancient Jewish Rabbis commentary on the Hebrew Bible (= Christian Old Testament)—the passage in Genesis 9:26–27 reveals that the Messiah will come from the family line of Noah's son Shem.[6]

In the New Testament, Luke 3:36, the genealogy of Jesus Christ comes through the family line of Noah's son Shem. (Luke 3:36)

III. Closing Thoughts

Humankind Gets Another Chance

Shem, Japheth and Ham's families multiply and spread over all the earth. Sadly, sin and curses did not die in the flood. They were still in the heart of people as evidenced in the story of Ham's sin.

Yet God promised never to destroy the earth again by flood. (Gen. 9:8-17)

God also promised that a future descendant of Eve would bruise the head of her enemy, who tricked her into losing paradise. (Gen. 3:15)

Read on to see the amazing way God keeps His promises!

Noah's Sons and Wives Populate the Earth

[6]Appendix C

Reading Assignment:
Genesis 11:1–26
I Chronicles 1:24–27
Genesis 11:27–14:24

Lesson 1.4

I. Lesson Exercise: Power in Agreement

The Tower of Babel's story in Genesis 11:1–9 gives us insight on the power a group of people have when they agree to work together to accomplish a goal (unity).

- People need to understand each other to agree.
- People need to agree on a project they want to accomplish together.
- People who agree are powerful; there are no limits to what they can accomplish.
- People can agree together that they will *not* do God's will.

13) Why was the Tower of Babel project *not* in agreement with God's will for the people? (Compare Gen. 9.1 with Gen. 11:4)

____

14) Why did God give people different languages? (Gen. 11:7–8)

____

Bible Story: Tower of Babel – Historical Fact or Mythical Fiction?

There are those who believe the Bible account of the Tower of Babel is a myth, a fiction short story. However, there is evidence to support it being a historical fact.

This evidence exists in the form of ancient language studies, historical literature, and archeological findings. Internet references exist for further research such as the Biblical Archaeology.org.uk website.

God blesses people who work in agreement on activities that are His will.
(Psalm 133:1, 3, Matthew 18:19)

God Calls Abram (Abraham)

The history of Shem's family narrows in focus to the family of Terah, with final focus turning to Terah's son Abram. In a way, you could say that the rest of the entire Bible is focused on the family of Abram, who will later be called Abraham.

God specifically calls Abram to establish a special relationship with him.

✞

This relationship will be called a covenant relationship with partner obligations on the part of God and Abram.

There are blessings for keeping covenant with God and curses for breaking covenant agreements.

At seventy-five years old, Abram took his wife Sarai, his nephew Lot, and all his wealth, and departed from his father's house as the Lord instructed him. God led Abraham to the land of Canaan (Gen. 12:4–5; Gen. 17:5)

In Genesis 12:1–9 we learn the first details of the covenant God made with Abram:

- God told Abram to leave his country, his relatives, his father's house, and go to a land that God would show him. *(A new land that Abram had never seen before.)*
- God would make Abram a father of a great nation.
- God would bless Abram, make him famous and a blessing to others.
- God would bless those who bless Abram and curse those that curse Abram
- All the families of the earth would be blessed through Abram's seed.

✞

Lot had to separate from his Uncle Abram (Gen. 13:5–9)

God had blessed Abram to be rich. He also blessed his nephew Lot with so much wealth—in sheep, cattle, tents and workers—the land could no longer support both of their camps.

Abram told Lot to select land away from him so they could separate. Lot chose the beautiful looking Jordan Valley area where Sodom, Gomorrah and Zoar were located. However, the beauty will soon fade...

Warring Kings Take Lot, but Abram Saves the Day!

War broke out in the ancient Middle Eastern area. Five Kings went to war against four kings, one king dominated many for twelve years, there were valleys with tar pits, and people escaped to the mountains. In the flurry of activity, Abram's nephew Lot, who had chosen to live in the Sodom and Gomorrah area, was captured along with the other inhabitants of the city. In Gen. 14:14 Abram takes his 318 trained servants to do what five Kings could not do; he rescues Lot and the other captives.

15) Who helped Abram to conquer his enemies? (Gen. 14:20)

____

II. Find Jesus in the Lesson

Jesus Is the Final King of Peace

Melchizedek is called the King of Salem and a priest of God Most High. After Abram rescues Lot, Melchizedek pronounces blessings on Abram, who in turn gives Melchizedek a tenth of all the goods he had recovered from the war. (Gen. 14:18–20)

In Hebrews Chapters 5 and 7 Jesus' priesthood is said to be from Melchizedek's line of priesthood.

Christ did not exalt himself to become high priest...
God said to him,

"You are a Priest Forever
in the line of Melchizedek."

Hebrews 5:5–6

Salem means peace, so Melchizedek was the King of Peace (Hebrews 7:1–2). Jesus Christ, who is a priest after the likeness of Melchizedek, is the final King of Peace.

III. Closing Thoughts

Adam and Eve's sin brought a curse on all humankind. Through Abram all humankind received new hope for being blessed. Abram's personal blessings from being in covenant relationship with God are also evident. Abram was wealthy. When he went to war against many kings, he won.

Abram credited all of his blessings to the hand of God. Yet Abram was an old man, married to an old woman *(and still good-looking),* who had no child to pass on his blessings. That was the next challenge God would address.

God cut a Blood Covenant…

Reading Assignment:
Genesis 15:1–17:27

Lesson 1.5

I. Lesson Exercise

In Genesis Chapters 15 and 17, God gives Abram more information about the covenant He made with him in Genesis 12.

Key points from all three chapters

- Abram will be a father of a great nation and his name will be great (famous)
- Those who bless Abram will be blessed, those who curse him will be cursed
- God will give the land of the Canaanites to Abram's offspring
- God will protect Abraham and his reward will be great
- Abram's name is changed to Abraham because he is a father of many nations
- Sarai's name is changed to Sarah because she will be a mother of many nations
- All these blessings will pass on to a son from Abraham and Sarah's own body
- Abraham's offspring will be too numerous to count (like sand and stars)
- The covenant God made with Abraham is everlasting, continuing with his offspring

Spiritual Signing of the Covenant (Gen 15:1–21)

When God promised to give old man Abram his own son, then…

Abram believed God.

He acted on that belief by obeying and trusting God.

God declared that Abram is a righteous person because of his faith in God's Word.

God cut a blood covenant with Abram.

- Abram brought specific animals as instructed by God. All but the birds were cut in half and laid out on the ground. After dark, God supernaturally sent a smoking pot and flaming torch to represent His passing through the middle of the dead animal halves.

- These actions were the blood covenant ritual, in which God used the poured-out blood of animals to represent His life and death binding commitment to fulfill His promises to Abram.
- If God would break any of His covenant agreements, then He would become like the dead animals. Therefore, the covenant was confirmed as binding forever. God entered into an everlasting covenant agreement with Abram.

This is what a blood covenant relationship is all about— it is life to keep the commitment, but death if you break it. With the shedding of the animal's blood, God and Abram were signing their covenant agreement in a spiritual sense.

Physical Signing of the Covenant (Gen. 17:9–14)

The covenant was signed in a physical sense when Abram obeyed God's instructions to circumcise every male in his household, and all future male descendants.

- In Gen. 17:5, God told Abram he was changing his name to Abraham as a part of their covenant agreement. *(Abrahamic Covenant)*
- In Gen. 17:9, God told Abraham his descendants would have the continuous responsibility to keep the terms of the covenant agreement between God and Abraham. The male reproductive organ is used to produce these descendants. When the foreskin of this organ is cut, then blood is shed in the actual instrument used to make new members of the covenant family. Through this act of circumcision, the blood covenant is renewed physically with each male responsible for reproducing new covenant members in the family.[7]
    - Note: Circumcision is the cutting away of the foreskin of the male's reproductive organ.

Ishmael is not the Son of Promise (Genesis 17:15–16 and Galatians 4:22–23)

- Sarah was not acting in faith when she convinced her husband to have a son by her Egyptian servant Hagar.

  In ancient times, they were all following a common custom that allowed for the birth of a child in this manner, when the woman of the house could not give birth.[8] Yet God made it very clear Abraham and Hagar's son was not the long awaited son of promise. Sarah, in spite of her old age, would have her own son.

... with Abraham

Abraham's Descendants' Future Oppression as Slaves Is Foretold

God gave Abraham advance knowledge that his descendants would serve as slaves away from the Promised Land of Canaan. After that time, God would punish their oppressors, and cause them to come out of slavery with great wealth. God also told Abraham he would die in peace. (Gen. 15:13–16)

16) Read Gen. 15:16. What did God say was to happen to the Amorites before Abraham's descendants could return to the Promised Land?

____

II. Find Jesus in the Lesson

Jesus and Israel's Return to the Promised Land

God made an everlasting covenant with Abraham in which He promised to give his descendants the Canaanite land (referred to as the "Promised Land," which is the Palestinian area of the Middle East today).

Abraham's descendants became a great nation (Israelites) who lived in the land until they were kicked out because of their sin. In modern times the Israelites (also known as Hebrews and Jews) moved back into this area in 1948 after being dispersed away from it for over 1,900 years.[9]

Today the land does not totally belong to the Israelites (Jews). However, this does not mean God has forgotten His promise to Abraham. Jesus talked to His disciples about this in the New Testament.

When the apostles were with Jesus, they kept asking him, "Lord, are you going to free Israel now and restore our kingdom?"

Jesus gave them this response,

"The Father sets those dates," he replied, "and they are not for you to know."

Acts 1:6–7

III. Closing Thought

Meaning of Abraham and Sarah's New Names

- **Abram's name is changed to Abraham, which means "Father of many,"** because God promised to make Abraham a father of many nations (Genesis 17:4–6).
- **Sarai's name is changed to Sarah, which means "princess," for she will be the mother of many nations.** Kings will be among their descendants." (Genesis 17:15–16)

[9]Appendix C

Bible Tidbits

❋ One language was spoken by every person in the beginning.

- In the early days of people on earth, all of humankind spoke one language. (Gen. 11:1)
- One can assume that Adam spoke the oldest language which was learned and communicated to his descendants. This language was the only one until God's intervention at the Tower of Babel.
- Some scholars conclude the oldest language is Semitic, the language of the Hebrews, which is Abraham and his descendants' language. Some scholars conclude the Sumerian or Egyptian language is the oldest.[10] Some say an exact answer is not known.

❋ The normal lifespan of humankind was significantly reduced after Noah's generation.

- Prior to Noah and the flood, people lived to be hundreds of years old. Methuselah fathered Lamech when he was 187 years old. Then he lived another 782 years when he fathered more sons and daughters. (Gen. 5:1–32; 6:1–3)
- By the time of Abraham, he was considered old at the age of 75. It was considered a miracle for Abraham to have a child at the age of 100 years old and for Sarah to have a child at 90 years old. (Gen. 17:17; 21:6–7)

❋ Abraham was not circumcised when he fathered Ishmael, but he was circumcised when he fathered Isaac.

- Abraham and Ishmael were circumcised at the same time, when Abraham was 99 years old, and Ishmael was 13 years old. On the other hand, Isaac was conceived after Abraham was circumcised, and he was circumcised on the eighth day of his life according to God's instructions for every male of the covenant. (Gen. 16:1–4; Gen. 17:9–14, 23–27, Gen. 21:1–5)
- Isaac was the firstborn son of the fully instituted Covenant relationship between God and Abraham.

[10]Appendix C

Lesson 1.6

Reading Assignment:
Genesis 18:1–21:7

I. Lesson Exercise

Abraham, the Friend of God

Friends visit each other, eat together, exchange gifts and talk intimately. This describes the exact relationship between God and Abraham.

In James 2:23, it plainly says that Abraham was called "the friend of God". This friendship is clearly demonstrated in today's lesson (Genesis 18:1–33).

- The three men that visited Abraham were really God and two angels.
- Abraham prepared bread, roasted meat, cheese curds and milk
- God told Abraham he and Sarah would have a son by the next year
- The Lord told Abraham He was planning to destroy Sodom and Gomorrah after the angels confirmed that the wickedness deserved total destruction.
- Abraham boldly pleaded for mercy on those towns. Abraham changed the number to use in determining God's mercy six times counting down from fifty to ten.

17) Why did God say He "singled out" Abraham from everyone else? (Gen. 18:18–19) ____

✞

Sodomy comes from Sodom

The word "sodomy" refers to "the sin of Sodom."

Based on Genesis 19:1–29, the sin of sodomy describes the type of sin which led to God's destruction of the cities of Sodom and Gomorrah.

- Genesis 19:5–9 describes the relations that the men of Sodom wanted to engage in with Lot's male guests as being wicked.
- 2 Peter 2:6–8 explains that Lot was a righteous man who was vexed by the "filthy conversation of the wicked" and his righteous soul was vexed "from day to day with their unlawful deeds" (KJV).

Lot's wife, Lot's plight

18) Why did Lot's wife turn into a pillar of salt? (Gen. 19:17, 26) ________

More Sinful Relations…

God gives detailed instruction on forbidden relations in Leviticus Chapter 18.

- In a family, only a married man and woman (husband and wife) are to look on each other's nakedness.
- This includes inappropriate touching or looking at each other, such as Ham did to his father Noah in Genesis 9:20–25.

… By Lot's Daughters

When Lot's daughters lay with their father, this was a sin. (Gen. 19:30–38)

- From their actions, two sons, Moab and Ben-ammi, were born.
- These boys' descendants became known as the Moabites and Ammonites. They grew into wicked nations that troubled Abraham's descendants.

But Keep Reading…

In "Find Jesus in the Lesson" learn of a story of God's loving grace for a Moabite descendant.

- This story reveals how God's loving grace is available for all who decide to turn away from sinful actions and turn to Him.

Okay, So Abraham Was Not Perfect, But God Is Faithful

Sarah may have been old, but she was beautiful. She was so beautiful Abraham would not admit she was his wife in new lands, so kings would not kill him to take her for their wife. Abraham was wrong for lying. Despite his sin, God intervened in order to protect the fulfillment of His promise that Abraham and Sarah would have a special child. God would not allow Abimelech to have relations with Sarah.

19) God told Abimelech that Abraham was a what? (Gen. 20:7)

____

After all they had been through, Isaac, the son of promise, is finally born to Abraham and Sarah. What a happy, I mean, funny ending!

20) What did Isaac's birth cause Sarah to do? (Gen. 21:6)

____

II. Find Jesus in the Lesson

Moabite in Jesus' Family Tree

The Moabites and Ammonites became such enemies of Abraham's descendants, that God instructed the following concerning them in Deuteronomy 23:3—

" No Ammonites or Moabites,
or any of their descendants for ten generations,
may be included in the assembly of the Lord."

But, guess what?

A Moabite woman is in the family tree of Jesus Christ (Matthew 1:5).

Her name is Ruth.

We will learn all about her in the Bible book named for her. This is an example of God's magnificent grace in His salvation plan, which is to all and for all through Jesus Christ.

III. Closing Thoughts

Today's Lesson Highlighted Lawful and Unlawful Relations

Lawful Relations

For God's promise to Abraham to be fulfilled, Abraham had to engage in lawful relations with his wife, so they could have baby Isaac. God prevented King Abimelech from having unlawful relations with Sarah. This ensured God got all the glory from the lawful actions.

Unlawful Relations

On the other hand, wicked Sodom and Gomorrah were destroyed. Part of their wickedness involved men engaging in unlawful relations. Then, Lot's daughters engaged in unlawful relations with their father, which eventually led to the birth of wicked nations.

The moral of the story is, engaging in relationships God's way, brings joy, happiness, and laughter...

...as with the birth of Isaac, whose name means laughter...

but engaging in unlawful relationships brings destruction in many ways.

✞

Lot's Wife's Pillar of Salt Body Was Seen Still Standing About 2000 Years Later

According to the New Living Translation Bible, the Bible story describing Lot's family's flight during the destruction of Sodom and Gomorrah occurred around 2067 (or 1901) BC.

When Lot's wife disobeyed the angel of the Lord's instructions by looking back upon the cities' destruction, she instantly turned into a pillar of salt.

First century Jewish historian Flavius Josephus reported seeing the pillar of salt body of Lot's wife during his lifetime (AD 37–100) which was almost 2000 years after the event occurred.

Read about Josephus and his eyewitness report at the end of this week's study pages.

Lesson 1.7

Reading Assignment:
Genesis 21:8–23:20
Genesis 11:32
Genesis 24:1–67

I. Lesson Exercise

Sarah's Faith

Do you wonder how Sarah could treat Hagar and Ishmael so harshly when she caused this messed up situation in the first place? But now Sarah is acting in faith, and God supports her decision (Gen. 21:12). Ishmael cannot share the family inheritance with Isaac. God promised Abraham He would take care of Ishmael.

21) When it appeared Hagar and Ishmael would die in the wilderness, God helped them. In Gen. 21:17, what did God hear that prompted him to help? ______________________________

Abraham's Faith

Abraham has been living by faith in God. He left behind his Father's family, he left behind the wealth of others, and he sent away the son he had grown to love, all in obedience to God. Now God has one final test of Abraham's faith. (Gen. 22:1–19)

22) Was Abraham willing to sacrifice Isaac—his beloved Son of Promise, the only son born to him and Sarah, and the son of his old age—at God's request?

____

The New Testament book **Hebrews** gives insight on Abraham's thoughts when he was willing to sacrifice Isaac.

> **"It was by faith that Abraham offered Isaac as a sacrifice when God was testing him. Abraham, who had received God's promises, was ready to sacrifice his only son, Isaac, though God had promised him, 'Isaac is the son through whom your descendants will be counted.'"**
>
> **"Abraham believed that if Isaac died, God was able to bring him back to life again. And in a sense, Abraham did receive his son back from the dead." Hebrews 11:17–19**

Important note concerning human and animal sacrifices

God tested Abraham's faith to see if he was willing to sacrifice Isaac, but God sent the ram in the bush to replace Isaac as the true sacrifice.

> **God never required any human sacrifice except for Jesus Christ. The only other physical sacrifices offered to God were certain animals in the Old Testament.**

Jesus Christ has satisfied all God's requirement for sacrifice (Hebrews 10:10-14). Today, we offer God spiritual sacrifices by the way we live.

It Was Love at First Sight!

After Sarah died, God prepared a new beauty to brighten Isaac's life. From Genesis 24:1-67, we read how Rebekah became Isaac's wife. It was love at first sight!

II. Find Jesus in the Lesson

Abraham's willingness to sacrifice Isaac, and Isaac's willingness to be sacrificed are a divine "type" of God's willingness to sacrifice Jesus, and Jesus' willingness to be sacrificed.

"By faith Abraham, when he was tried, offered up Isaac: and he that had received the promises offered up his only begotten son, Of whom it was said, That in Isaac shall thy seed be called: Accounting that God was able to raise him up, even from the dead; from whence also he received him in a figure." Heb. 11:17–19 KJV

In testing Abraham's faith, God experienced someone showing Him the same kind of love He has for humankind. John 3:16 describes God's sacrificial love.

"For God so loved the world that he gave his only begotten Son, so that everyone who believes in him will not perish but have eternal life." John 3:16

Isaac's sacrifice experience is an Old Testament pointer to the New Testament event when Jesus would sacrifice his life on the cross for the sins of all humankind. This means many of Abraham's obedient plans to sacrifice his son Isaac, are similar (not identical) to God's plan to sacrifice His Son Jesus. Here are some of the similarities:

- Isaac was Abraham's only begotten son–meaning his beloved, covenant son–whom Abraham was willing to sacrifice in obedience to God. (Genesis 17:19–21, Hebrews 11:17)
- **Jesus Christ is God's only begotten Son** [pre-existent, beloved, unique in kind], **who God willingly gave in sacrifice to provide salvation for all humankind.** (John 3:16, Hebrews 1:5–6)
- Isaac carried the wood on which he was to be sacrificed. (Gen. 22:6)
- **Jesus carried the wooden cross on which he was to be sacrificed. (John 19:17)**
- Isaac was bound by his father to the wood for the sacrifice, as if he were a sacrificial lamb. (Genesis 22:6–8)
- **Jesus was sent by His Father to be the sacrificial lamb to take away the sin of the world. (John 1:29)**
- Isaac is not recorded as giving his father any trouble when he learned he was the sacrifice. (Genesis 22:8–12)

- **Jesus willingly laid down his life in obedience to God's requirement to sacrifice his life for humankind. (Matthew 26:42, John 10:17-18)**
- Isaac was resurrected from the dead "in a sense" on the third day. In Hebrews 11:17–19, it says Abraham believed that if Isaac died, God would raise him from the dead. In that Abraham was willing to let Isaac die, Isaac was as good as dead from the moment Abraham set out to sacrifice him. Therefore, when the ram appeared to substitute for the sacrifice, this could be thought of as Isaac's "resurrection" from the dead in a sense. This occurred three days after Abraham and Isaac began the journey to the place of sacrifice on Mount Moriah. (Gen. 22:4-6)
- **Jesus was resurrected from the dead on the third day after he died on the cross. (Matthew 12:40, Luke 24:19–21)**

III. Closing Thoughts

Abraham, the Friend of God and Father of Faith

Abraham was not only the "Friend of God" (James 2:23), but also the "Father of Faith" (Romans 4:16–17). Faithful Abraham is a great example of the type of faith each Christian needs to have in their walk with God.

Most importantly, Abraham's faith was not going to die with him. God knew he would faithfully teach his son, and his entire household to follow the True and Living God (Gen. 18:19). In Isaac the promises of God for humankind would continue.

Antiquities of the Jews: Testimony of Pillar of Salt
by Flavius Josephus, 1st Century Jewish Historian (AD 37–100)[11]

Flavius Josephus

Ancient Jewish Historian: First Century (AD 37–100)
Eyewitness to Events Recorded in the New Testament

THE GENUINE

WORKS

OF

FLAVIUS JOSEPHUS,

THE

JEWISH HISTORIAN.

Tranflated from the ORIGINAL GREEK, according to *Havercamp*'s accurate EDITION.

CONTAINING

Twenty Books of the *JEWISH* ANTIQUITIES,

WITH THE

APPENDIX, or LIFE of *JOSEPHUS*, written by himfelf:

Seven Books of the *JEWISH* WAR:

AND

Two Books againft *APION*.

ILLUSTRATED

With new PLANS and DESCRIPTIONS of the TABERNACLE of *Mofes*; and of the TEMPLES of *Solomon*, *Zorobabel*, *Herod*, and *Ezekiel*; and with correct MAPS of *Judea* and *Jerufalem*.

Together with

Proper Notes, Obfervations, Contents, Parallel Texts of Scripture, five compleat Indexes, and the true Chronology of the feveral Hiftories adjufted in the Margin.

To this BOOK are prefixed eight DISSERTATIONS, viz.

I. The Teftimonies of *Jofephus* vindicated.
II. The Copy of the Old Teftament made ufe of by *Jofephus*, proved to be that which was collected by *Nehemiah*.
III. Concerning God's Command to *Abraham*, to offer up *Ifaac* his Son for a Sacrifice.
IV. A large Enquiry into the true Chronology of *Jofephus*.
V. An Extract out of *Jofephus*'s Exhortation to the *Greeks*, concerning *Hades*, and the Refurrection of the Dead.
VI. Proofs that this Exhortation is genuine; and was no other than a Homily of *Jofephus*'s, when he was Bifhop of *Jerufalem*.
VII. A Demonftration that *Tacitus*, the *Roman* Hiftorian, took his Hiftory of the *Jews* out of *Jofephus*.
VIII. A Differtation of *Cellarius*'s againft *Harduin*; in Vindication of *Jofephus*'s Hiftory of the Family of *Herod* from Coins. Tranflated into *Englifh*.

With an ACCOUNT of the *Jewifh* Coins, Weights, and Meafures.

By *WILLIAM WHISTON*, M.A.
Some time Profeffor of the Mathematicks in the Univerfity of *Cambridge*.

LONDON,
Printed by W. BOWYER for the AUTHOR: and are to be fold by JOHN WHISTON, Bookfeller, at Mr. *Boyle*'s *Head* in *Fleetftreet*. MDCCXXXVII.

Ancient Greek Text Translated into English
by William Whiston, London, 1737

[11]Appendix C

Antiquities of the Jews: Testimony of Pillar of Salt by Flavius Josephus, 1st Century Jewish Historian (AD 37–100)[11]

Book I. CONTAINING THE INTERVAL OF THREE THOUSAND EIGHT HUNDRED AND THIRTY-THREE YEARS.

FROM THE CREATION TO THE DEATH OF ISAAC.

CHAPTER 11.

HOW GOD OVERTHREW THE NATION OF THE SODOMITES, OUT OF HIS WRATH AGAINST THEM FOR THEIR SINS.

4. But God was much displeased at their impudent behaviour, so that he both smote those men with blindness, and condemned the Sodomites to universal destruction. But Lot, upon God's informing him of the future destruction of the Sodomites, went away, taking with him his wife and daughters, who were two, and still virgins; for those that were betrothed to them were above the thoughts of going, and deemed that Lot's words were trifling. God then cast a thunderbolt upon the city, and set it on fire with its inhabitants; and laid waste the country with the like burning, as I formerly said when I wrote the Jewish war. But Lot's wife continually turning back to view the city as she went from it, and being too nicely inquisitive what would become of it, although God had forbidden her so to do, was changed into a pillar of salt; *for I have seen it, and it remains at this day. Now he and his daughters fled to a certain small place, encompassed with fire, and settled in it. It is to this day called Zoar, for that is the word which the Hebrews use for a small thing. There it was that he lived a miserable life, on account of his having no company, and his want of provisions.

✞

** The following footnote to this text, which is recorded at the bottom of the page in the book "The Complete Works of Josephus" was written by William Whiston, who translated these works into English:*

This pillar of salt was, we see here, standing in the days of Josephus; and he had seen it. That it was standing then, is also attested by Clement of Rome, contemporary with Josephus; as also that it was so in the next century, is attested by Irenaeus, with the addition of an hypothesis, how it came to last so long, with all its members entire. Whether the account that some modern travelers give be true, that it is still standing, I do not know. Its remote situation, at the utmost southern point of the Sea of Sodom, in the wild and dangerous deserts of Arabia makes it exceedingly difficult for inquisitive travelers to examine the place; and for common reports of country people, at a distance, they are not very satisfactory. In the meantime, I have no opinion of Le Clerc's dissertation or hypothesis about this question, which can only be determined by eye-witnesses. When Christian princes, so called, lay aside their foolish and unchristian wars and quarrels, and send a body of fit persons to travel over the East, and bring us faithful accounts of all ancient monuments, and procure us copies of all ancient records, at present lost among us, wemay hope for full satisfaction in such inquiries, but hardly before.

[11]Appendix C

Josephus' Life and Works
Excerpt from Flavius Josephus Home Page, by G.J. Goldberg[12]

Josephus was a priest, a soldier, and a scholar.

He was born Joseph ben Mattathias in Jerusalem in 37 CE [AD], **a few years after the time of Jesus, during the time of the Roman occupation of the Jewish homeland.** In his early twenties he was sent to Rome to negotiate the release of several priests held hostage by Emperor Nero. When he returned home after completing his mission, he found the nation beginning a revolution against the Romans.

Despite his foreboding that the cause was hopeless, he was drafted into becoming commander of the revolutionary forces in Galilee, where he spent more time controlling internal factions than fighting the Roman army. When the city of Jotapata he was defending fell to the Roman general Vespasian, Josephus and his supporters hid in a cave and entered into a suicide pact, which Josephus oddly survived.

Taken prisoner by Vespasian, Josephus presented himself as a prophet. Noting that the war had been propelled by an ancient oracle that foretold a world ruler would arise from Judaea, Josephus asserted that this referred to Vespasian, who was destined to become Emperor of Rome. Intrigued, Vespasian spared his life. When this prophecy came true, and Vespasian became Emperor, he rewarded Josephus handsomely, freeing him from his chains and eventually adopting him into his family, the Flavians. Josephus thus became Flavius Josephus.

During the remainder of the war, Josephus assisted the Roman commander Titus, Vespasian's son, with understanding the Jewish nation and in negotiating with the revolutionaries. Called a traitor, he was unable to persuade the defenders of Jerusalem to surrender to the Roman siege, and instead became a witness to the destruction of the city and the Holy Temple.

Living at the Flavian court in Rome, Josephus undertook to write a history of the war he had witnessed. The work, while apparently factually correct, also served to flatter his patron and to warn other provinces against the folly of opposing the Romans. He first wrote in his native language of Aramaic, then with assistance translated it into Greek (the most-used language of the Empire). It was published a few years after the end of the war, in about 78 CE [AD]. He was about forty years old.

Josephus subsequently improved his language skills and undertook a massive work in Greek explaining the history of the Jews to the general non-Jewish audience. He emphasized that the Jewish culture and Bible were older than any other then existing, hence called his work the *Jewish Antiquities*. Approximately half the work is a rephrasing of the Hebrew Bible, while much of the rest draws on previous historians. This work was published in 93 or 94 CE [AD], when he was about fifty-six years old.

Josephus wrote at least two smaller books, including his autobiography, in which he recounts his life from birth until the writing of the Antiquities. The year he died is unknown.

[12]Appendix C

Josephus' Life and Works
Excerpt from Flavius Josephus Home Page, by G.J. Goldberg[12]

The Works of Josephus

Josephus is our only [non-Bible, non-Christian] **source of knowledge for much of the history of Judaism in the first century CE** [AD].

His books provide essential background for an understanding of both the beginning of modern Judaism and of the New Testament in its historical setting.

Four of his works have survived:

The Jewish War
The history of the Jewish revolt against the Roman Empire in the years 66–74 CE [AD], as experienced by Josephus himself.

Antiquities of the Jews
The history of the Jews prior to the revolt, based on the Bible, other Jewish writings, and the works of previous historians.

Against Apion
A defense of Judaism, answering an attack by a Roman author.

The Life
Josephus' autobiography.

These works can be read on the Internet in English and in Greek.

- **The Works of Flavius Josephus**:
  The complete text of the Whiston translation.

- **The Works of Josephus in Greek**:
  The Greek text of B. Niese, with textual analysis and translation links, located at the Perseus Project Website.

Additional Notes:

- Flavius Josephus home page by G. L. Goldberg includes a special section on **"Josephus' Account of Jesus': The Testimonium Flavianum,"** which addresses concerns with the authenticity of Josephus' testimony of Christ

- **The book *The Complete Works of Josephus* can be purchased.** Flavius Josephus, ***The Complete Works of Josephus*, Translated by William Whiston** (Edinburgh, Scotland: William P. Nimmo; Philadelphia, Pennsylvania: Porter and Coates; Kregel Publications, a division of Kregel, Inc., 1960, 1978, 1981).

[12]Appendix C

MAPS

For Events in Book of Genesis

Maps

Sources[13]

- World Map from picryl_public domain
- Middle East: Then and Middle East Now maps, ***Rose Book of Charts, Maps & Time Lines***; (Torrance, CA: Rose Publishing, 2005 RW Research, Inc.), 120, 121
- Thomas V. Briscoe, ***Holman Bible Atlas***, Maps 16 (text and maps), 3, 20, 21, 22, 23 used by permission (Nashville, TN: Broadman & Holman Publishers, 1998), pages 4, 36, 46–48, 50

[13]Appendic C

World Map (modern day)

Middle East
(Israel, Palestine)

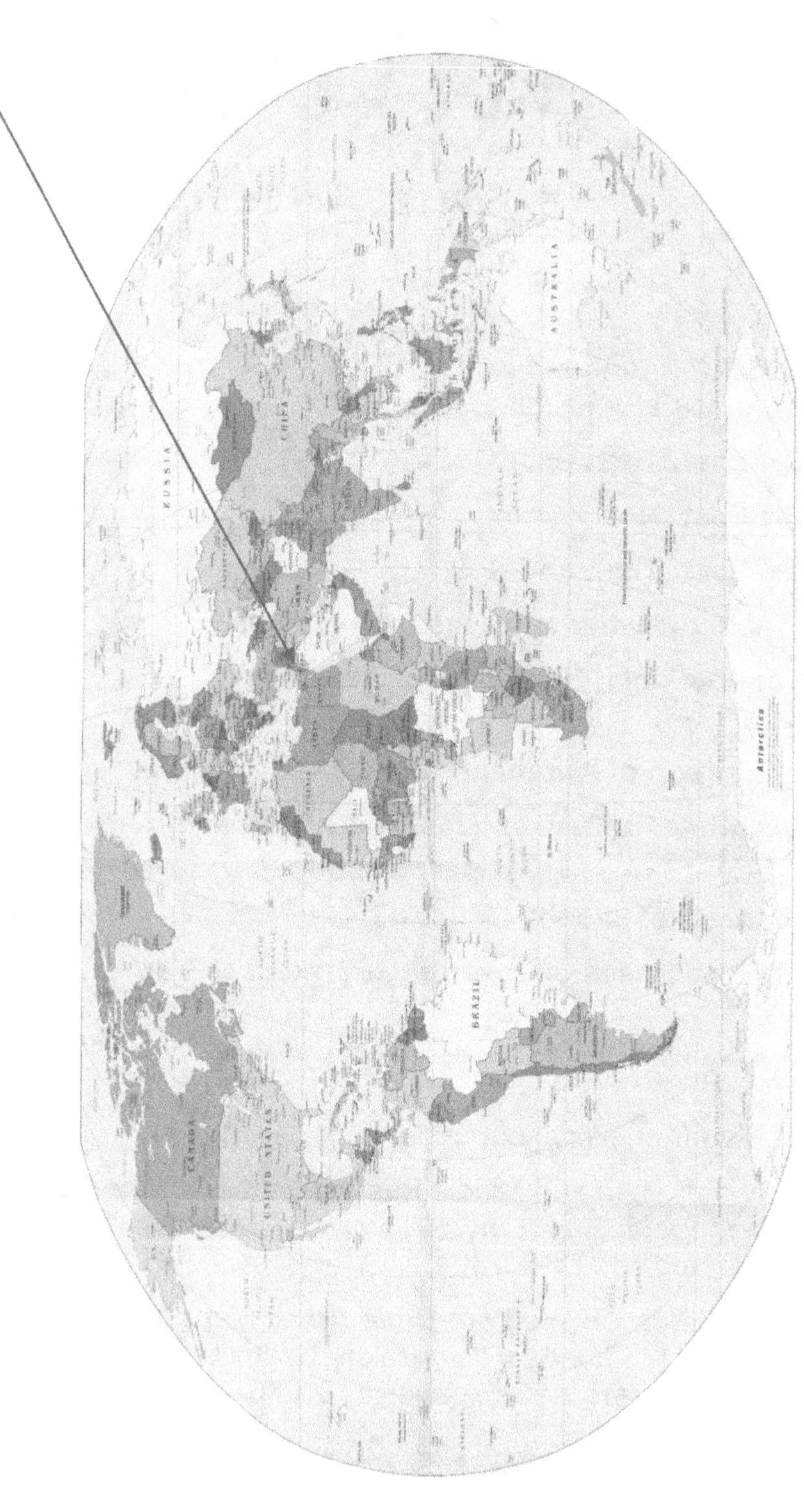

Middle East: Then (BC)

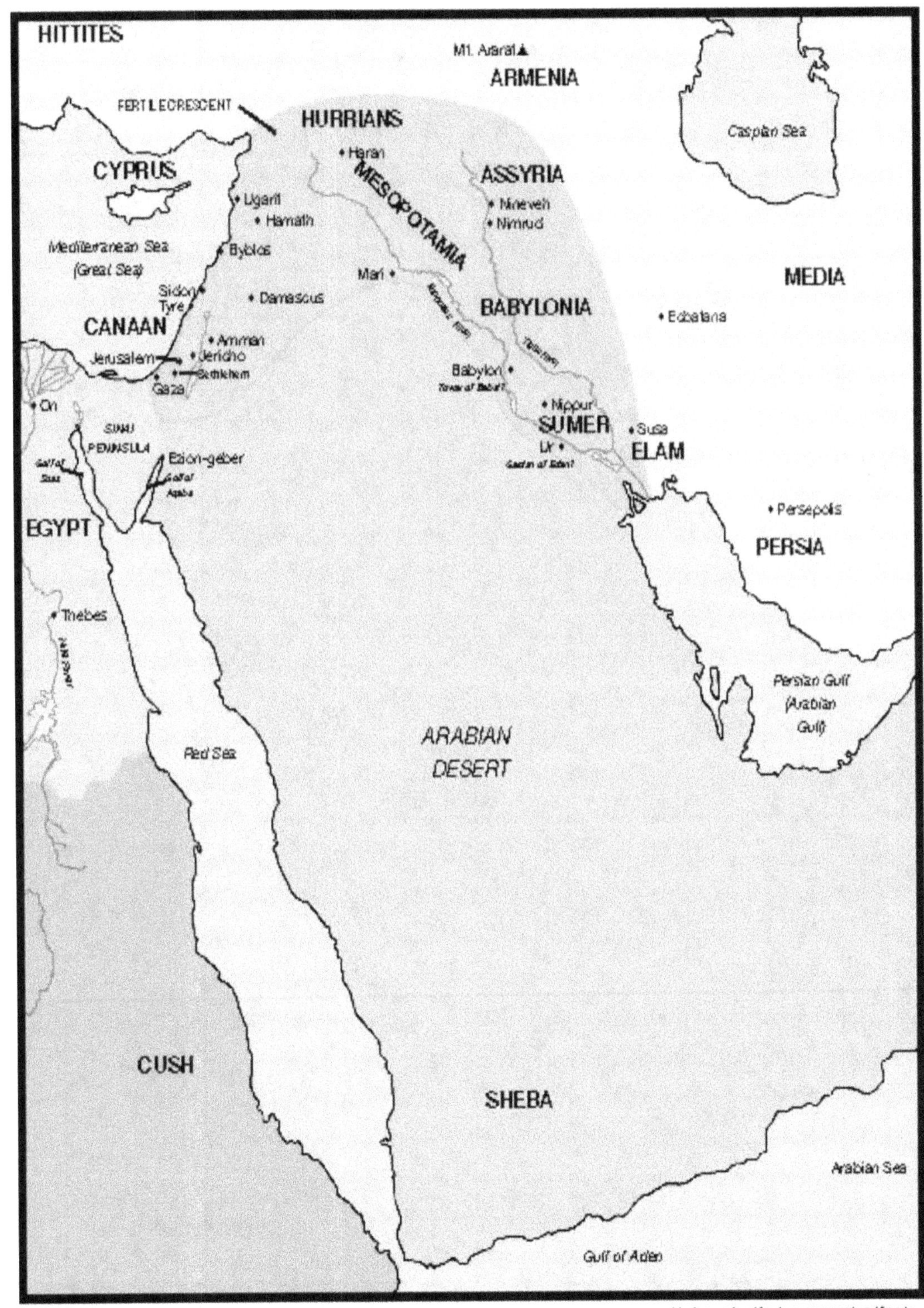

Middle East: Now

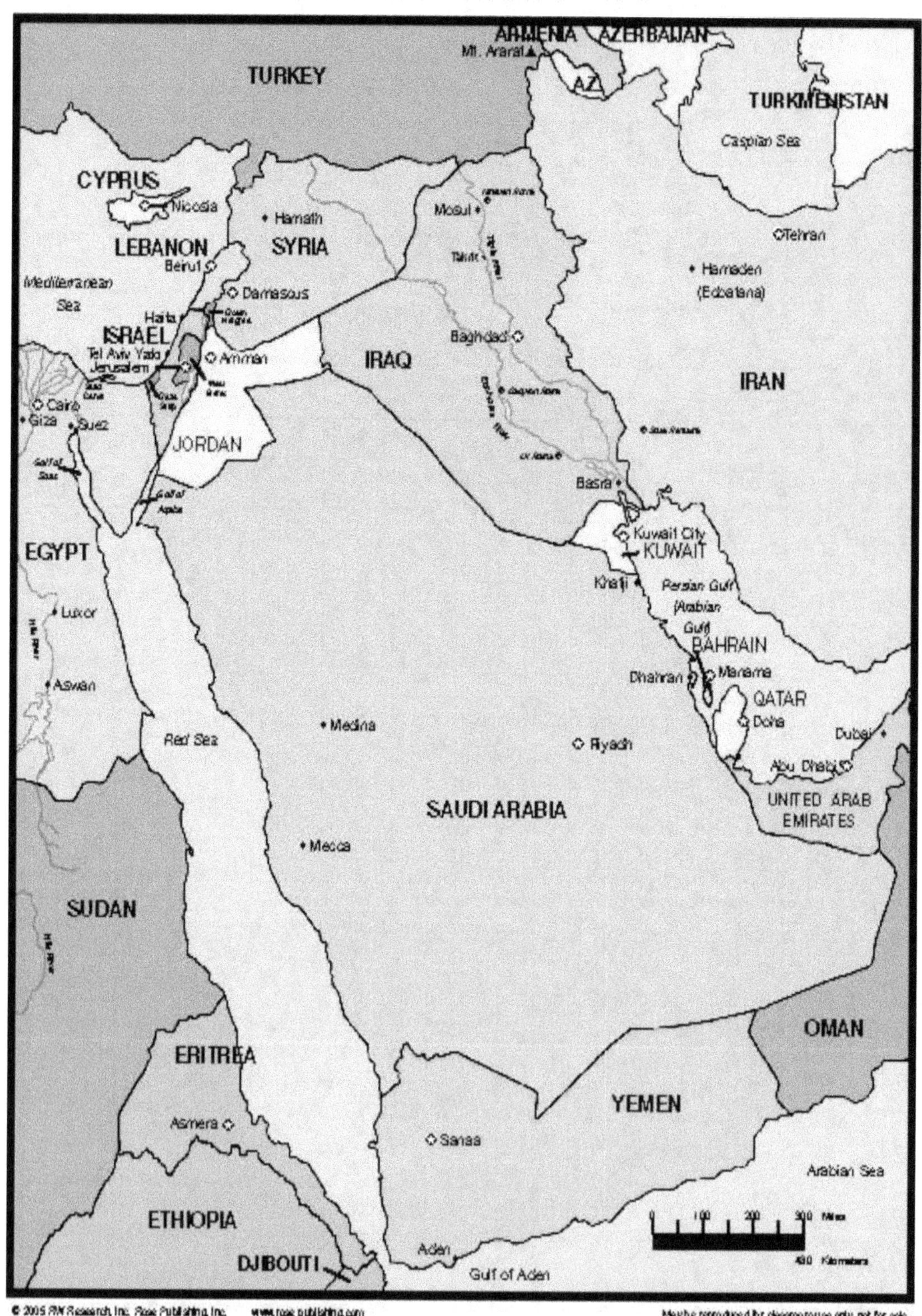

Middle East: Now

TURKEY
ARMENIA
AZERBAIJAN
AZ
Mt. Ararat
TURKMENISTAN
Caspian Sea
Tehran
Hamadan (Ecbatana)
IRAN
CYPRUS
Nicosia
LEBANON
Beirut
SYRIA
Hamath
Damascus
Mosul
Baghdad
IRAQ
Basra
Kuwait City
KUWAIT
Persian Gulf (Arabian Gulf)
BAHRAIN
Manama
Dhahran
QATAR
Doha
Abu Dhabi
Dubai
UNITED ARAB EMIRATES
OMAN
Mediterranean Sea
ISRAEL
Haifa
Tel Aviv-Yafo
Jerusalem
Amman
JORDAN
EGYPT
Cairo
Giza
Suez
Luxor
Aswan
Nile River
Red Sea
SUDAN
ERITREA
Asmera
ETHIOPIA
DJIBOUTI
Medina
Mecca
Riyadh
SAUDI ARABIA
Khafji
Sanaa
YEMEN
Aden
Gulf of Aden
Arabian Sea

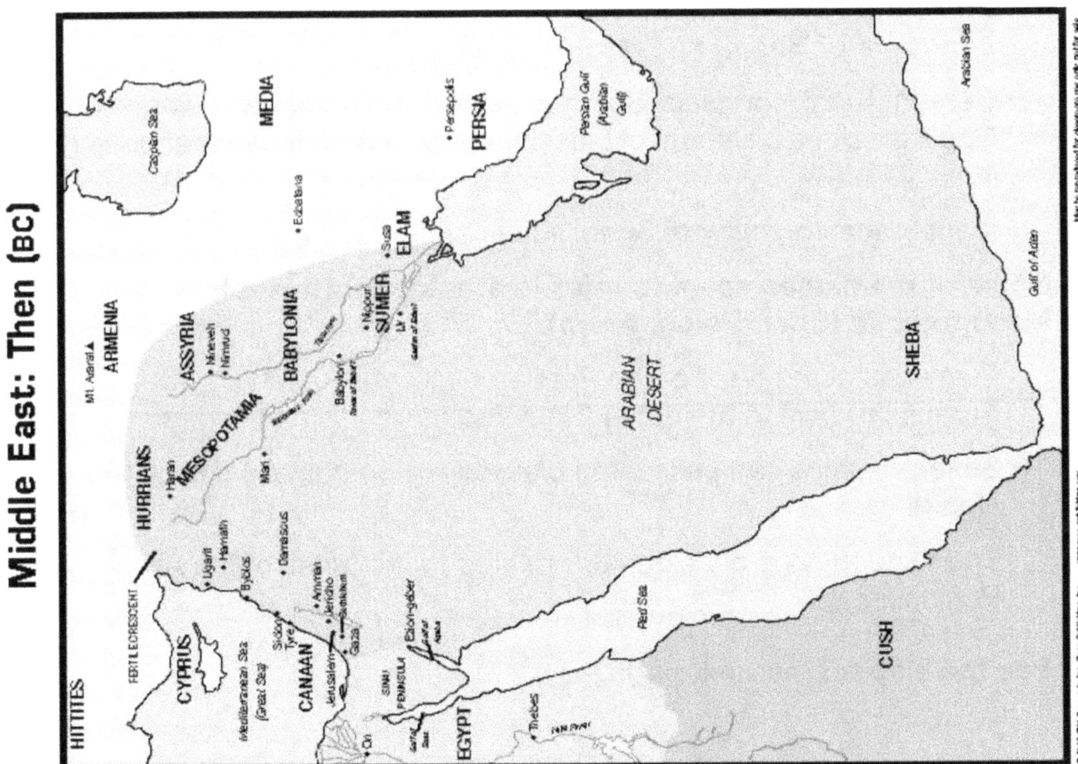

The Table of Nations

Genesis 10 presents a list of nations descended from the three sons of Noah: Japheth, Ham, and Shem.

This "Table of Nations" is unique in the ancient world. It contains seventy names of ancestral heads of nations and peoples known to Israel.

The fourteen descendants of Japheth are named first.

Japheth's descendants generally are associated with areas north and northwest of Canaan, including mainland Greece, Asia Minor (modern Turkey), certain Mediterranean islands (Crete, Cyprus, and Rhodes), and the mountainous areas from Armenia to the Caspian Sea.

The list next names thirty descendants of Ham.

The Hamites generally are located in North Africa (Egypt and the Sudan), along the coast of Somaliland and the west Arabian coasts, and in certain sections of Mesopotamia. Canaan along with many of the people groups Israel encountered as she entered the promised land (Amorites, Jebusites, Perizzites, Hivites, Girgashites, and others) are listed as Hamites.

The last and most extensive part of the list contains twenty-six descendants of Shem, ancestor of Israel.

Gen 11:10-26 connects Shem with Abram (Abraham), who received God's gracious covenant of blessing and hope for the human race (Gen 12:1-3).

Identification of many of Shem's descendants remains uncertain.

Some of the names seem to refer to areas of northwest Mesopotamia (Eber, Peleg, Aram).

Elam was at the head of the Persian Gulf, while Asshur and Arpachshad are in the upper Tigris region.

Several names can be located plausibly in Somaliland (Havilah, Ophir).

The thirteen sons of Joktan are related to the tribes of the Arabian Peninsula.

See the Map on the next page.

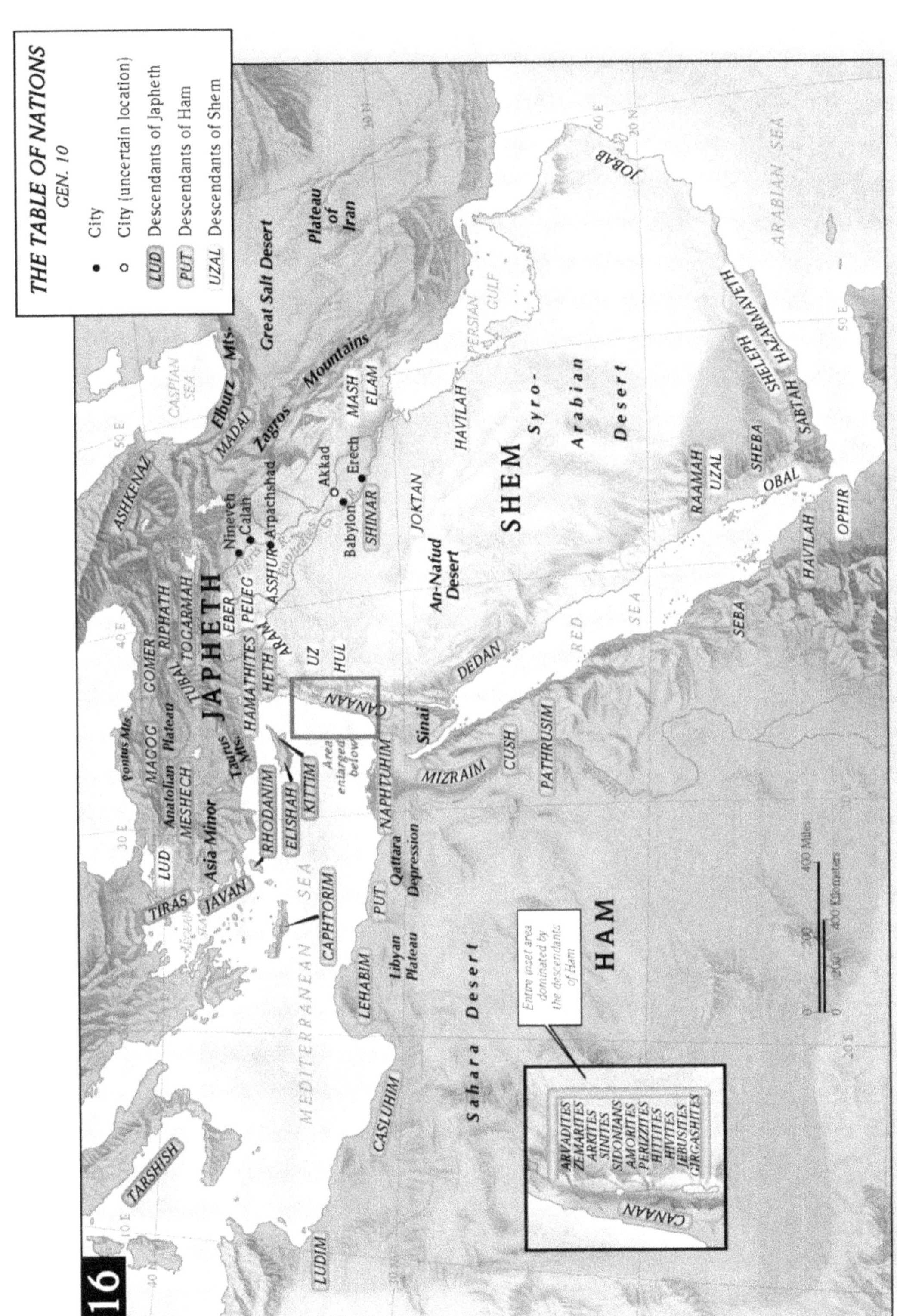
16
THE TABLE OF NATIONS
GEN. 10
City
City (uncertain location)
LUD Descendants of Japheth
PUT Descendants of Ham
UZAL Descendants of Shem
JAPHETH
SHEM
HAM
TARSHISH
TIRAS
LUD
JAVAN
MESHECH
MAGOG
GOMER
TUBAL
RIPHATH
TOGARMAH
ASHKENAZ
MADAI
RHODANIM
ELISHAH
KITTIM
CAPHTORIM
HAMATHITES
HETH
EBER
PELEG
ARAM
ASSHUR
UZ
HUL
CANAAN
Nineveh
Calah
Atrpachshad
Akkad
Babylon
Erech
SHINAR
MASH
ELAM
JOKTAN
HAVILAH
DEDAN
RAAMAH
UZAL
SHEBA
OBAL
SABTAH
SHELEPH
HAZARMAVETH
JOBAB
OPHIR
HAVILAH
SEBA
PATHRUSIM
CUSH
MIZRAIM
NAPHTUHIM
PUT
LEHABIM
CASLUHIM
LUDIM
Asia Minor
Anatolian Plateau
Pontus Mts.
Taurus Mts.
Elburz Mts.
Zagros Mountains
Great Salt Desert
Plateau of Iran
CASPIAN SEA
PERSIAN GULF
ARABIAN SEA
RED SEA
MEDITERRANEAN SEA
Syro-Arabian Desert
An-Nafud Desert
Sinai
Qattara Depression
Libyan Plateau
Sahara Desert
Area enlarged below
Entire inset area dominated by the descendants of Ham
ARVADITES
ZEMARITES
ARKITES
SINITES
SIDONIANS
AMORITES
PERIZZITES
HITTITES
HIVITES
JEBUSITES
GIRGASHITES
400 Miles
400 Kilometers

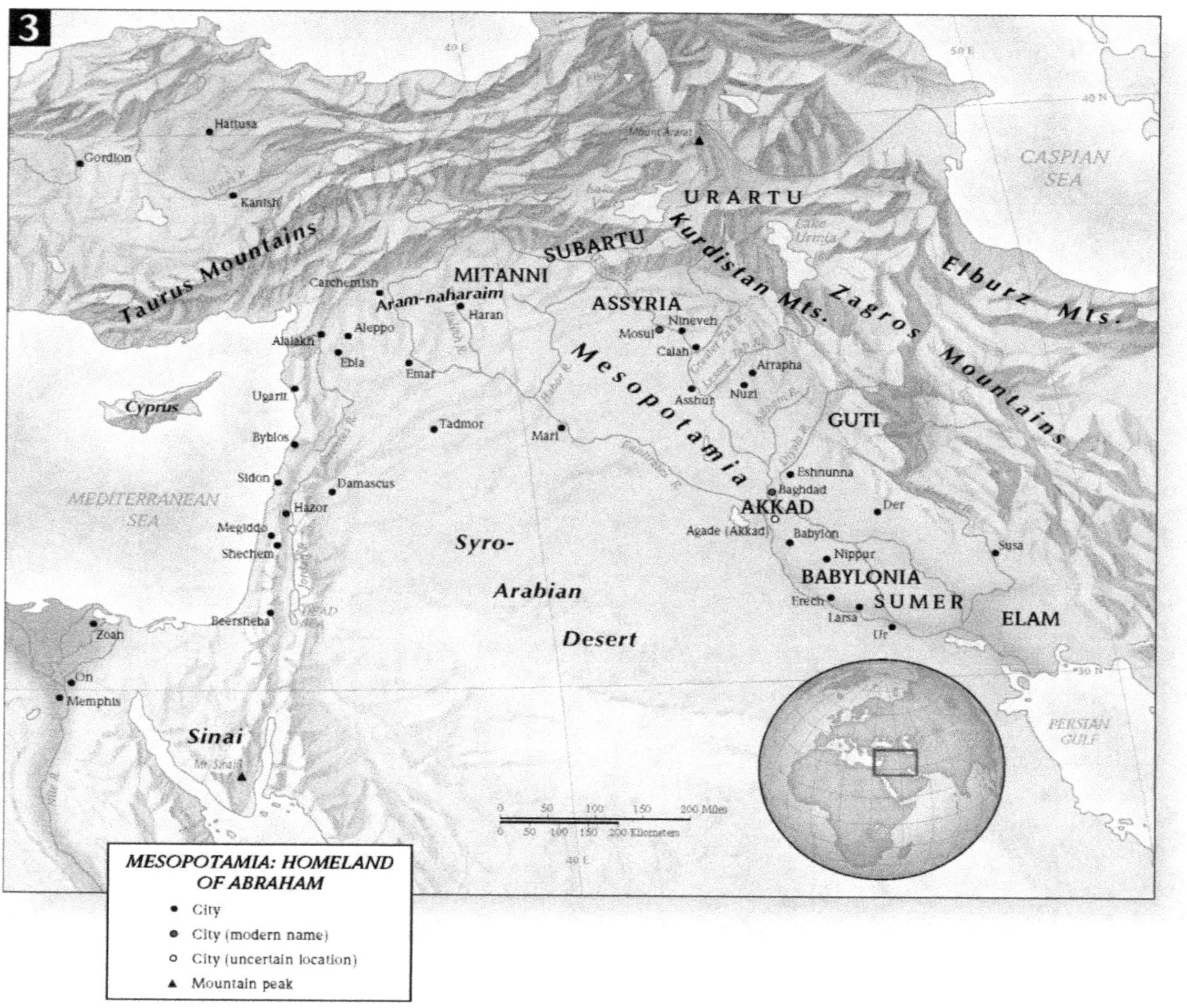
3
MESOPOTAMIA: HOMELAND OF ABRAHAM
City
City (modern name)
City (uncertain location)
Mountain peak
CASPIAN SEA
PERSIAN GULF
MEDITERRANEAN SEA
Elburz Mts.
Zagros Mountains
Kurdistan Mts.
Taurus Mountains
URARTU
SUBARTU
ASSYRIA
MITANNI
Aram-naharaim
Mesopotamia
GUTI
AKKAD
BABYLONIA
SUMER
ELAM
Syro-
Arabian
Desert
Cyprus
Sinai
Hattusa
Kanish
Gordion
Carchemish
Alalakh
Aleppo
Ebla
Emar
Haran
Tadmor
Mari
Ugarit
Byblos
Sidon
Damascus
Hazor
Megiddo
Shechem
Beersheba
Zoan
On
Memphis
Mosul
Nineveh
Calah
Asshur
Nuzi
Arrapha
Eshnunna
Baghdad
Agade (Akkad)
Babylon
Nippur
Erech
Larsa
Ur
Der
Susa
0 50 100 150 200 Miles
0 50 100 150 200 Kilometers

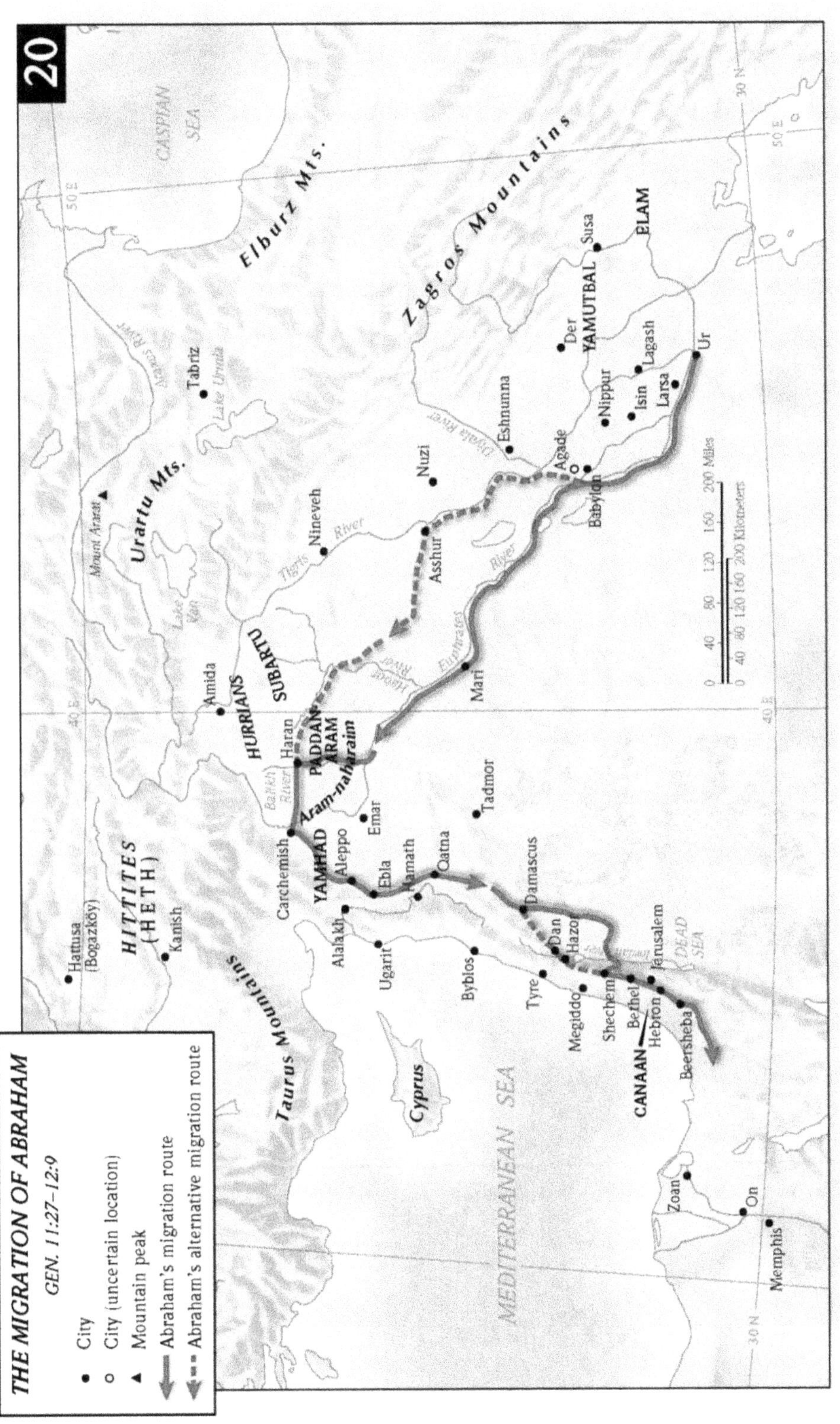
20
THE MIGRATION OF ABRAHAM
GEN. 11:27–12:9
City
City (uncertain location)
Mountain peak
Abraham's migration route
Abraham's alternative migration route
CASPIAN SEA
Elburz Mts.
Zagros Mountains
ELAM
Susa
YAMUTBAL
Der
Lagash
Ur
Larsa
Isin
Nippur
Eshnunna
Diyala River
Agade
Babylon
Tabriz
Lake Urmia
Araxes River
Urartu Mts.
Mount Ararat
Nuzi
Nineveh
Tigris River
Asshur
Euphrates River
Lake Van
SUBARTU
Habor River
Mari
Amida
HURRIANS
Haran
PADDAN-ARAM
Aram-naharaim
Balikh River
Tadmor
Emar
Carchemish
YAMHAD
Aleppo
Ebla
Hamath
Qatna
Damascus
Dan
Hazor
Jordan
DEAD SEA
Jerusalem
Bethel
Hebron
Beersheba
Shechem
Megiddo
Tyre
Byblos
Ugarit
Alalakh
CANAAN
HITTITES
(HETH)
Hattusa
(Bogazköy)
Kanish
Taurus Mountains
Cyprus
MEDITERRANEAN SEA
Zoan
On
Memphis
0 40 80 120 160 200 Miles
0 40 80 120 160 200 Kilometers
50 E
40 E
30 N

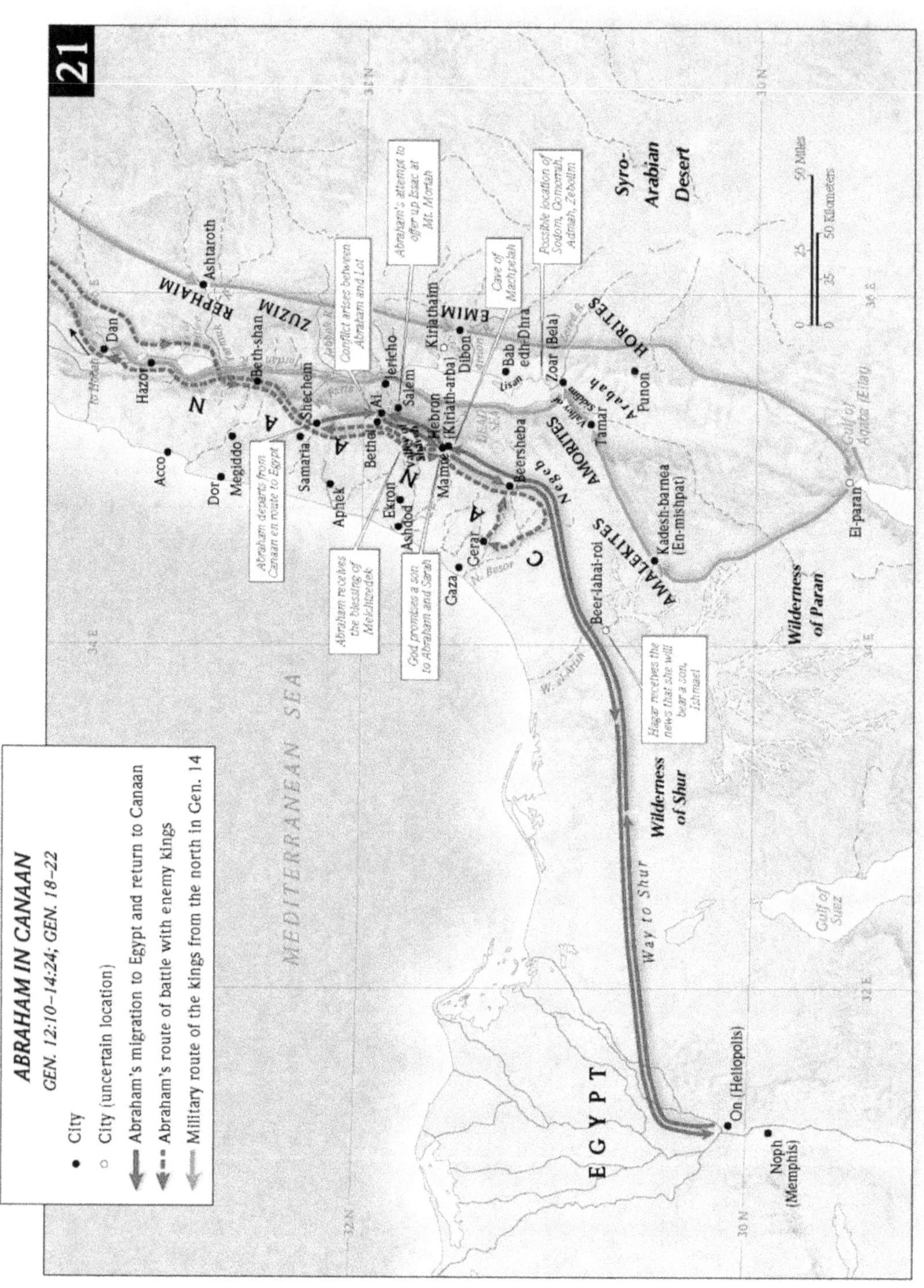
21
ABRAHAM IN CANAAN
GEN. 12:10–14:24; GEN. 18–22
City
City (uncertain location)
Abraham's migration to Egypt and return to Canaan
Abraham's route of battle with enemy kings
Military route of the kings from the north in Gen. 14
MEDITERRANEAN SEA
EGYPT
On (Heliopolis)
Noph (Memphis)
Way to Shur
Wilderness of Shur
Wilderness of Paran
Syro-Arabian Desert
Gulf of Suez
Gulf of Aqaba (Eilat)
El-paran
Kadesh-barnea (En-mishpat)
Beer-lahai-roi
Hagar receives the news that she will bear a son, Ishmael
AMALEKITES
AMORITES
HORITES
EMIM
ZUZIM
REPHAIM
Negeb
Gaza
Gerar
Ashdod
Ekron
Aphek
Samaria
Shechem
Bethel
Ai
Jericho
Salem
Hebron (Kiriath-arba)
Mamre
Beersheba
Tamar
Punon
Zoar (Bela)
Bab edh-Dhra
Lisan
Dibon
Kiriathaim
Ashtaroth
Dan
Hazor
Beth-shan
Megiddo
Dor
Acco
Abraham departs from Canaan en route to Egypt
Abraham receives the blessing of Melchizedek
God promises a son to Abraham and Sarah
Conflict arises between Abraham and Lot
Abraham's attempt to offer up Isaac at Mt. Moriah
Cave of Machpelah
Possible location of Sodom, Gomorrah, Admah, Zeboiim
50 Miles
50 Kilometers

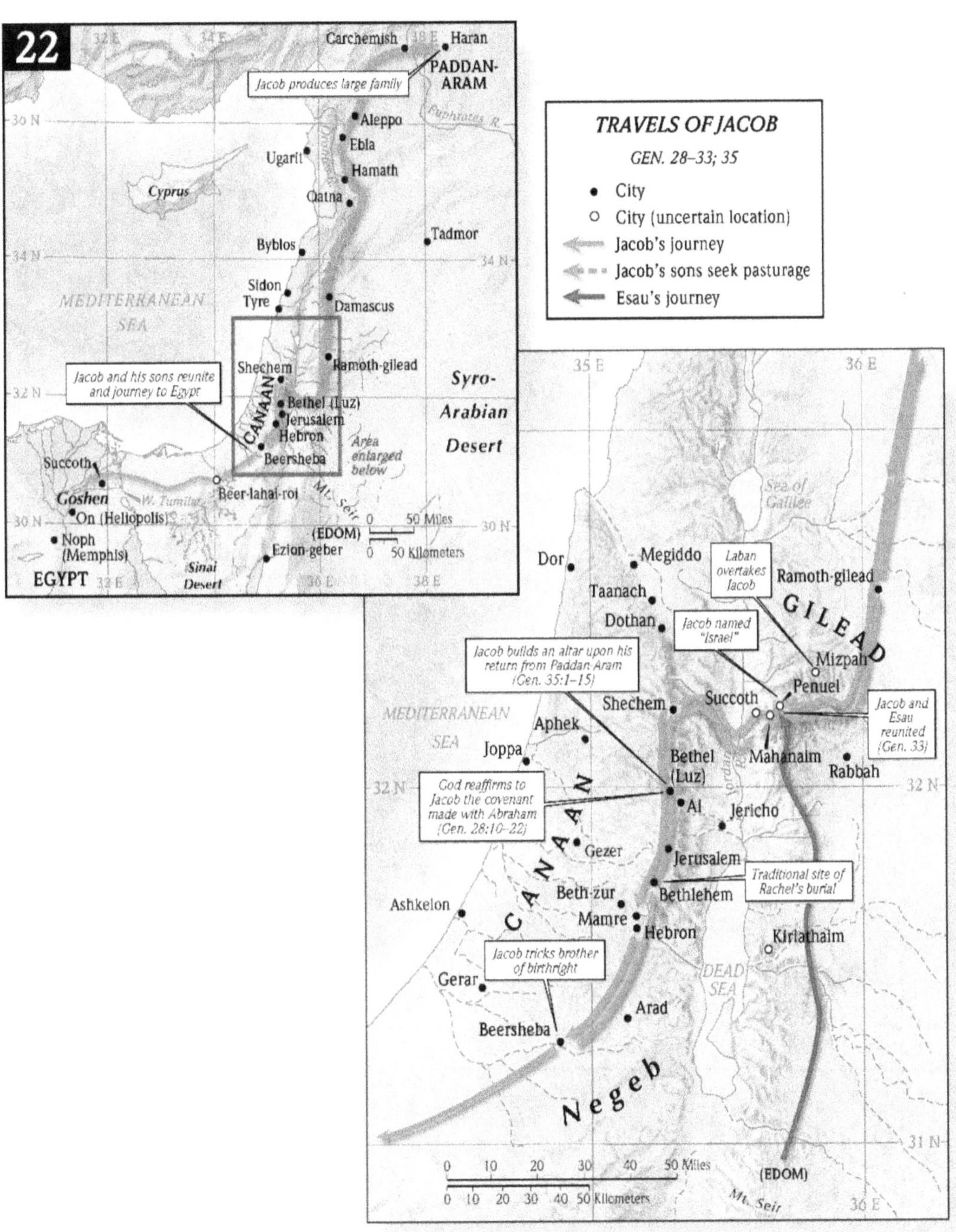
22
Carchemish
Haran
PADDAN-ARAM
Jacob produces large family
Euphrates R.
Aleppo
Ebla
Ugarit
Hamath
Cyprus
Qatna
Tadmor
Byblos
Sidon
Tyre
Damascus
MEDITERRANEAN SEA
Shechem
Ramoth-gilead
Jacob and his sons reunite and journey to Egypt
CANAAN
Bethel (Luz)
Jerusalem
Hebron
Beersheba
Syro-Arabian Desert
Area enlarged below
Succoth
Goshen
W. Tumilat
Beer-lahai-roi
Mt. Seir
On (Heliopolis)
(EDOM)
Noph (Memphis)
Ezion-geber
EGYPT
Sinai Desert
0 50 Miles
0 50 Kilometers
TRAVELS OF JACOB
GEN. 28–33; 35
City
City (uncertain location)
Jacob's journey
Jacob's sons seek pasturage
Esau's journey
Sea of Galilee
Dor
Megiddo
Laban overtakes Jacob
Ramoth-gilead
Taanach
GILEAD
Dothan
Jacob named "Israel"
Jacob builds an altar upon his return from Paddan-Aram (Gen. 35:1–15)
Mizpah
Penuel
Shechem
Succoth
Jacob and Esau reunited (Gen. 33)
MEDITERRANEAN SEA
Aphek
Joppa
Bethel (Luz)
Mahanaim
Rabbah
Jordan R.
God reaffirms to Jacob the covenant made with Abraham (Gen. 28:10–22)
Ai
Jericho
CANAAN
Gezer
Jerusalem
Traditional site of Rachel's burial
Beth-zur
Bethlehem
Ashkelon
Mamre
Hebron
Kiriathaim
Jacob tricks brother of birthright
Gerar
DEAD SEA
Arad
Beersheba
Negeb
0 10 20 30 40 50 Miles
0 10 20 30 40 50 Kilometers
(EDOM)
Mt. Seir

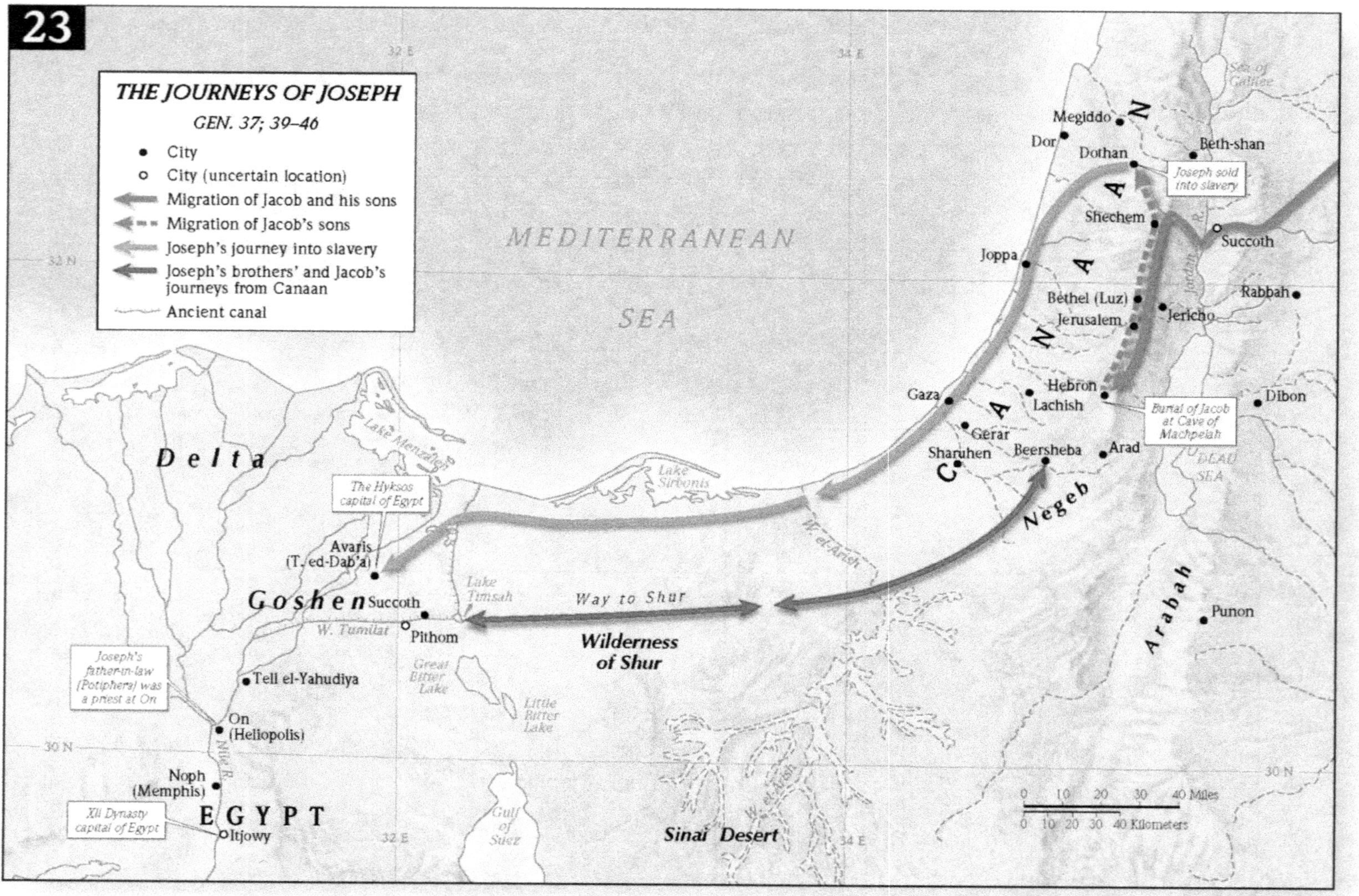

23
THE JOURNEYS OF JOSEPH
GEN. 37; 39–46
City
City (uncertain location)
Migration of Jacob and his sons
Migration of Jacob's sons
Joseph's journey into slavery
Joseph's brothers' and Jacob's journeys from Canaan
Ancient canal
MEDITERRANEAN
SEA
Sea of Galilee
Megiddo
Dor
Dothan
Beth-shan
Joseph sold into slavery
Shechem
Succoth
Jordan R.
Joppa
Bethel (Luz)
Jerusalem
Jericho
Rabbah
Hebron
Lachish
Gaza
Gerar
Sharuhen
Beersheba
Arad
Burial of Jacob at Cave of Machpelah
Dibon
DEAD SEA
C A N A A N
Negeb
Arabah
Punon
Delta
Lake Menzaleh
The Hyksos capital of Egypt
Lake Sirbonis
W. el-Arish
Avaris (T. ed-Dab'a)
Goshen
Succoth
Lake Timsah
Way to Shur
W. Tumilat
Pithom
Wilderness of Shur
Joseph's father-in-law (Potiphera) was a priest at On
Tell el-Yahudiya
Great Bitter Lake
Little Bitter Lake
On (Heliopolis)
Nile R.
Noph (Memphis)
XII Dynasty capital of Egypt
Itjowy
EGYPT
Gulf of Suez
Sinai Desert
0 10 20 30 40 Miles
0 10 20 30 40 Kilometers
32 E
34 E
32 N
30 N

Week 2

Featured Book:

Genesis,

with a few passages from 1 Chronicles Chapters 1 and 2

Contents:

Peek at the Week

Lesson	Key Events	Find Jesus
2.1	Abraham's Family Tree	Isaac's Son in Jesus' Family Tree
2.2	Jacob Steals Birthright and Blessing, then Jacob's Flight	God's Choice of Isaac's Son in Jesus' Family Tree
2.3	Jacob's Family	Jesus' Family Tree from Judah
2.4	Jacob's Flight, then Laban and Jacob Reunite	Animal sacrifices symbolic of Jesus' sacrifice
2.5	Esau and Jacob Reunite, then Jacob's Flight Again	Rachel's Death and Jesus' Birth
2.6	Edomites are Esau's descendants	Jesus is King of all kings
2.7	Joseph in Bondage	Judah's Son in Jesus' Family Tree

Chronological Notes

*Timetable	Key Events
2006 (or 1840) BC	Birth of Isaac's sons: Jacob and Esau
1991 (or 1825) BC	Death of Abraham
1929 (or 1763) BC	Jacob flees to Paddan-Aram
1909 (or 1743) BC	Jacob returns home to Canaan with 11 children
1898 (or 1732) BC	Joseph is 17 years old

**All dates are approximate.*

Reading Assignment:
Genesis 25:1–4
I Chronicles 1:32–33
Genesis 25:5–6, 12–18
I Chronicles 1:28–31, 34
Genesis 25:19–26, 7–11

Lesson 2.1

I. Lesson Exercise

Before Abraham Dies at 175 Years Old, He Has More Children

Genesis 24:1 says Abraham was a very old man. In today's lesson, we read that although he was very old, Abraham had more children. After Sarah's death, he has six sons with his concubine Keturah (secondary wife). These sons also produce nations of people just as Ishmael does through his twelve sons.

In future lessons the Ishmaelite (descendants of Abraham and Hagar) and Midianite (descendants of Abraham and Keturah) nations will play important roles in the life of the chosen descendants of Abraham and Sarah.

Abraham's descendants from Hagar and Keturah do not receive the covenant promises of special blessings God promised to Abraham, which included spiritual promises of great wealth, nations, and land. These special blessings are passed to Isaac alone, the son of Abraham and Sarah. (Gen. 25:5–6)

- Abraham has eight (8) total sons by Sarah, Hagar, and Keturah
- Isaac and Ishmael buried Abraham in the Cave of Machpelah, near Mamre, in the field of Ephron son of Zohar the Hittite. This is the property Abraham had purchased to bury Sarah. He was buried next to her. (Gen. 25:9)

Isaac has Children

After twenty years of marriage, Isaac finally has children at sixty years old.

- God answers Isaac's prayer for his wife Rebekah to have children (Gen. 25:21)
- Rebekah becomes pregnant with twin boys, who God reveals to her will become two rival nations. The younger boy will produce the stronger nation (Gen. 25:22)
- From the footnotes in the New Living Translation Bible, we learn the meaning of the names of Isaac and Rebekah's twin boys:
- Esau: The older twin was red and very hairy at birth. They named him "Esau," which means "hair" or "hairy."
- Jacob: The younger twin was holding on to Esau's heel when he was born. This child was named "Jacob," which means "he grasps the heel," a figure of speech that means "he deceives" or "supplanter."

Esau and Jacob Were about Fifteen Years Old When Abraham Died

- Abraham was 100 years old when Isaac was born (Gen. 21:3–5)
- Isaac was sixty years old when Jacob and Esau were born, and Abraham was 160 years old (Gen. 25:26)
- Abraham was 175 years old when he died (Gen. 25:7)

Esau and Jacob were about fifteen years old when Abraham died.

II. Find Jesus in the Lesson

Isaac's Son in Jesus' Family Tree

In Gen. 25:23, the text explains that Isaac's younger son will produce a stronger nation than his older son. This is the first indication of which son of Isaac the Messiah will be a descendant.

1) Look at Matthew 1:2 and Luke 3:34 to find out which of Isaac's sons is in Jesus' family tree. ______________________________

Abraham's Family Tree Is Very Important Throughout the Bible

III. Closing Thoughts

Abraham's Family Tree

Abraham's family tree is very important throughout the Bible. Although God instructed Abraham to move away from his father Terah's family, we will read references to this family again when Abraham's descendants are looking for the right wife.

For example:

- Abraham sent his servant to find a wife for Isaac from among his father's family living in Haran in the land of Aram. Look at the map "Migration of Abraham." Find the location of Ur where Abraham's family started, and Haran in Aram country, where the family moved.
- Abraham had more confidence in arranging marriages from within his family tree at Haran, than with his nearby neighbors the Canaanites.

Abraham's Religious Belief Passes to His Descendants

Joshua 24:2 explains that Abraham's father Terah worshiped many gods. When the one True and Living God communicated to Abraham to move away from his father's family, Abraham chose to follow this one God, which was different than what his father taught. As the head of his household, Abraham taught his family and servants about the one God (Gen. 18:19). The impact of Abraham's teaching is evident as God begins to interact with other members of Abraham's family.

For example:

- God honored Sarah's words to Abraham (Genesis 21:10–12)
- God heard Ishmael crying, then sent an angel to speak with his mother Hagar (Genesis 21:17–18)
- God answered Isaac's prayer (Genesis 25:21)
- God spoke with Rebekah (Genesis 25:22–23)

After Abraham's death, God will continue to interact with his descendants.

Abraham's Inheritance Passes Down to Specific Descendants

Abraham had obtained great wealth and great promises from God, which would be passed down to his descendants long after his death. God told Abraham these promises would last forever (Gen. 17:19).

What we discover in today's reading is that God's covenant with Abraham (meaning His inheritance of wealth and promises) was to be handed down to specific descendants of Abraham.

For example:

- Up to this point, we have seen that Isaac is the son of promise who received all of Abraham's inheritance. Now, Isaac has two sons, but only one of them will receive this inheritance.
- In Bible times, the normal custom was for the oldest son to get the inheritance by birthright. This means the right to the inheritance is his because of being born first. But, read on to see what becomes of the inheritance with Isaac's sons.

Abraham's Inheritance Passes Down to Specific Descendants

Abraham's Father's Family Tree

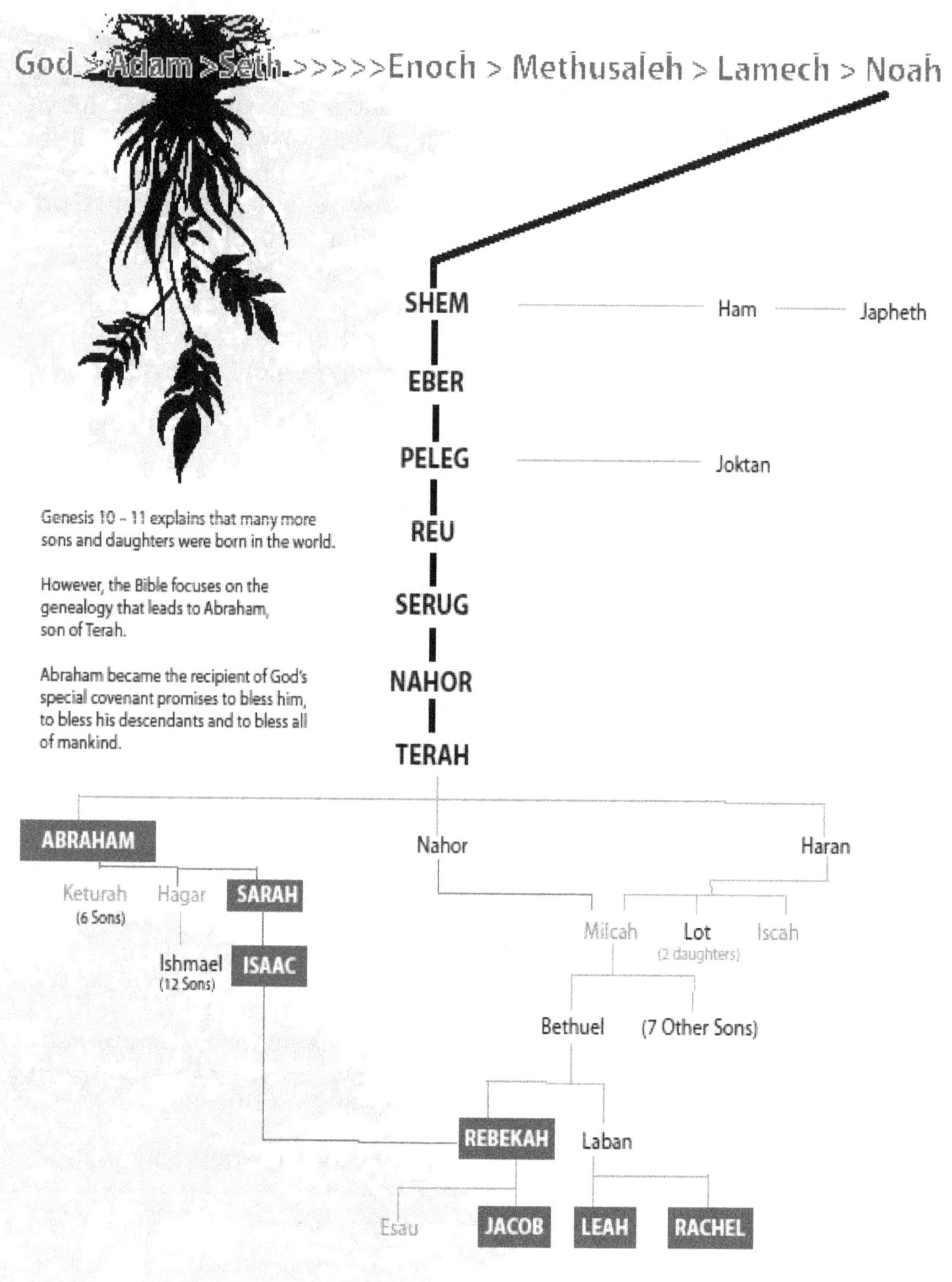

God > Adam > Seth >>>>>Enoch > Methusaleh > Lamech > Noah
SHEM
Ham
Japheth
EBER
PELEG
Joktan
REU
SERUG
NAHOR
TERAH
Genesis 10 – 11 explains that many more sons and daughters were born in the world.
However, the Bible focuses on the genealogy that leads to Abraham, son of Terah.
Abraham became the recipient of God's special covenant promises to bless him, to bless his descendants and to bless all of mankind.
ABRAHAM
Nahor
Haran
Keturah
(6 Sons)
Hagar
SARAH
Milcah
Lot
(2 daughters)
Iscah
Ishmael
(12 Sons)
ISAAC
Bethuel
(7 Other Sons)
REBEKAH
Laban
Esau
JACOB
LEAH
RACHEL

Abraham, Isaac, and Jacob's Family Tree

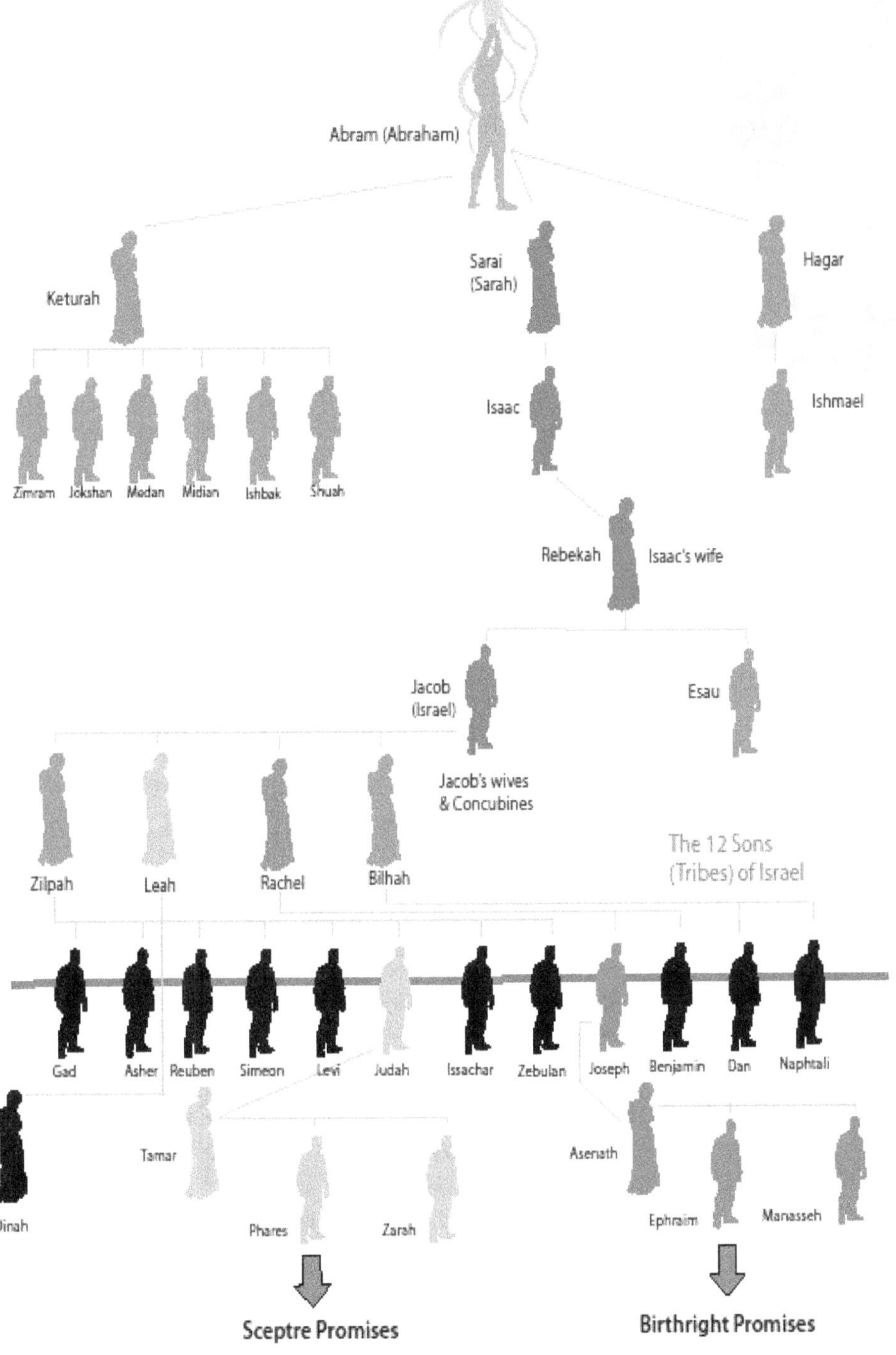

Abraham, Isaac and Jacob's Family Tree
Abram (Abraham)
Keturah
Sarai (Sarah)
Hagar
Zimram
Jokshan
Medan
Midian
Ishbak
Shuah
Isaac
Ishmael
Rebekah
Isaac's wife
Jacob (Israel)
Esau
Jacob's wives & Concubines
Zilpah
Leah
Rachel
Bilhah
The 12 Sons (Tribes) of Israel
Gad
Asher
Reuben
Simeon
Levi
Judah
Issachar
Zebulan
Joseph
Benjamin
Dan
Naphtali
Dinah
Tamar
Phares
Zarah
Asenath
Ephraim
Manasseh
Sceptre Promises
Birthright Promises

Lesson 2.2

Reading Assignment:
Genesis 25:27–28:5

I. Lesson Exercise: Like Father, Like Son

Famine describes a condition when there is an extreme scarcity (lack) of food over a large geographical area. Abraham experienced famine in his new homeland.

- In Genesis 12:10–20, there was a famine in the land of Canaan that affected Abraham. At that time, Abraham temporarily moved to Egypt until the famine was over. Then he returned to his home in Canaan country.

- In Genesis 20:1–18 another famine occurs in Canaan. This time Abraham moved to Gerar in southern Canaan, where the Philistines lived, and Abimelech was king.

In today's lesson, Isaac experiences a famine in his Canaanite homeland, similar to his father Abraham.

Compare Isaac's Experiences in Genesis Chapter 26 to His Father Abraham's

- God told Isaac not to go to Egypt during the time of famine. He was to say in the territory of Canaan, which included Philistine area of Gerar. (Gen. 26:1–3)

- Similar to Abraham's deception to the Abimelech King of the Philistines (Gen. 20:1–18), Isaac lied and said Rebekah was his wife. In Abraham's case, Sarah was his half-sister, but this was not the case with Isaac and Rebekah.

- Isaac reopened the wells his father Abraham had dug when he was in Gerar and gave them the same names. When trouble came from the Philistines, Isaac moved locations and opened new wells until the Philistines stopped troubling him.

- God blessed Isaac. He became a rich man, surpassing the prosperity of his father, and his wealth kept increasing. King Abimelech, who recognized God's blessing on Isaac's life, decided to make a peace treaty with Isaac.

- Gen. 26:23–25 says that God bestowed the covenant blessing of Abraham on Isaac. Because of this, like his father, Isaac built an altar where he worshiped God.

Birthright and Blessing

Nelson's Illustrated Bible Manners and Customs book[2] explains how in bible times, the person with the **birthright (inheritance)** would:

- Become head of the family
- Perform the priestly or religious leadership of the family
- Inherit all the material property of the family (which in the case of Abraham and Isaac meant inheriting great wealth)
- Inherit the covenant promises between God and their forefathers

Traditionally, the person receiving the birthright was the oldest son. If the head of the household did not have a son, then other arrangements would be made.

Additionally, fathers spoke **special blessings** over their children. We have already seen God honoring the father's blessings (or curses) as His own words.

Esau Sells His Birthright

Esau Gives Away His Birthright as the Firstborn Son

Isaac's firstborn son Esau should have received the birthright inheritance. But in a moment of hunger and weakness, Esau sold his birthright to his brother Jacob. Jacob understood the full value of possessing the family birthright.

Read Hebrews 12:16 to see how Esau is described as an immoral, godless person for trading his birthright as the oldest son for a single meal.

Esau Loses His Blessing as the Firstborn Son, Too

Rebekah guided her son Jacob into a tricky scheme to deceive Isaac, who bestowed his father's blessing on Jacob instead of rightful firstborn Esau. (Gen. 27). The first time Isaac prayed for Jacob, he thought he was Esau. But the second time he prayed, he knowingly bestowed upon Jacob his blessing, and gave him a warning and instruction. (Gen. 28:1-4) From this time forward, Jacob's name is listed ahead of Esau's.

2) To marry the "right" type of person, where did Isaac send Jacob? (Gen. 28:1–5) ________________________________

   (Hint: Look at Abraham's family tree)

[2]Appendix C

II. Find Jesus in the Lesson

God's Choice of Isaac's Son in Jesus' Family Tree

The scriptures are narrowing down which descendents of Abraham will be the ancestors of the Messiah. Consider the following passage from Romans 9:6–13:

> ***Well then, has God failed to fulfill his promise to the Jews? No, for not everyone born into a Jewish family is truly a Jew!***
>
> ***Just the fact that they are descendants of Abraham doesn't make them truly Abraham's children. For the Scriptures say, "Isaac is the son through whom your descendants will be counted," though Abraham had other children, too.***
>
> ***This means that Abraham's physical descendants are not necessarily children of God. It is the children of the promise who are considered to be Abraham's children.***
>
> ***For God had promised, "Next year I will return, and Sarah will have a son."***
>
> ***This son was our ancestor Isaac. When he grew up, he married Rebekah, who gave birth to twins.***
>
> ***But before they were born, before they had done anything good or bad, she received a message from God. (This message proves that God chooses according to his own plan, not according to our good or bad works.) She was told, "The descendants of your older son will serve the descendants of your younger son."***
>
> ***In the words of the Scriptures, "I loved Jacob, but I rejected Esau."***

3) Based on what you have learned so far, the Messiah will come through the descendent of Abraham, Isaac and _______________

Review the genealogy of Jesus Christ in Matthew 1:2 and Luke 3:34 to confirm the patriarchs of Israel listed in His family tree.

III. Closing Thoughts

Deception keeps playing a destructive role in the lives of all who give in to it.

As a result of Rebekah and Jacob's deceptive acts, the chosen family of God is torn apart. Esau plans to murder his brother, so Jacob runs away from his homeland of promise.

Yet, God will be faithful to His covenant with Abraham.

Read on to discover how God continues the Abrahamic covenant promises through Jacob.

Reading Assignment:
Genesis 28:6–30:24

Lesson 2.3

I. Lesson Exercise: Esau Tries to Find Favor

Although he cried bitterly after his brother stole his birthright and blessing, Esau could not get either of them back. Then, after realizing his father despised his Canaanite wives, Esau tried to marry someone he thought his Father would like.

4) Thought question: Why do you think Esau chose to marry another wife, this time from the descendant of Ishmael? (Gen. 28:8–9)

____

Bethel, the House of God

In the Maps section, look at Map 22 "Travels of Jacob." Follow Jacob's journey from his Canaanite home in Beersheba to Haran of Paddan-Aram country, the homeland of Abraham's father's family. Look for Bethel.

Bethel is first mentioned in Genesis 12:8 as the second place Abraham stopped to build an altar and worship the Lord. After Abraham returned to Canaan safely from his temporary stay in Egypt, he stopped at Bethel again to worship the Lord at that same altar.

Now Jacob's first stop, while running away from home, is Bethel. This is where Abraham had traveled before Jacob was born. Here God speaks to Jacob in a dream with a vision of angels going up and down on a ladder that reached from earth to heaven.

- God assured Jacob that the covenant of Abraham would continue through him.
- God confirmed He would one day safely bring Jacob back to the land of Canaan, his homeland of covenant promise.

5) After Jacob's first personal encounter with God in his dream, what did he name the place of this encounter? (Gen. 28:19) ____________

Jacob's Family

In Old Testament Bible times, travelers did not have the types of modern-day maps and other resources to help them arrive in places directly. But just as God blessed Abraham's servant to arrive at Abraham's homeland directly, Jacob was just as successful in finding it.

Laban (Rebekah's brother) is now head of the household. He has two daughters who are of marrying age. In Bible times, the custom was for Fathers to make arrangements for their daughter's marriage.

Marriage arrangements involved:

- The prospective husband paying money (or property) to the prospective bride's family; and
- The prospective bride's family gives a gift with the bride to assist in establishing her new family. The gift was a special blessing for the children to come.[3]

6) What payment did Jacob offer Rachel's father to marry her? (Gen. 29:18) ____

Jacob, who had deceived his brother and father, was now deceived by his new father-in-law.

On the morning after his wedding night, Jacob discovered he was married to Leah and not Rachel. But Laban smoothly convinced Jacob on what to do.

7) What price did Jacob end up paying for Rachel, which included the unexpected bonus of marrying Leah, too? (Gen. 29:25–30)

____

Jacob wanted to marry the one woman he loved, but he ends up having children through two sister-wives and their handmaids.

Look at the family tree charts on Page 2-6 and 2-7 for a pictorial representation of which woman had which child for Jacob. Jacob's two wives had the marriage custom rights to name all the children.

All the names have special meaning. In the New Living Translation One-Year Chronological, you can read the meaning of these names in the footnotes for each verse (Gen. 29:32–35; 30:6, 8, 11, 13, 18, 20, 24).

[3]Appendix C

Meaningful Names

The meaning of names for Jacob's eleven sons born to him in Haran:

1—Reuben	"look, a son"	7—Gad	"good fortune"
2— Simeon	"one who hears"	8—Asher	"happy"
3 —Levi	"feeling affection for"	9—Issachar	"reward"
4 —Judah	"praise"	10—Zebulun	"honor"
5 —Dan	"to vindicate/judge"	11—Joseph	"may he add"
6 —Naphtali	"my struggle"		

II. Find Jesus in the Lesson

Jesus' Family Tree from Judah

Jacob's son "Judah" is in Jesus' family tree, which is recorded in Matthew 1:2 and Luke 3:33–34.

8) What does the name Judah mean? (Gen. 29:35) ________________

Fun exercise: Compare Jacob's dream about angels ascending and descending from heaven to earth in Genesis 28:12 with Jesus' statement about angels ascending and descending from heaven in John 1:51.

III. Closing Thoughts

The Old Testament Bible often focuses on the male side of a story. Yet in today's lesson God reveals His love, care and personal consideration for the women.

Although Jacob's wife Leah did not have her husband's love, she had God's love. God opens her womb allowing her to have many sons until her sorrow turns to praising God for His care.

Then, when Jacob's wife Rachel needed personal consideration, God remembered her, allowing her to have a child also.

At this time in history, God often used customs for His purposes, such as the custom of having children through handmaidens.[4]

Although we never get insight on how Leah and Rachel's handmaids feel about what was going on, God blesses their sons to become a direct part of His covenant plans through Jacob.

Praise God for His love, care, and personal consideration of women!

[4]Appendix C

Lesson 2.4

Reading Assignment:
Genesis 30:25–31:55

I. Lesson Exercise

It Is Time for Jacob to Return Home

You can say that Jacob "paid his dues." He worked for Laban for twenty years.

> For fourteen years he worked for "free" to give his service as payment to Laban for marrying his two daughters.
>
> Then, he worked another six years at Laban's request, but this time he would be paid.
>
> Although Laban intended to cheat Jacob, God allowed Jacob to acquire great wealth at Laban's expense.

According to the customs of the time, Laban owed his daughters a wedding gift, which was a portion of his inheritance given to them to help with their families. **Since Laban never gave such a gift, Leah and Rachel agreed with Jacob that the wealth he gained in working for Laban was rightfully theirs anyway.**

9) After twenty years of faithful service to Laban, what reason does Jacob give his wives for wanting to return home? (Gen. 31:10–13)

____

10) Why did Jacob prosper in spite of his father-in-law's mistreatment as his boss? (Gen. 31:7–9) ______________________________

11) When Jacob and his family secretly stole away from Laban, what item did Rachel steal from her father? (Gen. 31:19)

____

Laban Catches up with Jacob and Company

- God warned Laban in a dream to be careful how he speaks to Jacob. (Gen. 31:24)
- Jacob pronounced the curse of death on the person who stole Laban's household gods. (Gen 31:32) At the time Jacob spoke this curse, he was unaware that his wife Rachel had stolen the gods.
- Before returning to his home, the last thing Laban does in his role as a father to his daughters and grandfather to their children is bless them. (Gen. 31:55)

II. Find Jesus in the Lesson

Animal Sacrifices Symbolic of Jesus' Sacrifice

Jacob makes his oath with Laban binding before God by offering a sacrifice. (Gen. 31:53–54) Jacob learned from his grandfather Abraham and his father Isaac the proper way to approach God. (Gen. 22:1–14)

Covenant promises required a sacrificial offering.

> God had Noah save seven pairs of certain animals that were approved by God for use in eating and sacrifices (Gen. 7:2). We do not know which animal was sacrificed in today's lesson, but we can be sure the animal was one approved by God.

In general, the Old Testament approved sacrifices were symbolic of the future one-time sacrifice of Jesus Christ. Christ's sacrificial death on the cross was necessary to give humankind proper access to God.

12) According to John 1: 29, which type of animal sacrifice was Jesus identified as; and what would His sacrifice do for the world?

____

III. Closing Thoughts

Reunions

Twenty (twenty-six) years is a long time to be away from home with no idea of what has been happening there. No doubt things had changed in Canaan since Jacob left. Then there is the little matter of Jacob's brother previously wanting to kill him.

**Having peaceably resolved his offenses with Laban,
Jacob now had to face his unresolved offenses with his brother.**

Through his encounter with Laban, Jacob learned first-hand what it feels like to be deceived and denied what is rightfully yours. Maybe this would help him in his approach to resolving his differences with Esau.

Most of all, Jacob had God's promise of bringing him home safely.

Certainly, the same God that helped Jacob with the reunion of Laban, would help Jacob with his reunion with Esau.

Curses

One more serious incident occurred in today's lesson that will come up again. Jacob spoke a curse of death on the person who stole Laban's handmade idol gods.

We have already seen how blessings and curses spoken by heads of households have the same impact as if God had spoken to them Himself.

Consider Proverbs 18:21 insight…

***Death and life are in the power of the tongue:
and they that love it shall eat the fruit thereof. (King James Version)***

***Those who love to talk will experience the consequences,
for the tongue can kill or nourish life. (New Living Translation)***

- Although neither Laban nor Jacob knew that Rachel had stolen the gods, God knew.
- The curse Jacob spoke set into motion spiritual laws that would cause Rachel's early death to come to pass.
- The lesson to learn from Rachel's unnecessary early death, because of her husband's rash curse, is that we all need to watch what we say. We need to be careful to speak words of "life" and "not death", even when we are experiencing the worst or toughest of times.

Bible Tidbits

❋ Beersheba means "Well of the Oath" or "Well of the Seven" or "Well of the Sevenfold Oath."

- The city of Beersheba is first introduced in Genesis 21:31. It will become the southernmost part of the Promised Land that God gave to Abraham.
- Abraham set aside seven lambs to give to Abimelech. He had Abimelech accept the lambs as part of an agreement (oath) in which Abimelech acknowledged Abraham dug the well; therefore, it belonged to Abraham. Then Abraham named the place where the oath was made Beersheba, which means "well of the seven" or "well of the oath" or "well of the sevenfold oath." (Gen. 21:22–34)
- Beersheba will be mentioned again and again in the Old Testament.

❋ Jacob honored God by paying tithes.

- In Gen. 28:22, Jacob agreed to present to God a tenth of his earnings on everything God gave to him. This practice is known as tithing. The act of paying tithes was first recorded in the Bible as an act by Abraham. He gave a tenth of his victory spoils to Melchizedek, who was the king of Salem and a priest of God Most High. (Gen. 14:17–20)
- According to the commentary on Gen. 28:22, in *Torah and Commentary* by Sol Scharfstein[5], the institution of collecting tithes is linked to Jacob's commitment to God in this passage. The money was given to God by being given to the poor and those in need. Eventually, the Law of Moses would instruct the Israelites to give their tithes to the Priests, who would then distribute it appropriately.

❋ Jacob carefully discussed his reasons for wanting to move the family with his wives.

- This included sharing with them his instructions from God. (Gen. 31:1–21)

[5]Appendix C

Reading Assignment:
Genesis 32:1–35:27

Lesson 2.5

I. Lesson Exercise

Jacob's Encounters with Angels of God

When Jacob started on his way home again after leaving Laban, Gen. 32:1 says "**angels of God" came to meet him**. Imagine that!

Jacob's hope for a safe return home turned to fear for his entire family's life when messengers told him his brother Esau was bringing 400 men to meet them. Jacob's fear of Esau's revenge first led him to divide his family up so Esau could not kill them all at once. Then he **turned to God in earnest prayer (**Gen. 32:6–32).

To calm Jacob's fears and change his life forever, God sent another visitor from heaven to Jacob. This time, Jacob's encounter with his heavenly visitor turned into an all-night wrestling match. The scriptures say the "man" knocked Jacob's hip out of joint at the socket when he could not win the struggle. Jacob still would not let him go.

Jacob explained, **"I will not let you go unless you bless me."** Next the "man" blessed Jacob because he said Jacob had **"struggled with both God and men and [had] won."** God changed Jacob's name to reflect his victory in his struggles. (Gen. 32:22–32)

13) What does Jacob's new name of "Israel" mean? (Gen. 32:28)

____

14) What does the name "Peniel" mean? (Gen. 32:30) ____________________

"No Revenge" : Forgiven

In the case of Esau and Jacob's story, it turns into a happy ending. God kept his word of bringing Jacob home in peace.

It is heartwarming how **Esau forgave** his brother,
choosing "no revenge".

- Consider how Jacob bows low seven times (Gen. 33:3).
- Consider Esau and Jacob's brotherly embrace with tears (Gen. 33:4).

Only God can heal such situations if we trust Him to help us. With God's help, the wrongs of the past were forgiven and both men were blessed.

"Revenge" : Not Forgiven

On the other hand, **Jacob's sons did not forgive**. They **chose "revenge,"** which caused Jacob to have to go on the "run" again.

Jacob's only daughter Dinah was violated by the Prince of Shechem. After violating her, the prince wanted to marry her. But Dinah's brothers were outraged!

15) Why did Dinah's brothers ask all Shechem men to be circumcised? (Gen. 34: 14–17; 24–29) ______________________________

Note: Circumcision is the process of cutting away the overhanging skin at the tip of the male's reproductive organ. This skin is also called the foreskin. In today's society, newborn boys who are circumcised usually have this procedure done before leaving the hospital after birth. This is a painful procedure, but as a baby they have no remembrance of the pain. When this procedure is performed on a man, the pain is so intense it prevents the man from even walking until the cut heals.

Blessings and Curses

God blesses Jacob.

God told Jacob to return to Bethel, the place where God first talked with Jacob, when he was on the run from Esau. Jacob cleansed his household of all things that offended God, and he worshiped God at Bethel. God saved Jacob from his enemies again. He put terror in their hearts, so no one attacked them. (Gen. 35:1–15)

God tells him again his new name is Israel. Jacob meant supplanter, but Israel meant he is a prince, who has wrestled with God and man and won. God repeated that the covenant blessings of Abraham were now given to Jacob (Israel) and his descendants.

God blesses Rachel.

God honored Rachel's words when she named her firstborn son Joseph, which means "may he add, or multiply." He blessed Rachel to have another son added to her.

However, Rachel died as her second son was being born. Some scholars believe Rachel's early death was the outcome of the curse that her husband Jacob spoke on the person who had stolen Laban's idols (Gen. 31:32)**. If this is true, then a person should choose their words carefully, speaking words that give life instead of words that bring death.** (Proverbs 18:21, Proverbs 26:2)

- Rachel named her son, "Ben-oni," which means "son of my sorrow."
- Jacob renamed him "Benjamin," which means "son of my right hand." (Gen. 35:18)

II. Find Jesus in the Lesson

Rachel's Death and Jesus' Birth

"So Rachel died and was buried on the way to Ephrath (that is Bethlehem). So Jacob set up a stone monument over her grave, and it can be seen there to this day."
Gen. 35:19–20

The town of Rachel's burial would play an important role in the birth of Jesus Christ. In Micah 5:2, there is a prediction about this town's future importance,

"But you, O Bethlehem Ephrathah, are only a small village in Judah. Yet a ruler of Israel will come from you, one whose origins are from the distant past." Micah 5:2

The ancient Rabbis identify Micah 5:2 as a Messianic passage. Appendix 9 of the book *The Life and Times of Jesus the Messiah* by Alfred Edersheim is entitled "List of Old Testament Passages Messianically Applied in Ancient Rabbinic Writings." It identifies the specific ancient rabbinic sources that admit Micah 5:2 is a messianic passage.

16) From Matthew 2:1–6, what does the town of Bethlehem have to do with Jesus Christ? ______________________________

III. Closing Thoughts

Stone Monuments and Other Landmarks

The stone monument Jacob placed over Rachel's grave (called a "pillar" in the King James Bible) will be a landmark for future generations of Israel's descendants.

Landmarks are noticeable objects on land that serve as a guide to travelers to help them know where they are. We will read about landmarks again.

Israel and the Israelites

More and more you will see Jacob referred to as Israel. Soon, all his offspring will be known as the Israelites.

God calls the Israelites His covenant people in the Old Testament.

- This means the descendants of Abraham, Isaac and Israel are God's chosen people to accomplish a unique work for Him in the earth.

Jacob => Israel => Israelites

Reading Assignment:
Genesis 36:1–19
I Chronicles 1:35–37
Genesis 36:20–30
I Chronicles 1:38–42
Genesis 36:31–43
I Chronicles 1:43–2:2

Lesson 2.6

I. Lesson Exercise

Edomites

Esau's descendants grew into a very large nation.

Genesis 25:30 explains how Esau also became known as Edom.

- Edom means "red."
- When Esau ate Jacob's red stew in exchange for his birthright, then he started being called Edom.
- The descendants of Esau (Edom = red) became known as the Edomites.

After Jacob's return to the land of Canaan, Esau took his wives, children, household servants, cattle, flocks and all his wealth—which he had gained in Canaan—and moved away from Jacob, to the hill country of Seir.

- Genesis 36:7 explains that the land could not support both brothers who had an abundance of cattle and livestock.
- Based on inheritance rights, the Edomites also had to move away because Jacob had the birthright.
- Jacob was to continue in the land of Canaan in fulfillment of the covenant God made with Abraham, Isaac and now Jacob (Israel).

The original tribes in Seir descended from "Seir the Horite", but the Edomites were rulers of that land. (Gen. 36:20)

- The fact that the Edomites became many kings (called dukes in KJV), began fulfillment of the promise God made to Abraham in Gen. 17: 6 and Sarah in Gen. 17:16. God promised that kings would be among their descendants.
- One purpose for today's lesson is to explain who the Edomites are since they became a strong nation that conflicted with the Israelite nation later.

When references are made to Mount Seir and Edom, remember these terms are different ways of talking about Esau's descendants.

ESAU => EDOM => Edomites

II. Find Jesus in the Lesson

Jesus Christ is King of All Kings

God promised Abraham and Sarah that many nations and kings of people would come from their descendants, which has begun to be fulfilled in today's lesson. Their descendant Jesus is the King who is King of all the kings of all the nations on earth. Consider these New Testament passages that continue the story of Abraham's special descendant.

God gave the promise to Abraham and his child.
And notice that it doesn't say the promise was to his children,
as if it meant many descendants.

But the promise was to his child—and that, of course, means Christ.

Galatians 3:16

❧

And the seventh angel sounded;
and there were great voices in heaven, saying;

The kingdoms of this world are become the kingdoms of our Lord,
and of his Christ; and he shall reign for ever and ever.

Revelation 11:15 KJV

❧

These shall make war with the Lamb,

and the Lamb shall overcome them:
for he is Lord of lords, and King of kings:

and they that are with him are called, and chosen, and faithful.

Revelation 17:14 KJV

III. Closing Thoughts

Some Ancient Civilizations besides Israel

Our current Bible text focuses on God's chosen people during the approximate dates of 2166 BC to 1700 BC. However, there were other nations in the world.

The chart on the following page is reproduced by permission of Pearson Education, Inc. publishing. It includes insight into some of the other ancient nations and their approximate dates of existence.

Some Ancient Civilizations[6]

Name	Approx. dates	Location	Major cities
Akkadian	2350–2230 BC	Mesopotamia, parts of Syria, Asia Minor, Iran	Akkad, Ur, Erich
Assyrian	1800–612 BC	Mesopotamia, Syria	Assur, Nineveh, Calah
Babylonian	1728–1686 BC (old) 625–539 B.C. (new)	Mesopotamia, Syria, Palestine	Babylon
Cimmerian	750–500 BC	Caucasus, northern Asia Minor	—
Egyptian	2850–715 BC	Nile valley	Thebes, Memphis, Tanis
Etruscan	900–396 BC	Northern Italy	—
Greek	900–200 BC	Greece	Athens, Sparta, Thebes, Mycenae, Corinth
Hittite	1640–1200 BC	Asia Minor, Syria	Hattusas, Nesa
Indus Valley	3000–1500 BC	Pakistan, Northwestern India	—
Lydian	700–547 BC	Western Asia Minor	Sardis, Miletus
Mede	835–550 BC	Iran	Media
Minoan	3000–1100 BC	Crete	Knossos
Persian	559–330 BC	Iran, Asia Minor, Syria	Persepolis, Pasargadae
Phoenician	1100–332 BC	Palestine (colonies: Gibraltar, Carthage, Sardinia)	Tyre, Sidon, Byblos
Phrygian	1000–547 BC	Central Asia Minor	Gordion
Roman	500 BC–AD 300	Italy, Mediterranean region, Asia Minor, western Europe	Rome, Byzantium
Scythian	800–300 BC	Caucasus	—
Sumerian	3200–2360 BC	Mesopotamia	Ur, Nippur

[6]Appendix C

Reading Assignment:
Genesis 37:1–38:30
I Chronicles 2:3–6, 8
Genesis 39:1–23

Lesson 2.7

I. Lesson Exercise: Jacob's Favored Son

Seventeen-year-old Joseph was born to Jacob and his beloved wife Rachel (who was now dead), when Jacob was in his old age. This caused Jacob to love Joseph more than his other children.

When Jacob gave Joseph the beautiful multi-colored tunic, Joseph stood out among the crowd. The common attire of the times was plain, white tunics. Joseph looked like royalty compared to others.

Besides this, Joseph, second to youngest of Jacob's twelve sons, was what some today might call a "tattletale."

As a result, Jacob's favored son was not so favored by his brothers:

- Jacob's partiality to Joseph caused his brothers to hate him (Gen. 37:4)
- The message of Joseph's dreams was that his own brothers and even his parents would bow down to him as if he were a king. Joseph's brothers quickly understood the dreams' meaning, which made them hate him more (Gen. 37:8, 10)
- Joseph's brothers' hatred eventually made them want to kill him. They ended up selling him into slavery instead. Then they deceived their father into believing he was dead.

Interestingly, a dead goat was used by Jacob to deceive his father (Gen. 27:1–40), and a dead goat is used by Jacob's sons to deceive him (Gen. 37:18–36).

Joseph Was Sold Out by His Own Brothers

Potiphar's Favored Servant

Pharaoh is the title for the King of Egypt.[7] The captain of Pharaoh's palace guard is Potiphar.

Ishmaelite/Midianite spice traders, traveling from up north in the Gilead area—through Canaan—on their way to Egypt (see map of the Journeys of Joseph), purchased Joseph from his brothers. They sold him as a slave to Potiphar.

Joseph, who began as slave boy for his Eqyptian master Potiphar, soon became Potiphar's favored servant as Joseph managed all the business dealings for Potiphar's household.

17) What made it possible for Joseph to become favored, despite his start as a slave in a foreign land? (Gen. 39:2–5) ________________

18) Why did Joseph attract Potiphar's wife's favor? (Gen. 39:6–7)

____

Jailer's Favored Prisoner

Joseph did not give in to the temptation presented to him by Potiphar's wife. Yet his faithfulness to God cost him dearly. Seemingly Joseph was back in another pit of a situation. With God's help, Joseph responded positively to his unfortunate turn of events. Soon he became the jailer's favored prisoner.

19) What made it possible for Joseph to become favored, despite being unjustly thrown in prison? (Gen. 39:21–23) ________________

<u>II. Find Jesus in the Lesson:</u> Judah's Son in Jesus' Family Tree

Judah and Tamar

While the Bible text highlights Joseph's life story, there are many things happening in Jacob's family that are not shared. However, a specific story about Jacob's son Judah almost seems odd as it is included in the middle of telling Joseph's story. From Genesis 38:1–30 we learn:

- Judah had married a Canaanite woman who gave him three sons.
- Tamar was Judah's daughter-in-law; married to Judah's oldest son Er.
- Because of their wicked behavior, Er died and his brother Onan after him. Judah promised to give Tamar his youngest son, Shelah, to marry and have children by, once he became of age. But the scripture explains Judah had no intention of keeping his promise.
- Tamar devised a plan. Disguised as a harlot, Tamar slept with her father-in-law Judah. She became pregnant with twin sons for Judah.

[7]Appendix C

In Matthew 1:3 and Luke 3:33–34, Judah and Tamar's son Perez (Pharez in KJV) **is in Jesus' family tree, along with his mother Tamar. Tamar is one of a few women named in Jesus' genealogy.**

The story of Judah and Tamar is included in the Bible to reveal interesting details about the family tree of the Messiah.

In general, the Old Testament keeps preparing us for the Messiah's coming.

III. Closing Thoughts

By the end of Week 2, many significant Bible events have occurred.

Here are some key events for review:

- **God created everything.**
- **God made man in His image, meaning to be like Him.**
- **Adam and Eve sinned against God by disobeying His "do not" command.**
- **Sin caused humankind to lose their right relationship with God and paradise.**
- **God allowed animal sacrifice to give humankind a way to approach Him again.**
- **During the time of Seth, men began to worship the Lord.**

Humankind became so evil God decided to destroy all living things.

- **Noah was righteous and found grace with God for himself and his family.**

Noah's family was saved from the worldwide destruction by flood.

After the flood, God directed people to spread out over all the earth.

- **God called Abraham to leave his father's family and homeland, and go to Canaan.**
- **God made a covenant with Abraham, Abraham's son Isaac and Abraham's grandson Jacob.**
- **Jacob's name was changed to Israel.**
- **God's covenant or chosen people are then known as Israelites, a covenantal community.**

Week 3

Featured Book:

Genesis,

with a few passages from 1 Chronicles Chapters 1 and 2
and beginning the book of

Job

Contents:

Peek at the Week

Lesson	Key Events	Find Jesus
3.1	Joseph in the Palace	Joseph's Life is a "type" of Jesus' life
3.2	Joseph Reunites with his family	Joseph's Life foreshadows events in Jesus' life
3.3	Jacob's Family move to Egypt	Judah's Grandson in Jesus' Family Tree
3.4	Jacob Blesses His Sons	Jesus, Lion of the Tribe of Judah
3.5	Righteous Job's Tragedy	Jesus Overcomes satan
3.6	Job and Friends First Set of Discussion Debates	Great Agony Led Job and Jesus to Question God
3.7	Job and Friends First Set of Debates continued	Jesus Christ is Emmanuel

Chronological Notes

Timetable	Key Events
1887 (or 1721) BC	Joseph interprets cup-bearer and baker's dream
1885 (or 1719) BC	Joseph interprets Pharaoah's dream and is appointed second ruler in Egypt
1876 (or 1710) BC	Jacob and family move to Egypt
1859 (or 1693) BC	Jacob dies
1805 (or 1639) BC	Joseph dies
Date not known for sure: Possibly before time of Mosaic Law, in time of Abraham, Isaac or Jacob ~ between 2000–1600 BC	Life of Job

**All dates are approximate.*

Reading Assignment:
Genesis 40:1–23
Genesis 35:28–29
Genesis 41:1–57

Lesson 3.1

I. Lesson Exercise: Interpretation of Dreams

When Joseph was seventeen years old, he had two special dreams he shared with his family. The family was able to understand the basic meaning of the dreams, so much so that his brothers became angry, while his father wondered about their full meaning.

In today's lesson we read about three more dreams. The meanings of these dreams were not understandable when hearing them. However, each dreamer had a strong sense that their dreams had a special meaning. The dreamers could not rest until they discovered the meaning (interpretation) of their dreams.

- Joseph explained interpreting dreams is God's business. (Gen. 40:8)
- God used Joseph to give His dream interpretations which described near and long-term future events. (Gen. 40:12–13; 18–19; 41:25–32)
- Based on what happens at the end of today's lesson, we learn that God's purpose for having Joseph interpret the cupbearer and baker's dreams was: a) so they could know that Joseph had the gift from God to interpret dreams; and b) so the cupbearer would remember Joseph's gift and tell Pharaoh. (Gen. 40:14–15; 41:9–13)
- God's purpose for interpreting Pharaoh's dreams was to let Pharaoh know the future, and to move Joseph into the palace in a position of influence in Egypt.

In this week's lesson, we will learn how God had an overall purpose to save Joseph's family from destruction during the upcoming famine.

Pharaoh's Favored Administrator

Not only did Joseph interpret Pharaoh's dreams, but his business management skills showed. He immediately advised Pharaoh on how to handle the upcoming seven years of great prosperity, to be followed by seven years of great famine.

- Joseph recommended Pharaoh put the wisest man in Egypt in charge of a nationwide program. Then Joseph gave details on what this nationwide program should include, with a food collection and storage plan during the good years to provide for the nation during the years of famine. (Gen. 41:33–36)

- Pharaoh concluded that since God had revealed the dreams to Joseph, he must be the wisest man in the world. He appointed Joseph to be second ruler in the kingdom managing the nationwide food program and all government activities.

1) How old was Joseph when he became the highest administrator over all the land and people of Egypt, second only to Pharaoh? (Gen. 41:46) _______________

II. Find Jesus in the Lesson

Joseph's Life is a "type" of Jesus' Life[1]

Joseph's life story is considered a "foreshadowing" type of the life of Jesus Christ. Although Joseph is not personally mentioned in the New Testament as a type of Christ, one can look at events from his life and find similarities with the type of events that happen in Jesus' life.

> Example: As Joseph was hated by his brothers and sold into slavery for money, Jesus was hated by his fellow Israelites and sold for money into the hands of those who crucified him.
>
> Example: As Joseph was lifted from prison and elevated to the highest dignity, Jesus was elevated to the highest position at God's right hand after His resurrection from the dead. (Rom. 8:34)

Compare the ages when Joseph began his public service for Pharaoh in Egypt and the age when Jesus will begin his public service for God.

2) How old was Joseph when he began service for Pharaoh? (Gen. 41:46) ________

3) How old was Jesus when He began public service for God? (Luke 3:23a) ________

[1]Appendix C:

III. Closing Thoughts

Isaac dies at the ripe old age of 180 years old.

Of the top three men who started the nation of Israel, the Bible text gives the least focus on Isaac. And yet it turns out that Isaac lives longer than his father Abraham, who died at 175 years, and longer than his son Jacob whose death we will read about in the upcoming lessons. Not bad for a person who as a young child was almost sacrificed like a lamb on an altar before God. Not bad at all!

✞

Prophetic Dreams

Prophetic Dreams, *not* demonic fakes!

Here is a word of caution about "prophetic dreams," meaning dreams from God that foretell events that will happen in the future.

> **As we learn from today's lesson, God is in the business of giving and interpreting dreams with messages that He wants known for His purposes.**

Deceptively, God's enemy, who we learned early in Genesis is satan (also called the devil), **has a fake of everything real that comes from God.**

> God gives specific instructions and warnings (laws) on why His children are not to go to **psychics, fortune-tellers, palm-readers, etc.** Reference Leviticus 19:26–28, 31 and Deuteronomy 18:10–12.

Warning:

> **Do not confuse God's beautiful gift of prophetic dreams, with the fake things that come from satan's influence that bring harm into our lives.**

Keep reading the whole Bible to understand what things are approved by God as compared with those things that are not approved by God.

Joseph's Boyhood Dreams Come to Pass

Lesson 3.2

Reading Assignment: Genesis 42:1–45:15

I. Lesson Exercise

Joseph's Boyhood Dreams Come to Pass

In Gen. 37:5–10, Joseph told his family about his two dreams.

- In the first dream, his brothers' bundles of grain gathered around and bowed low before Joseph's bundle of grain, which stood tall.
- In the second dream the sun, moon, and eleven stars bowed low before Joseph. Now that Joseph is second in charge in Egypt, those dreams he had at seventeen years old are finally coming to pass.
- In today's lesson Joseph's brothers really do bow low to him.
- In Joseph's first boyhood dream, there was a reference to the bowing of bundles of grain. In today's lesson, it turns out Joseph's brothers bow low to him because they need Joseph's grain.
- In the book of Revelation, we will see a reference to the second dream's symbols of sun, moon and stars (Revelation 12:1). We will revisit the meaning of the second dream at that time.
- Joseph's brothers did not recognize him because he looked, talked, and acted like an Egyptian.
- Notice how he spoke to them with the aid of an interpreter, as if he only spoke in Egyptian and did not understand the Israelite language.
- They bowed to him as if he were a king, because of his high position in Egypt. They knew he would decide whether to help them.

Joseph Tests His Brothers Love

Joseph put his brothers through some very uncomfortable moments before letting them know who he was. It was as if Joseph were testing their love for the family and their love for his only full brother Benjamin by his dead mother Rachel.

Joseph's uncomfortable, testing moments of his brothers included:

- Putting all his brothers in jail for three days (Genesis 42:17)
- Keeping Simeon tied up in custody for a longer time (Genesis 42:24, 33–36)
- Secretly returning the grain payment so they appeared to be thieves (Genesis 42:27–28)
- Making it appear Benjamin had stolen his personal cup (Genesis 44:12–17)

4) What did the brothers decide was the reason for all the trouble they were having in getting simple grain like everybody else? (Gen. 42:21–22 and 44:16) ____

5) Which two brothers were willing to allow harm to themselves or their children to protect Benjamin? (Genesis 42:37) _________; (Genesis 44:18, 33) _________________

Consider this: Judah stepped up to conduct himself like the leader of the family during this time of family testing. Some might even consider him kingly in the way he approached things. However, the firstborn son Reuben was ineffective in leading the family out of their trouble.

Family Reunion Time

After witnessing his brothers' love and protection of their father Jacob and his brother Benjamin, Joseph could no longer hold back the truth. He reveals who he is.

It's Family Reunion Time!

What an emotional moment for these men! With a full understanding of things, Joseph tries to explain to his brothers why God allowed them to mistreat him. It was so he could be placed in his current position to save their lives. (Gen. 45:1–8)

II. Find Jesus in the Lesson and III. Closing Thoughts

Events in Joseph's life continue to foreshadow (be a type of) **events that will happen in Jesus' life.**

In today's lesson, we see how the brother who was thought to be dead, was alive and in a position to save his family.

On the day Jesus was crucified and then buried, the hopes of many of being delivered from their enemies through Jesus Christ died along with Him.

After His resurrection from the dead, Jesus explained to His disciples how His death and burial were necessary. This is so He could be resurrected from the dead, and then save many people through His new life. (Luke 24:44–49)

Our Brother, Who Was Dead, Is Alive!

Read Jesus' explanation in Luke 24:15–26; 45–47 below.

Suddenly, Jesus himself came along and joined them and began walking beside them. But they didn't know who he was, because God kept them from recognizing him.

"You seem to be in a deep discussion about something," he said. "What are you so concerned about?"

They stopped short, sadness written across their faces. Then one of them, Cleopas, replied, "You must be the only person in Jerusalem who hasn't heard about all the things that have happened there the last few days."

"What things?" Jesus asked.
"The things that happened to Jesus, the man from Nazareth" they said.

"He was a prophet who did wonderful miracles. He was a mighty teacher, highly regarded by both God and all the people. But our leading priests and other religious leaders arrested him and handed him over to be condemned to death, and they crucified him. We had thought he was the Messiah who had come to rescue Israel. That all happened three days ago.

Then some women from our group of his followers were at his tomb early this morning, and they came back with an amazing report.

They said his body was missing, and they had seen angels who told them Jesus is alive! Some of our men ran out to see, and sure enough, Jesus' body was gone, just as the women had said."

Then Jesus said to them, "You are such foolish people! You find it so hard to believe all that the prophets wrote in the Scriptures. Wasn't it clearly predicted by the prophets that the Messiah would have to suffer all these things before entering his time of glory?"

...

Then he opened their minds to understand these many Scriptures.

And he said, "Yes, it was written long ago that the Messiah must suffer and die and rise again from the dead on the third day.

With my authority, take this message of repentance to all the nations, beginning in Jerusalem:

`There is forgiveness of sins for all who turn to me.'

Reading Assignment:
Genesis 45:16–47:27

Lesson 3.3

I. Lesson Exercise

Jacob's Family (The Israelites) Move to Egypt

Joseph had so much favor with Pharaoh that Pharaoh was excited to find a place for all of Joseph's family in Egypt.

- When Jacob set out to move his family to Egypt, he stopped in Beersheba to offer sacrifices to God. In a night vision, God spoke words of comfort to Jacob, giving him specific insight concerning his family's move to Egypt.
- God told Jacob not to be afraid of going down to Egypt where he would die with Joseph at his side. He assured Jacob that his descendants would return to the land of Canaan, which is the covenant land of promise that God gave to Abraham's descendants, through Isaac and Jacob. (Gen. 46:2–4)
- Jacob and his family moved to the land of Goshen in Egypt. (Gen. 46:28)
- There were sixty-six descendants of Jacob who traveled from Canaan with him. The total number with Jacob came to seventy people. (Gen. 46:26-27)
- Joseph's business skills benefited Pharaoh by eventually purchasing all the land and people of Egypt in exchange for providing the people with food.
- Joseph's business skills benefited his family by causing them to live in the best land in Egypt, supplying them with enough food to feed everyone throughout the famine. This enabled his family to prosper and grow quickly.

From Canaan to Egypt

II. Find Jesus in the Lesson: Judah's Grandson in Jesus' Family Tree

Genesis 46:1-25 lists the names of all the Israelites (descendants of Jacob), who went to Egypt. The names are organized based on each son of Jacob.

In verse 12, the sons of Judah are listed. We learned in an earlier lesson that Judah's son Perez is in Jesus' family tree. Perez has two sons, Hezron and Hamul.

6) From Matthew 1:3 and Luke 3:33, which son of Perez is in Jesus' family tree? ____________________

III. Closing Thoughts: God Fulfills Every Detail of His Prophecies

God forewarned Abraham that his descendants would live as slaves in a land foreign to their covenant Promised Land of Canaan. After 400 years, they would return to the Promised Land. (Gen.15:13–16)

In today's lesson, Jacob and his family move to this foreign land which is Egypt. God assures Jacob, just like he assured Abraham, that his descendants will return to live in the land of Canaan. (Gen.15:13–16; 46:1–4)

But the Israelites will not be oppressed as slaves until after Joseph is dead.

Historical Timeline of Ancient Egypt:

TIMELINE OF EVENTS & SIGNIFICANT PEOPLE[2]

Timeline of Events and Kingdoms in Ancient Egypt	Dates	Significant Events
I. Archaic Dynasties 1–2	3100–2800 BC	Unification of all Egypt.
II. Old Kingdom Dynasties3–6	2800–2250 BC	Construction of the pyramids begins.
III. First Intermediate Dynasties 7–9	2250–2000 BC	Political chaos. Abraham comes to Egypt.
IV. Middle Kingdom Dynasties 9–12	2000–1786 BC	Recovery and political stability. Joseph and Jacob come to Egypt.
V. Second Intermediate Dynasties13–17	1786–1575 BC	Hyksos "invasion"
VI. New Kingdom Dynasties 18–20	1575–1085 BC	Creation of the Egyptian Empire, and Akhanaten's religious strategy begins. The Exodus (1446 BC)
VII. Third Intermediate	1085–663 BC	Sheshonk I ("Shishak") sacks the temple (927 BC)
VIII. Late Period Dynasties 26–31	663–332 BC	The Exile (586 BC): refugees flee to Egypt.
IX. Ptolemaic Period	332–30 BC	
X. Roman Era	30 BC–AD 395	Mary and Joseph escape to Egypt (4 BC)

Dr. Joel A. Freeman is author of this table which is reprinted with his permission.

[2]Appendix C

Lesson 3.4

Reading Assignment:
Genesis 47:28–50:26

I. Lesson Exercise

Before his death, Jacob blesses Joseph's sons

Jacob enjoyed his son Joseph for seventeen years as a child. Now, Jacob spends the last seventeen years of his life with Joseph as a successful man.

Just before his death, Jacob has special blessings for Joseph's sons.

- Manassah, First born son of Joseph (*Gen. 41:51)*
  Manassah means "God has made me forget" *(all my troubles and father's family)*
- Ephraim, Second born son of Joseph *(Gen. 41:52)*
  Ephraim means "God has made me fruitful" *(in this land of my suffering)*
- Jacob adopted Joseph's first two sons as his own. Ephraim and Manassah would receive family inheritance in equal portions to Jacob's other sons. (Gen. 48:5)
- Just as Jacob, the younger brother, received the greatest blessing from his father, Jacob prayed for Joseph's younger son Ephraim to receive the greatest blessing over Manassah. Ephraim would become a multitude of nations, being very fruitful just as his name implied. (Gen. 48:12–20)

Before his death, Jacob blesses his own sons

Prophecies Concerning Their Future

❑ **Reuben (Gen. 49:2–4):**

Jacob told Reuben he knew Reuben had slept with his concubine wife Bilhah (Gen. 35:22), who was the mother of his half-brothers Dan and Naphtali. Because of this, Reuben lost his rights of inheritance as the first-born son. The birthright was passed to Joseph instead. (Genesis 49:26)

❑ **Simeon and Levi (Gen. 49:5–7):**

Jacob's remembrance of Simeon and Levi's revengeful act on the men of Shechem (Gen. 34:25–26), shaped the words he spoke over them. Jacob said their descendants would be scattered throughout Israel. Simeon's Promised Land inheritance was embedded in the inheritance of Judah. (Joshua 19:1, 9) The tribe of Levi did not receive land like the other tribes. Instead, they became the nation's priests who were scattered to live and serve among all the tribes. (Joshua 13:33; Leviticus 3; Numbers 35:1–8)

- ❑ **Judah (Gen. 49:8–12):**
  Judah's blessing includes Messianic prophecies that will be fulfilled by Jesus: a) Judah's brothers will praise him; b) Judah will defeat his enemies; c) all Judah's relatives will bow before him; d) Judah's tribe was represented by a lion; e) the scepter of kingship would not depart from Judah until the one to whom it belongs comes to get it *(King James Version says "until Shiloh comes")*
- ❑ **Zebulun (Gen. 49:13)**
  The people of Zebulun would settle on the shores of the sea
- ❑ **Issachar (Gen. 49:14–15):**
  The people of Issachar will be laborer type people
- ❑ **Dan (Gen. 49:16–18):**
  The type of animal that represents the Danites is a snake, a poisonous viper. The tribe will be a small but dangerous one
- ❑ **Gad (Gen. 49:19):**
  The people of Gad will eventually overturn those who try to conquer them and the Gadites will conquer them instead
- ❑ **Asher (Gen. 49:20):**
  Asher will be prosperous producing rich, highly prized foods
- ❑ **Naphtali (Gen. 49:21):**
  The deer is used to describe the people of Naphtali. The future territory of Naphtali included beautiful hills and valleys.
- ❑ **Joseph (Gen. 49:22–26):**
  Joseph is described as a prince among his brothers with a great amount of blessings pronounced on his descendants. His sons Ephraim and Manassah will produce powerful tribes. Because of Jacob's blessing, Ephraim and Manassah will replace Levi and Joseph in the count of the twelve tribes of Israel.
- ❑ **Benjamin (Gen. 49:27)**
  The type of animal that represents the Benjamites is the wolf. The tribe becomes known for its courage in fighting.

A Good Ending

After his death, Jacob is buried with great fanfare by his sons

7) Where was Jacob buried? (Gen. 49:29–32) ____________________
   [Note: Jacob is the last of the Israelite Patriarchs and Matriarchs to be buried in this location.]
8) Where was Joseph buried? (Gen. 50:26) ______________________
9) Before Joseph died, what did he make the Israelites promise to do with his dead body (bones) in the future? (Gen 50:25)

   ____

II. Find Jesus in the Lesson

The Messiah in Judah's Blessing

Jacob pronounced his blessing on his son Judah in Genesis 49:9–12. According to the ancient Rabbinic writings this passage contains several prophetic emblems for the Messiah. For example, the lion, Shiloh, and the kingly scepter are all messianic symbols. (For more details reference this passage listing in Appendix 9 of *The Life and Times of Jesus the Messiah* by Alfred Edersheim, 1993, Hendrickson Publishers, Inc.)

Jesus, Lion of the Tribe of Judah

At the beginning of Revelation Chapter 5, a strong angel asked if there was anyone worthy to open the seals of a special book in the hand of God. John, the author of Revelation and eyewitness of these heavenly events, began to cry when learning there was no man. Then, Revelation 5:5 explains that someone was found worthy.

But one of the twenty-four elders said to me, "Stop weeping!

Look, the Lion of the tribe of Judah, the heir to David's throne, has conquered.

He is worthy to open the scroll and break its seven seals." Revelation 5:5

The person found worthy is **a) called the Lion of the tribe of Judah,**
b) said to be an heir to the throne of David, which indicates kingship, just like the scepter in Gen. 49:10 represents kingship, and
c) the person has conquered, meaning defeated all his enemies.
The passage Revelation 22:16 reveals that this descendant of Judah and King David (Rev. 5:5) is Jesus Christ. He fulfills all and finishes all in His second coming to earth.

Jesus: Lion of the Tribe of Judah

III. Closing Thoughts

After Jacob died, his sons were all afraid the powerful, influential Joseph would finally turn on them all, and get revenge for the wrong they had done to him. Joseph honestly did not blame his brothers because he understood that all their actions were the work of God through them. Joseph explains this in Genesis 50:20—

As far as I am concerned, God turned into good what you meant for evil.

He brought me to the high position I have today so I could save the lives of many people.

Key Word(s)	Key Chapters
Sovereign	42

Title

"Job" means "one who suffers". Suffering Job is the main character of the book.

Key word "sovereign" refers to how God is sovereign, which means God can permit things to happen, even to the righteous, that we do not always understand. (1 Chron. 29:11-12, Psalm 115:3, Psalm 147:5, Jeremiah 32:27, Romans 11:33, Colossians 1:16, Romans 8:28)

Summary

Job is presented as a man who is righteous, meaning perfect and upright, in the eyes of God. Yet God allows Job to experience great, tragic suffering. Job's friends do not believe God would allow a truly righteous person to suffer so greatly. They try to convince Job to confess the wicked sin they believe he has done, which is the real reason he deserves so great a punishment from God. Job maintains he has lived as a righteous man. Finally, Job suffers with the lack of comfort he receives from anyone, including God.

There is a lot of detailed discussion about the "real" reason behind Job's suffering between a) Job and his three friends—Eliphaz, Bildad and Zophar; and b) from the young man Elihu, who listens to Job and his friends long enough until he is compelled to share his own thoughts. **In the end, God speaks to Job to clear up the matter once and for all.** God's answer totally satisfies Job, but his answer is not anything that anyone would expect. After much heartache and suffering, there is a happy ending for righteous Job.

Through Job's amazing story, with its exchange of ideas on why a person suffers, there are many lessons to be learned by all who read it.

Timetable: Timing is unknown

- **Timing of Job's events is unknown, but there are good guesses**
  Some Bible scholars believe Job lived sometime during the lifetime of Abraham, Isaac or Jacob. This is because his wealth is measured in flocks and herds, and the overall lifestyle and longevity of Job are most similar to persons described in Genesis.

  Also, there are no references to the Law of Moses. For example, Job was not condemned for performing sacrifices away from the Tabernacle and without the priest. (Lev. 17:3–9) This is why Job follows Genesis and is before Exodus in this chronological study.

  However, there are some scholars who propose that Job was an Edomite. This means he was a descendant from within Abraham's grandson Esau's family. This might explain why there are no references to the Mosaic law in the book of Job. Additionally, this could support the historical placement of this writing at a later time in history, such as around the time of the biblical wisdom books (e.g. Psalms, Proverbs). For more details on this view, refer to "Transition: The Book of Job,*" Chronological Study Bible* (Thomas Nelson, Inc.., 2008), p. 901.

- **Timing for how long Job suffered is unknown**
  Also unknown is how long Job's suffering lasted. There is a reference to months of pain in Job 7:3 but no other insight into the total amount of time.

- **Author:** Unknown for certain

- Some guesses for possible authors are Moses, Solomon, Isaiah, Hezekiah, Elihu (a character in Job), Job himself, or some non-Israelite author.

- **Date of writing:** Unknown for certain

- The guesses on dates are related to the thoughts on who wrote the book.

- **Major Events in Job:**

Events	Job
• Introduction to Job	1:1–5
• Introduction to Job's tragic tests of suffering	1:6–22 (Test 1) 2:1–10 (Test 2)
• Introduction to Job's three friends: Eliphaz the Temanite, Bildad the Shuhite, and Zophar the Naamathite	2:11–13
• Job tells his friends of his great pain and sorrow	3
• First set of discussion debates between Job and his friends about why Job is suffering	4–14
• Second set of discussion debates between Job and friends	15–21
• Third set of discussion debates between Job and friends	22–27
• Debate break time: Hymn to Wisdom	28
• Job gives a long speech expressing his thoughts and feelings about his suffering	29–31
• Elihu, a person who has listened silently to Job and his three friends, gives a long speech about his thoughts on Job's suffering	32–37
• God speaks to Job from the whirlwind	38–41
• Job responds to God in awe, respect, and repentance	40:3–5, 42:1–6
• God rebukes Job's three friends. He tells them to have Job pray for them so he can forgive them for the wrong way they represented God's views	42:7–9
• God restores Job's health, wealth and family, blessing him doubly in every area of his life	42:10–15
• Happy ending for Job	42:16–17

Reading Assignment:
Job 1:1–4:21

Lesson 3.5

I. Lesson Exercise: Like a Theatrical Play or Movie

The book of Job is presented almost like theatrical plays or movies are presented. We have characters on earth and in heaven.

The characters in heaven have conversations about the characters on earth that affect their lives, but the characters on earth do not know about the heavenly conversations.

On the other hand, we, the readers, view what both the heavenly and earthly characters are doing. Our point of view is to watch all the characters in action and learn from them.

In spite of the book of Job's movie-like presentation style, Bible scriptures that refer to Job give credence to him being a real, historical person and his book relaying real events. Read Ezekiel 14:12–20, James 5:10–11.

❑ **Introducing the Heavenly Characters**

- **Lord God**
  - Creator of the universe and all living things (Job 1:6; 2:1; 38–42)
- **Angels (Sons) of God**
  - Presented themselves before God on certain days (Job 1:6; 2:1)
- **Satan the Accuser**
  - Came with the angels before God (Job 1:6–7; 2:1)
- **The Lord boasts about the man Job**
  - God said Job was the finest man in all the earth; Job feared God (honored, respected and obeyed him); with no evil in his life.
- **Satan accuses God of protecting and blessing Job in such a way that he has earned Job's right to fear him**
  - Satan threatened that if God would stop protecting and blessing Job, then Job would no longer live for God.
- **First Heavenly Test Issued**
  - God gave satan permission to do whatever he wanted to with Job's possessions, but he did not have permission to hurt Job.
- **Second Heavenly Test Issued**
  - God gave satan permission to attack Job's health, but he had to spare Job's life.

Introducing Job

❑ Introducing the Earthly Characters

The main earthly character presented at the beginning of the story is Job.

- **Job**
  - The richest person in the entire area.
- **Job's children**
  - Celebrate birthdays together because they had a good relationship with each other. Job was always concerned if they sinned or not.
- **Job's wife**
  - She did not maintain her reverence for God when great trouble came.
- **Job's friends**
  - Came to visit Job when they heard of the tragedy he had suffered; they traveled from their homes supposedly to comfort Job.
- **Elihu**
  - A young man who listened in on Job and his three friends' conversation.

✞

❑ Introducing the Opening Scene in This Tragic Drama

10) In Job's First Test, summarize his losses (Job 1:13–19)

____

11) In Job's Second Test, summarize his loss (Job 2:5–8)

____

✞

Job's Initial Reactions

After Job's First Test, his initial reactions ended with his praising the name of the Lord. Job 1:22 explains that Job did not sin by blaming God.

Job's Second Test left him in intense physical pain in addition to his great heartache and financial distress from the first test. Yet God-fearing Job refused to curse God and die as his wife suggested. Job 2:10 again explains Job did nothing wrong in the way he reacted to his second test.

Discussion Debates Between Job and His Three Friends Begin

Over the next few days, we will read the detailed discussions between Job and his friends. The friends try to understand why Job is going through such great suffering. Disturbingly, these discussions turn into debates because Job and his friends have different points of view.

None of the earthly characters know of the heavenly conversations that are the real reasons behind Job's suffering. So what we view are the earthly characters trying to figure it out.

First Set of Discussion Debates Between Job and Friends

Speaker	Chapter in Job	Week in Daily Study
Eliphaz speaks	4–5	Week 3
Job responds	6–7	
Bildad speaks	8	
Job responds	9–10	
Zophar speaks	11	
Job responds	12–14	Week 4

II. Find Jesus in the Lesson and III Closing Thoughts

Jesus Overcomes satan

Satan was introduced to us in Genesis as the enemy of God and the enemy of all the descendants of Eve. Now he is introduced as an "accuser," who accuses the good man Job to God.

In Revelation 12:9–11, the scriptures describe satan as an accuser of all the people who believe in Jesus Christ. The good news is that Jesus Christ overcomes satan and helps all those who believe in Him to overcome satan.

You may not fully understand the meaning of the below passage but read it and keep its encouraging words in mind for future reference.

This great dragon—the ancient serpent called the Devil, or Satan, the one deceiving the whole world—
was thrown down to the earth with all his angels.

Then I heard a loud voice shouting across the heavens,
"It has happened at last—the salvation and power and kingdom of our God, and the authority of his Christ!

For the Accuser has been thrown down to earth—the one who accused our brothers and sisters before our God day and night.

And they have defeated him because of the blood of the Lamb and because of their testimony. And they were not afraid to die.
Revelation 12:9–11

Reading Assignment:
Job 5:1–7:21

Lesson 3.6

I. Lesson Exercise: Eliphaz Speaks

In yesterday's lesson, the text revealed that in Job's initial response to his tests he said nothing wrong. When Job finally tries to describe his great pain and sorrow to his friends, he curses the day he was born (Job 3:3–10). Then Job begins to ask the "why" questions (Job 3:20–25). He wants to know why God does not just let him die. After listening to Job, Eliphaz begins to rebuke Job for the way he feels.

- Eliphaz believes Job lacks faith in God when Job says he wishes God had not let him be born. (Job 4:3–6)
- From Job 4:8, 12–16, Eliphaz thinks two things qualify him to give Job advice. First, his experience qualified him, and secondly, his ghostly or spirit-like night vision qualified him to advise Job.
- From Job 5:8–16, Eliphaz just wants Job to "pray" about his situation, so everything will be fixed, because God fixes the problems of the righteous and punishes the wicked. Really, Eliphaz wanted Job to admit his sins and repent to God. He believed Job had hidden sin that delayed God from fixing everything.

Job Responds to Eliphaz

- Sadly, Job believes God, the Almighty, has struck him down. So he feels there is no help from God (Job 6:4).
- Job did not get the comfort from his friend Eliphaz that he expected. Eliphaz's quick accusations have made him an unreliable friend. He clearly explains that Eliphaz has been of no help. (Job 6:14–21)
- Finally, Job also did not get any physical relief. In describing the intensity of his suffering, it seems as if Job's pain feels unbearable. He says he gets no sleep, but instead during the day he longs for the night, and during the night he longs for the day. He further explains his skin is filled with worms and scabs, with his flesh open and full of pus. (Job 7:1–5)

Job Cries out to God

Job switched from talking to Eliphaz to talking to God in Job 7:6–21.

12) What did Job say to God about how he felt about his life, as a result of his present condition? (Job 7:16) ____________________________

13) Did Job understand God's view of what was going on? (Job 7:17–21)

____

II. Find Jesus in the Lesson

Great Agony Led Job and Jesus to Question God

In his great agony and distress, Job questions God. Jesus also questioned God when He experienced great agony and distress on the cross. (Matt 27:42–46)

This lets us know that when a person is experiencing intense suffering, they may not feel God's presence and help (although God's word says He will never leave or forsake His children). We need to keep this in mind when we witness someone going through tragic suffering, or when we go through such suffering ourselves.

"He saved others," they scoffed, "but he can't save himself!

So he is the king of Israel, is he?
Let him come down from the cross, and we will believe in him!

[4]He trusted God—let God show his approval by delivering him!
For he said, "I am the Son of God."

And the criminals who were crucified with him also shouted
the same insults at him. "

At noon, darkness fell across the whole land until three o'clock.

At about three o'clock, Jesus called out with a loud voice,
"Eli, Eli, lama sabachthani?" which means,

"My God, my God, why have you forsaken me?"

Matt 27:42–46

III. Closing Thoughts

Job believes God is punishing him and he does not know why.

Job's feelings reflect how many righteous people feel when they go through suffering they do not understand. The lesson the book of Job tries to teach us is that we do not always know the whole story behind why we are suffering. Although our suffering may cause us to question God, we need to continue to trust Him, seek Him for answers and wait on His deliverance.

Also, the friends who come to comfort those who are suffering need to be slow to give advice. When we do not feel someone else's pain, we can easily say words that add to their pain instead of bringing comfort.

Read on to see what more we can learn from this unique story of pain and triumph.

Reading Assignment:
Job 8:1–11:20

Lesson 3.7

I. Lesson Exercise

Bildad Speaks

- Bildad assumed Job's children obviously sinned against God, which is why their punishment (of an early death) was well deserved. (Job 8:4)
- Bildad believes Job has not been a man of complete integrity. (Job 8:5–6)
- Bildad believes expert advice comes from the previous generations, older people, who share from having a lifetime of experiences on earth. (Job 8:8–10)

Job Responds to Bildad

From Job's words to Bildad, we get some insight on what type of knowledge the people in Job's time had about the heavens and earth and God as Creator of all.

- In Job 9:5–6, Job's description sounds a lot like an earthquake
- In Job 9:9, Job describes star constellations, "Bear," "Orion," and, "Pleiades" and the constellations of the southern sky
- In Job 9:10, Job understood it was possible for God to perform an unlimited number of miracles

Job Pleads with God

Because Job was disgusted with his life, he asks to be allowed to complain bitterly.

- Job believed God was oppressing him, rejecting him, and punishing him without letting him know the reason why. (Job 10:3–7)
- Job was in such great pain, that he desperately asked God to give him a little comfort before he dies. (Job 10:20)

Zophar Speaks

Like Eliphaz and Bildad before him, Zophar is harsh and cruel in talking to Job because he believes Job is guilty of some wrong. He is attempting to defend God, but in his defense of God he accuses Job of being a sinner worthy of this suffering.

In Job 11:3, we read how Zophar intended to make Job feel ashamed because he thought Job was wrong and was mocking God.

II. Find Jesus in the Lesson: Jesus Christ is Emmanuel

In Job 9:32, Job complains that God is not a human being like he is. In other places, Job describes God as being beyond human reach or understanding, because He is high and mighty in heaven. Job feels God is unable to understand the human feeling and condition.

God eventually sent Jesus Christ, who is the Son of God, who is a part of the Trinity or Triune God (meaning one God in three divine persons), to live among us. In fact, one of Jesus' names is Emmanuel.

14) Look in Matthew 1:23 to see what the name Emmanuel (also Immanuel) means. ______________________________

III. Closing Thoughts

Jesus was not just the Son of God when He came to earth to live among us. He was also fully human, being born of the Virgin Mary. As a man, Jesus experienced all the pain and agony that humankind can experience. Right now, Jesus Christ is on the right hand of Father God. From that position, Jesus is ready to help us to go through every type of earthly life experiences. Consider the great assistance we can get through Jesus Christ as described in Hebrews 4:14–16.

Christ Is Our High Priest

That is why we have a great High Priest who has gone to heaven, Jesus the Son of God.
Let us cling to him and never stop trusting him.

This High Priest of ours understands our weaknesses, for he faced all of the same temptations we do, yet he did not sin.

So let us come boldly to the throne of our gracious God. There we will receive his mercy, and we will find grace to help us when we need it. (NLT)

Seeing then that we have a great high priest, that is passed into the heavens, Jesus the Son of God, let us hold fast our profession.

For we have not an high priest which cannot be touched with the feeling of our infirmities; but was in all points tempted like as we are, yet without sin.

Let us therefore come boldly unto the throne of grace, that we may obtain mercy, and find grace to help in time of need. (KJV)

Week 4

Featured Book: Job

Contents:

Peek at the Week

Lesson	Key Events	Find Jesus
4.1	Job and Friends First Set of Discussion Debates End	Life after Death through Jesus Christ
4.2	Job and Friends Second Set of Discussion Debates	Jesus Christ Understands our Human Suffering and is Ready to Help
4.3	Job and Friends Second Set of Discussion Debates End	Jesus Christ as Redeemer and Resurrection
4.4	Job and Friends Third Set of Discussion Debates	Through Jesus, God is with us, even when we do not feel or hear him
4.5	Job and Friends Debates End, Job's Hymn to Wisdom	Jesus Christ is the Power of God and Wisdom of God
4.6	Job's Long Speech	Job's actions reflect the actions Jesus describes for Christians
4.7	Young Man Elihu Speaks Out	Jesus Christ is Humankind's Intercessor

Chronological Notes

Timetable	Key Events
Date not known for sure: Possibly before time of Mosaic Law, in time of Abraham, Isaac or Jacob ~ between 2000–1600 BC	Life of Job

**All dates are approximate, with uncertainties from Bible scholars leading to early and late dates for some events.*

Lesson 4.1

Reading Assignment:
Job 12:1–14:22

I. Lesson Exercise

End of First Set of Discussion Debates between Job and Friends

Speaker	Chapter in Job	Week in Daily Study
Eliphaz speaks	4–5	Week 3
Job responds	6–7	
Bildad speaks	8	
Job responds	9–10	
Zophar speaks	11	
Job responds	**12–14**	**Week 4**

Job Responds to Zophar

Job begins his response to Zophar by basically calling him a "know-it-all." Job assures Zophar that he knows a few things, too. He insists he is blameless before God but knows his current suffering does not make it appear this is true right now.

Consider Job's view of his friends' reaction to his extreme suffering in Job 12:5:

People who are at ease mock those in trouble.
They give a push to those who are stumbling.

These words from Job basically describe how some people will "kick a person while they are down." Be thankful to God for the people who show you compassion and understanding from the beginning to end of your suffering. Overall, the challenge for the person who is suffering is to not get discouraged by all the poor comforters who will come your way. God is the only one who can supply the perfect comfort.

- God is the only one with true wisdom, power, counsel and understanding (Job 12:5)
- Job longs to speak directly to God, so he can argue his case with Him. (Job 13:3)
- Because his friends were poor comforters, Job told them the smartest thing they could do was shut up and leave him alone. (Job 13:5, 13)

Job Argues His Case with God

From Job 13:20–24, Job was not yet hearing God's response to his cries for help. This lets us know that in the midst of our suffering, we may not hear God at first.

Job 14 contains two popular passages as quoted from King James Bible:

"Man that is born of a woman is of few days
and full of trouble."
Job 14:1 KJV

"If a man die, shall he live again?
All the days of my appointed time will I wait,
till my change come."
Job 14:14 KJV

II. Find Jesus in the Lesson: Life after Death through Jesus Christ

Job is a man who is facing death's door, pondering what death will mean to him personally. By Chapter 14 he poses one of the most important questions to living and dying humanity, "If a man die, shall he live again?"

Through Jesus Christ, we can find the answer to that question. Read 1 Corinthians 15:3–4, 12–23 below.

> **I** *[Apostle Paul]* **passed on to you what was most important and what had also been passed on to me--that Christ died for our sins, just as the Scriptures said.**
>
> **4He was buried, and he was raised from the dead on the third day, as the Scriptures said.**

The Resurrection of the Dead

> **But tell me this--since we preach that Christ rose from the dead, why are some of you saying there will be no resurrection of the dead?**
>
> **For if there is no resurrection of the dead, then Christ has not been raised either. And if Christ was not raised, then all our preaching is useless, and your trust in God is useless.**
>
> **And we apostles would all be lying about God, for we have said that God raised Christ from the grave, but that can't be true if there is no resurrection of the dead.**
>
> **If there is no resurrection of the dead, then Christ has not been raised.**

> **And if Christ has not been raised, then your faith is useless, and you are still under condemnation for your sins. In that case, all who have died believing in Christ have perished! And if we have hope in Christ only for this life, we are the most miserable people in the world.**
>
> **But the fact is that Christ has been raised from the dead. He has become the first of a great harvest of those who will be raised to life again.**
>
> **So you see, just as death came into the world through a man, Adam, now the resurrection from the dead has begun through another man, Christ. Everyone dies because all of us are related to Adam, the first man. But all who are related to Christ, the other man, will be given new life.**
>
> **But there is an order to this resurrection: Christ was raised first; then when Christ comes back, all his people will be raised."**

III. Closing Thoughts

We do Not Have "All the answers"

In Job 13:7, Job challenges his friends with the following statement,

"Are you defending God by means of lies and dishonest arguments?"

This is certainly a comment for each of us to think about. We cannot assume we understand all the ways of God. We do not have "all the answers."

We need to pray carefully about every situation, seeking "God's true wisdom, power, counsel and understanding." This is so we are led by His Spirit in the right way to respond.

When we do not really understand a situation, it is better to do as Job says: "Please, be quiet." This is so we are not guilty of speaking wrong things in an effort to defend God.

Reading Assignment:
Job 15:1–18:21

Lesson 4.2

I. Lesson Exercise

Second Set of Discussion Debates between Job and Friends

Speaker	Chapter in Job	Study Week
Eliphaz speaks 2nd time	15	Week 4
Job responds	16–17	
Bildad speaks 2nd time	18	
Job responds	19	
Zophar speaks 2nd time	20	
Job responds	21	

Eliphaz speaks the second time

You would think after Job told his friends to ***"be silent now and leave me alone,"*** they would quit. But not so!

Today's lesson begins round two of the discussion debates, with a third one to occur after this set.

- Eliphaz resorts to name-calling as he calls Job a" windbag" (Job 15:2)
- After harshly rebuking Job, who is already physically and emotionally depressed, Eliphaz continues to try and "help Job" by giving more advice. This is because Eliphaz believes his advice is wise since it comes from his own experience and that of other wise men. (Job 15:17–18)
- Then Eliphaz explains that wicked people are in pain all their lives.

Job responds to Eliphaz

1) What type of comforters does Job call his friends? (Job 16:2)

____

2) What type of comfort does Job say he would give? (Job 16:5)

____

(*Note: This is the type of comfort all Christians should give.*)

In Job 16:7–17, Job describes what he believes God has done to him. But Job Chapters 1 and 2 revealed the real reason behind Job's suffering.

> Job is suffering because of the tragedies satan put on him after God gave satan permission to test Job's love for God.
>
> Satan is the one who designed and administered the tragedies, which God allowed because he knew Job was a man of complete integrity.
>
> God was working through Job to prove to satan that God was right about Job's integrity and pure love for Him.

Although Job truly believes God is wrongfully bringing all this terror into his life, he still pours out his tears to God; he still looks to God for his help.

In Job 13:15 King James Version (KJV), Job makes the following statement:

"Though he slay me, yet will I trust in him: but I will maintain mine own ways before him."

3) Thought Question: When we do not understand why God allows suffering in our life, what can we learn from Job's words in Job 13:15 about how to approach God? ____

Bildad speaks the second time

"Terrors surround the wicked and trouble them at every step"
Bildad, Job 18:11.

Matthew 5:45 is one of many scriptures that lets us know God allows good to happen to those who are evil. So Bildad's belief that the wicked are surrounded by trouble every step of their way is not true.

Job's story is but one example of how God allows evil to happen to those who are good. Those who are righteous have God to help them overcome all troubles in their lives (Psalm 34:19)

II. Find Jesus in the Lesson

Jesus Understands Our Human Suffering and Is Ready to Help Us!

Job did not have the comfort of the scriptures describing God's saving help for all through Jesus Christ. He had his own knowledge of God which was strong. This led him to seek God's help in spite of thinking God was unjustly punishing him.

Today, we can look to Jesus Christ who understands human suffering, because He experienced it first-hand. Consider the below passage from Hebrews. May God bring this to your remembrance when you are in a time of trouble. Jesus understands and is ready to provide grace and mercy to help us with every problem.

> **"That is why we have a great High Priest who has gone to heaven, Jesus the Son of God. Let us cling to him and never stop trusting him.**
>
> **This High Priest of ours understands our weaknesses, for he faced all of the same temptations we do, yet he did not sin.**
>
> **So let us come boldly to the throne of our gracious God. There we will receive his mercy, and we will find grace to help us when we need it." Hebrews 4:14–16**

III. Closing Thoughts

Clarification on "The Retribution Principle"

From Old Testament poetry and wisdom books—Job, Psalms, Proverbs, and Ecclesiastes—one might notice this idea: "The obedient are good and will have a good life, but the disobedient are wicked and will have a miserable life."[1]

The idea that everyone gets what they deserve in this life is known as "The Retribution Principle."

However, Job's experience with suffering caused him to rethink this idea.

He wondered why he was experiencing misery like someone who was wicked, when he had been obedient to God.

He also realized some people who he considered "wicked," were having what seemed a good life, at least sometimes.

What we learn through the story of Job is that in this life on earth, God may allow bad things to happen to good people for His purposes. Also, God may allow wicked people to experience good, because of His grace, mercy, longsuffering, and loving-kindness which He extends to everyone in hopes all will come to be saved (becoming His children).

This is the character of "Sovereign God," who is supreme ruler over all.

Only after this life will the righteous experience only good eternally while the wicked experience God's punishment eternally. (Revelation 20:11–21:8)

[1]Appendix C

Lesson 4.3

> **Reading Assignment:**
> **Job 19:1–21:34**

I. Lesson Exercise: Job Responds to Bildad

Job tells his friends they should be ashamed of themselves for the harsh way they are treating him. His open humiliation should not be used by them to accuse him of living in sin. Job, once a highly admired man about town, is now abandoned, rejected, humiliated, mocked and mistreated by family, friends and strangers.

4) In Job 19:28-29, what warning did Job give his friends about the danger of their fault-finding attitude of him, an innocent man? ____________

Zophar Speaks the Second Time

It is amazing that Zophar does not want to endure Job's "insults", but Zophar keeps insulting Job. He gives a detailed description of the well-deserved punishment of the wicked, which he believes is what Job is experiencing right now.

5) What is the negative type of prayer Zophar speaks concerning the wicked? (Job 20:23) ____________________________________

Job Responds to Zophar

No matter how much Job's three friends try to convince him of guilt and make him feel ashamed, Job has an assurance in his heart of the pure life he has lived before God. No number of accusations against him can change that. Only a blameless man could maintain such a confident testimony when things do not look so good.

6) In Job 21:34, what does Job say about his friends' explanations?

____

II. Find Jesus in the Lesson and III. Closing Thoughts

Job speaks about His redeemer and Resurrection after Death

> **But as for me, I know that my Redeemer lives, and that he will stand upon the earth at last. And after my body has decayed, yet in my body I will see God! I will see him for myself. Yes, I will see him with my own eyes. I am overwhelmed at the thought!" Job 19:25–27**

Did Job have a revelation of Jesus Christ when speaking the above?

New Testament passages explain that Jesus redeems those who believe in Him with His blood (Gal. 3:13; Rev. 5:9). In John 11:25 Jesus said,

> ***"I am the resurrection and the life, Those who believe in me, even though they die like everyone else, will live again."***

We will read more on **Jesus Christ as Redeemer and Resurrection** in the New Testament. Job's Old Testament hope of redemption and resurrection from the dead points to Christ's coming.

Reading Assignment:
Job 22:1–25:6

Lesson 4.4

I. Lesson Exercise

Third Set of Discussion Debates between Job and Friends

Speaker	Chapter in Job	Study Week
Eliphaz speaks 3rd time	22	Week 4
Job responds	23–24	
Bildad speaks 3rd time	25	
Job responds	26–27	
Zophar does not speak	Not applicable	

Eliphaz speaks the Third Time

Eliphaz now directly accuses Job, ***"It is because of your wickedness! Your guilt has no limit!" (Job 22:5).*** Eliphaz tries to help Job find his wickedness by describing the types of sins Job must have committed, since Job must think God cannot see them.

7) List four types of sins Eliphaz says Job "must have" committed to deserve God's punishment (Job 22:6–9):
vs. 6___________________________, vs. 7___________________________,
Vs. 9a___________________________, vs. 9b___________________________

Job responds to Eliphaz

Job wants to find God because he believes if he could speak directly to God, God would give him a fair hearing. Alas, Job is unable to find, feel or hear from God.

"I go east, but he is not there. I go west, but I cannot find him.
I do not see him in the north, for he is hidden.
I turn to the south, but I cannot find him." Job 23:8–9

Bildad speaks the third time

Bildad's last words rightfully magnify God's power but wrongfully minimize God's love for humankind by saying, ***"people… are nothing but worms in his sight."*** (Job 25:1–6)

II. Find Jesus in the Lesson and III. Closing Thoughts

**Jesus Helps Us to Know the Truth that
God Is With Us Even When We Do Not Feel or Hear Him**

Just like Job in the above scriptures said he could not find God *(meaning to feel or hear Him)* , sometimes we are unable to feel God.

Our assurance that God is near us at all times needs to come from Jesus' promise in Matthew 28:20.

"…And be sure of this:
I am with you always,
even to the end of the age."

Unlike what Bildad said in Job 25:1–6, where he says people are but worms in God's sight, God has a very high view of humankind.

In fact,…

God loves mankind so much
He sent his only begotten Son,
Who is Jesus Christ,
To provide salvation for us
(John 3:16);
And to bring all who believe in Jesus
Into a glorious state
(Hebrews 2:9–10).

Reading Assignment:
Job 26:1–29:25

Lesson 4.5

I. Lesson Exercise: Job Responds to Bildad

Job responds to Bildad, and he has the last words in this third set of discussion debates with his three friends. Zophar is not recorded as speaking the third time.

Job and his three friends, Eliphaz, Bildad and Zophar, have been struggling with three basic topics:

1. trying to describe God's greatness, wisdom and power
2. trying to describe who can be blameless before God
3. trying to describe the destruction of the wicked

In Job's last response to his friends, he speaks with great clarity on these topics. Job's descriptions are also the most correct in God's eyes as we will see confirmed by God later on in Job, and by other Bible scriptures.

Job describes God's greatness in Job 26:5–14 (compare with Gen. 1)

- God stretches the northern sky over empty space and hangs the earth on nothing
- God wraps rain in thick clouds; clouds do not burst with the water
- God shrouds His throne with His clouds
- God created the horizon when He separated the waters
- God set the boundaries for day and night
- At God's rebuke, the foundations of heaven tremble
- By God's great power the sea grew calm
- By God's skill He crushed the great sea monster
- God's Spirit made the heavens beautiful
- God's power pierced the gliding serpent

Job describes how he is blameless before God in Job 27:2–6

In Job 27:5, Job said he will never say his friends are right when they utter their wrong accusations against him. He said he will defend his innocence until he dies.

Job describes the destruction of the wicked in Job 27:7–23

Job acknowledges that the wicked can become rich while living on earth. However, in the long run, if the wicked do not turn to God, their family, money, clothes, houses, and peace of mind will eventually be destroyed.

Job's "ODE to Wisdom"

Hymn to Wisdom

There is a break from the discussion debates. Job's friends are finally silent. Job uses this time to summarize all his thoughts.

He precedes his summary by pondering how one could find wisdom and understanding. Through Job, we get insight on mining type of work man had become successful in doing at this time.

8) In Job 28:1–5, Job describes how man explores the deepest, farthest, darkest regions of earth, using light, shafts, and rope to do what? ______________________________

9) In Job 28: 6–10, Job describes how man can overturn the roots of mountains and tunnel in deep rocks, to find what? ______________

10) In Job 28:12–18, what did Job say man could not find or afford to buy; but God knew where to find it because He established it? _____

II. Find Jesus in the Lesson

Jesus Christ Is the Power of God and the Wisdom of God

All who believe on Jesus Christ as their Lord and Savior have Jesus working in them to reveal God's wisdom to them. Rejoice in this truth.

So where does this leave the philosophers, the scholars, and the world's brilliant debaters? God has made them all look foolish and has shown their wisdom to be useless nonsense.

Since God in his wisdom saw to it that the world would never find him through human wisdom, he has used our foolish preaching to save all who believe.

God's way seems foolish to the Jews because they want a sign from heaven to prove it is true.

And it is foolish to the Greeks because they believe only what agrees with their own wisdom.

So when we preach that Christ was crucified, the Jews are offended, and the Gentiles say it's all nonsense.

But to those called by God to salvation, Jews and Gentiles, Christ is the mighty power of God and the wonderful wisdom of God.

God alone made it possible for you to be in Christ Jesus. For our benefit God made Christ to be wisdom itself.

***He is the one who made us acceptable to God.
He made us pure and holy, and
he gave himself to purchase our freedom.***

1 Corinthians 1:20–24, 30

Job's "ODE to Wisdom"

III. Closing Thoughts

"The fear of the Lord is true wisdom; to forsake evil is real understanding."
Job 28:28

Job recognized the great advances in man's knowledge taking place in his day.

This allowed man to do things such as:

- Tunnel through mountains and dig deep into the earth to mine for precious stones of silver, gold and sapphire, or iron and copper
- Dam up rivers to look for treasures in streams such as gold

But with all the industrial advances of that time, Job also recognized none of this made man a wise man.

Job explained that having wisdom was far more valuable than gold and all the precious stones of the earth.

The only place to find true wisdom is to get it from God.

This is still true today! Read James 1:5; 3:13-18.

Reading Assignment:
Job 30:1–31:40

Lesson 4.6

I. Lesson Exercise: Job's Long Speech

Job gets it all out of his system now by taking his time to summarize all his thoughts and feelings about his suffering. He does this by:

- Speaking about his former blessings (Job 29:1–25)
- Speaking about his current suffering (Job 30:1–31)
- Speaking about his innocence before God (Job 31:1–40)

Job speaks about his former blessings

"Oh that I were as in months past, as in the days when God preserved me… As I was in the days of my youth, when the secret of God was upon my tabernacle" Job 29:2–4 KJV

Job remembers the time in his life when he felt God's friendship, counsel and protection. This reminds one of what satan said to God in Job 1…

"You have always protected him and his home and his property from harm. You have made him prosperous in everything he does. Look how rich he is!" Job 1:10–11

Job did not stop honoring God when his great blessings were taken from his life as satan had predicted, but Job did long for his blessed past.

When God's "secret" was on Job's life, Job was admired by young, old, rich, poor, great and small. His actions were just; his advice was valued.

11) Based on Job's belief he had lived right before God, for which he had enjoyed God's choicest blessings, how had Job expected to die? (Job 29:18) ____

Job speaks about his current suffering

Job is now mocked, scorned, shunned and even spit on because of his horrible condition. What a big difference from the way he was treated when he had God's former blessings on his life.

12) What does Job say about his Life? (Job 30:16) _______________

Job speaks about his innocence

Through it all, Job maintains he is innocent before God. He reexamines the way he has lived, how he has treated others with respect out of his fear of God. In the end, he finds himself blameless of any wrong doing.

Note: To "fear God" means to respect, honor and obey God, not to be terrified of Him.

Consider Job's actions that he uses to confirm his innocence in Job 31:1–34:

- Not looking with lust on any other woman
- Not lying or deceiving anyone
- Helped the poor
- Helped widows and orphans
- Provided clothes for the homeless
- Never put his trust in his wealth or material blessing
- Never worshipped false gods, such as worshipping the sun or moon
- Never rejoiced over the misfortune of his enemies
- Never cursed anyone or tried to get revenge
- Endeavored to be a good boss, treating his workers right
- Never turned away from helping a stranger
- Openly and quickly confessed any sins whenever committed

II. Find Jesus in the Lesson

Job's actions as described in Job 31:1–34 reflect the kind of actions Jesus describes for Christians. By these actions Christians demonstrate they are the children of God. For example, Jesus said,

- In Matt. 5:28 not to lust after another woman
- In Matt. 5:8 to be pure in heart
- In Matt. 25:31–40 to help the hungry, homeless, and stranger
- In Matt. 5:44 to love and bless your enemies
- In Matt. 22:37 to love God with all your heart, soul and mind
- In Matt. 6:19–21 to not make your treasures of earthly things, but in heavenly

III. Closing Thoughts

Christians are not righteous because of the good works we do

Christians do good works because they are made righteous before God through faith in Jesus Christ our Lord (2 Corinthians 5:17–21). Our new nature progressively transforms us to be like Jesus.

Yet, Job's actions are commended by God. In Ezekiel 14:14, Ezekiel uses Job as one of three examples of righteous men on earth.

"Even if Noah, Daniel, and Job were there,
their righteousness would save no one but themselves,
declares the Sovereign LORD."
Ezekiel 14:14

Heavenly Intercessor

Lesson 4.7

Reading Assignment:
Job 32:1–34:37

I. Lesson Exercise: Elihu Speaks

Elihu is a young man who has listened quietly to Job and his three friends. Out of respect for his elders, he did not break into their conversation. Now Elihu has built up anger because of all he has heard. He can no longer hold back his opinion.

Elihu Responds to Job's Friends

Job 32:2–3 explains Elihu is angry because...

- Job refused to admit he had sinned, and God was right in punishing him for it
- He felt Job's friends condemned God by their inability to answer Job's arguments.

Elihu Presents His Case against Job

From Elihu, we gain additional insight on beliefs and environment of ancient times.

13) What did Elihu believe man was formed from? (Job 33:6)

____

14) What was one way Elihu says God speaks to man? (Job 33:15)

____

Elihu accuses Job of Arrogance

Elihu says everyone knows God does not sin and he cannot do any wrong (Job 34:10). He also expresses his belief that God is a fair judge (Job 34:16–20).

While these statements are true, everyone does not believe them. It is even more difficult for someone who feels they are suffering wrongfully to believe God is fair.

II. Find Jesus in the Lesson

Jesus Christ Is Humankind's Intercessor

In the midst of his discomforting discourse in Job 33:24, Elihu makes a very interesting "if statement" concerning the work of a heavenly intercessor for humankind. When this passage is compared to Romans 8:33–34, then it can be seen how Jesus Christ serves as humankind's intercessor before God.

III. Closing Thoughts

In the book of Job, we get insight into what knowledge, industry and beliefs people had in ancient times. Remarkably, some of these customs are familiar to us today although the book of Job was written thousands of years ago.

- **Star Constellations** (Job 9:9, 38:31), such as...
  - **Orion**
  - **Pleiades**
  - **Arcturus**
- **Mining** (Job 28:1–11) for precious stones and minerals deep in the earth and in streams and rivers of water, such as looking for...
  - **Gold**
  - **Sapphire silver**
  - **Copper**
  - **Iron**
- **Writings** such as in a...
  - **Book** (Job 19:23, 31:35)
  - **Stone** (Job 19:24)

✞

Bible Tidbits

The Bible describes true occurances of the below. This supports the thinking of some that elements of mythological stories were derived from a fantastical stretch of true historical events.

- **Land Monsters** (Job 40:15–24; 41:1)
- **Sea Monsters** (Job 41:1; Isaiah 27:1)
- **Dragons** (Psalms 74:13–14), all defeated by God
- **Giants** (Gen. 6:4)
- **Castles** (Gen. 25:16 in KJV, 1 Chron. 11:5, 7 in KJV)

Week 5

Featured Books: Finish Job, Begin Exodus,
plus short excerpt from 1 Chronicles Chapter 6

Contents:

Peek at the Week

Lesson	Key Events	Find Jesus
5.1	Elihu's Long Speech	Jesus Makes Us Righteous
5.2	The Lord Speaks	Voice of Christ = Voice of God = Word of God
5.3	Job's Happy Ending	Jesus Explains Sin is not Source of all Sickness (or trouble in one's life)
5.4	God Calls Moses	Stephen, a Jewish Christian, speaks of Moses and his faith in Jesus
5.5	Moses Introduces God as "I AM"	Jesus and the Names of God
5.6	God Sends Ten Plagues to Egypt	Pharaoh's Hardened Heart is Like Heart of non-believers in Christ
5.7	Showdown's Over—God Wins!	Christ, our Passover Lamb

Chronological Notes

Timetable	Key Events
Date not known for sure: Possibly before time of Mosaic Law, in time of Abraham, Isaac or Jacob ~ between 2000–1600 BC	Life of Job
1526 (or 1360) BC	About 300 years after Joseph's death; Moses is born
1486 (or 1320) BC	Moses runs away from Egypt at about 40 years old; Moses goes to Midian
1446 (or 1280) BC	Moses was 80 years old when he returns to Egypt from Midian to face Pharaoh with God's message

**All dates are approximate.*

Reading Assignment:
Job 35:1–37:24

Lesson 5.1

I. Lesson Exercise: Elihu's Long Speech finished

After five chapters, Elihu finishes his long speech to Job and his friends. He is an angry young man who begins by rebuking Job's friends, who in his view failed in defending God's character and getting Job to repent. Elihu picks up where they left off. With full confidence that he is right, Elihu attempts to do what he believes Job's friends should have done.

1) In Job 36:3-4, why does Elihu believe he is qualified to speak with authority about God and Job's situation? ______________________________

II. Find Jesus in the Lesson and Closing Thoughts

Jesus Makes Us Righteous

Elihu asked Job an important question in Job 35:2 *NLT/KJV*

"Do you think it is right for you to claim,
'My righteousness is more than God's?'"

Through Jesus Christ, we are made the righteousness of God, which is not based on any works on our part but based solely on our confession of faith in Jesus Christ's Lordship over our lives. The following scriptures explain this.

God saved you by his special favor when you believed. And you can't take credit for this; it is a gift from God. Salvation is not a reward for the good things we have done, so none of us can boast about it.

For we are God's masterpiece. He has created us anew in Christ Jesus,
so that we can do the good things he planned for us long ago.
Ephesians 2:8–10

What this means is that those who become Christians become new
persons. They are not the same anymore, for the old life is gone.
A new life has begun!

All this newness of life is from God, who brought us back to himself
through what Christ did. And God has given us the task of reconciling
people to him. For God was in Christ, reconciling the world to himself,
no longer counting people's sins against them.
This is the wonderful message he has given us to tell others.

We are Christ's ambassadors, and God is using us to speak to you.
We urge you, as though Christ himself were here pleading with you,
"Be reconciled to God!"

For God made Christ, who never sinned, to be the offering for our sin,
so that we could be made right with God through Christ."
2 Corinthians 5:17–21 NLT

For he hath made him to be sin for us, who knew no sin;
that we might be made the righteousness of God in him.
2 Corinthians 5:21 KJV

Lesson 5.2

Reading Assignment: Job 38:1–40:5

I. Lesson Exercise

The Lord Speaks

God finally speaks to Job. God's words are clarifying and satisfying.

- God speaks to Job from the whirlwind.
- God says ignorant words had been used to question His wisdom.
- God's questions to Job are basically related to His work in creation. He asks where all the "experts" were when wisdom guided Him in creating the universe.
- Job is at a loss for words, right after he explains to God that he is nothing.

When God was not speaking, Job had many questions he wanted to ask God; he had a strong defense of his case he wanted to present to God. Finally, the moment Job has been waiting for has come. God is talking, but He is asking Job the questions.

2) In Job 40:3-5, what response did Job give God? ________________

II. Find Jesus in the Lesson

Voice of Christ = Voice of God = Word of God

It is tough to be in a position like Job was, when you desperately want to hear from God, but you do not hear Him. God speaks to humankind through Jesus Christ, the Son of God, who is also the Word of God (John 1:1–3, 14-18). Even when we cannot hear God's voice, we have the written Word of God, the Holy Bible, which today we can read for instruction in what is right and correction from wrongdoing. (2 Tim. 3:16)

> ***Long ago God spoke many times and in many ways to our ancestors through the prophets. But now in these final days, he has spoken to us through his Son. Hebrews 1:1–2***

III. Closing Thoughts: Hearing the Voice of God

It is awesome to experience hearing (and know you are hearing) the voice of God. When God finally spoke, it left Job speechless. All Job's complaints, all his concerns with God disappeared because of the authority and wisdom in God's response.

For Christians, we have the Word of God in the Bible (2 Tim. 3:16), and the Spirit of God (John 16:13) to help us hear God through Christ. Like Job, when God finally speaks to us, His voice and His words bring peace to our troubled souls.

Lesson 5.3

> **Reading Assignment:**
> **Job 40:6–42:17**

I. Lesson Exercise

Happy Ending

We give great honor to those who endure under suffering.

Job is an example of a man who endured patiently.

From his experience we see how the Lord's plan finally ended in good, for he is full of tenderness and mercy.

James 5:11

3) God restored Job's fortunes, after Job did what? (Job 42:10)

____

4) How was Job blessed after his suffering had ended? (Job 42:12–17)

____

From Job's experience we see
how the Lord's plan finally ended in good,
for he is full of tenderness and mercy.
James 5:11

II. Find Jesus in the Lesson

Jesus Explains Sin Is Not the Source of All Sickness

Job kept telling his friends his suffering was not punishment for sin in his life. In the end God showed everyone Job was correct.

Similarly, Jesus explained how a man was not born blind because of sin, but so God's glory could be revealed.

Read Jesus' response to his disciples' question about this man in John 9:1–3.

III. Closing Thoughts

Lessons Learned

When we began our study of Job, it was as if we were observing a play or movie where we had more insight into what was happening than the characters involved.

As viewers of the story, we have been able to observe everyone's reactions and then learn something.

Let us explore some of the things we can learn from Job's story.

- **True wisdom, power, counsel, and understanding come from God.**

We need God's insight on what is really happening in any situation, because what we see is also affected by things we do not see, such as happenings in the spirit world.

- **Show compassion without judgment.**

A person's suffering may not be the result of sin. Without God's insight, just show compassion with loving-kind service.

- **Think about how you would like to be treated if you were in the suffering person's position.**

Treat them like you would want to be treated.

- **Human experience and wisdom from the young or old can be helpful but may not have the total correct guidance for you.**

Seek God for final guidance / answers.

- **Be patient in your suffering. Honor God by not blaming Him.**

Continue to trust God in the midst of suffering. Seek God for help, relief and answers.

The Bible represents God's truth, but every passage in the Bible read alone may not relay a truth of God.

> **For example, everything Job's friends said was not truth, and everything Job said was not truth.** You need to fully read a topic, and then seek God for proper interpretation of what you have read, before concluding that what you have read is truth.

1 Corinthians 2:9–16 explains we need the Spirit of God to help us understand the things of God (meaning His word, His ways, His will).

Key Word	Key Chapters
Redemption	12, 20

Intro to Exodus

Title

The title “Exodus” comes from the Greek language and means "going out" or "exit." The book of Exodus tells of Israel’s going out of (exiting) from Egypt.

Key word “redemption” refers to the Israelite nation’s deliverance from slavery in Egypt. It also refers to Israel’s coming into covenant relationship with God.

Summary

The book of Exodus describes the redemption of Israel in two parts.

- **First:** The book describes God’s miraculous deliverance of the children of Israel from their bondage of slavery in Egypt as oppressed Hebrew slaves.
- **Second**: The book describes Israel’s transformation into God’s specially chosen nation to live in covenant relationship with Him and represent God to the world.

The hero of the book of Exodus is the Prophet Moses.

Moses’ life is a miracle as God protects him from death as a baby, and then causes his enemies to raise and train him as the royal prince of Egypt for forty years.

After running away from palace life, Moses lives as a humble shepherd for forty years in the wilderness.

With the unique background of palace and wilderness training, God returns Moses to Egypt to rescue the Israelites.

The Israelites had been living in Egypt 430 years; and as slaves for some of that time. The children of Israel had grown from seventy-five in Egypt, when Jacob’s son Joseph was second in command of Egypt.

At the time of Moses, the Israelites, who were known as Hebrew slaves by the Egyptians, had grown to 600,000 men. This means they were probably two million strong when you count women and children, too.

God’s deliverance, by His miracle working power through His prophet Moses, proved to Egypt and the world that the God of the Israelites (or Hebrews) is the only true God.

God told Moses to inform Israel that it was time for them to enter the Promised Land in Canaan, which God had promised to give them. This was because of His covenant with their forefathers Abraham, Isaac and Jacob (Israel).

But before Israel could enter the Promised Land, they needed to become a holy nation.

After their exodus from Egypt, the book of Exodus begins to describe the Israelites transformation from a slave nation to God's holy nation.

Israel's Exodus Story is a "Type" of Sinful Humankind's Redemption Process

Israel's "exodus" is a beautiful illustration of God's plan of redemption for all people from the bondage of sin.

When a person accepts God's plan of salvation, they are set free from a lifestyle of enslavement to their sinful nature.

Just like Old Testament Israelites had to believe in Moses and follow his instructions to be delivered, New Testament people must believe in Jesus Christ and follow His Word.

Then they will be set free from sin and transformed into the holy children of God.

❑ **Timetable:** *All dates are approximate, with early and late dates for uncertainties from Bible scholars, such as timing of the exodus. Some calculate it occurred during the 1400s, others the 1200s B.C.*

- Time between Israel's entering and exiting Egypt: 430 years

Dates	**Key Events**
1876 (or 1710) BC	Jacob and family enter Egypt
1486 (or 1320) BC	Moses leaves Egypt, Escapes to Midian
1446 or 1280 BC	Moses returns to Egypt; Israelites exit Egypt

❑ **Author: Moses**

Moses is the stated author of Exodus (Exodus 17:14; 24:4–8; 34:27; Josh. 8:31–35). Jesus verified Mosaic authorship (Mark 12:26). Moses was personally connected with events in Exodus, Leviticus, Numbers and Deuteronomy. Jewish and Christian tradition holds that Moses was the writer of these books (and Genesis), with the exception of the death of Moses in Deuteronomy. However, some scholars believe there were several authors for the Pentateuch (first five books of the Bible).

❑ **Date of Writing:** ~ 1425 BC
For more details on differing views concerning the authorship and date for the Pentateuch, with support for the traditional view of Moses' authorship, read the "Author" section in the Intro to Genesis.

❑ **Major Events in Exodus:**

Israel in Egypt (Chapters 1–12:36)	**Journey from Egypt to Sinai** (Chapters 12:37–18)
Slavery in Egypt (1)	Exodus from Egypt (12:37–14:31)
Birth, Early Life, Call of Moses (2–4)	Song of Moses (15:1–21)
Pharaoh Oppresses Israel (5–6:13)	Wilderness of Shur (15:22–27)
Family Tree of Moses & Aaron (6:14–27)	Wilderness of Sin (16)
Plagues and Passover (6:28–12:36)	Rock at Rephidim (17)
	Jethro and Moses (18)

Covenant and Law at Sinai (Chapters 19 – 24)	**The Tabernacle** (Chapters 25 – 40)
Preparations for Covenant (19)	Design Specifications (25–27)
Ten Commandments (20:1–17)	Priests (28–29)
Covenant Laws (20:18–23:33)	Furniture (30)
Israel Accepts God's Covenant (24)	Craftsmen (31:1–11)
	Sabbath (31:12–18)
	Israel's Breach of Covenant: Golden Calf (32)
	God and Moses (33)
	Covenant Renewal (34)
	Construction of Tabernacle (35–38)
	Priestly Garments (39)
	Completion and Dedication of Tabernacle (40)

Historical Locations: See Map (4) "Egypt Land of Bondage."

Israel in Egypt Until the Fourth Generation: 400–430 Years

Background

Genesis 12–17 describes the covenant agreement God made with Abraham. As part of this agreement, God promised to give Abraham's descendants the land of the Canaanites (also called Amorites).

> Abraham's specific descendants to partake in God's covenant were the offspring of Abraham's son Isaac and grandson Jacob (Israel). These covenant descendants became known as the Israelites. They were also called the Hebrews, and in later years become known as the Jews.

Prior to the birth of Isaac, God told Abraham that although He promised to give Abraham's descendants the land of Canaan, they would temporarily live in a foreign land for four hundred years (Genesis 15:13–16).

> **God also forewarned Abraham that his descendants would be afflicted as slaves while in the foreign land.**

✞

Part I. God's Purpose for Temporarily Planting Israel in Egypt

After four generations,
your descendants will return here to this land,
when the sin of the Amorites has run its course.
Genesis 15:16

The above prophetic words God spoke to Abraham include insight on His reason for eventually removing the people living in the land of Canaan. The Amorites were a sinful people whose sin would reach a point of wickedness that would invoke God's full judgment. When the time came, God would give the land to the Israelites.

To protect the Israelites from becoming like the wicked people of Canaan, God temporarily planted Israel in the land of Egypt. In his book, *Survey of the Old Testament*[1], Dr. Paul Benware describes how God used Israel to protect Israel.

Egypt now became the protector of the infant nation.
God was placing His baby nation into the incubator of Egypt until it was grown up enough to fend for itself. Egypt protected Israel in three ways.

First, it protected Israel physically.
Although the Egyptian army was unaware of it, they were guarding Israel against countless kings and robber bands that could have wiped out this young nation in a matter of hours.

[1]Appendix C

Second, Egypt shielded Israel morally.

Although Egypt may not have been known for its righteousness, it was superior to the wicked Canaanites. By removing Israel from the degrading influence of these perverse Canaanites people, God was preserving His people from moral failure, which surely would have come if they had been left in Canaan.

Third, Egypt secured Israel's racial purity.

Israel would certainly have intermarried with the Canaanites (as Genesis 34 reveals), but they would not intermarry with the Egyptians. The Egyptians looked down on the Israelites because of their occupation of shepherding (Genesis 46:34), and this was a key factor in keeping these two peoples apart.

Additionally, because of the Egyptians advanced achievements in writing, mathematics, and science, God used Egypt to help prepare Moses to become Israel's first great deliverer, leader, and prophet (Acts 7:22; Hebrews 11:23–26).

Part II. Length of Time Israel Lived in Egypt and Israel's Egyptian Bondage

Then the Lord told Abram,
"You can be sure that your descendants will be strangers in a foreign land, and they will be oppressed as slaves for four hundred years. Genesis 15:13

One of the scriptural challenges among Bible scholars and critics is the reckoning of the length of time Israel lived in Egypt, along with how much of that time was actually spent in bondage.

> At first reading, passages describing these events appear to give conflicting reports. For example, Genesis 15:13 and Acts 7:6 use the number "**400,**" while Exodus 12:40–41 and Galatians 3:17 use the number "**430** "

Passages such as 1 Chronicles 6:1; 1 Chronicles 23:6–13 and Exodus 6:16–20 point to a time of 350 years.

> In addition, the ages of Levite family members mentioned in Exodus 6:18–20 added together with Moses' age (Exodus 7:7), point to a sojourn of 350 years.

Furthermore, some studies, as well as Jewish traditions, conclude the Israelite nation was only in Egypt for 215 years.

Israel in Egypt Until the Fourth Generation: 400–430 Years

Diligent study of all the passages reveal that the durations are different because they are calculated from different start times.

> There is a detailed explanation on this topic provided by **Bible Apologists / Alden Bass, Bert Thompson, Ph.D., and Kyle Butt, M.A. in their article "How Long Was the Israelites Egyptian Bondage[2]."**

Examples of the clarifications the above article and others similar to it provide are:

- Each passage must be read carefully to determine at what point the time clock begins counting. For example, does the passage start the count from the time God made the covenant with Abraham, or with Abraham's descendants, or with the actual time Jacob and his family moved into Egypt.
- The punctuation provided by the translators of Genesis 15:13 should have been placed to indicate Abraham's descendants would be in the foreign land for 400 years, and they would be oppressed as slaves; not that they would be oppressed as slaves for 400 years in the foreign land.
- A review of the oldest versions of the Hebrew and Greek text, along with reliable ancient historians such as Flavius Josephus, are critical to resolving any apparent discrepancies in the English translations.

✞

Part III. Time's Up!

But I will punish the nation that enslaves them,
and in the end they will come away with great wealth.
Genesis 15:14

God promised Abraham He would make his descendants a great nation. This included returning them to the Promised Land with great wealth. The time has come!

Read on!

[2]Appendix C

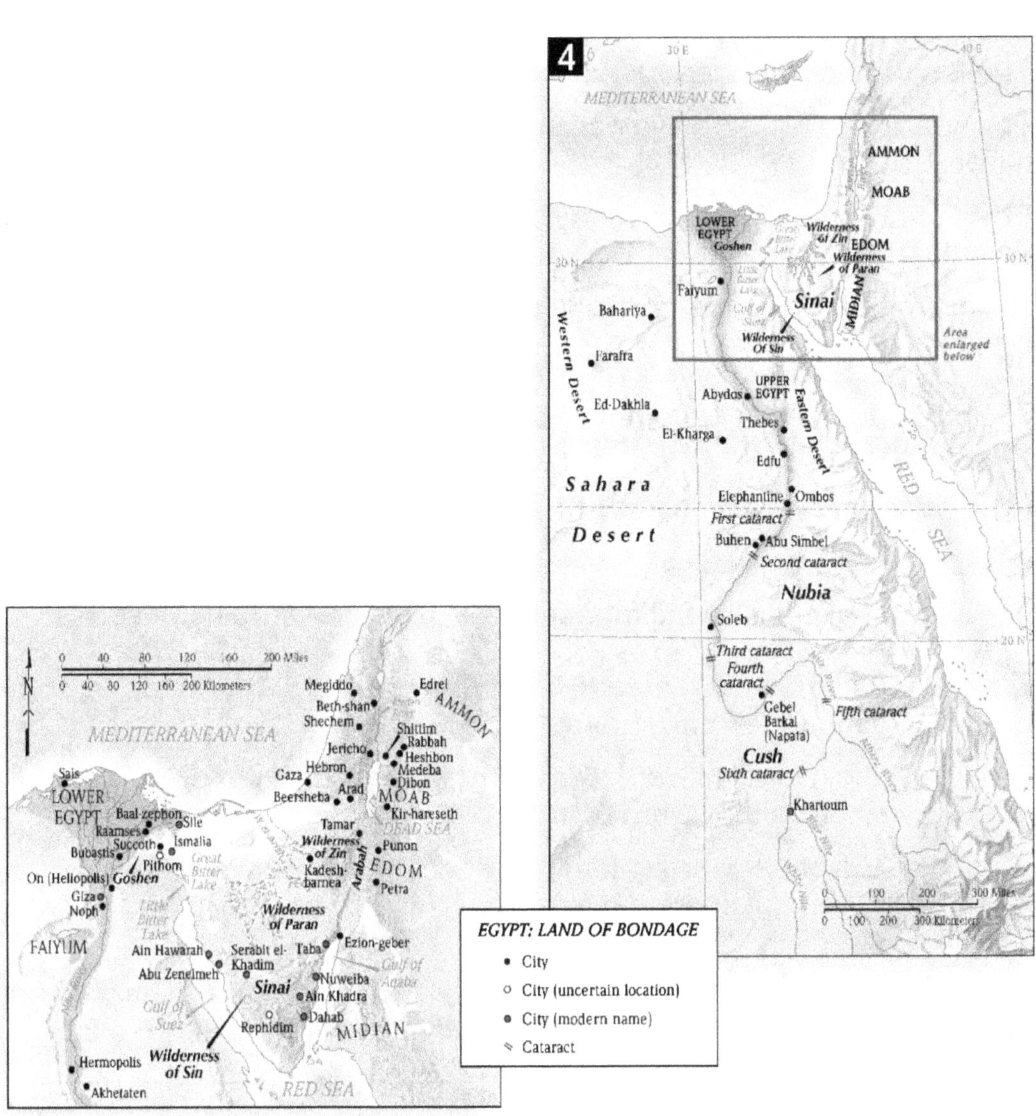
4
MEDITERRANEAN SEA
AMMON
MOAB
LOWER EGYPT
Goshen
Wilderness of Zin
EDOM
Wilderness of Paran
Faiyum
Sinai
MIDIAN
Bahariya
Western Desert
Farafra
Wilderness Of Sin
Area enlarged below
UPPER EGYPT
Abydos
Ed-Dakhla
Thebes
Eastern Desert
El-Kharga
Edfu
Sahara
Desert
Elephantine
Ombos
First cataract
RED SEA
Buhen
Abu Simbel
Second cataract
Nubia
Soleb
Third cataract
Fourth cataract
Gebel Barkal (Napata)
Fifth cataract
Cush
Sixth cataract
Khartoum
0 100 200 300 Miles
0 100 200 300 Kilometers
0 40 80 120 160 200 Miles
0 40 80 120 160 200 Kilometers
N
Megiddo
Edrei
Beth-shan
AMMON
Shechem
MEDITERRANEAN SEA
Shittim
Jericho
Rabbah
Heshbon
Hebron
Medeba
Gaza
Dibon
Sais
Arad
LOWER EGYPT
Beersheba
MOAB
Baal-zephon
Sile
Kir-hareseth
Raamses
Tamar
DEAD SEA
Succoth
Ismalia
Wilderness of Zin
Punon
Bubastis
Pithom
Great Bitter Lake
Arabah
On (Heliopolis)
Goshen
Kadesh-barnea
EDOM
Petra
Giza
Noph
Little Bitter Lake
Wilderness of Paran
FAIYUM
Ain Hawarah
Serabit el-Khadim
Taba
Ezion-geber
Abu Zenelmeh
Gulf of Aqaba
Sinai
Nuweiba
Ain Khadra
Gulf of Suez
Rephidim
Dahab
MIDIAN
Wilderness of Sin
Hermopolis
Akhetaten
RED SEA
EGYPT: LAND OF BONDAGE
City
City (uncertain location)
City (modern name)
Cataract

Reading Assignment:
Exodus 1:1–2:25
I Chronicles 6:1–3a
Exodus 3:1–4:17

Lesson 5.4

I. Lesson Exercise

Israel as Hebrew Slaves in Egypt: A Nation within a Nation

The Israelites increased in numbers until they became nation sized.

They were the Hebrew slave nation living among the powerful Egyptian nation.

Pharaoh, King of Egypt in today's lesson, did not know about Joseph.

He felt threatened by the multitude of these non-Egyptians living in his kingdom.

- **In Exodus 1:11–14 we read how the Egyptians cause the Israelites to:**
  - become their slaves
  - build their cities of Pithom and Rameses
  - make bricks and mortar to use in all their building projects
- **In Exodus 1:15–22, we read what Pharaoh told Egyptians to do to the Israelites' newborn boys:**
  - the midwives were to kill all newborn male Hebrew babies as soon as they were born
  - Egyptians were to throw newborn Israelite boys in the Nile River, but spare the girls

❑ **Introducing Moses: Moses' Birth**

5) Why did newborn Moses escape death in the Nile River? (Ex. 2:1–10) ______________________________

❑ **Man on the Run: Moses escapes to Midian**

- From Exodus 2:11–15 we read about Moses running away from Egypt. After Moses murdered an Egyptian to help an Israelite, he discovered everyone knew what he had done. He ran away before Pharaoh could kill him for his actions.[4]
- Moses ran into the Midianite people. He lived with a Midianite Priest's family for the next forty years of his life. He married one of the priest's daughters.

6) The Midianites were the offspring of whom? (Gen. 25:1–2)

____

[4]Appendix C

❑ God Calls Moses to Israel's Rescue

- The Angel of the Lord appeared to Moses as a blazing fire in a bush. From a distance Moses saw that the blazing burning bush never burned up, so he went near to investigate. (Exodus 3:2)
- God called Moses to go back and lead His people Israel out of Egypt. (Exodus 3:9–10)
- God told Moses that when he brought the Israelites out of Egypt, he was to...
  - First, bring them to the mountain he was talking to God on to worship Him (12)
  - Finally, lead them to their own good and spacious Promised Land in Canaan (8)

7) God told Moses to inform the Israelite leaders that God's name is what? (Exodus 3:14–15) ______________________________

❑ God Prepares Moses for His Return to Egypt

God instructs Moses on how to persuade the Israelites he was their God-sent Deliverer. Moses was to...

- Tell God's promise - He would lead them out of Egyptian bondage. (Exodus 3:17) God also brought them out with great wealth in keeping with His promise. (Read Exodus 3:22 and Exodus 12:35–36; with Genesis 15:14)
- Show three signs of God's power
  - Moses' staff could turn into a snake and back into a staff (Exodus 4:2)
  - Moses' hand could become leprous and return back to normal (Exodus 4:6)
  - Moses could cause water from the Nile to turn into blood (Exodus 4:9)
- God gave Aaron to Moses to be Moses' spokesperson to the people (Exodus 4:14–15)

II. Find Jesus in the Lesson and III. Closing Thoughts

Stephen, a Jewish Christian, speaks of Moses and his faith in Jesus

After Jesus rose from the dead and returned to heaven, many Israelites (called Jews in New Testament) believed in Jesus' resurrection. They accepted the risen Jesus Christ as Lord and Savior of their lives. Stephen was one such Jewish Christian.

Before being stoned to death for his belief in Jesus Christ, Stephen summarized the history of the Jewish people in Acts 7:15-35

From Acts 7:15–35

A portion of Stephen's summary words describing Moses' life up to the point in today's Exodus lesson.

So Jacob went to Egypt. He died there, as did all his sons. All of them were taken to Shechem and buried in the tomb Abraham had bought from the sons of Hamor in Shechem.

As the time drew near when God would fulfill his promise to Abraham, the number of our people in Egypt greatly increased. But then a new king came to the throne of Egypt who knew nothing about Joseph. This king plotted against our people and forced parents to abandon their newborn babies so they would die.

At that time Moses was born–a beautiful child in God's eyes. His parents cared for him at home for three months. When at last they had to abandon him, Pharaoh's daughter found him and raised him as her own son. Moses was taught all the wisdom of the Egyptians, and he became mighty in both speech and action.

One day when he was forty years old, he decided to visit his relatives, the people of Israel. During this visit, he saw an Egyptian mistreating a man of Israel. So Moses came to his defense and avenged him, killing the Egyptian. Moses assumed his brothers would realize that God had sent him to rescue them, but they didn't.

The next day he visited them again and saw two men of Israel fighting. He tried to be a peacemaker. "Men," he said, "you are brothers. Why are you hurting each other?"

But the man in the wrong pushed Moses aside and told him to mind his own business. "Who made you a ruler and judge over us?" he asked. "Are you going to kill me as you killed that Egyptian yesterday?" When Moses heard that, he fled the country and lived as a foreigner in the land of Midian, where his two sons were born.

Forty years later, in the desert near Mount Sinai, an angel appeared to Moses in the flame of a burning bush. Moses saw it and wondered what it was. As he went to see, the voice of the Lord called out to him, "I am the God of your ancestors--the God of Abraham, Isaac, and Jacob." Moses shook with terror and dared not look.

And the Lord said to him, "Take off your sandals, for you are standing on holy ground. You can be sure that I have seen the misery of my people in Egypt. I have heard their cries. So I have come to rescue them. Now go, for I will send you to Egypt."

And so God sent back the same man his people had previously rejected by demanding, "Who made you a ruler and judge over us?"

Through the angel who appeared to him in the burning bush,
Moses was sent to be their ruler and savior.

Reading Assignment:
Exodus 4:18–7:13

Lesson 5.5

I. Lesson Exercise

Moses Returns to Egypt

- ❑ **God gives Moses insight on what to expect when he returns to Egypt**
  - Those who wanted to kill Moses were all dead. (Ex. 4:19)
  - Moses will use God's miracles in interacting with Pharaoh for the release all the Israelites.
  - God will make Pharaoh's heart stubborn so he will refuse to let them go. (Ex. 4:21) (Read "Closing Thoughts" on Lesson 5.6 for an explanation of this.)
  - Moses was to warn Pharaoh that God was willing to kill his firstborn to cause him to release God's firstborn (Ex. 4:23)

- ❑ **God was ready to punish Moses during his family's return journey to Egypt**
  - Moses' son was an Israelite descendant by Moses. In order to be a legal member of the covenant nation, Moses' son had to be circumcised (refer to Genesis 17:9–14).
  - From what little text we read in Exodus 4:24–26, Moses' son had not been circumcised. The exact reason is unknown, but there seems to have been some contention between Moses and Zipporah concerning this practice. Before the boy could join the other Israelites, he must be circumcised, or Moses would be punished.
  - Finally, Moses' wife Zipporah took a knife and circumcised their son. The punishment for breaking the covenant was avoided.

- ❑ **Israel's Leaders First Response to Moses Was Good; Pharaoh's Was Not Good**
  - In Ex. 4:29–31 we read how the Israelites' first response to Moses was positive. They worshipped God because of the good news.
  - Pharaoh, on the other hand, commanded that the Hebrew slaves work harder, and they were to be treated worse than ever. He commanded that they make the same number of bricks without being supplied with the straw. (Exodus 5:6–9)
  - Pharaoh also called his magicians in to turn their staffs into snakes just like Moses did. However, Moses' huge snake ate the magician's snakes displaying God's superior power. (Ex. 7:10–13)

Hebrews = Descendants of Jacob = Israelites = Jews

Aaron and Moses told Pharaoh that the God of the Hebrews had met with them (Ex. 5:3).

"Hebrews" is another name for the Israelites.

This name has been used several times now (Genesis 40:15; 43:32, Exodus 2:13; 3:18, 5:3).

The name Israelites and Hebrews are used a lot in the Old Testament for the same group of people. Near the end of the Old Testament and in the New Testament, these people will be called "Jews."

- "Hebrew" comes from "Eber"[5], a descendant of Noah's son Shem. Gen. 10:21 says Shem was the ancestor of all descendants of Eber.
- In Gen. 11:10–26, the history of Shem's family down to Abram (Abraham), through Eber, is listed. Descendants of Abraham, Isaac and Jacob are known as children of Eber, and then the "Hebrews".
- According to the *Torah and Commentary—The Five Books of Moses* by Sol Scharfstein,[6] the name Hebrew comes from the word *Ivrim*, which means "those who came from the other side." When Abram (Abraham) left his homeland Ur to go to the new homeland God led him to, he had to cross the Euphrates River. This is when Abraham's family became known as the people who came from the other side => Ivrim => Hebrews.
- After the Babylonian exile, the Israelites will become known as the Jews, but this will be discussed in more detail at a later point in the Bible.

Children of Eber =

Hebrew children =

Descendants of Jacob,

Whose name was changed to Israel =

Israelites =

Jews

[5,6]Appendix C

God Is Ready to Be Known

Moses and Aaron went to see Pharaoh. They told him,

"This is what the LORD, the God of Israel, says:

`Let my people go, for they must go out into the wilderness to hold a religious festival in my honor.' "

"Is that so?" retorted Pharaoh.

"And who is the LORD that I should listen to him and let Israel go?

I don't know the LORD, and I will not let Israel go."

Exodus 5:1–2

The Egyptian people were very religious, worshipping over eighty different gods.

This involved worship of different things in creation such as the Nile River, the sun and animals. The Egyptians even worshipped their Pharaoh King as a god.

- **Worship of many gods is called polytheism** (e.g. Egyptians)
- **Worship of one God is monotheism.**[7] (e.g. Hebrews)

The True and Living God Is One God.

The one God was ready to be known worldwide.

Through Moses, He presented himself as God of the Hebrews (Israelites). He was getting ready to introduce Himself to Egypt as the only true and living God.

The nation of Egypt was a great nation in the earth during the time of Moses. In fact, when Moses was raised in the palace as a royal child (as a prince of Egypt), he received the best education available to humankind in his time.

Through royal tutors, Moses had an opportunity to learn to write, and he learned advanced medical knowledge, elaborate building techniques, and great mathematical knowledge.

Also, because of Egyptian religious beliefs, Moses was exposed to an organized worship system with temples, priests and religious rituals.

According to Acts 7:22, Moses learned all the wisdom of the Egyptians, and was mighty in words and in deeds.

[7]Appendix C

Moses Introduces God

A shepherd's life may have humbled him, but Moses was well-educated. After forty years in the palace of Egypt (Acts 7:23) and forty years a wilderness shepherd, at eighty years old (Exodus 7:7), God uses Moses to introduce Himself to Israel and Egypt.

8) God said Moses would be as a ______________ to Aaron his brother. (Exodus 4:16)

9) God said Aaron would be Moses' _________________ to the people. (Exodus 4:16)

10) God said Moses would seem like ________ to Pharaoh. (Exodus 7:1)

11) God said Aaron would be like Moses' ______________. (Exodus 7:1)

<u>II. Find Jesus in the Lesson and III. Closing Thoughts</u>

Review the Charts on the "Names of God" and "Jesus and the Names of God"

> ***God replied, "I AM THE ONE WHO ALWAYS IS. Just tell them, 'I AM has sent me to you.'"***
>
> ***God also said, "Tell them,***
> ***'The LORD, the God of your ancestors--the God of Abraham, the God of Isaac, and the God of Jacob--has sent me to you.'***
>
> ***This will be my name forever; it has always been my name, and it will be used throughout all generations." Ex. 3:14–15***
>
> ***"And God continued,***
>
> ***"I am the LORD. I appeared to Abraham, to Isaac, and to Jacob as God Almighty, though I did not reveal my name, the LORD, to them." Exodus 6:2–3***

God uses different names to give unique insight on who He is and how He interacts with humankind.

Jesus, as God with us, continues to give insight on God by His names.

Study "Jesus and the Names of God" and "Names of God" charts on the following pages [8]

[8]Appendix C

Jesus and the Names of God

The New Testament alludes to Jesus' divine nature by comparing Jesus to several names and attributes used for God. Here are a few examples of Jesus being compared to God:

Jesus is God	In the beginning was the Word, and the Word was with God, and the Word was God. ...(John 1:1-5)
Jesus is one with God	"I and my Father are one." (John 10:30)
Jesus is eternal	[Jesus] said, "Fear not; I am the First and the Last." (Revelation 1:17b)
Jesus is omnipresent Omnipresent means "present everywhere"	And [God] hath put all things under his feet, and gave him to be the head over all things to the church, which is his body, the fullness of him that filleth all in all. (Ephesians 1:22, 23)
Jesus is omniscient Omniscient means "all-knowing"	"Lord, thou knowest all things...." (John 21:17)
Jesus is life giving	In him was life; and the life was the light of men. (John 1:4)
Jesus is El Olam	The Beginning and the End: "I am Alpha and Omega, the beginning and the end, the first and the last." (Revelation 22:13)
Jesus is YHWH-Jireh	The Lord will Provide: ..."I am the bread of life. He that cometh to me shall never hunger, and he that believeth on me shall never thirst." (John 6:35)
Jesus is YHWH-Rohi	The Lord is my Shepherd: "I am the good shepherd: the good shepherd giveth his life for the sheep." (John 10:11)
Jesus is YHWH-Tsidkenu	The Lord is Righteousness: For he hath made him to be sin for us, who knew no sin; that we might be made the righteousness of God in him. (2 Corinthians 5:21)
Jesus is YHWH-Rapha	The Lord Who Heals: Who his own self bare our sins in his own body on the tree, that we, being dead to sins, should live unto righteousness: by whose stripes ye were healed. (1 Peter 2:24)
Jesus is El Shaddai	The All Sufficient One: ..."My grace is sufficient for thee: for my strength is made perfect in weakness..." (2 Corinthians 12:9)
Jesus is Immanuel	God With Us: ...they shall call his name Emmanuel, which being interpreted is, God with us. (Matthew 1:23)
Jesus is YHWH-Shalom	The Lord is Peace: "Peace I leave with you; my peace I give unto you...." (John 14:27)

Name of God	Meaning	Application
ADONAI	The Lord My Great Lord	God is the Master and majestic Lord. God is our total authority.
EL	The Strong One	He is more powerful than any false god. God will overcome all obstacles. We can depend on God.
EL ELOHE YISRAEL	God, the God of Israel	The God of Israel is distinct and separate from all false gods of the world.
EL ELYON	The God Most High	He is the Sovereign God in whom we can put our trust. El Elyon has supremacy over all false gods.
ELOHIM	The All-Powerful One Creator	God is the all-powerful creator of the universe. God knows all, creates all, and is everywhere at all times. The plural of "El".
EL OLAM	The Eternal God The Everlasting God	He is the Beginning and the End, the One who works His purposes throughout the ages. He gives strength to the weary.
EL ROI	The God Who Sees me	There are no circumstances in our lives that escape His fatherly awareness and care. God knows us and our troubles.
EL SHADDAI	The All Sufficient One, The God of the Mountains, God Almighty	God is the all-sufficient source of all of our blessings. God is all-powerful. Our problems are not too big for God to handle.
IMMANUEL	God With Us "I AM"	Jesus is God in our midst. In Him all the fullness of Deity dwells in bodily form.
JEHOVAH (YHWH, see comments)	"I AM," The One Who Is The Self-Existent One	God never changes. His promises never fail. When we are faithless, He is faithful. We need to obey Him.
JEHOVAH-JIREH	The Lord Will Provide	Just as God provided a ram as a substitute for Isaac, He provided His son Jesus as the ultimate sacrifice. God will meet all our needs.
JEHOVAH-MEKADDISHKEM	The Lord Who Sanctifies	God sets us apart as a chosen people, a royal priesthood, holy unto God, a people of His own. He cleanses our sin and helps us mature.
JEHOVAH-NISSI	The Lord is My Banner	God gives us victory against the flesh, the world and the devil. Our battles are His battles of light against darkness and good against evil.
JEHOVAH-RAPHA	The Lord Who Heals	God has provided the final cure for spiritual, physical, and emotional sickness in Jesus Christ. God can heal us.
JEHOVAH-ROHI	The Lord is My Shepherd	The Lord protects, provides, directs, leads, and cares for His people. God tenderly takes care of us as a strong and patient shepherd.
JEHOVAH-SABAOTH	The Lord of Hosts The Lord of Armies	The Lord of the hosts of heaven will always fulfill His purposes, even when the hosts of His earthly people fail.
JEHOVAH-SHALOM	The Lord is Peace	God defeats our enemies to bring us peace. Jesus is our Prince of Peace. God brings inner peace and harmony.
JEHOVAH-SHAMMAH	The Lord is There The Lord My Companion	God's presence is not limited or contained in the Tabernacle or Temple, but is accessible to all who love and obey Him.
JEHOVAH-TSIDKENU	The Lord Our Righteousness	Jesus is the King who would come from David's line, and is the one who imparts His righteousness to us.
YAH, OR JAH	"I AM," The One Who Is The Self-Existent One	God never changes. His promises never fail. When we are faithless, He is faithful. God promises His continuing presence.
YHWH	"I AM," The One Who Is The Self-Existent One	God never changes. His promises never fail. When we are faithless, He is faithful.

Bible Reference	Comments
Psalm 8; Isaiah 40:3-5 Ezekiel 16:8; Habakkuk 3:19	**Pronounced: ah-doe-NI** *Adonai* (plural) is derived from the singular *Adon* (Lord). This term was pronounced in substitution of *YHWH* (considered too sacred to be uttered).
Exodus 15:2; Numbers 23:22 Deuteronomy 7:9 (Mark 15:34)	**Pronounced: el** Occurs more than 200 times in the Old Testament (including compounds). Generic Semitic name for God, used by other cultures to refer to their gods. *El* is used in compound proper names such as Isra-*el* (wrestles with God), Beth-*el* (House of God), and *El*-isha (God is salvation).
Genesis 33:20; Exodus 5:1 Psalm 68:8; Psalm 106:48	**Pronounced: el el-o-HAY yis-raw-ALE** The name of the altar that Jacob (Israel) erected after his encounter with God and God's blessing upon him. (Genesis 32:24-30; Genesis 33:19, 20)
Genesis 14:17-22; Psalm 78:35 Daniel 4:34 (Acts 16:17)	**Pronounced: el EL-yuhn** Melchizedek, the king of Salem (Jeru "Salem") and the priest of God Most High, referred to God as "El Elyon" three times when he blessed Abram.
Genesis 1:1-3; Deuteronomy 10:17 Psalm 68 (Mark 13:19)	**Pronounced: el-o-HEEM** Plural form of *El*. This name is usually associated with God in relation to His creation. Some people use the plural word "Elohim" as proof for the Trinity. (Genesis 1:26) *Elohim* is also used to refer to false gods and even human judges. (Psalm 82:6, 7; John 10:34)
Genesis 21:33; Psalm 90:1, 2 Isaiah 40:28 (Romans 1:20)	**Pronounced: el o-LAHM** Jesus Christ possesses eternal attributes. He is the same yesterday and today and forever. (Hebrews 13:8) He obtained eternal redemption for us. (Hebrews 9:12)
Genesis 16:11-14; Psalm 139:7-12	**Pronounced: el ROY** Hagar called the LORD by this name beside a fountain of water in the wilderness. God knows all of our thoughts and feelings. Jesus knew the thoughts of those around him, demonstrating that he is *El Roi*. (Matthew 22:18; 26:21, 34; Luke 5:21-24)
Genesis 17:1-3; 48:3; 49:25 Genesis 35:11; Psalm 90:2	**Pronounced: el-shaw-DIE** Some scholars suggest that *Shaddai* refers to God's power evident in His judgment. Others suggest that *El Shaddai* means "God of the Mountains." God refers to Himself as "El Shaddai" when he confirms his covenant with Abraham.
Isaiah 7:14; 8:8-10 (Matthew 1:23)	**Pronounced: ih-MAN-u-el** This name indicates that Jesus is more than man. He is also God. Isaiah said that the child born to the virgin would be called "Immanuel." (Isaiah 7:14; 9:6) He is the radiance of God's glory and the exact representation of His nature. (Hebrews 1:3)
Exodus 3:14; Exodus 6:2-4 Exodus 34:5-7; Psalm 102	**Pronounced: juh-HO-vah** A 16th century German translator wrote the name *YHVH (YHWH)* using the vowels of *Adonai* because the ancient Jewish texts from which he was translating had the vowels of *Adonai* under the consonants of *YHVH*. By doing this, he incorrectly came up with the name Jehovah (*YaHoVaH*).
Genesis 22:13, 14; Psalm 23 (Mark 10:45; Romans 8:2)	**Pronounced: juh-HO-vah JI-rah** Also known as YHWH-Jireh. Abraham called the place "The Lord will provide" where God provided a ram to be sacrificed instead of his son Isaac. Jesus said that He was the bread of life and anyone who comes to Him will be provided for. (John 6:35)
Exodus 31:12, 13 (1 Peter 1:15, 16 Hebrews 13:12; 1 Thessalonians 5:23, 24)	**Pronounced: juh-HO-vah mek-KAH-dish-KIM** Also known as YHWH-Mekaddishkem. We have been set apart, made holy, and redeemed by the blood of Jesus Christ, our *Jehovah-Mekaddishkem*. Therefore, we are to continue to live our lives holy and pleasing to God. (1 Peter 1:13-25)
Exodus 17:15, 16; Deuteronomy 20:3, 4 Isaiah 11:10-12 (Ephesians 6:10-18)	**Pronounced: juh-HO-vah NEE-see** Also known as YHWH-Nissi. Name of the altar built by Moses after defeating the Amalekites at Rephidim. Isaiah prophesies that the "Root of Jesse" (Jesus) will stand as a banner for the peoples. (Isaiah 11:10)
Exodus 15:25-27; Psalm 103:3 Psalm 147:3 (1 Peter 2:24)	**Pronounced: juh-HO-vah RAH-fah** Also known as YHWH-Rapha. Jesus demonstrated that He was *Jehovah-Rapha* in his healing of the sick, blind, lame, and casting out demons. Jesus also heals His people from sin and unrighteousness. (Luke 5:31, 32)
Psalm 23:1-3; Isaiah 53:6 (John 10:14-18 Hebrews 13:20; Revelation 7:17)	**Pronounced: juh-HO-vah RO-hee** Also known as YHWH-Ra'ah (RAH-ah). Jesus is the good shepherd who lay down His life for all people.
1 Samuel 1:3; 1 Samuel 17:45; Psalm 46:7 Malachi 1:10-14 (Romans 9:29)	**Pronounced: juh-HO-vah sah-bah-OATH** Also known as YHWH-Sabaoth. Many English versions of the Bible translate *Sabaoth* as Almighty. "Jehovah-Sabaoth" is often translated as *The Lord Almighty*. *Sabaoth* is also translated as *Heavenly Hosts* or *Armies*.
Numbers 6:22-27; Judges 6:22-24 Isaiah 9:6 (Hebrews 13:20)	**Pronounced: juh-HO-vah shah-LOME** Also known as YHWH-Shalom. Name of the altar built by Gideon at Ophrah to memorialize God's message "Peace be unto thee." Isaiah tells us that the Messiah will also be known as the "Prince of Peace," our *Jehovah-Shalom*. (Isaiah 9:6)
Ezekiel 48:35; Psalm 46 (Matthew 28:20; Revelation 21)	**Pronounced: juh-HO-vah SHAHM-mah** Also known as YHWH-Shammah. God revealed to Ezekiel that the name of the New Jerusalem shall be "The LORD is there." Through Jesus Christ, the Spirit of God dwells in us. (1 Corinthians 3:16)
Jeremiah 23:5, 6; 33:16; Ezekiel 36:26, 27 (2 Corinthians 5:21)	**Pronounced: juh-HO-vah tsid-KAY-noo** Also known as YHWH-Tsidkenu. All people sin and fall short of God's glory, but God freely makes us righteous through faith in Jesus Christ. (Romans 3:22, 23) God promised to send a King who will reign wisely and do what is just and right. The people will live in safety. (Jeremiah 23:5, 6)
Exodus 3:14; 15:2; Psalm 46:1 Psalm 68:4; Isaiah 26:4	**Pronounced: Yah** Shorter form of *Yahweh*. It is often used when combined with other names or phrases. *Hallelujah* means "Praise Yah (the Lord)," *Elijah* means "God is Yah (the Lord)," and *Joshua* means "Yah (the Lord) is my salvation."
Exodus 3:14; Malachi 3:6	**Pronounced: YAH-way** God's personal name given to Moses. Also called the tetragrammaton ("four letters"). Occurs about 6,800 times. Translated "LORD" in English versions of the Bible, because it became common practice for Jews to say "Lord" (Adonai) instead of saying the name *YHWH*.

Reading Assignment:
Exodus 7:14–9:35

Lesson 5.6

I. Lesson Exercise

It's Showdown Time!

Pharaoh is very stubborn, refusing to let God's people the Israelites go.

Today's lesson describes seven of ten plagues God sends in Egypt. Then Pharaoh lets them go.

> ***The LORD said to Moses, "Get up early in the morning. Go to Pharaoh and tell him, 'The LORD, the God of the Hebrews, says:***
>
> ***Let my people go, so they can worship me. If you don't, I will send a plague that will really speak to you and your officials and all Egyptian people. I will prove to you that there is no other God like me in all the earth.***
>
> ***I could have killed you all by now. I could have attacked you with a plague that would have wiped you from the face of the earth.***
>
> ***But I have let you live for this reason--that you might see my power and that my fame might spread throughout the earth.'" Exodus 9:13–16***

From Exodus 9:13–16, God identified the reasons He chose to do ever increasing plagues instead of just killing all the Egyptians.

Through the plagues, God would reveal to the Egyptians that there are no other gods besides the God of the Hebrews. And God's fame would spread over the earth for His mighty defeat of great Egypt in its time.

Review the chart "Moses' Ten Plagues."

Of the over eighty gods the Egyptians worshipped, God's miracles demonstrated to Egypt those gods were nothing.

II. Find Jesus in the Lesson and III. Closing Thoughts

Pharaoh's Hardened Heart Is Like Hardened Hearts of Non-Believers in Christ

With complete accuracy, God told Moses, Moses told Aaron, and Aaron told Pharaoh when each plague would start, when it would stop, who it would affect or not affect.

The Egyptian magicians were only able to copy the first two plagues. After that they exclaimed to Pharaoh the plagues produced by Moses were the "finger of God".

Pharaoh Continued Refusing to Let God's People Go

The text says Pharaoh hardened his heart (Exodus 8:32; 9:34–35), but it also says God hardened Pharaoh's heart (Exodus 4:21, 7:3, 14:4) against letting them go, so God could do more miracles.

L. Richards explains in *Bible Reader's Companion* that God did not change the natural tendency of Pharaoh's heart, nor did God force him to act against his will.[9]

It was God's act of revealing Himself to Pharaoh that caused Pharaoh's heart to harden.

God Still Hardens and Softens Hearts by the Same Means.

When God reveals Himself to us by Jesus Christ, those who choose to believe are softened, and respond to God. Those who refuse to believe become hardened, never accepting Jesus Christ.

Although the world was made through him [Jesus], the world didn't recognize him when he came.

Even in his own land and among his own people, he was not accepted.

But to all who believed him and accepted him, he gave the right to become children of God. John 1:10–12

[9]Appendix C

Lesson 5.7

Reading Assignment:
Exodus 10:1–12:51

I. Lesson Exercise

Pharaoh's Arms Are Too Short to Box With God

Showdown's over - God wins!

With the victory in today's lesson, some specific prophecies God gave to Abraham and Jacob were fulfilled as Israel is redeemed (meaning set free or delivered) from the hand of their enemies.

Exodus 12:40 identifies 430 years as the time the Israelites lived in Egypt since entering the land with Jacob (Gen. 46:3–4). In Genesis 15:13–14, God told Abraham that his descendants would be there about that long.

First Time for "The Lord's Passover"

Many Jewish people still celebrate the Lord's Passover each year. This annual celebration is a reminder of the specific events described in Exodus Chapter 12.

12) Explain what the phrase "The Lord's Passover" is truly describing based on the events in today's lesson. (Ex. 12:12–13; 28–30) ____________________

II. Find Jesus in the Lesson and III Closing Thoughts

Christ, Our Passover Lamb

The next day John saw Jesus coming toward him and said,

"Look! There is the Lamb of God who takes away the sin of the world!
John 1:29

For God so loved the world that he gave his only Son, so that everyone who believes in him will not perish but have eternal life.

John 3:16

Christ, our Passover Lamb, has been sacrificed for us.
I Corinthians 5:7

The events in Exodus Chapter 12 were a symbol of future events to happen through Jesus Christ. Jesus is symbolized by the lamb sacrificed during the first Passover. The lamb was killed, and its blood placed over the doorposts of obedient Israelites doors, causing the death angel to pass over their homes.

Similarly, Jesus was sacrificed to save all humankind. Jesus' blood that was shed on the cross paid God's price for sin. For all who believe on the work of Jesus Christ, our sins are taken away as the blood of Jesus is supernaturally applied to the doorposts of our sinful hearts. When death comes, it cannot hurt believers.

The death angel passes over us when it sees the blood of Jesus in our hearts. Because of the eternal life believers possess through faith in Jesus Christ, death simply becomes a transport vehicle, delivering us to live with God forever.

This truth will continue to be revealed as you keep reading through the Bible.

Passover, Passover Celebration and Pesach Seder[10]

[2] This month shall be unto you the beginning of months:
it shall be the first month of the year to you.
[3] Speak ye unto all the congregation of Israel, saying,
In the tenth day of this month they shall take to them every man a lamb,
according to the house of their fathers, a lamb for an house:
[4] And if the household be too little for the lamb,
let him and his neighbour next unto his house take it according to the number of the souls;
every man according to his eating shall make your count for the lamb.
[5] Your lamb shall be without blemish, a male of the first year:
ye shall take it out from the sheep, or from the goats:
[6] And ye shall keep it up until the fourteenth day of the same month:
and the whole assembly of the congregation of Israel shall kill it in the evening.
[7] And they shall take of the blood, and strike it on the two side posts
and on the upper door post of the houses, wherein they shall eat it.
[8] And they shall eat the flesh in that night, roast with fire, and unleavened bread;
and with bitter herbs they shall eat it.
[12] For I will pass through the land of Egypt this night,
and will smite all the firstborn in the land of Egypt, both man and beast;
and against all the gods of Egypt I will execute judgment: I am the LORD.
[13] And the blood shall be to you for a token upon the houses where ye are:
and when I see the blood, I will pass over you, and the plague shall
not be upon you to destroy you, when I smite the land of Egypt.
[14] And this day shall be unto you for a memorial;
and ye shall keep it a feast to the LORD throughout your generations;
ye shall keep it a feast by an ordinance for ever. ***Exodus 12:2 –8, 12–14 KJV***

Passover (Pesach)

- Pesach means "passing over" or "protection" in the Hebrew language. It is derived from Exodus 12:1–30.
- For the tenth plaque against the Pharaoh who refused to let God's people (Israelites) go, God planned to kill the firstborn of both man and beast. To protect the Israelites, God gave Moses instructions on how the Israelites were to mark their dwellings. This is so God could identify and "pass over" their homes.

Passover (Pesach) Celebration

- Of all the Jewish holidays, Pesach is the one most observed.
- Many of the Passover observances are instituted in Exodus 12:1–15.

Passover (Pesach) Seder

- The Pesach Seder is both a retelling and a reliving of the Jewish ancestors' exodus from slavery in Egypt more than 3,000 years ago.
- Seder takes place the first two nights of eight-day Passover=Pesach holiday
- Seder is considered the most important event in the Passover Celebration. It is steeped in long held traditions and customs as whole families and friends gather to celebrate it together.
- Leading up to the first night of Passover, the home is cleaned and cleared of all yeast foods, called hametz (chametz). All hametz is either eaten before Passover begins or sold to non-Jewish neighbors and friends.
- Special dishes and utensils for the Passover holiday are taken out of storage, cleaned, and used.
- Only foods that are "Kosher for Passover" are allowed.
- The "Haggadah," which contains the Passover Story from the book of Exodus, is read. The history is celebrated with stories, songs and prayers.
- When Messianic Jews and Christians celebrate the Seder, symbolism that points to Yeshua the Messiah (Jesus Christ) is explained.

[10]Appendix C

Moses' Ten Plagues: True God of Israel against False gods of Egypt[11]

I** [God of Hebrews] **will prove to you** [Pharaoh King of Egypt] **that there is no other God like me in all the earth." Ex. 9:14b

"I will execute judgment against all the gods of Egypt, for I am the LORD!" Exodus 12:12b

Moses' Plague	Description	Scripture	Against Egyptian gods	What was affected
#1: Water to Blood	When Moses' staff hit water in Nile river, water turned to blood. When Aaron pointed staff toward waters of Egypt, all water in rivers, canals, marshes, reservoirs and stored in people's homes all turned to blood.	Exodus 7:14– 25	Osiris— false god of Nile which supposedly gave life to Egypt Hapi— false spirit god of the Nile which was supposedly lord of fishes, birds and marshes	Nile river was the source of life of Egyptians; they worshipped it as a god. Fish died, river stank, Egyptians not able to drink water from Nile. Egyptian magicians could also turn water to blood. Plague lasted one week.
#2: Frogs	Hordes of frogs sent across all Egypt from one border to other, in all land and all water. Did not stop until Moses said so, at Pharaoh's request.	Exodus 8:1–15	Heqt—false frog god was a symbol of fertility and resurrection	Overwhelming swarms of frogs in Nile river, over all land, in houses, bedrooms& cooking areas. Magicians could also make frogs come on land.
#3: Lice (Gnats)	Aaron struck dust with staff, swarms of lice (gnats) rose from dust covering all Egypt, people and animals. Homes and ground were filled with them.	Exodus 8:16–19	Geb (Seb) —false earth god, which supposedly gave good soil for growing crops	All the dust in the land of Egypt turned into lice (or gnats). Magicians could NOT do this; they told Pharaoh this was the "finger of God".
#4: Swarms	Swarms of flies were sent throughout Egypt, ground and homes filled with them.	Exodus 8:20–32	Kheper— false insect god Amon-Ra—false creator god, still seen in Egypt today.	All Egypt had flies including palace. NO flies in Goshen with Israel, but Egyptians in chaos.
#5: Livestock Diseased	At the time announced, God sent a deadly plague that destroyed Egyptian horses, donkeys, camels, cattle, and sheep. They all began to die.	Exodus 8:9:1–7	Apis—false sacred bull god supposed protector of livestock and prosperity Hathor—false cow goddess Mnevis-ram's head; Khnum-bull	To the Egyptians the bull was sacred, but this plague destroyed their sacred bull. Israel's livestock was NOT affected, not a single one died.

Notes:

1) Moses did all actions based on God's instructions. God made the miracles happen through Moses and Aaron's obedient actions.
2) Egyptians worshipped over eighty gods. This chart highlights main gods, but ALL gods were proven false by plagues and miracles.

References[11]: "Against all the Gods of Egypt" by D. Padfield; "Against All Gods: Purpose of the Ten Plagues" by T. Sliedrecht

Moses' Ten Plagues: True God of Israel against False gods of Egypt[11]

I [God of Hebrews] ***will prove to you*** *[Pharaoh King of Egypt]* ***that there is no other God like me in all the earth." Ex. 9:14b***

"I will execute judgment against all the gods of Egypt, for I am the LORD!" Exodus 12:12b

#6: Boils	Moses tossed soot from a furnace in the sky while Pharaoh watched. It spread like fine dust over all Egypt, causing terrible boils to break out on people and animals.	Exodus 9:8–12	Serpis— false god of healing Thoth— false god of intelligence & medical learning Imhotep— god of medicine Isis - magic/medicine Sekhmet —epidemics & healing	Boils were like open sores with puss running out of them. On the bodies of all people and animals in Egypt, including on magicians/priests. No one in Israel was affected.
#7: Hail	Moses lifted his staff to the sky; God sent thunder, hail and lightening struck earth. God sent a great hailstorm against all Egypt. Never in Egypt's history had there been a storm like that, with severe hail and continuous lightening.	Exodus 9:13–-35	Nut— false sky goddess Horus— false sky god of Upper Egypt Shu— false god of wind Tefnut—false goddess of rain, dew and moisture	Hail fell over all of Egypt on people, animals and crops, leaving Egypt in ruins. All in fields destroyed –people, crops and animals. Trees destroyed. The only spot without hail that day was land of Goshen, where people of Israel lived.
#8: Locusts	Moses raised his staff, God caused an east wind to blow all day and night; next morning swarms of locusts were everywhere	Exodus 10:1–20	Emutet —lady of fertile land and granaries Nepri— false god of grain Seth— false god of crops	Pharaoh's officials begged him to let the Israelites go serve their God, saying "Don't you realize Egypt lies in ruins?" Locusts devoured all hail left.
#9: Darkness	Moses lifted his hand to heaven and a terrifying darkness fell over entire land of Egypt for three days.	Exodus 10:21–29	Amon-Ra (Re) —false sun and creator god; Ptah—creator of moon and stars; Tem—god of sunset; Shu—sunlight and air	During darkness Egyptians barely moved because they could not see. But Israelites had light as usual.
#10: Death of Firstborn	About midnight God passed through Egypt; firstborn sons died in every family in Egypt, even Pharaoh, and animals	Exodus 11:1–10	All false gods related to giving and protecting life Pharaoh— false god who could not save his own son	In prep for leaving after this, God had Israel ask Egyptians for silver & gold; then eat Passover meal with sandals on

Note: After plague #8, Pharaoh agreed to let Israel go under his terms. Moses would not accept anything less than release on God's terms – all Israel and everything belonging to Israel would leave out of Egypt together - which happened after plague #10.

References[11]: "Against all the Gods of Egypt" by D. Padfield and "Against All Gods: Purpose of the Ten Plagues" by T. Sliedrecht

Archaeology and Exodus

According to the Introduction of the Archaeological Study Bible, our current generation has the unique ability to correlate Bible events and persons with historical settings. This is due to the large number of archaeological exploration successes in the ancient Near East, especially those discoveries from the 20th century that are also continuing into the present.

As a result of the quantity, quality, and relevancy of these newly discovered archaeological finds, it has become easier to understand and confirm the accuracy of many Bible events. Yet not all events are confirmed in this way.

The Archaeological Study Bible provides a great benefit to biblical studies by linking archaeological findings side by side with Biblical scripture.

There are also many books, pamphlets, Internet articles, and DVD's that provide insight on these great archaeological finds, which can be researched by Bible topics. While there are conflicting opinions about the conclusions on some findings, there is enough material to give evidence to the authenticity of many Bible events.

Below are example references that are reasonably priced and easily accessible for further study of archaeological findings and their confirmation of events in the book of Exodus.

⇒ **Bibles**

New International Version (NIV) Archaeological Study Bible, [12] book of Exodus articles on "Archaeological Sites," "Ancient Texts and Artifacts," "Cultural and Historical Notes," "Ancient Peoples, Lands and Rulers"

Chronological Study Bible (Thomas Nelson, Inc., 2008)

⇒ **Books**

Israel in Egypt: The Evidence for the Authenticity of the Exodus Tradition (Paperback) by James K. Hoffmeier (Author), 1996, Oxford University Press

Ancient Israel in Sinai: The Evidence for the Authenticity of the Wilderness Tradition (Hardcover), by James K. Hoffmeier (Author), 2005, Oxford University Press

Riddle of the Exodus: Startling Parallels Between Ancient Jewish Sources and the Egyptian Archaeological Record (Paperback) by James D. Long (Author), 2006, LightCatcher Books

⇒ **Pamphlet**

Archaeology and the Bible—Old Testament by Rose Publishing, Inc., Torrance, California (hendricksonrose.com)

⇒ **Internet Articles**

Archaeology and the Book of Exodus: Exit From Egypt by Mario Seiglie, Good News Magazine Mar/Apr and May/Jun 1997 (ucg.org/good-news)

⇒ **DVD**

The Exodus Revealed: Searching for the Red Sea Crossing (2001) by Questar Video

[12]Appendix C

Week 6

Featured Book: Exodus

Contents:

Peek at the Week

Lesson	Key Events	Find Jesus
6.1	Exodus complete with Miracle at Red Sea	Jesus our Deliverer
6.2	God tests Israel's faithfulness in the wilderness	Jesus our Healer
6.3	God presents terms of Covenant agreement	Jesus and the Ten Commandments
6.4	Israel accepts God's Covenant	Jesus and Three Yearly Covenant Festivals
6.5	Moses spends 40 days and night with God and receives Covenant Tabernacle design	Jesus in the Tabernacle Design
6.6	Instruction for Priests' Dedication Ceremony	Jesus our Anointed Priest
6.7	Israel breaks and remakes Covenant with God	Jesus our Intercessor

Chronological Notes

* Timetable	Key Events
1446 or 1280 BC	Passover Celebration and Exit from Egypt Miracle at the Red Sea
1 Month after Exodus from Egypt	Israel at Elim in Sin Desert (Manna and Quail) (Exodus 16:1)
2 Months after Exodus	Israel arrives in Wilderness of Sinai (Exodus 19:1)
During 1st year after Exodus from Egypt	Israel's faithfulness to God is tested (Ex. 15:25–26) Israel makes, breaks & remakes Covenant with God Israel organized into a Covenant nation (chosen people) with laws, priests, worship tabernacle, God's presence
In beginning of the 2nd Year after Exodus 1445 (or 1279) BC	Israel leaves wilderness of Sinai (Numbers 10:11) Israel from Egypt should have entered Promised Land Unbelieving Israel from Egypt wanders in wilderness
40 Years after Exodus 1405 (or 1239) BC	Second generation Israel enters Promised Land

**All dates are approximate, with uncertainties from Bible scholars leading to early and late dates for some events.*

Reading Assignment:
Exodus 13:1–15:27

Lesson 6.1

I. Lesson Exercise

Exodus Always Remembered

Moses gave the Israelites God's instructions for always remembering their exodus from Egypt. When they did three activities, they would remember the day God brought them out and pass on what they remembered to future generations.

Activity instructions are in Exodus 12:1–30; 43–51 and 13:1–16:

- Passover Festival
- Unleavened Bread Festival
- Dedication of firstborn sons and firstborn male animals

God's Key Instructions for Yearly Festivals in Exodus 12, 13

Passover Month: "Abib" or "Nisan"[1]

(This month occurs around March or April)

Day 1 Start of a new year as a nation Ex 12:2	Day 8	**Day 15** **Passover** **- Eat Lord's Passover** On night of Day 14 which is when Day 15 begins after sundown, Eat roast lamb, bitter herbs & bread without yeast Ex 12:8
Day 2	Day 9	Day 16 Eat no bread with yeast
Day 3	**Day 10** **Choose lamb or young goat to sacrifice Ex 12:3**	Day 17 Eat no bread with yeast
Day 4	Day 11	Day 18 Eat no bread/yeast
Day 5	Day 12	Day 19 Eat no bread/yeast
Day 6	Day 13	Day 20 Eat no bread/yeast
Day 7	**Day 14** **- Kill sacrifice lamb Ex. 12:6** - At evening begin to celebrate Festival of Unleavened Bread by eating no bread with yeast for the whole week Ex. 12:17–20	**Day 21** Eat no bread/yeast - From evening of Day 14 until Day 21, no yeast in homes or anywhere in the borders of the land Ex. 12:18-20, Ex. 13:7 - During festivals tell children why you are celebrating Ex. 13:8

[1]Appendix C

Dedication of Firstborn Sons and Firstborn Male Animals

- God told the Israelites to tell their children that the firstborn sons and male animals belonged to Him. This is because God had spared Israel's firstborn when He killed the Egyptians' firstborn, which resulted in Israel's exodus from Egypt. (Ex. 4:22-23; 13:1-2, 12-16)
- Firstborn sons were offered by providing redemption payment to God's leaders. (Numbers 3:40-51)

Israel's Exodus from Egypt Ended with Miracle Crossing at Red Sea

When Pharaoh and his officials realized the Hebrew slaves were not coming back, they decided to go after them to force their return. It seemed to them like the Hebrews were trapped at the Red Sea by a God who did not know how to lead them. But God did everything on purpose!

1) Why did God not lead the Israelites on the shortest way from Egypt to the Promised Land? (Ex. 13:17) ________________________________

2) Why did God make it look to everyone that the Israelites were trapped between the wilderness and sea? (Ex. 14:1–4) ____________

3) What foolish statement did the Israelites make when upset about what appeared to be a bad situation? (Ex. 14:12) _________________

4) What miracle did God perform to complete the Israelites' victorious exodus from their enemies? (Ex. 14:15–31) _______________________

5) What did the Egyptian warriors shout before they died? (Ex. 14:25)

____

II. Find Jesus in the Lesson

Song of Moses and Song of the Lamb, who is Jesus our Deliverer

In Exodus 15:1–21 Moses led Israel in singing a song of deliverance to the Lord. What an amazing musical experience! There was possibly a million or more voices singing triumphant praise to God, who gave them miraculous victory over their enemies.

The last book of the Bible, Revelation, speaks of earth's final events before transitioning to the new heavens and earth. **In Revelation 15:3 the Song of Moses is sung again. This time it is sung along with the Song of the Lamb, who is Jesus Christ.**

These songs are sung by the delivered saints of God who experience victory over their beastly enemy. The power of their victory comes from faith in Jesus Christ.

✞

I saw before me what seemed to be a crystal sea mixed with fire. And on it stood all the people who had been victorious over the beast and his statue and the number representing his name. They were all holding harps that God had given them.

And they were singing the song of Moses, the servant of God, and the song of the Lamb Rev. 15:2–3

✞

And the Crowd Goes Wild!

III. Closing Thoughts

And the Crowd Goes Wild!

In addition to Moses' song, the women went forth in spontaneous praise dance with tambourines, rhythm and celebration dances.

Miriam, who is Moses' and Aaron's sister, is called a prophetess as she leads this activity. (Exodus 15:20–21)

God is worthy of our spontaneous, exuberant, emotional praise, especially when He does great things in our lives.

The praise we give to God should be greater than the praise of cheering crowds at sports events. Think about it!

Reading Assignment:
Exodus 16:1–19:25

Lesson 6.2

I. Lesson Exercise

God Tests Israel's faithfulness in the Wilderness

Moses led the Israelites to Mt. Sinai (also known as the mountain of God) to worship the Lord, before going to the Promised Land. God had foretold him to take them there in Exodus 3:12.

Review the chart **"Key Events in Israel's Journey from Egypt to Sinai"** to review activity that occurred along the way.

Look at **"The Exodus" map** to follow Israel's journey from their slave home in Egypt (Rameses and Goshen) to the Promised Land of freedom and prosperity in Canaan.

Moses' Father-in-Law's Wise Advice

Moses' father-in-law Jethro brought Moses' wife Zipporah and their two sons back to join Moses now that God had safely delivered Moses and Israel out of the hands of the Egyptians. While with them, Jethro observed Moses' interaction with Israel.

6) Briefly describe the wise advice Jethro gave to Moses. (Ex. 18:24–26) ____

God Officially Introduces Himself to Israel

God planned for Israel to become "God's Covenant people" (specially chosen ones). He would be to them the "Covenant God of Israel." In preparation for Israel agreeing to enter this covenant relationship with God, God reveals (introduces) Himself directly to all the Israelites at Mt. Sinai.

Moses, who has been the middleman between God and Israel, now gave Israel God's instructions on what to do before meeting God.

7) How did the people have to prepare for hearing God at Mt. Sinai:

   a) Wash ______________ (Exodus 19:10–11)

   b) Set ________________ (Exodus 19:12)

   c) Abstain from _________________ (Exodus 19:15)

8) When God came down on top of Mt. Sinai to speak to Moses and the people, briefly describe what happened to the mountain because of God's presence? (Exodus 19:16–19) ________________________

II. Find Jesus in the Lesson: Jesus Our Healer

At Marah, God announces to Israel,

"I am the Lord who heals you"

Exodus 15:26

In Hebrew God is known as "Jehovah-Rapha" (YHWH-Rapha), which is derived from Exodus 15:26 and means "The Lord who heals." In the Old Covenant (Old Testament), Israel had access to YHWH-Rapha by obeying all God's commandments and laws.

Review the chart "Names of God" in Week 5.

Under the New Covenant (New Testament), the Church of God in Jesus Christ has access to YHWH-Rapha by faith in Jesus, who is our Healer, also known as YHWH-Rapha. (1 Peter 2:24)

Review the chart "Jesus and the Names of God" in Week 5.

╬

But he was wounded for our transgressions, he was bruised for our iniquities: the chastisement of our peace was upon him: and with his stripes we are healed.

Isaiah 53:5 KJV

Who his own self bare our sins in his own body on the tree, that we, being dead to sins, should live unto righteousness: by whose stripes ye were healed.

1 Peter 2:24 KJV

III. Closing Thoughts

First Five Books in Old Testament are like "ABC's" of the Bible

The first five books of the Bible are referred to as the books of "Law". Many details from these books will be seen again and again in other Bible books. Therefore, although it may seem tedious now, studying the details in this part of Israel's life will greatly benefit your understanding of future Bible reading.

In general, reading the Bible can be compared to learning to read. First you must learn the ABC's, then words, then sentences. In a similar manner, you will need to be familiar with the first five books to understand later sections of the Bible.

Key Events in Israel's Journey from Egypt to Sinai

On the map "The Exodus," find the "Land of Goshen" where the Israelites ate the Passover meal, sprinkled the lamb's blood on their doorposts, and from which they removed the bones of Joseph to carry with them as they exited Egypt.

Next find the location for the "Crossing at the Red Sea."

Look for key locations of the Israelites' journey after the Red Sea crossing:

- ❑ **At "Marah," Israel begins to complain:**
  - The water at Marah was bitter (Ex. 15:22–23)
  - The people turned against Moses (Ex. 15:24)
  - God had Moses throw a branch in the water to make it drinkable (Ex. 15:25)
  - Israel was tested to see if they would obey all of God's commands (Ex. 15:25–26)
- ❑ **At "Elim" Israel camped by twelve springs of water and seventy palm trees:** (Ex. 15:27)
- ❑ **At the area "between Elim and Mt. Sinai" Israel complains again:**
  - Israelites spoke bitterly against Moses and Aaron (Ex. 16:2)
  - They foolishly said it would have been better if they had died in Egypt (Ex. 16:3)
  - God rained down "manna" from heaven by morning and quail for meat at evening for the Israelites to eat while in the wilderness (Ex. 16:4; 12–14)
  - God gave instructions on gathering food to test Israel's obedience (Ex. 16:4)
- ❑ **At "Rephidim", there is more complaining by the Israelites:**
  - There was no water at Rephidim (Ex. 17:1)
  - People grumbled and complained to Moses (Ex. 17:2)
  - People questioned why Moses brought them to the wilderness to die (Ex. 17:3)
  - Moses struck the rock with his staff and water came pouring out (Ex. 17:6)
  - Moses called the place "Massah" (the place of testing) and "Meribah" (the place of arguing) (Ex. 17:7)

Israel's First Fight!

- ❑ **At Rephidim, Israel had their first fight with Amalekites**
  - Joshua led the Israelites in battle (Ex. 17:9)
  - As long as Moses held staff up with his hands, Israel would win (Ex. 17:11)
  - Aaron and Hur helped Moses keep his hands up when he got tired (Ex. 17:12)
  - Moses told Joshua to write down God's words that He will blot out every trace of Amalek from under heaven (Ex. 17:14)
  - Moses called the altar "The Lord is my Banner"—Jehovah-Nissi (Ex. 17:15)

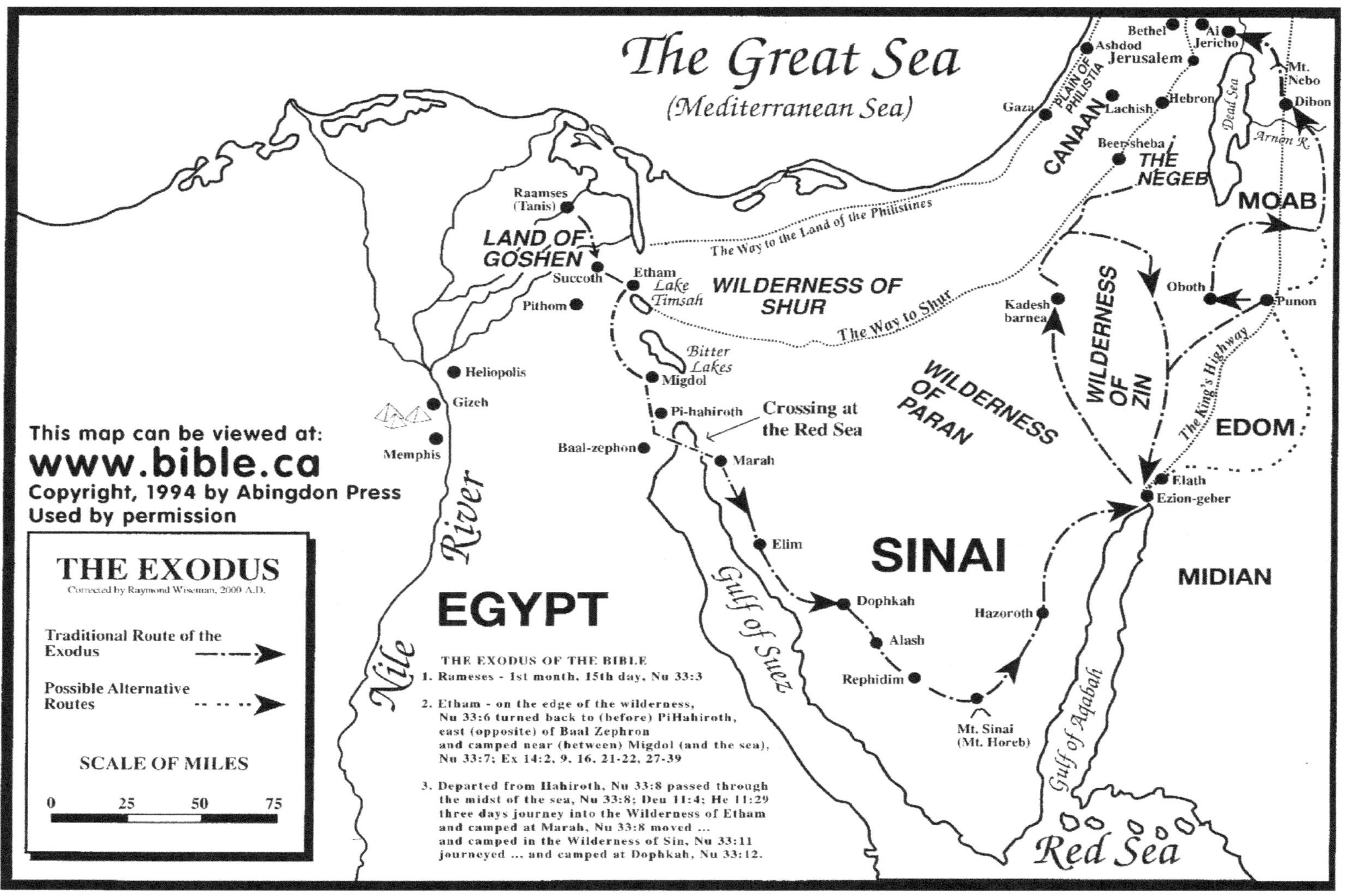
The Great Sea
(Mediterranean Sea)
This map can be viewed at:
www.bible.ca
Copyright, 1994 by Abingdon Press
Used by permission
THE EXODUS
Corrected by Raymond Wiseman, 2000 A.D.
Traditional Route of the Exodus
Possible Alternative Routes
SCALE OF MILES
0 25 50 75
EGYPT
Nile River
Memphis
Gizeh
Heliopolis
LAND OF GOSHEN
Raamses (Tanis)
Pithom
Succoth
Etham
Lake Timsah
Bitter Lakes
Migdol
Pi-hahiroth
Baal-zephon
Crossing at the Red Sea
Marah
Elim
Gulf of Suez
Dophkah
Alash
Rephidim
Mt. Sinai (Mt. Horeb)
Hazoroth
SINAI
WILDERNESS OF SHUR
The Way to the Land of the Philistines
The Way to Shur
WILDERNESS OF PARAN
Kadesh barnea
WILDERNESS OF ZIN
Gaza
PLAIN OF PHILISTIA
CANAAN
Ashdod
Bethel
Jerusalem
Lachish
Beersheba
Hebron
THE NEGEB
Ai
Jericho
Dead Sea
Mt. Nebo
Dibon
Arnon R.
MOAB
Punon
Oboth
EDOM
The King's Highway
Elath
Ezion-geber
MIDIAN
Gulf of Aqabah
Red Sea
THE EXODUS OF THE BIBLE
1. Rameses - 1st month, 15th day, Nu 33:3
2. Etham - on the edge of the wilderness, Nu 33:6 turned back to (before) PiHahiroth, east (opposite) of Baal Zephron and camped near (between) Migdol (and the sea), Nu 33:7; Ex 14:2, 9, 16, 21-22, 27-39
3. Departed from Hahiroth, Nu 33:8 passed through the midst of the sea, Nu 33:8; Deu 11:4; He 11:29 three days journey into the Wilderness of Etham and camped at Marah, Nu 33:8 moved ... and camped in the Wilderness of Sin, Nu 33:11 journeyed ... and camped at Dophkah, Nu 33:12.

Bible Tidbits

❋ God promised to totally wipe out the memory of the Amalekites from under the heavens.

- In Exodus 17: 8–16, we read that the Amalekites chose to go to war against God's newly delivered Israelite people. God, working through Moses' raised staff, empowered the Israelite army—commanded by Joshua—to defeat the Amalekite army. As long as Moses held up his staff, Israel had the advantage.
- Aaron and Hur, who accompanied Moses to the hill-top to watch the battle, helped keep Moses' hands raised once he became tired. As a result Israel won. After the victory, God told Moses to write on a scroll and read aloud to Joshua His judgment on the Amalekites.
- God would erase the memory of Amalek from under heaven. This is because the Amalekites were known for the unprovoked attacking of the weak, sick and helpless Israelites lagging behind, which was evidence of their cruelty and cowardice, and their lack of fear for Israel's God. Since they showed no mercy on Israel, God would show no mercy to them. Deut. 25:17–19.[3]

❋ God becomes known to Israel as "Adonai Nissi—the Lord is my Banner"

- As part of war, those who fight typically identify a banner, flag or rallying cry that represents who or for what they are fighting. In the case of the Israelites' first battle against the Amalekites, God used Moses to reveal Israel's banner.
- "Moses built an altar there and named it Jehovah-Nissi (which means 'The LORD is my banner')." (Exodus 17:15)

❋ God keeps His promise hundreds of years later

- ~ 1900 BC Amalek is born. He is the grandson of Esau, who is the brother of Jacob, the father of the Israelites. (Genesis 36:12)
- ~1400 BC God told Israel to wipe out Amalek. This would take place after God gave Israel rest from their enemies, when they were living in the Promised Land. He told them "do not forget" to do this. (Deut. 25:17–19)
- ~ 1050 BC To fulfill the prophecy, God told Saul to destroy all the Amalekites, including their king, all the people and their cattle. Saul disobeyed God and as a result lost his own kingly position. (1 Samuel 15)
- ~ 1000 BC King David was successful in slaughtering many of the Amalekites. (2 Samuel 1:1)
- ~ 700 BC During King Hezekiah's reign the Amalekites were wiped out. (1 Chronicles 4:41–43)
- ~ 470 BC It is possible that Haman, who plotted to kill all the Jews in the book of Esther, was a descendant of the Amalekites through King Agag. If so, then he and his family were destroyed also. (Esther 3–10)

[3]Appendix C

Lesson 6.3

Reading Assignment:
Exodus 20:1–22:15

I. Lesson Exercise

God Presents the Terms of His Covenant Agreement

God instructs the Israelites on the terms of His covenant agreement. This means He described what He expected the people to do (their partner obligations) to be in covenant relationship with Him. God also described what he would do for Israel (His partner obligations).

If Israel agreed to God's Covenant, they would make a blood covenant commitment. This means...

God's Covenant is a
life-or-death partnership;

It is "life" to keep it and "death" to break it!

The Ten Commandments

The Ten Commandments are first listed in Exodus 20:1–17.

Review them in the chart "The Ten Commandments and You."[4]

The first four commandments describe how to show respect for God, while the remaining six describe how to show respect for people.

The chart includes modern examples of how to keep them.

After giving the first two commandments, God made it very clear in Exodus 20:5,

I, the LORD your God, am a jealous God
who will not share your affection with any other god!

God will:

- Punish those who hate Him down through their descendants, to the third and even to the fourth generation. (Ex. 20:5)
- Lavish His love on those who love Him to a thousand generations. (Ex. 20:6)

The fourth commandment tells Israel to keep the Sabbath day holy (Ex. 20:8).

- God's reason for making the Sabbath a rest day was because God created the whole world in six days. On the seventh day He rested, so God blessed the seventh day and set it aside as a holy day of rest for all (Ex. 20:11, Gen. 2:3).

God made a promise to those who keep the fifth command, "Honor your father and mother."

They will live long and prosper in the Promised Land! (cf. Eph. 6:3)

[4]Appendix C

The Ten Commandments and You

	Commandment	Bible Example	Modern Example
RESPECT FOR GOD You shall love the Lord your God with all your heart.	1. You shall have no other Gods before me.	The Exodus Exodus 34:11-14	Put God first! Today a "god" may be anything a person allows to rule his daily life: deities of other religions, superstitions, horoscopes, bad habits or addictions, friends, heroes, desire for money, fame or power.
	2. You shall not make for yourself an idol.	Golden Calf Exodus 32:1-8	Put your faith in God only. Worshipping or serving any man-made thing that is thought to have supernatural power: statues of gods of other religions, crystals, pictures, jewelry, amulets, charms, rabbit's foot, or objects thought to have power or "good luck."
	3. You shall not misuse the name of the LORD your God.	Don't use God's name in a false oath. Lev. 19:12	Treat God's name with respect. Don't use God's name lightly in making promises or in any other way. This is the name that raised people from the dead, caused blind to see, and made the paralyzed to walk. It is a powerful name and needs to be used with the right attitude.
	4. Remember the Sabbath day by keeping it holy.	God provides enough on the sixth day for the seventh. Exodus 16:23-30	In Jesus' time, very religious people obeyed this commandment by refusing to do any kind of work—even to the point of not helping people in need. Jesus said that Sabbath was made for man's benefit. People should rest from their normal work, but also be available to do good to others. Today Christians set aside the day to worship God and meet with other Christians.
RESPECT FOR PEOPLE	5. Honor your father and your mother so that you may live long in the land the LORD your God is giving you.	Jesus was obedient to Mary and Joseph. Luke 2:51	Treat your parents with respect no matter what. Your parents have made many sacrifices to raise you. They have changed diapers, lost sleep, bought food, toys and clothes, paid doctor bills and changed their schedules to help you. Even if you don't get along with your parents, they deserve your gratitude. If your parents ask you to do something wrong, respectfully tell them no and suggest a good alternative that they might consider.
	6. You shall not murder.	Each person is made in God's image. Genesis 9:6	Personal revenge belongs to God. God will make things right in the end. God has set up governments and rules to deal with murders. Life and death are in God's hands. Examples: no revenge killing, murder, suicide, abortion or euthanasia (mercy killing). Jesus said we should love our enemies and pray for them.
	7. You shall not commit adultery.	Joseph runs from temptation. Genesis 39:1-13	Stay true to your husband or wife. Marriage vows made before God should be kept in spite of difficulties. Sex only within marriage relationship. No rape or incest. Avoid sexual temptation: provocative videos, movies, television, magazines, computer games or programs, pictures and books. Jesus said that even thinking about another person lustfully is wrong.
	8. You shall not steal.	Achan steals. Joshua 6:17-19 Joshua 7:1-5	Respect other's possessions. Don't take things that don't belong to you. Examples: shoplifting (taking candy, toys, or anything from a store), taking money or valuables from others, cheating on tests and taxes, photocopying music or any printed material without permission.
	9. You shall not bear false witness against your neighbor.	Honesty toward neighbors. Leviticus 19:13	Be trustworthy. Don't falsely accuse or blame someone else. Don't lie about them or to them. Don't gossip. Don't lie to God and to yourself by believing you are perfect. Keep your promises.
	10. You shall not covet...anything that belongs to your neighbor.	Life is more than possessions. Eccl. 5:9-18; 6:12	Be content with what you have. Don't long for things that belong to others. Example: their house, car, job, bike, toys, jewelry, clothing, or friends. Ask God to give you what you need. He promises that He will take care of your needs! Seek wisdom and good character, not riches.

After God instructed Moses on the Ten Commandments, He then began to give Moses other commandments for Israel.

- **Commands for Proper Use of Altars**

  Israel was not to build an altar on top of steps. This is so they would avoid anyone looking under the altar worker's clothing and seeing their nakedness. (Ex. 20:26)

- **Commands for Fair Treatment of Slaves**

  When a slave's ear was pierced, it meant he was a slave permanently. (Ex. 21:21:6)

- **Commands for Cases of Personal Injury**

  Exodus 21:24 in KJV says, "Eye for eye, tooth for tooth, hand for hand, foot for foot." This means if one person caused another person to lose an eye, then the person who caused the injury would also have to lose an eye, etc.

- **Commands for Protection of Property**

  Interestingly, for God's covenant people, if people could not figure out who a thief was, God Himself would determine and reveal the thief. (Ex. 22:7–9)

II. Find Jesus in the Lesson

Jesus and the Ten Commandments

Jesus teaches us that keeping the Ten Commandments is not enough to inherit eternal life, but it is still the right way for Christians to live.

Consider Jesus' words from Matthew 19:16–21.

The Rich Young Man

The Man:	**Someone came to Jesus with this question: "Teacher, what good things must I do to have eternal life?"**
Jesus:	**"Why ask me about what is good?" Jesus replied. "Only God is good.**
	But to answer your question, you can receive eternal life if you keep the commandments."
The Man:	**"Which ones?" the man asked.**
Jesus:	**And Jesus replied: "Do not murder. Do not commit adultery. Do not steal. Do not testify falsely. Honor your father and mother.**
	Love your neighbor as yourself."
The Man:	**"I've obeyed all these commandments," the young man replied. "What else must I do?"**
Jesus:	**Jesus told him, "If you want to be perfect, go and sell all you have and give the money to the poor, and you will have treasure in heaven.**
	Then come, follow me."

III. Closing Thoughts

Details Are Coming

God's terms of the covenant agreement are presented in high-level overview in the Ten Commandments. The total list of over 600 commandments and laws will be presented in detail in Leviticus.

Reading Assignment:
Exodus 22:16–24:18

Lesson 6.4

I. Lesson Exercise

God's Terms of Covenant Agreement Continued: What Israel Must Do

God continues to give the detailed commandments and laws He expects Israel to follow because of their covenant relationship with Him. He describes their social responsibility and the type of just dealings they should have with fellow Israelites, strangers and foreigners. God also clarifies Israel's relationship with Him.

- Redeem firstborn sons by making necessary payment (Ex. 22:29)
- God called Israel ***"my own holy people"*** (Ex. 22:31)
- Every man in Israel was required to keep three festivals each year
  - **Festival of Unleavened Bread:** eat bread without yeast for seven days (Ex 23:15)
  - **Festival of Harvest:** bring God the first crops of the harvest (Ex. 23:16)
  - **Festival of the Final Harvest:** celebrated at end of harvest season (Ex. 23:16)

God's Covenant Agreement terms continued: What God Will Do

God's awesome, powerful, miracle-working presence would be with His covenant people Israel. He describes in overall terms the benefits of having His presence.

- God's angel will go before Israel to lead them safely to Promised Land (Ex. 23:20)
- God will be an enemy to Israel's enemies, opposing all who oppose them (Ex. 23:22)
- If Israel served only God, He will bless their food and water, keep them healthy, they would have no problems with childbirth; and they would live long, full lives (Ex. 23:25–26)
- God will send his terror on the people whose lands they would invade (Ex. 23:27)
- God will send hornets to drive the people out of Israel's Promised Land (Ex. 23:28)
- God would keep wild animals under control so as not to harm them (Ex. 23:29)

Israel Accepts God's Covenant

After Moses announced to the Israelites all the terms of God's covenant agreement, with all its teachings and regulations, then the Israelites responded,

> ***"We will do everything the Lord has told us to do." (Ex. 24:3)***

After Israel's positive response, it was time for the blood covenant commitment ceremony. Moses wrote all God's instructions down for future teaching.

Israel Accepts God's Covenant Continued: Blood Confirmation

- Moses read the Book of the Covenant to the people with God's instructions in it (Ex. 24:7)
- Moses directed young men to offer Burnt and Peace offerings to God (Ex. 24:5)
- Moses sprinkled one half of the blood against the altar (Ex. 24:6)
- Moses sprinkled the other half of the blood over the people, after he read the book to the people, and they repeated their commitment to do everything God had commanded (Ex. 24:7–8)
- The blood confirmed the covenant God made with Israel (Ex. 24:8)

Covenant Meal

The first part of making the Covenant Agreement official was making it a Blood Covenant, which is described above.

The next part of the ceremony involved sharing the Covenant Meal, which is described below.

- Aaron, Aaron's sons Nadab and Abihu, and seventy leaders of Israel represented all of Israel before God. These men went into the mountain with Moses to eat the covenant meal with God. (Ex. 24:1, 9)
- In the mountain, the leaders saw God, the God of Israel. They shared a meal together in God's presence. (Ex. 24:11)
- After the meal was over, God told Moses to come up closer to Him in the mountain. God planned to give Moses the tablets of stone with His commands and more instructions. (Ex. 24:12)
- Moses stayed in the mountain with God for forty days and forty nights.

9) Who did these leaders see in the mountain? (Ex. 24:10) __________

<u>II. Find Jesus in the Lesson and III. Closing Thoughts</u>

Jesus and the Three Yearly Covenant Festivals

In Jesus' lifetime, he attended the yearly festivals God commanded all the males of Israel to attend. One example of Jesus' participation is found in a story from when he was twelve years old.

Jesus attended the Passover festival in Jerusalem, which is what the Festival of Unleavened Bread was also called. Read Luke 2:41–52.

Here is New Testament insight on Jesus' participation in the festivals.

Three Pilgrimage Festivals: All Males Required to Celebrate in Jerusalem				
Name	**Hebrew Name**	**Alternate Name**	**Time of Year**	**Jesus and the Festival in the New Testament**
Passover	Pesach	Unleavened Bread (combined with Passover + Unleavened Bread + Firstfruits)	<u>Spring</u> Hebrew Calendar: Nisan 14 (or 14–21) Gregorian Calendar: March or April	Luke 2:41–52
Weeks	Shavuot	Harvest or Pentecost or Latter Firstfruits	<u>Late Spring or Early Summer</u> Occurs 50 days after Passover Hebrew Calendar: Sivan 6 Gregorian Calendar: May or June	Acts 2
Booths	Sukkot	Tabernacles or Tents (combined with Jewish New Year + Day of Atonement + Booths)	<u>Fall</u> Hebrew Calendar: Tishri 15–21 (or 1–21) Gregorian Calendar: September or October	John 7

Reading Assignment:
Exodus 25:1–28:43

Lesson 6.5

I. Lesson Exercise

Moses Receives God's Plans for the Tabernacle

"I want the people of Israel to build me a sacred residence where I can live among them. You must make this Tabernacle and its furnishings exactly according to the plans I will show you. Exodus 25:8–9

God gives Moses detailed instruction on:

- How to build the Tabernacle, which will be the place where God lives among Israel
- How to make clothing for the Priests, who will lead Israel in Tabernacle worship

God repeatedly tells Moses,

Be sure that you make everything according to the pattern I have shown you here on the mountain. Exodus 25:40

Today's lesson introduces the following pieces of Tabernacle design:

- **Ark of the Covenant and Mercy Seat** (= sacred chest and cover)—Ex. 25:10–22
- **Table of Showbread** (= Table of special Bread of the Presence)—Ex. 25:23–30
- **Golden Lampstand** (= lampstand of pure, hammered gold)—Ex. 25:31–40; Ex. 27:20–21
- **Tabernacle** (= structure including cloth coverings and framework)—Ex. 26:1–30
- **Veil** (= special curtain to separate Holy Place and Most Holy Place)—Ex. 26:31–33
- **Entrance to Tabernacle** (= embroidered curtain)—Ex. 26:36–37)
- **Brazen Altar** (= Altar of Burnt Offering)—Ex. 27:1–8
- **Tabernacle Courtyard** (= courtyard enclosed with the curtains)—Ex. 27:9–15
- **Courtyard Entrance** (= embroidered curtains)—Ex. 27:16–19

... And introduces the clothing for the priests, which were the garments of the High Priest Aaron and his sons:

- **Ephod**—Ex. 28:6–14
- **Breastpiece** (= Chestpiece)—Ex. 28:15–30
- **Gold cords with stones connect Ephod and Breastpiece**—Ex. 28:22–28
- **Robe**—Ex 28:31–-35
- **Turban** (= Mitre or Headdress) with engraved gold medallion—Ex. 28:36–38
- **Tunic** (= fine linen embroidered tunic)—Ex 28:39
- **Girdle** (= Sash)—Ex 28:39

II. Find Jesus in the Lesson and III. Closing Thoughts

Jesus in the Tabernacle Design

Review the charts on **"Shadows of the Messiah in the Tabernacle."**

Christians believe the Messiah is Jesus, who is the Christ, God's Anointed deliverer for Israel and all humankind.

The Tabernacle Design along with the priests' garments and functions in the Tabernacle worship are all believed to point to Messiah.

Another excellent reference to how the Tabernacle and the priestly garments portrays Jesus as Messiah is the pamphlet and study material for **"The Tabernacle"** published by the Rose Publishing, Inc.[5] This material is easy to understand and includes helpful pictures with detailed descriptions.

[5]Appendix C

SHADOWS OF MESSIAH IN THE TABERNACLE IN THE OLD COVENANT[6]

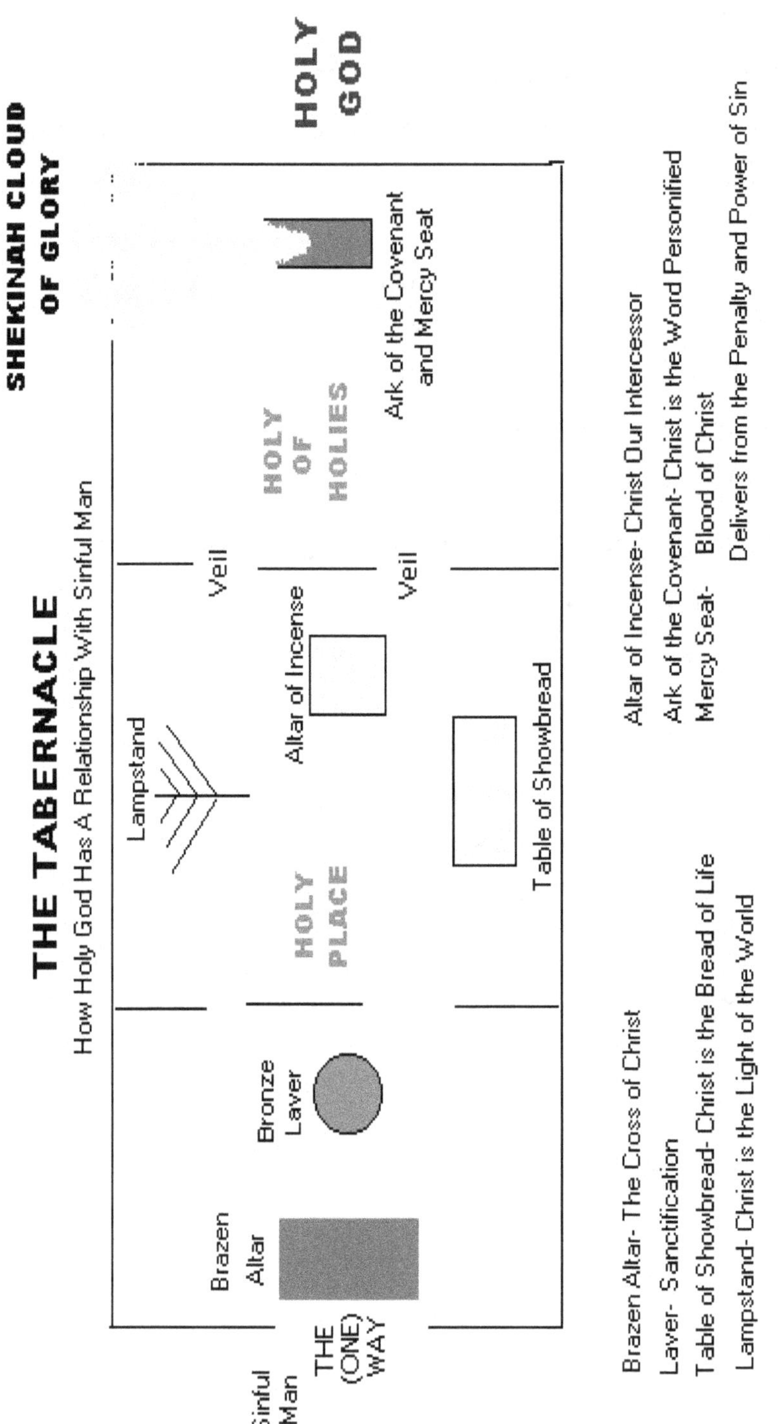

Reference[6]: **"Shadows of Messiah in the Tabernacle in the Old Covenant"** is reprinted by permission of Bruce Hart of Precept Austin (preceptaustin.org, Covenant: Abrahamic vs Mosaic)

Shadows of the Messiah in the Tabernacle in the Old Covenant – Scriptures and Notes[6]

Outer Court

The (ONE) Way

(Only one entrance way for sinful man; Door always faced east)

Jesus declared "I am the way, the truth, the life and no one comes to the Father but through Me." John 14:6

"I am the door; if anyone enters through me, he shall be saved, and shall go in and out, and find pasture." John 10:9

Brazen Altar

(The place where **SACRIFICE** of the lamb (or other animal) took place to bring about reconciliation for sin and to facilitate consecration)

(It foreshadowed the **reconciliation** one can have through the blood of the eternal covenant in Jesus Christ. Heb. 2:17)

Jesus is the sacrificial Lamb of God Who "takes away the sin of the world". (John 1:29)

Just as priests could not come before the LORD without a sacrifice, we too must receive by faith the **once for all sacrifice of Jesus Christ.** (Heb. 10:10)

Bronze Laver

(Priests would wash daily before entering Holy place)

Jesus is the Word and we are cleansed through Him. (John 15:3, Eph. 5:26)

Holy Place

Lampstand

(Seven branched candlestick on the south side of the Holy Place)

Jesus is the Light of the world
(John 1:4, John 8:12)

Altar of Incense

(It stood directly in front of the Ark of the Covenant in the Holy of Holies)

(It was to burn perpetually and symbolized prayer)

Jesus ever lives to continually make intercession in the true Tabernacle in Heaven (Heb. 7:25, Rom. 8:34)

Table of Showbread

(On the north side of the Holy place)

Jesus is the Bread of Life — Living Bread (John 6:48, 51)

The Veil

(The only entrance into the Holy of holies, which symbolized the Throne of God)

Jesus is the rent veil, His torn flesh giving us access to God so that now believers may boldly approach the Throne of Grace

(Matt. 27:50–51; Heb. 10:19–22; Heb. 4:14–16)

Holy of Holies

Shekinah Cloud of Glory

(Shekinah literally means "that which dwells". It was used in Jewish writings to describe the "glory cloud" that centered upon the mercy-seat, symbolizing the presence of God among His people.)

John beheld Jesus' glory, the Word made flesh as He dwelt or "tabernacled" among men. (John 1:14)

Ark of the Covenant

(The Ark of the Covenant contained the tablets of stone, a pot of manna, and Aaron's rod that budded. It was covered by the Mercy Seat)

Mercy Seat

(The Mercy Seat was a picture of the **propitiation** of God's anger. Jesus took the punishment for our sins and in so doing satisfied (propitiated) God's anger against all who place their faith in Him.)

Believers are in essence "covered by the blood of Christ" and can now meet with God at His Throne any time, any day. This is in contrast to the Jewish High Priest who could only go into God's presence once per year on the **Day of Atonement**. Rom. 3:25

The High Priest was meeting with Jehovah Who was also Jesus because He is the "I Am" and He and His Father are One. (John 8:58, John 10:30)

[6]Appendix C

Reading Assignment:
Exodus 29:1–31:18

Lesson 6.6

I. Lesson Exercise

God Continues Giving Moses Instructions Regarding the Priests and Furniture for the Tabernacle

Aaron and his sons will be ordained to be the High Priests for the nation of Israel. Their special duties will be described in detail in the book of Leviticus. God instructs Moses on the ceremony for dedicating Aaron and his sons to do this task.

10) What are the names of Aaron's four sons who will be ordained with Aaron? (Ex. 28:1) ________________, ________________,

____________________, ___________________

Review how a ram's blood and anointing oil were applied. (Ex. 29:19-21)

God's remaining instructions: Tabernacle furniture (see charts) and instructions today are:

- Altar of Incense (= Incense Altar)—Ex. 30:1–10
- Laver of Brass (= Bronze Laver or Washbasin)—Ex. 30:17–21
- Anointing Oil (God's holy anointing oil for furniture and people)—Ex. 30:22–33
- Incense (God's pure and holy incense only used in Tabernacle)—Ex. 30:34–38
- Sabbath Day (= holy day of worship)—Ex. 31:12–17

11) When God finished speaking to Moses on Mt. Sinai, what did He give Moses that was written by the finger of God? (Ex. 31:18)

____

Offerings are needed to build and maintain the Tabernacle

In yesterday's lesson, God told Moses to ask the Israelites to bring him specific types of offerings to use in building the Tabernacle and making the garments.

In today's lesson, God tells Moses the way to collect offerings from the people on a regular basis in order to pay for the upkeep of the Tabernacle over the years.

12) What was the age of people required to pay the census offering to the Lord? (Ex. 30:11,14) ______________________

13) How much was the census payment to be? (Ex. 30:13) ____________

Skilled people are needed to make the Tabernacle and Garments

God gave Moses the vision for the pattern of the work, but God did not intend Moses to do all the work. He showed Moses the skilled craftsmen who could build everything according to the pattern God gave to Moses.

14) Who were the two skilled craftsmen to oversee all the work to be performed?

    a) (Ex. 31:1) ____________________________

    b) (Ex. 31:6) ____________________________

II. Find Jesus in the Lesson and III. Closing Thoughts

Jesus Our Anointed Priest

Hebrews 5:1–5 explains that the high priest is chosen and anointed by God to represent people before Him.

It also explains that God chose:

- **Aaron to be High Priest for Israel under the Old Covenant**
- **Jesus to be our High Priest under the New Covenant**

✞

When Moses came down the mountain
carrying the stone tablets,
he wasn't aware that his face glowed
because he had spoken to the LORD face to face.
And when Aaron and the people of Israel
saw the radiance of Moses' face,
they were afraid to come near him.
Exodus 34:29–30

Reading Assignment:
Exodus 32:1–34:35

Lesson 6.7

I. Lesson Exercise

Israel Breaks the Covenant

God delivered Israel from Egyptian bondage after performing ten mighty acts of miracles and judgment on the Egyptian people.

When the great Egyptian army pursued Israel to the Red Sea, God let the angelic pillar of cloud be darkness to the Egyptians, stopping them in their tracks, while it was a bright light for Israel, who walked safely along the floor of the Red Sea.

In a showy display of God's miraculous power, the waters stood like tall walls on either side of the Israelites as they passed by on the ground of the Red Sea's water bed.

Then the waters collapsed to drown all of the Egyptian warriors and horses that pursued after the Israelites.

Within two months after their departure from Egypt, God led approximately two million Israelites—men, women and children—safely through the desert wilderness.

He provided drink, food, and healing for everyone, in spite of their constant complaints and foolish statements.

Finally, God dramatically displayed who He was on top of Mt. Sinai, where He spoke so all Israel could hear Him.

Israel accepted God's covenant. With this acceptance, God became the God of Israel and Israel became God's chosen people.

In today's lesson, Moses, who has wisely represented God to the people and the people to God, has been at the top of Sinai's mountain for some time.

Moses is getting detailed instructions from God, including direction for the next phase of Israel's Covenant relationship activity. The next phase will include establishing their Tabernacle worship.

Sadly, in spite of all that God has done, Israel quickly breaks their Covenant Agreement with God.

They did this because Moses, who has been serving as the middleman between God and the people, had stayed in the mountain a long time.

Israel lost focus as they entertained the thought that Moses might be dead.

With Moses gone so long, the people wanted a leader and gods they could see right now!

- At the request of the complaining people, Aaron made a "golden calf" from the gold earrings he told the people to bring him. The people proclaimed the golden calf was the god that brought Israel out of Egypt. (Ex. 32:3–4)
- The people sacrificed burnt and peace offerings to the golden calf, and celebrated with feasting, drinking, and indulging in ungodly actions. (Ex. 32:5–6)
- Because of their great sin against Him, God wanted to destroy all the Israelites and begin a new great nation from the offspring of Moses. (Ex. 32:9–10)

Moses Intercedes for Israel

Moses was very wise in the way he interceded for Israel when God was angry enough to destroy them all. "Interceding" means to ask God's mercy for someone else. Moses reminded God of two very important things which turned God's anger.

- Moses told God that the Egyptians would say He tricked the Israelites to come out to the wilderness just so He could kill them all. (Ex. 32:12)
- Moses reminded God of His covenant with Abraham, Isaac, and Jacob. (Ex. 32:13)

Moses Gets Israel Back on the Right Path

- When Moses saw the sinful actions of the Israelites as he was coming out of the mountain, he threw the stone tablets at the base of Mt. Sinai. (Ex. 32:19)
- After the golden calf was melted in the fire *(which was possibly a fire created by the broken tablets at the bottom of the mountain)*, Moses took the cooled metal, ground it into powder, and made the people drink it. (Ex. 32:20)
- When Moses asked all those on the Lord's side to stand by him, the Levites all came. Then they killed the men who chose not to be on the Lord's side. For their actions, the Levites were ordained by God for his special service. (Ex. 32:25–29)
- Next, the Lord sent a great plague on the sinful people. (Ex. 32:35)

Moses kept pleading Israel's case before God. He would not let God give up on them. In fact, Moses kept working on God until God agreed to personally lead the people for the rest of their journey to Promised Land.

- God called Moses His friend. (Ex. 33:17)
- Moses asked God to show him His (God's) Glory. (Ex. 33:18)
- God told Moses he could not look directly at God's face and live. (Ex. 33:20)

God Remakes the Covenant Agreement with Israel

After Moses' intercessory prayer to God for Israel, combined with Israel's change of actions, God told Moses to cut two more stone tablets similar to the ones God had given him before. He also invited Moses back into the mountain, where God once again described the terms of the covenant agreement.

15) How long was Moses in the mountain this time? (Ex. 34:28) ______

16) What did God write on the stone tablets? (Ex. 34:28) ____________

<u>II. Find Jesus in the Lesson and III. Closing Thoughts</u>

Jesus, Our Intercessor

After making a blood covenant with God (Ex. 24: 1–8)**, the Israelites messed up big time.** They broke the first 2 of the Ten Commandments. In keeping with the punishment for breaking the covenant, God had the right to destroy Israel. But Moses interceded, and God forgave them.

Similarly, after people commit their lives to Christ, any sin they commit deserves to be punished by death. But Romans 8:34 explains how Jesus, who intercedes for believers, helps us to get back right with God when we sin. We just need to ask Jesus to help us, and then follow His instructions as revealed in our hearts by the Holy Spirit of God.

Week 7

Featured Books:

Complete **Exodus**, a few passages from **Numbers**, **Leviticus**

Contents:

Peek at the Week

Lesson	Key Events	Find Jesus
7.1	Israel's Skilled Craftsman Build Tabernacle	Jesus in the Tabernacle Materials
7.2	Israel's Skilled Workers Make Priests Garments	Jesus in the Tabernacle Furniture
7.3	God's Glory Fills the Tabernacle Moses Sets Up	Jesus IS Tabernacle of God's Glory
7.4	Tabernacle Dedication Offerings	Jesus' Blood, More Precious than Silver and Gold
7.5	Levite Priests Dedicated for Tabernacle service	Jesus in the Sacrificial Offerings
7.6	Procedures for Sacrificial Offerings	Jesus in the Sacrificial Offerings
7.7	High Priests Ordination Service: Aaron	Jesus our High Priest

Chronological Notes

* Timetable	Key Events
During the 1st year after Exit from Egypt 1446 (or 1280) BC	Israel organized into a Covenant nation (chosen people) with laws, priests, worship tabernacle, God's presence - Builds the Tabernacle - Makes Tabernacle Priests clothing
At the beginning of the 2nd Year after Exodus 1445 (or 1279) BC	- Moses erects the Tabernacle and God's glory fills it - Israel's dedication celebration for the Tabernacle - Israel dedicates the Levi Priests - Moses dedicates and anoints High Priests: Aaron and sons - Israel celebrates the Passover Feast - Israel learns the Holy laws for Priests and People - Israel leaves wilderness of Sinai (Numbers 10:11) - Israelites from Egypt should have entered Promised Land - Unbelieving Israelites begin to wander in wilderness
40 Years after Exit 1405 (or 1239) B.C.	- Unbelieving Israelites from Egypt die in wilderness - Second generation Israel enters Promised Land

**All dates are approximate...*

Reading Assignment:
Exodus 35:1–36:38

Lesson 7.1

I. Lesson Exercise: Sabbath Rest

Moses told the Israelites again to set aside the seventh day of the week as a holy day of total rest before God. No work was to be done. It was a day for worship and fellowship. What a balanced lifestyle God directs for His people to live!

Giving to Support God's Vision—Gifts for the Tabernacle

From the Tabernacle construction story, let us consider lessons we can learn on how the vision God gives His leaders are fulfilled. Moses had the vision with the exact pattern for the Tabernacle (Sacred Tent of Worship) and for making the priests' garments. God intended the people to work with Moses. Moses told the people of God's invitational command to bring special offerings.

The people of God were to:

- Give purposefully — For building Tabernacle; making priests' garments
- Give specific things — For building plans/designs to God's pattern
- Give specific service — For implementing God's plans
- Give willingly — For God loves a cheerful giver

Plans were given by God in detail, but the people had to work the plans.
Provisions were given by God; but provided through willing people.

Finally, God prepared workers whom He anointed with his Holy Spirit, giving them the wisdom, intelligence and skill to do and lead all the work to be done.

> Bezalel was the leader; Oholiab was his assistant.
> All others worked under their leadership.

II. Find Jesus in the Lesson: and III. Closing Thoughts

Jesus in the Tabernacle Materials

Then he [Jesus] said,
"When I was with you before, I told you that everything written about me by Moses and the prophets and in the Psalms must all come true."
Luke 24:44

Jesus explained that in the Old Testament, including in the books of the covenant written by Moses, the scriptures gave insight to Jesus Christ's earthly ministry (They also give insight on Jesus second coming, too.)

The Tabernacle of Moses is filled with many symbols of Jesus Christ's ministry. Studying all of them would take a long time.

At the end of this week's daily study pages are a set of charts that describe some of the connection between Jesus and the Tabernacle of Moses.

The section immediately following this week's daily study pages is, "Jesus in the Tabernacle Reference Material." Within that section review:

- 🕮 **Jesus in the Tabernacle—Introduction**
- 🕮 **Table 1. Jesus in the Tabernacle—Materials**

Reading Assignment:
Exodus 37:1–39:31

Lesson 7.2

I. Lesson Exercise and II. Find Jesus in the Lesson

On Purpose, For Purpose

In Exodus 25–30, God gave Moses detailed instructions on how to build the Tabernacle of Worship, prepare the priests' garments and materials.

In Exodus 35, we see the people's overwhelming positive response to providing the raw materials for all.

In Exodus 36 and in today's lesson, the skilled craftsmen whom God chose to bring the entire vision together begin their work. God gave them special wisdom to make everything just as Moses had envisioned it.

Many New Testament scriptures reference Old Testament worship practices in presenting the new covenant message.

> This is because the physical structure of the Tabernacle, every aspect of the priesthood, and the entire Tabernacle worship experience represented spiritual principles.

Every detail had to be followed exactly as God gave it, because God gave them on purpose, for a purpose.

> One purpose was to establish Israel in their covenant relationship with God. It was also to prepare for the new covenant that was to come. Almost 1500 years after worship in the Tabernacle of Moses began, the New Testament scriptures reveal the new covenant that was established in the person and ministry of Jesus Christ, the Messiah.

In several charts to follow, some of these spiritual meanings and Messianic symbolisms are presented. For a more detailed study, review the references associated with each chart.

Following this week's study pages, there is a special section entitled **"Jesus in the Tabernacle Reference Material."** For today's lesson exercise, review **"Table 2. Jesus in the Tabernacle—Furniture."**

III. Closing Thoughts

Holy Anointing Oil and Fragrant Incense

Then he *[Bezalel]* **made the sacred anointing oil and the fragrant incense, using the techniques of a skilled incense maker. Ex. 37:29**

God gave Moses detailed instructions on the ingredients, formula and use of the holy anointing oil in Exodus 30:22–33, and the fragrant incense in Exodus 30:34–38.

> In today's lesson, the skilled craftsman Bezalel is seen functioning as a skilled alchemist or perfumer, as he prepares the oil and incense precisely as God intended.

Review the following charts describing some of the spiritual meanings and Messianic symbolism in the "Holy Anointing Oil" and "Fragrant Incense."

Holy Anointing Oil[1]
Exodus 30:22–33; 40:9–15; Psalm 133

Ingredients—Four Spices Mixed in Pure Olive oil

- **Spice #1: Pure Myrrh**
  - Spiritual symbolism—"Bitter" or "Suffering"
  - Background—Myrrh is a bitter plant, but sweetness is obtained after it is bruised. It was used as a perfume (Song of Sol. 1:13), purification (Esther 2:12), as a medicine for deadening pain (Mark 15:23), and for preparing the dead for burial (John 19:39-40).
  - Messianic symbolism—Isaiah 53:3–5, 1 Peter 2:21–24
- **Spice #2: Sweet Cinnamon**
  - Spiritual symbolism—"Sweet Smelling Savor"
  - Background—Cinnamon comes from the bark of a tree and has a warm, sweet, pleasing, and peculiar aroma (Song of Sol. 4:14). It is used for flavoring as it improves the flavor of bitter substances. It is also used as a medicine, and it is a stimulant. No doubt the sweet fragrance helped to counter-act the stink of the butchering, burning and cooking of the sacrificial animal offerings.
  - Messianic symbolism—Ephesians 5:2
- **Spice #3: Sweet Calamus**
  - Spiritual symbolism— "Stand Upright" or "Persevering in Righteousness and Truth"
  - Background—Calamus is a fragrant, sweet cane or reed whose root was highly prized as a spice (Song of Solomon 4:14, Isaiah 43:24, Jeremiah 6:20). The more the bark is beaten the sweeter its fragrance. The fragrance was obtained by crushing the plant. It usually grew in miry soil (hostile-like environment), growing up erect and fragrantly scenting the air.
  - Messianic symbolism—John 18:33–37
- **Spice #4: Cassia**
  - Spiritual symbolism— "Submission to and Worship of God" and "Victory"
  - Background—Cassia is from a plant family similar to cinnamon. But it comes from the bark of a shrub. It grows in high altitudes, flourishing where other plants could not grow. Some Bible scholars explain the root word means "to bowing down" or "shriveled" (Gen. 24:26, 1 Sam. 24:8). It was used for flavoring. It was also used as a bitter medicine, but one which purges that it may heal.
  - Messianic symbolism—Psalm 45:1–8 and Phil. 2:5–11

[1]Appendix C

Holy Anointing Oil[1]
Exodus 30:22–33; 40:9–15; Psalm 133

- **Mixing Vehicle: Pure Olive Oil**
  - Possible Spiritual symbolism— "Holy Spirit"
  - Background—Olive oil was produced by beating the trees with sticks to knock the olives off, and then bruising, crushing, and beating the olives until the pure beaten oil was produced. It served as the liquid vehicle in which all the holy anointing oil's ingredients were blended. The spices were evenly diffused in the oil, pervading all and uniting all. The spices gave fragrance to the olive oil with their combination of bitter and sweet properties used to produce their blended aroma.
  - Messianic symbolism—Isaiah 61:1–3; Luke 4:14–21, Acts 10:38; Psalm 45: 6–7; Hebrews 1: 8–9

📖 **Purpose**

- **It was used to set apart the objects it was poured or sprinkled on for sacred use.** (Exodus 30:26–31, 40:9, Psalm 133)
  - Anoint the Tabernacle
  - Anoint all the Tabernacle furniture
  - Consecrate the priests
- It was used to purify, consecrate and make holy the things or persons upon which it was placed.

📖 **Warnings—Exodus 30:32–33**

- **The Anointing Oil was holy, and it was to be treated in a holy manner. It was not to be used or blended in any other way than God instructed, or the offender would be cut off.**
  - It was not to be poured on plain flesh (only poured on the head)
  - It was not to be mixed for the priest's own use or for non-holy purposes or mixed with a different composition
  - It was not to be poured on strangers

"...This will always be my holy anointing oil... It is holy, and you must treat it as holy."
Ex. 30:31–32

[1]Appendix C

Fragrant Incense[2]

(Also known as "Sweet Incense" or "Sacred Perfume")

Exodus 30:34–38; Leviticus 16:12–13; Psalm 141:2

- **Ingredients— three kinds of powdered sweet spices mixed with pure frankincense, all in equal quantities**
  - Sweet spices—resin droplets, mollusk shell, and galbanum.
    - **Stacte (resin droplets)**
      - An aromatic gum that falls in drops
      - The root of the original Hebrew word means "to ooze," or "to distill gradually" or "fall in drops." This meaning is comparable to the idea of the clouds dropping water as in Judges 5:4 and the heavens dropping at the presence of God as in Psalm 68:8.
    - **Onycha (mollusk shell)**
      - An aromatic shell of a mollusk (e.g. snails, clams, oysters), which when burned emits a pleasant odor.
      - The root of the original Hebrew word means "to roar" or "fierce lion."
    - **Galbanum**
      - An odorous gum; the sap from a broken shrub.
      - The root of the original Hebrew word means "to be fat" or "the richest or choice part."
  - **Pure Frankincense**
    - A resin from the bark of a tree that was pierced and left so the sap could run. As the resin is left to dry, white dust forms on the drops of the frankincense.
    - The root of the original Hebrew word means "white" or "whiteness."
  - **Fragrant Smoke**
    - The sweet incense consisted of aromatic gums and spices that produced a fragrant smoke when they were burned.
    - The High Priest carried the golden censer with Him into the Holy of Holies on the Day of Atonement. (Lev.16:12–13)
      - The censer was full of burning coals of fire taken from the altar where the animals were sacrificed.
      - Once he went behind the veil, the priest put the incense upon the fire before the Lord.
      - Then the cloud of the incense covered the mercy seat.

[2]Appendix C

Fragant Incense[2]

(Also known as "Sweet Incense" or "Sacred Perfume")

Exodus 30:34–38; Leviticus 16:12–13; Psalm 141:2

📖 **Purpose**

- **Clouds of incense symbolized the glory of God** that is present as we worship Him (Exodus 19:6; 30: 7– 8).
- **Incense represents the rising of our prayers to God** (Ex. 30:7–8; Lev. 16:12–13; Psalm 141:2, Luke 1:10, Hebrews 9:4; Revelation 5:8; 8:3–4).
- **The fragrance of incense represents the spiritual principle that God's people produce an aroma that pleases God.** We are like a sweet-smelling incense in God's nostrils (Ephesians 5:1–2; 2 Corinthians 2: 14–16a).

📖 **Warnings—Exodus 30:9, 36b–38**

- **Always treat the incense as most holy**
  - Never make incense like this for personal use
  - Do not offer any unholy incense on the altar; do not use strange incense for the Tabernacle worship (Lev. 10:1–7)

✞

And the smoke of the incense,

Which came with the prayers of the saints, Ascended up before God

Out of the angel's hand.

Revelation 8:4
KJV

[2]Appendix C

Reading Assignment:
Exodus 39:32–40:38
Numbers 9:15–23

Lesson 7.3

I. Lesson Exercise

It Is Finished!

Bezalel, Oholiab, and all the other skilled craftsmen have finished the work God gave them to do. The Tabernacle built, the priests' garments made, the work was perfect. Moses blessed the workers. It is now Moses and God's turn to act.

1) On the first day of the New Year (one year after Israel's exodus from Egypt), what did God have Moses do to the Tabernacle now that the craftsmen had completed their work?

   a) (Ex. 40:2) ________________; b) (Ex. 40:9) ____________________

2) What did God have Moses do to Aaron and his sons?

   a) (Ex. 40:12) __________________; b) (Ex. 40:13)________________

   c) (Ex. 40:14) __________________; d) (Ex. 40:15)________________

3) What did God do when Moses finished his work? (Ex. 40: 34–35)

   ____

4) How did the heavenly cloud interact with the Israelite camp throughout all their wilderness journeys? (Ex. 40:36–38)

   ____

II. Find Jesus in the Lesson

Jesus, the Tabernacle of God's Glory

When Jesus Christ came to the earth from heaven, the scripture says that He was God dwelling among us.

The word for "dwelt," in John 1:14 KJV means "tabernacle" in the original Greek language the New Testament Bible was written.

If we replace the word dwelt with the word tabernacled, the passage reads like this...

And the Word was made flesh,
and [tabernacled] among us,
(and we beheld his glory,
the glory as of the only begotten of the
Father) full of grace and truth.
John 1:14 KJV

III. Closing Thoughts

The Tabernacle of Moses was an earthly model of the real Tabernacle in Heaven.

Just like the cloud from the glory of God filled the earthly tabernacle such that Moses could not stand, a similar incident happened in the heavenly tabernacle in Revelation 15:5–8.

Read verse 8 to confirm the truth of a heavenly tabernacle.

And the temple was filled with smoke from
the glory of God, and from his power;
and no man was able to enter into the temple,
till the seven plagues of the seven angels
were fulfilled.
Revelation 15:8

Reading Assignment:
Numbers 7:1–89

Lesson 7.4

I. Lesson Exercise

Twelve Tribes Dedication Offerings and Altar Gifts

For twelve days leaders from each of the tribes of Israel brought dedication offerings for the priests to use in their Tabernacle ministry work.

When we read further in the book of Numbers, the order of the tribes will become clear.

Look at Numbers Chapter 7 to find answers for the following exercise.

Complete the below list with the names of the missing tribes based on the order they brought their gifts in Numbers 7:

5) Day 1—Judah (verse 12)
   Day 2—Issachar (verse18)
   Day 3—___________ (verse 24)
   Day 4—___________ (verse 30)

6) Day 5—Simeon (verse 36)
   Day 6—Gad (verse 42)
   Day 7—__________ (verse 48)
   Day 8—__________ (verse 54)

7) Day 9—Benjamin (verse 60)
   Day 10—_________ (verse 66)
   Day 11—Asher (verse 72)
   Day 12—Naphtali (verse 78)

The Voice of God

8) Where did Moses now hear God's voice speak from in today's lesson? (Numbers 7:89) __________________________________

II. Find Jesus in the Lesson

Jesus' Blood, More Precious than Silver and Gold

The children of Israel brought an abundance of precious gifts for the beginning work of the Tabernacle—more gold and silver, animals and incense. All these gifts were necessary for the daily function of the Tabernacle, which was to atone for the nation's sins. This is so God's presence would continuously dwell among them.

Jesus came as a one-time offering, to redeem humankind from eternal death. The precious blood of Jesus is more precious than silver and gold.

Forasmuch as ye know that ye were not redeemed
with corruptible things, as silver and gold,
from your vain conversation
received by tradition from your fathers;

But with the precious blood of Christ,
as of a lamb without blemish and without spot.
1 Peter 1:18–19

III. Closing Thoughts

The Tabernacle was referred to by several different names in the Old Testament. The names are represented slightly differently between the King James Version of the Bible and the New Living Translation.

Names of the Tabernacle (KJV / NLT)

The Tabernacle (Exodus 25:9) /

Tabernacle

The Sanctuary (Exodus 25:8) /

Sacred Residence

The Tent of Testimony or Witness
(Numbers 9:15; 17:7; 18:2; Exodus 25:22, 26:33–34) /

Tabernacle of Covenant or Sacred Tent

The House of God
(Exodus 34:26, Deuteronomy 23:18; Joshua 9:23; Judges 18:31) /

House of the Lord your God

The Tent of the Congregation (Exodus 40:34–35) /

Tabernacle

Key Word	Key Chapters
Holy Living	19

Intro to Leviticus

Title

The English title "Leviticus" comes from the ancient Greek translation of this third book of the Old Testament which means, "Pertaining to the Priests."

The key words "holy living" refer to the book's main message. This describes Israel's priestly and community regulations for living in right relationship with their Holy God.

Summary

The activities in Leviticus take place in the first month of the second year after Israel's mass exodus out of slavery in Egypt.

Following the exodus, God's prophet Moses led Israel to Mount Sinai, where they became God's covenant people. As part of organizing the nation into His holy, covenant people, God directed Moses to lead them in building the worship Tabernacle. The Tabernacle became the central meeting place between God and Israel.

After Israel's first year post exodus, with the Tabernacle now completed, God directed Moses to give Israel laws and commandments.

The purpose of these regulations was to organize them into a holy nation, to represent God in the earth. Israel would experience God's choicest blessings in the Promised Land, but only as they lived by God's regulations.

Leviticus contains God's laws and commandments for Israel, which:

- Established the priesthood, who would facilitate the people's proper approach to God with sacrificial offerings, worship days. and worship celebrations.
- Instructed the people on how to care for their own bodies, defining what God said was clean versus unclean hygiene practices and diet.
- Instructed the Israelites on how to interact with each other, defining proper family, community, moral and social conduct.

God's holy living standards were in stark contrast to the practices of Egypt that Israel came out of and other heathen nations that would surround them in the Promised Land.

Some of the laws could not be performed until Israel lived in the Promised Land.

God's reason for giving the holy living regulations is explained in Leviticus 19:1–2:

The LORD also said to Moses,

"Say this to the entire community of Israel:

You must be holy because I, the LORD your God, am holy."

Leviticus Can Be Viewed as Organized in Two Main Sections

- Section one describes the procedures that describe the right way for the priests and people to approach their holy God. (Chapters 1–10)
- Section two gives regulations on how holy people are to interact with each other in their everyday lives. (Chapters 11–27)

As Israel follows God's laws and commands, they are transformed from a Hebrew slave nation to God's holy nation. In Chapter 26, the people are warned that if they do not follow all of God's regulations, then they will be cursed instead of blessed as God had planned.

Leviticus Chapter 23 describes the seven feasts of the Lord Israel was to celebrate each year. These feasts foreshadowed the ministry work of Jesus Christ in redeeming all humankind from sin's curse, and in fulfilling God's eternal covenant promises to Israel.

❑ **Timetable: Approximately 1445** (or 1279) **BC**

Leviticus takes place in the first month of the second year after Israel's exodus from Egypt. This is after the Tabernacle was set up, but before Israel left Mount Sinai to continue across the wilderness and go on to the Promised Land in Canaan.

❑ **Author:** Most Likely Moses

Most Bible scholars believe Moses is the author of Leviticus (and all the first five books of the Bible). His authorship of Leviticus is supported by the book's repeated references to God speaking directly to Moses. (Leviticus 1:1, 4:1, 6:1).

❑ **Date of Writing:**

The Book of Leviticus was possibly written between 1440 and 1400 BC, during the time of Israel's forty years of wandering in the wilderness.

There are some scholars that offer differing views concerning the authorship and dating of the Pentateuch. For more information on these views along with additional support for Mosaic authorship, review the "Author" section in the Intro to Genesis.

❑ **Major Events in Leviticus:**

Section 1. **Priestly regulations for worship** **(Chapters 1–10)**	**Section 2.** **Nation-wide regulations for holy living** **(Chapters 11–27)**
Regulation for Sacrificial Offerings (1–7)	Clean and Unclean Things (11–15)
Regulations for the Priests (8–10)	National Day of Atonement (16)
	Regulations about holy living (17–20)
	Regulations about celebrating Sabbaths, Holy Days and Festivals (21–25)
	Covenant Blessings and Curses (26)
	Regulations on Vows and Gifts (27)

Historical Location:

Mount Sinai on the southern tip of the Sinai Peninsula. Find this location at area #10 on the map in Week 6: "The Exodus."

Lesson 7.5

> **Reading Assignment:**
> **Numbers 8:1–9:14**
> **Leviticus 1:1–3:17**

I. Lesson Exercise

Let There Be Light!

- The Tabernacle Courtyard was lit by the light of day.
- The Holy Place, where the priests performed daily routines, was lit by the Golden Lampstand.
- But, the Most Holy Place (Holy of Holies), located at the far end of the Tabernacle, was lit by the brightness of God's presence when he came down on top of the Ark, over its cover, which was known as the Mercy Seat.

In preparation for the work to begin, God told Moses to set up the seven lamps in the lampstand so that the light would reflect forward. It was to illuminate the Table of Shewbread and the Altar of Incense where the priestly duties would be performed.

With the Golden Lampstand shining bright, it was time to dedicate the priests for Tabernacle service.

9) Who did God say the Levites substituted for by working in God's service in the Tabernacle? (Numbers 8:16) ____________________

10) At what age did the Levites begin serving in the Tabernacle? (Numbers 8: 24) ____

Second Passover

God instructed that all males were to celebrate the Passover at the appointed time each year. In today's lesson we learned that there is an exception to this rule.

11) What is the exception to the regulation on Passover? (Num. 9:9–12)

____

II. Find Jesus in the Lesson and III. Closing Thoughts

Jesus in Sacrifice Offerings—Materials

The section immediately following this week's daily study pages is, "Jesus in the Tabernacle Reference Material." Within that section review...

📖 **Table 2. Jesus in the Tabernacle—Furniture**

📖 **Table 3. Jesus in the Sacrifice Offerings—Materials**

Reading Assignment:
Leviticus 4:1–6:30

Lesson 7.6

I. Lesson Exercise

All Sin Must Be Atoned For

When anyone does something that is forbidden by the LORD, their actions are considered sin. This is true regardless of whether the person or congregation committing the sin does it unintentionally, unknowingly, or knowingly.

All sin must be atoned for through the procedures of the sin offering. Then God will forgive the person or persons for their sin.

> ***If any of them sin by doing something forbidden by the LORD, even if it is done unintentionally, they will be held responsible.***
> ***Leviticus 5:17***

- If the high priest sins, he brings guilt upon the entire community. (Lev. 4:3–12)
- If the entire community sins and they are not aware of it, all the people will be guilty. When they discover the sin, they must atone for it. The leaders of the community represent the entire community in the atonement procedures. (Lev. 4:13–21)
- If one of Israel's leader's sins, he is guilty even if he sinned unintentionally. When he discovers the sin, he must atone for it. (Lev. 4:22–26)
- If the common person(s) sins, they are guilty of sin, even if they sinned unintentionally. When they discover the sin, they must atone for it. (Lev. 4:27–31)

II. Find Jesus in the Lesson

The section immediately following this week's daily study pages is, "Jesus in the Tabernacle Reference Material." Within that section review…

🕮 **Table 4. Jesus in Sacrifice Offerings—Special Offerings**

🕮 **Table 5. Jesus in Sacrifice Offerings—Animals**

III. Closing Thoughts

Atonement Procedures Result in Forgiveness of Sin

The purpose of the atonement procedures is to obtain God's forgiveness for sins people commit, whether they were done in ignorance, or on purpose. Review the chart on the following page which summarizes the atonement procedures.

Atonement Procedures Result in Forgiveness of Sin[3]

The atonement procedures begin with transfer of the sins of the person to the substitute animal, followed by the death (sacrifice) of the animal. This is followed by sprinkling of the blood from the sacrifice in the Tabernacle by the priest.

The general procedures are:

- **Laying on of Hands**

  The person(s) who has sinned lays his hand on the head of the atoning sacrifice animal, which is an unblemished bull, goat, or lamb, depending on the type of sin that was committed. Then the person confesses his sin and prays for God to accept his sacrifice to atone for his sin.

- **Substitution**

  The responsibility for suffering the consequence of the sin, which is death, is transferred from the person to the sacrifice animal.

- **Bloody Sacrifice**

  The animal is slain on the altar of burnt offerings at the entrance of the Tabernacle. This is done in place of the person(s) deserving to be slain.

- **The Blood —Sprinkled and Poured Out**

  The priest takes some of the blood of the sacrificed animal into the Tabernacle. He then dips his finger in the blood and sprinkles it seven times before the Lord, in front of the inner curtain, in front of the incense altar before the Lord's presence. He places some of the blood on the horns of the incense altar.

- **Sweet-Smelling Sacrifice**

  Next, specific procedures must be carried out with handling the rest of the animal's blood and body parts, which is similar to the peace offering procedures. This fire offering is very pleasing to the LORD, a sweet-smelling sacrifice.

- **At-one-ment**

  This enables the person to be "at one" with God again by "covering" the sin.

- **Forgiveness**

  Once the "atonement" procedures are complete, God forgives the person of the sin they had committed. God will continue to bless the individual, leaders, congregation, or nation.

[3]Appendix C

AARON AND HIS SONS PREPARING A BURNT SACRIFICE.—LEV. i. and iv. 28.

Lesson 7.7

Reading Assignment:
Leviticus 7:1–8:36

I. Lesson Exercise

Ordination of the High Priests

Levi men served as priests, but their role was different from the priestly role of Aaron and his sons. Aaron and sons performed the duties of the High Priest. As briefly described in Numbers 8:19, Levites would work for the High Priest.

High Priests had the unique privilege of going beyond the Inner Veil, into the Holy of Holies, once per year to make atonement for the whole nation of Israel. Besides Moses, they were the only other persons allowed to come near the presence of God.

The High Priests ordination ceremony was more involved than the dedication of the Levi priests. One of the unique activities in the High Priests' ceremony was how Moses applied the blood of the second ram (consecration ram) to their bodies.

12) From Leviticus 8:22–24, where did Moses apply some of the second ram's blood on the body of Aaron and his sons? _______________, ___________________, and ____________________

13) Thought question: Why do you think Moses applied the blood on the High Priests in this unique way? ________________________________

II. Find Jesus in the Lesson

Jesus, Our High Priest

Jesus is humankind's High Priest under the New Covenant (New Testament) Church.

There are significant differences between the Old Covenant (Testament) Priesthood and Jesus' New Testament Priesthood.

These differences are described in Hebrews Chapter 9.

Review these verses in the charts "Old Rules of Worship," "Christ Is the Perfect Sacrifice," and "Christ Came Once for All."

III. Closing Thoughts

Set Apart, Dressed and Consecrated to Serve as God's High Priest

Review the charts "Set Apart to Serve," "Dressed to Serve" and "Consecrated to Serve" for additional insight on the significance of the High Priest's selection, dressing and preparation for service.

Set Apart to Serve[4]

The High Priest was set apart by God to represent the spiritual needs of the children of Israel before Him.

- "Set apart" means to be made "holy" and "sanctified" to perform a specific task. The High Priest was to draw near to God's holy presence in worship, intercessory prayer and thanksgiving on behalf of all Israel. He did this only for special ceremonies such as on the Day of Atonement. (Leviticus 16)
- Originally God wanted all Israel to be His kingdom of priests and holy nation. But, fear and sin prevented this. **(Ex. 19:4–8, 20:18–21; 24:4–5; 32)**

Only one High Priest could serve at a time.

- God chose Aaron and his sons—Nadab, Abihu, Eleazar and Ithamar—to minister to Him in the office of High Priest. (Ex. 28:1. Lev. 8:1–36)
- While only one High Priest served at a time, Aaron's sons assisted Him in handling the Tabernacle materials, such as when the Tabernacle was relocated during the wilderness journeys.

The first High Priest set apart for this position was Aaron.

- Aaron served as the first, one and only High Priest in the time of Moses.
- God confirmed Aaron in this position when later some of the Israelite leaders challenged Aaron's right to be the High Priest. (Numbers 17:1–13).

Aaron had four sons, but the High Priesthood only continued through two of them.

- Aaron's oldest two sinned against God and were killed. (Lev. 10:1–7)
- This left Eleazar, Ithamar and their male descendants to continue the High Priesthood ministry throughout the generations of Israel.
- After the death of Aaron, his oldest living son Eleazar was ordained to become the High Priest for the children of Israel. (Num. 20:22–29)
- After the death Eleazar, his eldest son Phinehas became the High Priest. (Numbers 25:10–13; Joshua 24:33; Judges 20:28)

The Priesthood was promised to the family of Eleazar's son Phinehas, but it was switched back and forth between Eleazar and Ithamar's descendants for several reasons. (Reference scriptures—1 Kings 2:26, 27, 35; 2 Kings 25:18–21; Haggai 1:1, 14, Zechariah 3:1; 1 Chronicles 9:10, 24:7)

In the New Testament, the Aaronic Priesthood ended when Jesus Christ became the Great High Priest for all humankind

- Christ follows after the family line of Melchizedek.
- He represents all humankind for all time before God. (Hebrews 5:5–10; 6:20; 7)

[4]Appendix C

Dressed to Serve[4]

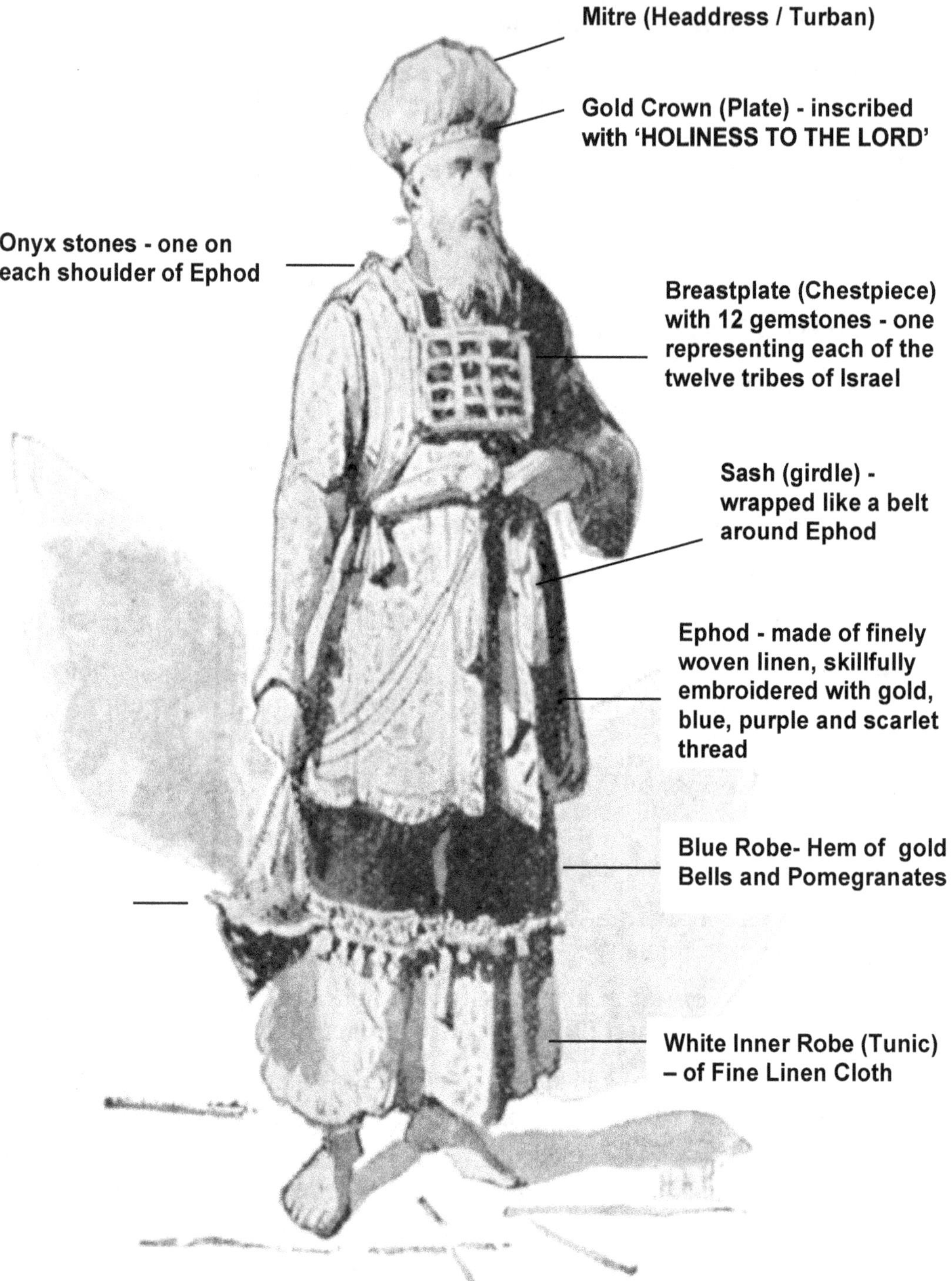

HIGH PRIEST IN ROBES AND BREASTPLATE.
—*Lev.* viii. 8.

[4]Appendix C

Dressed to Serve[4]

Exodus 28 describes the High Priest's sacred garments. They displayed God's glory and beauty (Exodus 2, 40) **as he stood before God to represent the people and before the people to represent God.**

- The detailed design of each garment piece was significant. God appointed men He filled with "the spirit of wisdom" to make them.
- The best materials were used to prepare them— fine linen cloth, gold, blue, purple and scarlet thread, and precious gemstones.
- These garments were only worn for service during special ceremonies.

Below is a brief description of the High Priest's garments that were his required dress to serve before the LORD.

- **White Inner Robe + Undergarments**: Made of fine linen cloth, the linen undergarments and the white inner robe were the first pieces put on by the priests. The linen undergarments made were required to cover their nakedness. Fine linen represents the purity and righteousness of the Messiah and of God's people. (Exodus 28:42; Leviticus 8:7; Isaiah 61:10; Revelation 15:5–6 and19:7–8)
- **Blue Robe**: The blue robe (also known as robe of the Ephod) was a single piece garment with slits in the sides for the arms and a hole in the top for the head. The hem was trimmed in alternating pure gold bells and pomegranates. People could follow the priest's movements in the Tabernacle by the sound of the bells. (Ex. 28:31–35)
- **Ephod + Sash (Girdle):** This special garment consisted of two pieces of material that were held together by gold wire that was skillfully embroidered together with blue, purple, scarlet, and fine-twined linen threads. The front piece and back piece were held together by gold-braided straps that were clasped together on the priest's shoulders. Later in Israel's history, the ephod would become the symbol of the priestly office. The ephod was held together by the sash, which was made of the same material. (Exodus 28:6–14; 1 Samuel 2:28)
- **Onyx Stones:** Two onyx stones were placed on the shoulders of the High Priest and attached to the gold straps of the ephod. One stone was engraved with six of the names of the tribes of Israel while the other stone contained the other six. These stones served as another reminder to the High Priest that when he went before God, he represented the twelve tribes of Israel in his ministry. This was a "type" of the ministry of Christ who is the Great High Priest that bears the believers' needs before God. (Ex. 28:9–14, Heb. 7:25, 9:24,1 John 2:1)
- **Mitre (Headdress / Turban) + Gold Crown (Band)**: The turban head wrap, with the gold plate that sat as a crown on the priest's head, served two purposes: 1) to represent the High Priest taking onto himself the guilt of the people of Israel when they consecrated their sacred offerings; and 2) to always wear it so the Israelites would be accepted before the Lord. (Exodus 28:38)

[4]Appendix C

Dressed to Serve[4]

- **Breastplate (Chestpiece) + Urim and Thummin**: The breastplate was used by the High Priests to seek a decision from God on behalf of the Israelites. Also known as "breastplate of judgment," it was made from the same material as the ephod. **It was a square cloth that was doubled over to form a pouch.** This pouch was strapped to the ephod by gold braided cords and gold settings of the ephod's shoulder pieces. Inside the pouch were the Urim and Thummim. **The High Priest carried this reminder to intercede for Israel over his heart. (Ex. 28:15–30)**
  - **There were four rows of precious stones across the breastplate. Within each stone was engraved the name of one of the tribes of Israel.** It is possible the names were written in the birth order of the sons of Jacob, but the scriptures do not explicitly say this.
  - The exact names of the precious stones are difficult to identify from ancient times to today. See the different names used in King James Version (KJV) and New Living Translation (NLT) Bibles. Compare with names of New Jerusalem's foundation stones in Rev. 21:19–20.

Names of Gemstones in KJV (NLT)

1st Row:
Sardius (red Carnelian) + Topaz (pale-green Peridot) + Carbuncle (Emerald)

2nd Row:
Emerald (Turquoise) + Sapphire (blue Lapis Lazuli) + Diamond (white Moonstone)

3rd Row:
Ligure (orange Jacinth) + Agate (Agate) + Amethyst (purple Amethyst)

4th Row:
Beryl (Beryl) + Onyx (Onyx) + Jasper (Jasper)

  - **This is a "type" of the ministry of Christ who bears believers close to His heart as He represents us before God.** Also, the people of God are like precious stones to the Lord, each being unique, colorful and beautiful. (Malachi 3:17; Romans 8:33–34, Ephesians 2:21–22; 1 Peter 2:5)
  - **The pouch contained the Urim and Thummin, which were used by the priests to know God's decision on a petition the Israelites would bring before Him.** While it is not clear exactly the Urim and Thummin were, the scripture is clear that they were objects used to determine the LORD's will for His people. The meaning of their names is insightful.
    - **Urim means "lights"**
    - **Thummim means "perfections"**

[4]Appendix C

Consecrated to Serve[4]

Aaron and his sons were consecrated to serve in the office of High Priest after completing sacred steps.

These steps included washing, dressing, anointing and sacrifice offerings, which were repeated over a seven-day period for completion. They were performed in full view of the people. (Lev. 8:3–5) They also received instructions on rules of conduct they must observe.

- **Washing** (Ex. 29:4; Lev. 8:6; Ex. 30:19–20; Titus 3:5; 1 John 1:9) Aaron and his sons were first thoroughly washed at the Tabernacle door by Moses. After that, the priest washed himself in prep for daily service.
- **Dressing** (Ex. 29:5–9, 40:13–14; Lev. 8:7–9; Ex. 28:39–42; John 15:16; Eph. 6:13-17) Aaron and his sons were stripped of their old clothing. Moses dressed Aaron in his priestly garment. Separately Moses dressed Aaron's sons. None of them dressed themselves in this first consecration ceremony.
- **Anointing** (Ex. 29:7, 21; Lev. 21:12, Psalm 133:2; 1 Cor. 12:13; Eph. 5:18) Moses poured the holy anointing oil over Aaron's head, which ran down his beard to the hem of his garment. It was sprinkled on Aaron's sons. The holy anointing oil was only used for anointing people and things that were separated for God's holy use.
- **Sacrifice Offerings** (Ex. 29:10–46; Lev. 8:31–32; Heb. 9:22; 2 Cor. 5:21; Heb. 9:22; 2 Cor. 2:15; Rev. 2:7; Eph. 4) Moses was the officiating priest as three animals were sacrificed as part of the consecration offerings: a young bullock for the sin offering; a ram for the burnt offering; and a ram of consecration. During the final sacrifice, the ram's blood was applied to the right ears, right thumbs and right large toes of Aaron and his sons. This symbolized that the priest was consecrated to hear, do and walk in God's will. The remaining blood was mixed with the anointing oil and sprinkled on Aaron and his sons and their garments. Then the wave offering of consecration was performed.
- **Seven Days for Completion** (Ex. 29:29, 35; Rom. 12:1) Aaron and his sons had to repeat the ceremony for seven days before their consecration for service was considered complete.
- **Rules of conduct** (Leviticus 21–22; 1 Peter 1:16) – After being ordained for service, the priest had unique daily rules of conduct that he must keep, or he would be disqualified for service.
  - Could have no physical defects or any of a number of ailments
  - Must observe strict rules concerning funerals, marriage, family
  - Could not mix holy things with unholy things

The priest's consecration process was physically symbolic of what the New Testament believer-priests must go through spiritually to be consecrated for service. Meditate on the New Testament passages above.

[4]Appendix C

Old Rules of Worship
Hebrews 9:1–10

Now in that first covenant between God and Israel, there were regulations for worship and a sacred tent here on earth.

There were two rooms in this tent.

In the first room were a lampstand, a table, and loaves of holy bread on the table.

This was called the Holy Place.

Then there was a curtain, and behind the curtain was the second room called the Most Holy Place.

In that room *[the Most Holy Place]* ***were a gold incense altar and a wooden chest called the Ark of the Covenant, which was covered with gold on all sides.***

Inside the Ark were a gold jar containing some manna, Aaron's staff that sprouted leaves, and the stone tablets of the covenant with the Ten Commandments written on them.

The glorious cherubim were above the Ark.

Their wings were stretched out over the Ark's cover, the place of atonement.

But we cannot explain all of these things now.

When these things were all in place, the priests went in and out of the first room regularly as they performed their religious duties.

But only the high priest goes into the Most Holy Place, and only once a year, and always with blood, which he offers to God to cover his own sins and the sins the people have committed in ignorance.

By these regulations the Holy Spirit revealed that the Most Holy Place was not open to the people as long as the first room and the entire system it represents were still in use.

This is an illustration pointing to the present time.

For the gifts and sacrifices that the priests offer are not able to cleanse the consciences of the people who bring them.

For that old system deals only with food and drink and ritual washing--external regulations that are in effect only until their limitations can be corrected.

Christ, the Perfect Sacrifice
Hebrews 9:11–20

So Christ has now become the High Priest over all the good things that have come.

He has entered that great, perfect sanctuary in heaven, not made by human hands and not part of this created world.

Once for all time he took blood into that Most Holy Place, but not the blood of goats and calves.

He took his own blood, and with it he secured our salvation forever.

Under the old system, the blood of goats and bulls and the ashes of a young cow could cleanse people's bodies from ritual defilement.

Just think how much more the blood of Christ will purify our hearts from deeds that lead to death so that we can worship the living God.

For by the power of the eternal Spirit, Christ offered himself to God as a perfect sacrifice for our sins.

That is why he is the one who mediates the new covenant between God and people, so that all who are invited can receive the eternal inheritance God has promised them.

For Christ died to set them free from the penalty of the sins they had committed under that first covenant.

Now when someone dies and leaves a will, no one gets anything until it is proved that the person who wrote the will is dead.

The will goes into effect only after the death of the person who wrote it. While the person is still alive, no one can use the will to get any of the things promised to them.

That is why blood was required under the first covenant as a proof of death.

For after Moses had given the people all of God's laws, he took the blood of calves and goats, along with water, and sprinkled both the book of God's laws and all the people, using branches of hyssop bushes and scarlet wool.

Then he said, "This blood confirms the covenant God has made with you."

Christ Came Once For All Time
Hebrews 9:21–28

And in the same way, he sprinkled blood on the sacred tent and on everything used for worship.

In fact, we can say that according to the law of Moses, nearly everything was purified by sprinkling it with blood.

- ✞ ***Without the shedding of blood, there is no forgiveness of sins.***

That is why the earthly tent and everything in it--which were copies of things in heaven--had to be purified by the blood of animals.

But the real things in heaven had to be purified with far better sacrifices than the blood of animals.

- ✞ ***For Christ has entered into heaven itself to appear now before God as our Advocate.***

He did not go into the earthly place of worship, for that was merely a copy of the real Temple in heaven.

Nor did he enter heaven to offer himself again and again, like the earthly high priest who enters the Most Holy Place year after year to offer the blood of an animal.

If that had been necessary, he would have had to die again and again, ever since the world began. But no!

- ✞ ***He came once for all time, at the end of the age, to remove the power of sin forever by his sacrificial death for us.***

And just as it is destined that each person dies only once and after that comes judgment, so also Christ died only once as a sacrifice to take away the sins of many people.

- ♦ ***He will come again but not to deal with our sins again.***
- ♦ ***This time he will bring salvation to all those who are eagerly waiting for him.***

Jesus in the Tabernacle

Reference Material

Contents:

Jesus in the Tabernacle—Introduction[1]

🕮 **God wanted a big family.**

He created Adam and Eve to produce that family. They all began in a loving family relationship (fellowship, communion).

🕮 **Adam lost fellowship with God**.

He lost humankind's family connection (blood relationship) to God.

🕮 **God made a temporary method for restoring humankind's fellowship with Him, through the shed blood of clean, perfect, innocent animals.**

- Select animals substituted for humankind, being offered up as a sacrifice in place of the person.
  - The animal died for punishment of the person's sin, in place of the person dying for their own sin.
  - This was necessary because God required death for sin. (Genesis 2:17)

🕮 **God chose one family to use to bring the message of restoration between God and humankind to the entire world.**

- Abraham's family > son Isaac > grandson Jacob (Israel) > descendants = Israelite nation = God's chosen people
- Then through Abraham's descendant Jesus Christ in the New Testament

🕮 **God established the proper way to access Him.**

- First, in the Old Testament the way was made through the Tabernacle of Moses' sacrifices and worship services led by the Aaronic Priesthood
- God dwelled among Israel in the Most Holy Place of the Tabernacle, between the Cherubims over the lid of the Ark of the Covenant (Mercy Seat)
- Tabernacle priests served as mediators between God and Israel, leading the proper approach to God
- Procedures and services had to be implemented exactly as God instructed.

[1]Appendix C

Jesus in the Tabernacle—Introduction[1]

- **The Tabernacle of Moses was a shadow (meaning figure or type) of the proper way to access God.**
  - In the New Testament it was revealed that the permanent way to access God is through Jesus Christ.
  - A restored blood relationship (fellowship) with God is provided for through the blood of Jesus Christ that was shed on the cross.
  - This restoration is available for all who exercise faith in Jesus Christ. (John 14:6)
- **Every aspect of the Tabernacle represents the ministry of Jesus Christ in restoring humankind's family relationship (fellowship, communion) with God.**
  - This includes all the Tabernacle materials and furniture, the Priesthood and their garments and sacrificial offerings
- **The charts that follow give some insight on the connection between the Tabernacle of Moses and Ministry of Jesus Christ**
- **Excellent resources for more details on the topic of Jesus in the Tabernacle are:**
  - *The Tabernacle: Shadows of the Messiah—Its Sacrifices, Services, and Priesthood* by David M. Levy
  - *The Tabernacle of Moses: The Riches of Redemption's Story as Revealed in the Tabernacle* by Kevin J. Conner

[1]Appendix C

Table 1. Jesus in the Tabernacle—Materials[1]

Tabernacle Materials	Materials Description	Jesus in the Tabernacle Materials
Gold (from jewelry in Egypt)	**Pure gold is the most valuable and most precious metal.** Used for furniture in Holy Place and Most Holy Place	**Pure gold represents Jesus' deity, who is Christ, eternal, divine Son of God.** John 1:1–18, Rev. 21:18
Silver (from jewelry in Egypt)	**Silver is a precious metal.** Used for structure bases, hooks. Silver represents ransom money for redemption.	**Jesus paid the ransom price to redeem mankind.** 1 Peter 1:18–19 *(Matt. 26:15)*
Brass (bronze, brazen) (from mirrors in Egypt)	**Brass symbolizes judgment.** (Deut 28:23) Overlaid wood on Sacrifice Altar and used in Washbasin (Laver). Represents judgment for and justification from sin.	**Brass overlaying acacia wood represents the divine righteousness** 1 John 3:5, 2 Cor. 5:21 **And judgment of Christ.** Rev. 1:15
Blue (from shellfish)	**Blue represents color of the sky, symbolizing heaven.**	**Blue represents Jesus came from heaven.** John:1,14
Purple (from purple snail)	**Purple is the color of royalty, associated with Kings**	**Purple represents Jesus' Kingship.** Luke 1:31–33
Scarlet (from worms)	**Scarlet, a bright red dye** Produced by worms or grubs	**Red symbolic Jesus' redeeming blood.** 1 Peter 1:18–19

[1]Appendix C

Table 1. Jesus in the Tabernacle—Materials[1]

Tabernacle Materials	Materials Description	Jesus in the Tabernacle Materials
Fine-Twined White Linen (from Egypt)	**Egyptian fine, white linen** is said to be twice as good as quality of linen made by modern technology *(Tabernacle of Moses-Levy p.74)*. Used in curtains, roof covering, and Priests' garments. Represents purity (Rev 15:5–6)	White represents purity and righteousness; Fine-ness represents faultless material. **These qualities represent purity of Jesus** who had no sin, fault-less, innocent until death. John 19:6, 1 Peter 1:19
Embroidered Linen 1st Covering = Roof (shaped the sacred tent)	**Fine-twined linen embroidered with Cherubim** made the roof or 1st covering of the Tabernacle. Embroidery mixed the blue, purple, scarlet and white colors	**Mixture of embroidery colors represent Jesus' Ministry work** which was holy (white), heavenly (blue), royal (purple) and saving (red). Col. 1:18–20
Woven Goats' Hair 2nd Covering = Tent	**Scapegoat (from goats in flocks) was used on Day of Atonement** to send nation's sins in wilderness. Lev. 16	**Through Jesus, our scapegoat, God wants to forgive and forget our sins** 1 John 3:5, Heb. 8:12
Tanned Ram Skin (Red) 3rd Covering = above Tent	**Rams (from flocks) are not naturally red;** **It was dyed red,** symbolizing atoning blood sacrifice, covering sin.	**Christ, as sacrificial lamb, shed blood to cleanse, cover our sins** Isaiah 53:7, Matt. 26:28, 1 Peter 1:18–19
Outer Covering 4th Covering = Protection	**This covering formed a thick, protective, weatherproof outer layer** over Tabernacle. No amount of baking heat, sun, wind, sand, or rain disturbed contents underneath	This covering looked unattractive but hid glorious treasure underneath. **God's glory dwelt among us** (tabernacled) **in Jesus' flesh.** Isaiah 53:2, John 1:14
Acacia (Shittim) Wood (from Sinai Desert)	**Hard, incorruptible, indestructible, non-decaying wood.** Used for structure frame, tables, altars.	**Gold overlaying acacia wood represents union of Jesus' divine and human natures.** Phil. 2:6–11

Table 1. Jesus in the Tabernacle—Materials[1]

Tabernacle Materials	Materials Description	Jesus in the Tabernacle Materials
Olive Oil (for Light)	**Golden Lampstand was filled daily with pure olive oil, empowering it to give light.** Olive oil represents God's Holy Spirit (1 Sam 16:13), which empowered Christ's earthly ministry, empowers/enlightens Church ministry, and enlightens believers spiritual walk. Eph. 5:16–26	**Jesus was filled and led by God's Holy Spirit in His earthly ministry** Luke 4:1,18–19 Pure olive oil is pressed hard. Jesus was placed in "olive press", agonizing in Gethsemane, beaten and crucified on Calvary. Matt 26:36–46; 27:1–50
Spices for Anointing Oil (Holy, Sacred) (Exodus 30:22–33)	**1) Pure Myrrh, 2) Sweet Cinnamon, 3) Sweet Cane, 4) Cassia, 5) Olive Oil;** All skillfully blended by perfumers. Mix involved crushing and sweetness.	**Jesus was anointed by God with Holy Spirit, empowered for earthly service** Acts 10:38 And empowered to raise up from dead Rom. 8:11
Spices for Sweet Incense (Holy, Fragrant, Pure) (Exodus 30:34–38)	**1) Resin droplets (stacte), 2) Mollusk scent (onycha), 3) Galbanum, 4) Pure Frankincense;** Skilled incense maker refined the mixture (beat to a fine texture and carefully mixed)	**Jesus is a sweet savor (sweet smelling perfume) of life for believers.** 2 Cor. 2:14–16 Savor made as beaten in suffering but sweetened by God's power

[1]Appendix C

Table 1. Jesus in the Tabernacle—Materials[1]

Tabernacle Materials	Materials Description	Jesus in the Tabernacle Materials
Precious Stones (for High Priest garments) **- Onyx stones (on Ephod shoulder piece)** **- Twelve Precious Stones (Chestpiece / Breastplate)** (Exodus 39:10-14)	**Attached to the outer shoulder piece of the High Priests' garments, the onyx stone was engraved with the twelve tribes of Israel** (six names in each stone on each shoulder). Worn on the chestpiece (breastplate), names of the twelve tribes of Israel were individually engraved on twelve unique stones. These engraved stones represented the entire tribe of Israel which the High Priest carried on his shoulders and in his heart. This reminded him he represented the entire nation of Israel in doing his Priestly duties.	**"And they shall be mine, saith the LORD of hosts, in that day when I make up my jewels; and I will spare them, as a man spareth his own son that serveth him." Malachi 3:17 KJV** Precious jewels represent all the children of God, who believe in Jesus Christ, causing their lives to be spared from God's punishment, and enabling them to become beloved children of God, forever! John 3:16, John 1:12

ණ✞📖✞ৡ

Gifts for the Tabernacle—Exodus 35:4–9

"Then Moses said to all the people, "This is what the LORD has commanded.

Everyone is invited to bring these offerings to the LORD:
gold, silver, and bronze; blue, purple, and scarlet yarn;
fine linen; goat hair for cloth; tanned ram skins and fine goatskin leather;
acacia wood; olive oil for the lamps; spices for the anointing oil and the fragrant incense;
onyx stones, and other stones to be set in the ephod and the chestpiece."

[1]Appendix C

Table 2. Jesus in the Tabernacle—Furniture[1]

Tabernacle Furniture / Location	Brief Description with New Testament Meaning	Jesus in the Furniture
1. Gate of the Courtyard (curtain) / East end of Tabernacle Courtyard Tribe of Judah is located at this end; Judah means "Praise"	**Enter gate and court through praise and thanksgiving (Ps 100:4).** This means enter God's presence rejoicing, because God provides way to restore fellowship with man.	**Jesus Christ, our Gate-Way to God** John 14:6—Jesus is the only way to access God; He brings Peace to man from God (Col 1:20); This is joy to the world (Luke 2:10–14)
2. Brazen Altar for Sacrifice Offerings / Tabernacle Courtyard First piece of furniture inside the gate (also called "Altar of Burnt Offering")	**Perfect sacrifice substitutes for people; Shed blood of the innocent atones for sin** Atone means to make "at one" with God by covering or blocking sin from God's view; Sacrifices also redeem mankind; Redeem means to pay the price to deliver from death and restore to life (Hebrew 9:22).	**Jesus Christ, our Sacrifice for Sins** John 1:29—Jesus, as a sacrificed lamb, died on the cross for our sins, restored the way for mankind to become at one with God; Jesus made atonement for our sins (Romans 5:11) and redeemed mankind (Hebrews 9:12). Jesus' followers are to be living sacrifices because of Jesus' sacrifice. (Rom. 12:1–2)

[1]Appendix C

Table 2. Jesus in the Tabernacle—Furniture[1]

Tabernacle Furniture / Location	Brief Description with New Testament Meaning	Jesus in the Furniture
3. Brazen Laver (for Washing) / **Tabernacle Courtyard Between Brazen Altar & Tabernacle Door** **(also called Washbasin)**	**Priests washed before entering Tabernacle** Washing represented cleansing from daily defilement of sin; A process that comes by - Regeneration by Holy Spirit - meaning made a new spiritual person (Titus 3:5) - Purification - washing and cleansing of heart and life by doing God's Word daily (Ephesians 5:6, John 15:3) - Sanctification - means "to set apart".	**Jesus Christ, our Sanctification** 1 Cor. 1:30; 1 Thess. 4:2–4 Through Jesus we receive initial purification before God. Then, He helps us daily cleanse our lives from sin as we learn to live by the Word of God, through Holy Spirit's power. Jesus sanctifies us by a) setting us apart from sin and b) setting us apart to do God's service.
4. Door of the Tabernacle (curtain) / **Courtyard entrance into Tabernacle**	**Blood sacrifice and cleansing from sin are required before entering into God's presence** (Heb. 10:19–22)	**Jesus Christ, our Door-Way to God** John 10:7–10, Jesus is true way; other ways that say they lead to God are false.
5. Golden Lampstand / **South end (left side) of Holy Place** **(also called Golden Candlestick)**	**Golden Lamp lit up entire room, powered by pure olive oil;** Represents divine direction, as light and power from God guide believers' way to please him. (Psalm 119:105)	**Jesus Christ, the Light of the World** Jesus is the light and life of men, providing God's divine vision, guidance and blessing John 1:4; John 9:5

[1]Appendix C

Table 2. Jesus in the Tabernacle—Furniture[1]

Tabernacle Furniture / Location	Brief Description with New Testament Meaning	Jesus in the Furniture
6. Table of Showbread (Bread of Presence) / **North end (right side) of Holy Place**	**Twelve loaves of Bread (two stacks of six) represented twelve tribes of Israel in God's presence.** The loaves, sprinkled with frankincense perfume, sat on the golden table along with the drink offering (wine). This represents the favored (perfumed) and fruitful (wine) life of the believer in God's presence (bread), sustaining earthly lives.	**Jesus Christ, the Bread of Life** John 6:51— Jesus is the bread from heaven which sustains the life of all those who choose to live by His Word and be led by His Spirit daily.
7. Altar of Incense (Prayer) / **In Holy Place directly in front of Ark of Covenant, but in front of the Veil**	**Sweet incense, made from four spices by skilled perfumers, was sprinkled over burning coals from the brazen altar on the altar of incense.** This produced a sweet fragrance and cloudy smoke which were to burn continually. This represents continual prayers of the saints of God. (Rev. 8:4)	**Jesus Christ, our Intercessor** Romans 8:34 and Hebrews 7:25— Jesus, who rose up from the dead, is now seated at the right hand of Father God. There he makes continuous intercession for believers in Him, until it is time for him to return for God's family and rule the earth.
8. Inner Veil (embroidered heavy curtain) / **Between Holy Place and Most Holy Place**	**Veil separated Holy God from sinful man.** Moses went beyond veil often, High Priest (Aaron and sons) entered once per year to make atonement for nation's sin over Ark. This represents limited access to God.	**Jesus Christ, our Direct Access to God** Heb. 4:14–16 and 10:19–20— Through Jesus, each believer has direct, continuous access to God to obtain God's divine mercy, help and fellowship.

[1]Appendix C

Table 2. Jesus in the Tabernacle—Furniture[1]

Tabernacle Furniture / Location	Brief Description with New Testament Meaning	Jesus in the Furniture
9. Ark of the Covenant / **In Most Holy Place** **(Holy of Holies) West end**	**The Ark represented God's throne and presence dwelling among God's covenant (chosen) people**; providing blessings, protection and power	**Jesus Christ, our New Covenant** Hebrews 8:6—Jesus provides for a better covenant with God, with better promises
10. Ark Cover (Mercy Seat of God) / **Lid for the Ark of Covenant** **(The Place of Atonement)**	Winged Cherubim were made a part of one-piece Mercy Seat, where God's presence would sit on the Ark Cover. **Atoning blood sprinkled over the Cover was a sweet-smell to God.** This represented Blood of Jesus on actual heavenly Ark around God's throne.	**Jesus Christ, God's Grace, Mercy, Peace, Divine Power and Glory towards Mankind** Romans 5:1–11—Jesus provides continuous access to God's glory, power and blessings by forgiveness and cleansing from sins of believers. Hebrews 4:14–16; 6:19–20; 9:3–15

❧✝📖✝☙

First Covenant Had a Worldly Sanctuary—Hebrews 9:1–5a KJV

"Then verily the first covenant had also ordinances of divine service, and a worldly sanctuary.
For there was a tabernacle made;
The first, wherein was the candlestick, and the table, and the showbread; which is called the sanctuary.
And after the second veil, the tabernacle which is ca;lled the Holiest of all;
Which had the golden censer, and the ark of the covenant overlaid round about with gold,
Wherein was the golden pot that had manna, and Aaron's rod that budded, and the tables of the covenant;
And over it the cherubims of glory shadowing the mercy-seat"

[1]Appendix C

Table 3. Jesus in the Sacrifice Offerings—Materials[2]

Offering Materials	Purpose	Jesus in Offering Materials
Offering **(Exodus 29:14, Heb. 7:27)**	**To bring near**, as in bringing near to God	Through the offering of Jesus Christ, mankind is brought near to God
Priests **(Exodus 31:10, Heb. 9:11)**	**Mediators**, meaning an in-between or middle person, **between God and people**	**Jesus is our heavenly mediator to give us access to God;** Jesus replaced the requirement for human priests.
Altar **(Exodus 20:24, Heb. 13:10-13)**	**Place of slaughter; made of acacia wood** (indestructible) **and brass** (judgment)	The cross was Jesus' place of slaughter; His shed blood for judgment of man's sin
Fire **(Lev. 1:7, Isa. 53:4-5, Heb. 12:29)**	**Judgment of sin on animals;** God is a consuming fire = life if repent or death	**Jesus' suffering persecution and death satisfied God's fiery judgment on mankind**

[2]Appendix C

Table 3. Jesus in the Sacrifice Offerings—Materials[2]

Offering Materials	Purpose	Jesus in Offering Materials
Horns of Altar **(Lev. 4:18, Heb. 12:24)**	**Horn symbolized power or strength** Deut 33:17; Psalm 89:17	**Animals blood applied to horns of altar; Power in Jesus' blood shed on cross**
Blood **(Lev. 17:11, Heb 9:22)**	**God requires shedding of innocent blood to atone for man's sin**	**Jesus shed blood once and for all, for all mankind (unlike yearly animal sacrifice)**
Ashes **(Lev. 6:10, Acts 2:31)**	**Ashes spoke of God's acceptance of the sacrifice, with finished death of animal**	**Human Jesus died, body placed in grave, soul went to Hell, satisfied man's debt**
Utensils: **shovels, basins, forks, firepans and a grate, meaning a network of brass** **(Exodus 27:3, John 18 and 19)**	**All made of brass, representing instruments of God's acts of judgment;** they assist in atonement process for man's sin by shed blood of the innocent	**Animal sacrifices were ugly, stinky business. This represented the ugliness Jesus experienced in substituting for man, so man is saved by faith in Him.**

Jesus Came to Do God's Will—Hebrews 10: 4–7 KJV

But in those sacrifices there is a remembrance again made of sins every year.
For it is not possible that the blood of bulls and of goats should take away sins.

Wherefore when he cometh into the world, he saith,
Sacrifice and offering thou wouldest not, but a body hast thou prepared me:
In burnt offerings and sacrifices for sin thou hast had no pleasure.

Then said I, Lo, I come (in the volume of the book it is written of me,) to do thy will, O God.

Table 3. Jesus in the Sacrifice Offerings—Materials[2]

[2]Appendix C

Table 4. Jesus in the Sacrifice Offerings—Special Offerings[2]

Sweet Smelling Sacrifices * Very Pleasing to God *(Restored Fellowship between God and Man is Sweet)*			
Sacrificial Offering	**Name Means…**	**Purpose**	**Jesus in the Offering**
1. **Burnt Offering** Lev. Chp 1, 6; Num 28-29	Name means "to go up", whole offering burned, smoke upward	**Total dedication** (surrender of self) **to God for His divine favor**	Jesus surrendered to Father's will, offering himself on cross
2. **Grain Offering** Lev. Chp 2 and 6; Num. 15 **(KJV = Meat Offering) (also = Meal Offering)**	Name means "to give a gift", to obtain God's favor on your life;	**Dedicated, daily, living relationship with God;** **General thanksgiving;** **Sin offering for very poor**	He was without sin, perfect and innocent, Jesus perfectly obeyed God *(Leaven represents sin, meal offering had no leaven in it)*
3. **Peace Offering** Lev. Chapters 3, 7, 22, 23 Num 6	Name means "sacrifices of peace"; Voluntary thanksgiving or freewill offering to God; Acknowledges God's deliverance or unexpected blessings	**Peace and wholeness because of fellowship, communion with God**	Jesus made peace with God for man on the cross; Believers have peace and fellowship with God (Phil. 2:6–11; Heb. 4:15; Rom. 5)

[2]Appendix C

Table 4. Jesus in the Sacrifice Offerings—Special Offerings[2]

Non-Sweet Smelling Sacrifices to God (*Sin Stinks*)			
Sacrificial Offering	**Name Means…**	**Purpose**	**Jesus in the Offering**
4. Sin Offering Lev. Chp 4 -5, 6; Num. 28-29	Name means “missing the mark”; Sacrifices for sins committed ignorantly or not “on purpose” (meaning you did not know it was wrong or you did not want to)	**Atonement and forgiveness for sin:** **Unintentional sin** (sins of omission) **Purification from sin**	Jesus substituted his life for all to pay debt for man’s sin; God forgives sin by faith in Jesus; Fellowship restored with God for believers in Jesus Christ
5. **Guilt Offering** Lev. Chp 5-6, 7 (KJV = Trespass Offering)	Name means “guilt or violation”; Sacrifices are for specific acts of sins committed against God and man; Atonement for damages and harm caused by specific sin once it is known and confessed	**Atonement and forgiveness for sin:** **Committed purposefully** (sins of commission); **Removes guilt of sin; the offerer goes from being cursed to blessed**	Jesus was offered on the cross for the guilty sins of others; Satisfied God’s judgment for wrongs done to God by mankind *(Heb. 9:23–10:18)*

[2]Appendix C

Table 5. Jesus in the Sacrifice Offerings—Animals[2]

Offering Animals	Purpose	Jesus in Offering Animals
Bull (Ox)	**Strong, serving animal** - Priests and leaders expected to use this animal for sacrifice	**Symbolic of Jesus as strong, enduring servant who was obedient unto death** (Phil. 2:5–8)
Ram (Lamb)	**Meek, gentle animal** - Priests and leaders expected to use this animal for sacrifice	**Symbolic of Jesus meekness;** He voluntarily surrendered his life to death (Isaiah 53:7; Heb. 10:5–10)
Goat	**Symbol for sinners** (Matt. 25:33)	**Symbolic of Jesus dying in shame** as if he were a sinner (criminal) at his death (Isaiah 53:12; Luke 23:33)
Turtledove	**Symbol of mourning** (Isa. 38:14), **and harmlessness** (Matt. 10:16)	**Jesus mourned over mankind** (Luke 19:41)
Pigeon	**Symbol of poverty**	**Jesus became poor, so we might be rich** (Matt. 8:20; 2 Cor. 8:9); **Jesus is the Poor's sacrifice** (Luke 2:24)

[2]Appendix C

Week 8

Featured Book: Leviticus

Contents:

Peek at the Week

Lesson	Key Events	Find Jesus
8.1	Holy God Gives Instructions for Holy Living	Jesus' Followers Must Be Holy like God
8.2	Instructions for Holy Living continued	Jesus and the Laws of Moses
8.3	Day of Atonement (Yom Kippur)	Jesus—High Priest, Sacrifice and Blood
8.4	Laws and Regulations on Forbidden Relations	Precious Blood of Jesus Atones for Sin
8.5	Consequences for Disobeying God's Laws	Jesus, Our Perfect Sacrifice for Sin
8.6	Instructions on the Seven Festivals of the Lord	Jesus and the Seven Feasts of the Lord
8.7	Kinsman Redeemer	Jesus our Kinsman Redeemer

Chronological Notes

* Timetable	Key Events
During the 1st year after Exit from Egypt 1446 (or 1280) BC	Israel organized into a Covenant nation (chosen people) with laws, priests, worship tabernacle, God's presence - Builds the Tabernacle - Makes Tabernacle Priests clothing
At the beginning of the 2nd Year after Exit 1445 (or 1279) BC	- Moses erects the Tabernacle and God's glory fills it - Israel's dedication celebration for the Tabernacle - Israel dedicates the Levi Priests - Moses dedicates and anoints High Priests: Aaron and sons - Israel celebrates the Passover Feast - Israel learns the Holy laws for Priests and People - Israel leaves wilderness of Sinai (Numbers 10:11) - Israelites from Egypt should have entered Promised Land - Unbelieving Israelites begin to wander in wilderness
40 Years after Exodus - 1405 (or 1239) BC	Unbelieving Israelites from Egypt die in wilderness Second generation Israel enters Promised Land

**All dates are approximate.*

Lesson 8.1

Reading Assignment:
Leviticus 9:1–11:47

I. Lesson Exercise

God Is a Consuming Fire

Tabernacle built, dedication ceremonies complete, priests anointed for service, Aaron and his sons prepare the first sacrifices as part of their high priestly duties.

They perform sacrificial offerings for the sins of themselves and their families. Then they perform the sacrifices for the whole nation of Israel.

They lifted the animal breasts and right thighs as an offering *(referred to as "wave" and "heave" offerings in King James Version of the Bible)*, then they blessed the people.

After completing one more set of offerings, they moved away from the altar, then WHOOSH!

Try to imagine a glorious cloud streaming from heaven down onto the Most Holy Place at the back of the Tabernacle.

Suddenly, fire zooms out from the back of the Tabernacle through the front entrance all the way to the brazen altar in the courtyard.

It completely consumed the offerings on the altar.

No wonder the people shouted with joy and immediately fell face down on the ground!

1) When God's consuming fire enveloped the offerings on the altar, was this a good thing or a bad thing? (Lev. 9:23–24) ________________

Strange Fire Meets Consuming Fire

Aaron's two sons Nadab and Abihu disobeyed God by burning a different kind of fire than what the Lord had instructed them to use for the altar of incense.

King James Version calls it a "strange fire."

We see God's consuming fire blaze forth a second time in response to these men's actions.

2) Read Leviticus 10:2
   a) What did the consuming fire of God do to Nadab and Abihu?

      ____

   b) Was this a good or bad thing? __________________

Instructions for Priests' Conduct

God gave instructions for Aaron and his descendants conduct as High Priests.

- Never drink wine or any alcoholic drink before performing Tabernacle duties
- Be Israel's experts on what is holy and what is unholy
- Be Israel's experts on what is clean and what is unclean
- Be teachers of the law that God gave to Israel through Moses
- Offer blood sacrifices. Review charts: "The Four Blood Sacrifices"

The Holy God Gives All Israel Instructions for Holy Living

God gave Moses and Aaron detailed instructions on what holy living means for His holy nation Israel. God defines clean and unclean, holy and unholy, and gives laws.

First God instructs them on what land animals, fish, birds and insects Israel can eat and what they cannot eat. Violation of these laws would result in disease or death. See the chart on "Instructions for Clean and Unclean Animals."

<u>II. Find Jesus in the Lesson and III. Closing Thoughts</u>

Jesus' Followers Must Be Holy

"Never defile yourselves by touching such animals.
After all, I, the LORD, am your God.

You must be holy because I am holy. …

I, the LORD, am the one who brought you up
from the land of Egypt
to be your God.

You must therefore be holy because I am holy."
Leviticus 11:43–45

God required holiness in the Old Testament under the Old Covenant. This was accomplished by the people following daily laws for worship, eating and living.

In the New Testament, God still requires holiness for believers in Christ. Holiness is accomplished by following the laws of love for God, self, and fellow humans according to God's Word and by the work of the Holy Spirit within their heart. Read 1 Peter 1:13–2

The Four Blood Sacrifices in the Old Testament[1]

reprinted by permission

Many people miss the significance of the different kinds of sacrifices in the Old Testament. These sacrifices are described in the beginning chapters of Leviticus and show up again and again in the Bible. For example…

When the Psalms refer to King David giving the Lord a thank offering, this tells us that David had experienced an unexpected deliverance.

When we read about peace offerings, we know that some of the offerings were shared with the community (like a huge potluck meal).

Old Testament offerings show us a lot about our salvation from God.

Salvation must deal with our original sin (our sinfulness), our specific sins, and our need for legal satisfaction. Then we can rejoice in our peace relationship with God and have fellowship with Him and others.

There are four types of Blood Sacrificial Offerings

1. Burnt Offerings
2. Sin Offerings
3. Trespass Offerings
4. Peace Offering

There were two types of Non-Blood Offerings

Grain offering (Leviticus 2; 6:14–23) and **drink offering** (Leviticus 23:13; Numbers 15:1–10; 28:31.)

These offerings usually accompanied the burnt offerings and peace offerings. A portion of grain offering was burned on altar, a portion eaten by priests.

- **Grain offering** (fine flour and pure olive oil) is for general thanksgiving and a sin offering for very poor; symbol of sinless-ness.
- **Drink offering** (wine) was a symbol of joy in Old Testament uses. It represented Christ's blood in the New Testament.

[1]Appendix C

The Four Blood Sacrifices in the Old Testament[1]

reprinted by permission

NAME	PURPOSE	VICTIM	GOD'S PORTION	PRIEST'S PORTION	OFFERER'S PORTION
1. Burnt Offering *('olah)* Lev 1; 6:8–13; 8:18–21; 16:24	To propitiate for sin in general, *original sin;* a means of approach by unholy people to a holy God	Male, unblemished: ox, sheep, goat, or dove (according to wealth)	Entire animal (hence called *kalil,* whole burnt offering)	Nothing	Nothing
2. Sin Offering *(hatta't)* Lev 4:1–5:13; 6:24–30; 8:14–17; 16:3–22	To atone for specific transgressions where no restitution was possible	Priest or congregation: bullock Ruler: he-goat Commoner: she-goat	Fatty portions (fat covering inwards; kidneys, liver, caul)	All the remainder (had to be eaten within court of tabernacle)	Nothing
3. Trespass Offering—also called a Guilt Offering *('asham)* Lev 5:14–6:7; 7:1–6	To atone for specific transgressions where restitution was possible, damages computed at six-fifths payable in advance. Legal *satisfaction*	Ram (only)	Fatty portions (fat covering inwards; kidneys, liver, caul)	All the remainder (had to be eaten within court of tabernacle)	Nothing

[1]Appendix C

The Four Blood Sacrifices in the Old Testament[1]

reprinted by permission

4. Peace Offering (*shelamin*)

Peace Offerings are also called Fellowship Offerings in some translations of the Bible. You can read more about them in Leviticus Chapter 3. These offerings represented fellowship with God and with other believers.

Peace Offerings were the only offering that the worshipper ate. In fact, they were a communion meal. In a symbolic sense everyone ate together: God, priest, worshipper, and others in the faith community. There were actually three types...

a. Thank Offering (*towdah*) Lev 7:12–15	For an unexpected blessing or deliverance already granted by God	Unblemished male or female ox/sheep/goat	Fatty portions	1. Wave offering; breast--to high priest 2. Heave offering; right foreleg--to officiating priest (to be eaten in any clean place)	Remainder (eaten in court, the same day) -- this was a community meal eaten with others.
b. Votive Offering (*neder*) Lev 7:16 (*for Special Vows*)	For blessing or deliverance already granted, when a vow had been made in support of the petition	Unblemished male or female ox/sheep/goat	Fatty portions	1. Wave offering; breast--to high priest 2. Heave offering; right foreleg--to officiating priest (to be eaten in any clean place)	Remainder (eaten in court, first or second day) -- this was a community meal eaten with others.
c. Freewill Offering (*nedabah*) Lev 7:16	To express general thankfulness and love toward God, without regard to specific blessings	Male or female ox/sheep/goat (minor imperfections permitted)	Fatty portions	1. Wave offering; breast--to high priest 2. Heave offering; right foreleg--to officiating priest (to be eaten in any clean place)	Remainder (eaten in court, first or second day) -- this was a community meal eaten with others.

[1]Appendix C

Instructions for Clean and Unclean Animals: Leviticus 11:1–47

Animal Types	Clean—Do Eat	Unclean—Do Not Eat or Touch Their Dead Bodies	How to Become Clean if Defiled
Land	Land Animals with divided hooves and chew the cud	Animals without both split hooves and chew cud: Camel, Rock badger, Hare, Pig. Animals that scurry on the ground or slither on bellies, with four legs or many feet: Mole, mouse, lizards, gecko, chameleon Animals that walk on all four legs with paws	If touch dead body of unclean animals, person is defiled. - Immediately wash clothes and remain defiled until evening, then person is clean. If unclean animal dies and falls on something, object is defiled. - Put object in water and it will be defiled until evening, then clean Contaminated pots are smashed and contents unclean. If dead animal falls in spring water or cistern, that water remains clean.
Fish	Fish with both fins and scales from fresh or salt water	Fish that do not have both fins and scales	
Birds	Birds not on detestable list	Eagle, vulture, osprey, buzzard, kites, ravens, ostrich, nighthawk, seagull, hawks, owls, cormorant, pelican, stork, herons, hoopoe, bat	
Insects	Insects jumping with hind legs — locusts, crickets, grasshoppers	All other swarming insects that walk or crawl	

Lesson 8.2

Reading Assignment:
Leviticus 12:1–14:32

I. Lesson Exercise

Instructions for Purification after Childbirth

After the birth of a child, the woman became "ceremonially" unclean.

This means she was restricted from participating in Tabernacle worship and from touching anything holy, until after a certain amount of "purification" time.

After this, she brought offerings to the Tabernacle where the priest made atonement for her, and then she became ceremonially clean.

- The woman was unclean after the birth of a son for seven days (Lev. 12:2)
- On the eighth day the newborn son was to be circumcised (Lev. 12:3)
- The woman's purification time after birth of a son was thirty-three days (Lev. 12:4)
- The woman was unclean after the birth of a daughter for fourteen days (Lev. 12:5)
- The woman's purification time after a daughter's birth was sixty-six days (Lev. 12:5)
- If the woman could not afford to bring a lamb for the whole burnt offering, she was able to bring two turtledoves or two young pigeons instead. (Lev. 12:8)

Instructions for Handling Contagious Skin Diseases (Leprosy)

In the King James Version of the Bible, these contagious skin diseases are called "leprosy." The significance of these skin diseases is that they prevented a person from worshiping at the Tabernacle and from normal living among people.

> ***Those who suffer from any contagious skin disease must tear their clothing and allow their hair to hang loose.***
>
> ***Then, as they go from place to place, they must cover their mouth and call out, 'Unclean! Unclean!'***
>
> ***As long as the disease lasts, they will be ceremonially unclean and must live in isolation outside the camp. Leviticus 13:45–46***

3) Who decided if a person was ceremonially clean or unclean? (Leviticus 13:2–4) ________________________________

Suspect skin conditions included

- swelling or a rash or a shiny patch on the skin
- some hair has turned white and an open sore in the affected area
- boil on the skin
- burn on the skin
- open sore on the head or chin with fine yellow hair in it
- shiny white patches on the skin
- hair balding on forehead with a reddish white infection

Priests had a delicate job of inspection, quarantine, and re-inspection.

4) Why did God require the people with contagious skin diseases to live isolated away from others, outside of the Israelite camp? (Lev. 13:46)

____

Even clothing could be declared unclean due to having leprous material.

If woolen, linen, or leather material had a bright green or reddish color in it, it was suspect.

5) What was done to material with an infectious mildew in it? (Leviticus 13:52) ____

Instructions for Purification after Contagious Skin Disease is Healed

It was possible to be healed from a contagious skin disease. However, the person who believed they were healed had to be examined by the priest outside the camp, who officially decides if they are healed.

If the priest confirms their healing, then a purification ceremony is performed.

> This ceremony included detailed steps such as special blood water sprinkled on them, washing clothes, shaving hair, and bathing their bodies.
>
> They lived seven more days outside the camp, with more shaving, washing, and bathing, followed by multiple sacrifice offerings to make atonement for them.

To complete becoming ceremonially clean, the persons healed from the contagious skin diseases experienced three things sprinkled, covering, and poured all over their bodies:

- **Blood was sprinkled** over the person (Lev. 14:7)
- **Water covered their whole bodies** as they bathe in it (Lev. 14:8)
- **Oil was poured over the head of** the healed person (Lev. 14:15–18)

II. Find Jesus in the Lesson

Jesus and the Laws of Moses

Mary, the Mother of Jesus, followed the Law of Moses for her purification process after the birth of her son Jesus Christ. Read Luke 2:21–24 with Leviticus 12:8.

6) What animals did Mary bring for her purification offering after Jesus' birth, and what did the animals reveal about her financial status?

   ______________________________, ______________________________

Ten lepers cried out from a distance for Jesus to heal them (Luke 17:11–19).

7) What instructions, from the Law of Moses, did Jesus give the lepers so they could receive their healing? (Luke 17:14 with Leviticus 13:17)

   ____

III. Closing Thoughts

Healthy Laws for Today, too!

Although the New Covenant no longer requires God's people to follow the strict laws of Moses, nutritional and medical communities have found health benefits in those laws.

> For example, if the hygiene and dietary instructions from those laws are properly understood and applied, the overall health of individuals can benefit today.

Also, for contagious diseases of any kind, isolation has proven to be one way to prevent the spread of this disease to others and to help the infected person's healing process.

> For example, schools today instruct parents to keep children with contagious diseases at home until their contagious period has passed.

Finally, the practice of washing clothes, washing hands thoroughly and thoroughly bathing our bodies on a regular basis is proven to have positive effects on keeping an individual healthy and preventing the spread of diseases.

There are many resources on the medical benefits found within the laws of Moses. Here are two excellent books with some of this information.[2]

- ***None of these Diseases*** by S. I. McMillen, M.D. and David E. Stern, M.D.
- ***The Maker's Diet*** by Jordan Rubin, N.M.D., Ph.D

[2]Appendix C

Lesson 8.3

Reading Assignment:
Leviticus 14:33–16:34

I. Lesson Exercise

Getting to Know:

"Jehovah-Rapha: The Lord Who Heals"

If you will listen carefully to the voice of the LORD your God and do what is right in his sight, obeying his commands and laws, then I will not make you suffer the diseases I sent on the Egyptians; for I am the LORD who heals you. Ex. 15:26

Shortly after the Israelites came out of Egypt, God identified Himself as Israel's healer.

He promised to take sickness away from within their community and no woman would be barren of having children.

God would always provide good food for them to eat, and they would have long, fulfilling lives (Exodus 23:25–26).

God also promised not to allow Israel to suffer with the diseases He had sent on Egyptians.

But receiving God's healing was conditional.

The condition was that Israel was to obey all God's commands (instructions, regulations and laws) for holy living.

8) What did the Law of Moses direct priests to do with houses they determined were unclean from an infectious mildew? (Leviticus 14:45)

____

Under the Law of Moses, a man with a genital discharge is ceremonially unclean until he is healed from the discharge.

Similarly, a woman with a menstrual discharge was ceremonially unclean until the menstrual period stops.

The people and things they touch were defiled.

Before the priests would declare affected persons clean again, they went through purification time and cleansing actions.

This included washing their clothes and bathing in fresh spring water (Leviticus 15:13, 21, 27).

Day of Atonement

On the appointed day in early autumn, you must spend the day fasting and not do any work.

This is a permanent law for you, and it applies to those who are Israelites by birth, as well as to the foreigners living among you.

On this day, atonement will be made for you, and you will be cleansed from all your sins in the LORD's presence.

It will be a Sabbath day of total rest, and you will spend the day in fasting. This is a permanent law for you.

In future generations, the atonement ceremony will be performed by the anointed high priest who serves in place of his ancestor Aaron.

He will put on the holy linen garments and make atonement for the Most Holy Place, the Tabernacle, the altar, the priests, and the entire community.

This is a permanent law for you, to make atonement for the Israelites once each year. Leviticus 16:29–34

God made it very clear to Moses that the high priests—Aaron, his sons and their male descendants who stand in the office of High Priest after their death—were never to enter into the Most Holy Place except on the Day of Atonement each year.

Leviticus 16:29 explains Day of Atonement occurred in early Fall, on the 10th day of the 7th month.

Scapegoat

As part of the Day of Atonement procedures, two goats played important roles in atoning for the people.

One goat was sacrificed to the Lord. But the other goat was called the "scapegoat."

The high priest would lay his hands on the head of the scapegoat.

This symbolized his laying the sins (blame, guilt) of people on the goat in substitute for the persons who performed the sins.

When the goat ran into the wilderness, this represented the goat removing the sins from the guilty persons and taking them to some unknown territory, forever.

Atonement

9) On Day of Atonement procedures, what five things were atoned for by the High Priest? (Lev 16:33) a)______________; b)______________; c) ________________, d) _________________, e) _________________

II. Find Jesus in the Lesson

Jesus and Atonement

The Most Holy Place was a place where the **high priest** would go in once a year, on the **Day of Atonement**, to **sprinkle the blood of an animal upon** the Ark of the Covenant and **the mercy seat, which sat on top of the ark.**

> The animal was sacrificed on the Brazen Altar and its blood was carried into the Most Holy Place by the priest.

Jesus became the High Priest; the Sacrifice and His Blood was on the Mercy Seat of the Ark in the True Tabernacle in Heaven.

> He performed Atonement procedures one time for all times, which is available for all humankind who will believe in Him.

Read Hebrews Chapters 9 and 10.

III. Closing Thoughts

Day of Atonement = Yom Kippur

> ***...On the appointed day in early autumn, you must spend the day fasting and not do any work.***
>
> ***This is a permanent law for you...***
>
> ***On this day, atonement will be made for you and you will be cleansed from all your sins in the Lord's presence.***
> ***Leviticus 16:29–30***

Yom Kippur is a Jewish holiday still celebrated today.

It was instituted by God's instructions in Leviticus 16:29 and 23:26. Yom Kippur is thought to be the holiest, most celebrated Jewish holiday.

The Hebrew words "Yom Kippur" mean "Day of Atonement."

It is so named because on this day the Jews repent for all the sins, they have committed the previous year against God and people.

> This day involves dedicated fasting, praying, and attending synagogue services.
>
> No outside work is performed.
>
> Although the day is a solemn day, it is nonetheless marked by joy because of the certainty of being forgiven.

Review the chart "Jewish Feasts and Holidays" to see an example of how Yom Kippur dates occur on the calendar over several years.

The Life of Every Creature is in the Blood

Lesson 8.4

Reading Assignment:
Leviticus 17:1–19:37

I. Lesson Exercise

Instructions on "The Blood"

For the life of any creature is in its blood.
I have given you the blood
so you can make atonement for your sins.

It is the blood, representing life, that brings you atonement.

The life of every creature is in the blood.

That is why I have told the people of Israel never to eat or drink it,
for the life of any bird or animal is in the blood.

So whoever eats or drinks blood must be cut off.
Lev. 17:11, 14

In fact, we can say that according to the law of Moses,
nearly everything was purified by sprinkling with blood.

Without the shedding of blood, there is no forgiveness of sins.
Hebrews 9:22

In today's lesson, God gives instructions on the right way to use the blood to obtain His forgiveness for sins, and the wrong way to use the blood, which would result in death (cut off) of the individual who disobeys God's instructions.

God's laws not only applied to the Israelites, but also to foreigners who chose to live among them.

- **Right Way** (Lev. 16:1–9)
  - Centralized worship—only bring sacrifices to the entrance of Tabernacle where priests sprinkle the blood around the altar
- **Wrong Way** (Lev. 16:1–9)
  - Sacrificing on your own in other places inside or outside the camp; or sacrificing to evil spirits in the open field
- **Right Way** (Lev. 16:13)
  - The blood of an animal approved for eating is drained on the ground and covered with dirt, before eating it.
- **Wrong Way** (Lev. 16:10, 14)
  - Never eat or drink blood in any form

Laws and Regulations on Forbidden Relations: Lev. 18

God instructed Israel not to act like the people in Egypt where they once lived. And they were not to act like the people of Canaan where He was taking them to live.

> **In Leviticus 18, God gave detailed instructions on the specific relations the Israelites were forbidden to do.**
>
> **He also explained that these unlawful relations were the reason the Canaanites were losing the land, so God was now giving the land to Israel.**

10) God said the Canaanites' unlawful relations did what to the land? (Lev. 18:25) ____

11) God said the land would soon do what to the Canaanites? (Lev. 18:25) ____

Finally, God warned the Israelites that if they committed the forbidden relations, then like the Canaanites the land would vomit them out also. (Leviticus 18:28)

Instructions for Holy Living in Everyday Life Activities

God gave more detailed instructions on what holy living looked like in everyday life.

He summarized again the proper way to approach Him and not idols.

He explained the proper way to treat family members and the proper way to interact with others not in the family.

These instructions included proper business practices and treatment of the poor.

He gave instructions on the proper way to talk and how to dress. God also gave instructions on matters of the heart.

- **Do not nurse hatred in your heart for any of your relatives**, but confront them and talk about the situation, in hopes of resolving the problem. (Lev. 19:17)
- **Never seek revenge or bear a grudge against anyone**. (Lev. 19:18)
- **Love your neighbor as you love yourself.** (Lev. 19:18) This implies you need to love yourself, meaning have a positive self-image, taking good care of yourself. (Matt. 5:43–46)

II. Find Jesus in the Lesson and III. Closing Thoughts

Only the Precious Blood of Jesus Atones for Humankind's Sin

Priests did the following types of actions with the blood of animals:

- **Sprinkled the Blood on people, on furniture**
  (Examples: Exodus 24:8, Leviticus 4:5; Leviticus 16:18–19, Leviticus 14:51–52)
- **Poured the Blood out**
  (Examples: Leviticus 1:15, Leviticus 4:7, Leviticus 8:15)
- **Strategically applied the Blood to parts of furniture, or parts of people**
  (Leviticus 4:7, Leviticus 8:23–24, Leviticus 14:14)

Sin separated man from God.

In the Old Testament, God gave power to the life-giving blood of specific animals, properly applied as He instructed, to atone for humankind's sin.

By a decision of God's mercy and grace, this allowed God to forgive man for his sin, so God and man could be in fellowship.

The blood of animals was a temporary solution until the blood of Jesus was shed in a one-time human sacrifice.

In the New Testament, God still requires the blood properly applied to atone for humankind's sin.

God only approves of the Precious Blood of Jesus (1 Peter 1:18–19) **as the powerful atoning blood agent**.

Through the crucifixion experience, where Jesus' blood was shed before and on the cross, **Jesus' blood was sprinkled, poured out and strategically applied as God required for humankind's redemption.**

Jesus' blood lives today on the Mercy Seat of the Heavenly Ark.

It obtains God's mercy and grace for all those who believe in Jesus (Hebrews 9:11–14; 10:10, 12:24).

The Saving, Cleansing, Healing, Resurrecting
Powerful Blood of Jesus
is applied to one's life today
by the prayer of faith.

(John 3:16, Rom. 3:21–25, Heb. 4:14–16)

Blessings for Obedience

Reading Assignment:
Leviticus 20:1–22:33

Lesson 8.5

I. Lesson Exercise

You must carefully obey all my laws and regulations;
otherwise the land to which I am bringing you will vomit you out.

Do not live by the customs of the people whom I will expel before you.
It is because they do these terrible things that I detest them so much.

But I have promised that you will inherit their land,
a land flowing with milk and honey.

I, the LORD, am your God, who has set you apart from all other people.
Leviticus 20:22–24

Consequences for Disobeying God's Laws and Regulations

The Good News is...

the awesome benefits of following God's instructions were health, wealth, and joyous times for all in Israel, natives and foreigners alike.

The Bad News is...

the punishment for disobeying God was severe, in most cases, death. Lev. 20:1–27 details when death is the punishment for disobeying laws.

- Do not offer children as sacrifice to idol god Molech / to disobey = death
- Do not commit prostitution by worshipping idol god / to disobey = death
- Do not consult mediums and psychics, meaning those with familiar (evil) spirits who try to contact the dead or predict the future using "magic," such as witches, palm readers and occult games / to disobey = death
- Do not curse father or mother / to disobey = death
- Do not commit adultery with another's man's wife / to disobey = death
- Do not commit forbidden relations with family members, including those married into the family / to disobey = death
- Do not commit forbidden relations with the same gender / to disobey = death
- Do not commit forbidden relations with animals / to disobey = death
- Do not have relations with a woman on menstrual period / to disobey = death
- A man is not to marry his living brother's wife / to disobey = childless
- Do not eat animals or birds God has defined as unclean / to disobey = health problems, and isolation from God and others

12) What was to happen to men and women who act as mediums or psychics? (Leviticus 20:27) ____

Consequences for Disobedience

More Instructions for the Priests

The Priests' punishment for disobeying God's laws was death. (Lev 21:1–22:16)

- Priests do not touch dead relatives unless immediate family members.
- Priests do not shave beards, trim the edges of beards or cut their bodies
- Priests do not marry harlot, or divorced women; daughter who becomes a harlot, must be put to death.
- High Priests, who have anointing oil on them, do not wear hair loose or tear clothing as in mourning, and do not attend family funerals while consecrated.
- High Priests must marry virgins from within the tribe of Levi. Do not marry harlot, divorced, or widowed women.
- High Priests cannot have physical defects
- Priests who are unclean may not eat of the sacred offerings, until clean again
- Only the priests' immediate family can eat the sacred offerings
- Priests and people had to give great care to bringing the proper offerings, such as animals with no physical defects of any kind and at least eight days old

13) God had one other very important command for all Israel, priests and common folk alike in Leviticus 22:32. What is this command? ____________________

<u>II. Find Jesus in the Lesson and III. Closing Thoughts</u>

Jesus, Humankind's Perfect Sacrifice for Sin

The perfect animal sacrifices, with no physical defects, were a symbol of the perfect, sinless, blameless, faultless life of Jesus Christ, who died as a lamb without blemish or spot, in substitute payment for the sins of humankind. (1 Peter 1:19)

Although he died on the cross like a criminal, Jesus was not guilty of any wrongdoing. (Isaiah 53:12, 1 Peter 2:21–24)

Consider the testimony of the Roman governor, Pilate, who struggled with the final sentence he was pressured into giving to crucify Jesus.

What is truth?" Pilate asked.
Then he went out again to the people and told them,
"He is not guilty of any crime.
But you have a custom of asking me to release someone from prison
each year at Passover. So if you want me to, I'll release the King of the Jews."

But they shouted back, "No! Not this man, but Barabbas!"
(Barabbas was a criminal.)

***

Then Pilate had Jesus flogged with a lead-tipped whip.
The soldiers made a crown of long, sharp thorns and put it on his head,
and they put a royal purple robe on him. "Hail! King of the Jews!" they
mocked, and they hit him with their fists.

Pilate went outside again and said to the people,
"I am going to bring him out to you now,
but understand clearly that I find him not guilty."
John 18:38–40, 19:1–4

Seven Festivals of the Lord

Reading Assignment:
Leviticus 23:1–25:23

Lesson 8.6

I. Lesson Exercise: Instructions on the "Seven Festivals of the Lord"

There was a holy day every seventh day of every week, called the **Sabbath Day**. This day was a time of no work and worshipful assembly. In addition to the weekly Sabbath days, God established seven festivals, which were holy occasions with **special Sabbath Days**. Israel was to observe them at specific times every year.

God directed Israel to keep Seven Festivals in Leviticus 23.

- Festival of Passover (Lev 23: 4–5)
- Festival of Unleavened Bread (Lev 23:6–8)
- Festival of Firstfruits (Lev 23:9–14)
- Festival of Harvest (Lev 23:15–22)
- Festival of Trumpets (Lev 23:2—25)
- The Day of Atonement (Lev 23:26–32)
- Festival of Shelters (Lev 23:33–43)

Sabbath Years

Not only were there Sabbath Days of rest for the people, but God also established Sabbath Years of rest, which provided for restoration of the land and families.

Every seventh year, the land was to have one full year of total rest, in which the Israelites were not to plant or store anything that grew naturally.

14) What were the Israelites and their animals to eat during the Sabbath Year? (Lev. 25:6-7) ______________________________

The year after seven Sabbath years (7 x 7 = 49th year), was known as the Year of Jubilee. On the Day of Atonement of the forty-ninth year, trumpets were blown loud and long to kick off the Jubilee celebration for the start of the fiftieth year.

In this year debts were forgiven, slaves released, property returned to original family owners and again no farming.

15) What was God going to do to ensure the people had plenty to eat despite not farming the land in the Sabbath Years? (Lev. 25:21—22)

____

II. Find Jesus in the Lesson and III. Closing Thoughts

Review the charts:

- **God's Work/Rest Plan for Israel**
- **Feasts and Holidays of the Bible** (shows Jesus participation)
- **Jewish Feasts & Holidays**

Lesson 8.7

Reading Assignment:
Leviticus 25:24–26:46

I. Lesson Exercise: Kinsman Redeemer

A close relative is called a kinsman, being in close kinship by blood relationship. A redeemer is a person who buys back something by paying the correct price and restoring it to the original owner.

The idea of a kinsman redeemer is a close relative who buys back person(s) or property that was sold by his relative who fell into "hard times" in life, and then restores the relative to original status.

In today's lesson, we learn how a kinsman redeemer is allowed to help his close relative by buying back the land or lives of his relatives. This is necessary when it is not the Year of Jubilee, when the release would happen automatically.

16) Were the foreigners in Israel, who became rich and purchased Israelites as slaves, required to abide by the laws of the Year of Jubilee and Kinsman Redeemer? (Lev. 25:47–53) ______________________

Redemption of Property and Poor, enslaved people

- Land and houses were eventually returned to original owners in Jubilee Year, except for one exception. (Lev. 25:24–30)
- The Israelites were not allowed to charge their relatives with interest on anything they lent to them, whether money or food. (Lev. 25:35–37)
- The Israelites were not allowed to treat relatives who sold themselves to them as slaves, but as hired servants. They only served until Jubilee. (Lev. 25:40–43)

*** **Review the chart: God's Economic Plan for Israel** ***

Blessings for Obedience, Curses for Disobedience

God made it clear that if Israel kept His laws and carefully obeyed His commands, the nation would experience health, wealth, peace, and joy, because of God's blessings and presence among them. They would walk free with their heads held high!

On the other hand, if they did not obey God's laws and commands, then the curses on their lives would be severe and increase until they returned to a state of obedience. Sickness, disease, and poverty were at one level, but if the Israelites still disobeyed God, they would eventually eat their own children (Lev. 26:29).

Finally, the Israelites would be scattered in shame among foreign nations, until they learned to honor God in their lives again. Yet, God did make it clear He would never forsake them forever, because of His covenant with their ancestors. (Lev 26:44–45)

II. Find Jesus in the Lesson and III. Closing Thoughts

Jesus Is Humankind's Kinsman Redeemer

When Jesus took on human flesh, he became the Kinsman (brother) Redeemer (savior) "brother-savior" for humankind. He saves us from eternal perishing and gives us eternal life if we believe in Him. (Heb. 2:9–15, John 3:16–17)

God's Economic Plan for Israel

Definition: Economic

"of or having to do with the production, distribution, and consumption of wealth"
"of or having to do with the satisfaction of material needs of people"
Webster New World College Dictionary: Fourth Edition

God's covenant agreement with Israel included an overall economic plan that enabled the nation as a whole to live prosperously.

If Israel would keep God's commands, then His blessings would result in tremendous benefits to meet the needs of all.

God would send seasonal rains so the land would yield a surplus of crops and fruit, even during days and years of Sabbath rest. All Israel would live happy and safe in the land God gave them. (Lev. 26:1–13)

The below highlights key areas of God's economic plan for Israel.

<u>God's Economic Plan for providing for the Tabernacle, Priests and Levites</u>

- Tithe—all goes to Levites as their inheritance — Numbers 18
  Lev. 27:30–33, Deut. 14:22–29, Deut. 26:1–15
- Tithe of tithes—go to High Priest — Num. 18:21–29
- Census tax — Ex. 30:11–16
- Firstborn tax — Numbers 3:40–51
- A portion of offerings for the priests — Lev. 7:28–38
- Holy gifts for the Lord given to priests and Levites — Num. 18:8–32
- Towns for the Levites — Num. 35:1–8
- Gifts for the priests and Levites — Deut. 18:1–8

<u>God's Economic Plan for providing for the Family</u>

- Work six days, Rest one day and Refresh — Lev. 23:3, Deut. 5:14
- Land assigned to Israel and tribes in Promise Land — Num. 34:1–29
- Women who inherit property — Num. 36: 1–13
- Power to get wealth to establish covenant — Deut. 8:18
- Rights of the firstborn — Deut. 21:15–17
- Inheritance remains in family after death — Num. 27:8–11
- God abundantly prospers covenant-keepers — Deut. 28:1–14; 29:9

<u>God's Economic Plan for providing for Poor and those on Hard Times</u>

- Sabbath year rest of land so poor can eat — Ex. 23:11
- Leave excess food for poor and strangers — Lev. 19:9–10
  Lev. 23:23
- Temporary Hired Servant or Enslaved status — Lev. 25: 25–55
  Lev. 19:13, Ex. 21:1–11, Deut. 24:10-12
- Redemption of property — Lev. 25: 24–34
- Jubilee Year of restored inheritances and freedoms — Lev. 25: 8–23
- Release of debtors and Hebrew slaves — Deut. 15: 1–18
- Third year tithe goes to Levite, poor, fatherless, etc — Deut. 26:12

God's Work / Rest Plan for Israel

In Leviticus Chapters 23 and 25, Moses instructs Israel on God's work/rest plan for the entire nation. God's plan allowed time for all the people to rest, as well as providing rest for the land God had given them. During the rest times, the people were to spend quality time in worship to God and in fellowship with one another. No one was to do work. This allowed the work animals to also rest. For their obedience, Israel's families would be healthy and prosperous. The below diagram highlights the work/rest cycle.

		Scripture References
Weekly	**6-day Work Week** — **7th Day Sabbath Rest = No Work**	**Leviticus 23:3**
Monthly	**6d Work / 7d Rest** · **6d Work / 7d Rest** · **6d Work / 7d Rest** · **6d Work / 7d Rest**	**Leviticus 23:1–4**
Yearly	**Spring Festival**: No Work · **Summer Festival**: No Work · **Fall Festival**: No Work	**Leviticus 23:5–44**
Sabbath Year	**6-Work Years** ▢▢▢▢▢▢ **7th Year Sabbath Rest**: No Work (**NW**) · **6-Work Years** ▢▢▢▢▢▢ **7th Year Sabbath Rest**: **NW**	**Leviticus 25:1–7**
Jubilee Year	▢▢▢▢▢▢ N W · ▢▢▢▢▢▢ N W · ▢▢▢▢▢▢ N W ▢▢▢▢▢▢ N W · ▢▢▢▢▢▢ N W · ▢▢▢▢▢▢ N W ▢▢▢▢▢▢ N W · N W **= 49th Year Sabbath of Sabbath Yrs + 50th Jubilee Year**	**Leviticus 25:8–23**

HOLIDAY	DATE OBSERVED	SCRIPTURE BASIS	GENERAL INFORMATION
PASSOVER (Pesach) and	**14 NISAN** *(MARCH OR APRIL)*	Leviticus 23:4, 5 Exodus 12:1-4	**Passover and Unleavened Bread: Commemorates God's Deliverance of Israel Out of Egypt** *Pesach* (PAY-sahk) means to "pass over." The Passover meal, seder (SAY der), commemorates the Israelites' deliverance from slavery in Egypt. The LORD sent Moses to lead the children of Israel from Egypt to the Promised Land. When first confronted by Moses, Pharaoh refused to let the people go. After sending nine plagues, the LORD said the firstborn males of every house would die unless the doorframe of that house was covered with the blood of a perfect lamb. That night, the LORD "passed over" the homes with blood on the doorframes. The tenth plague brought death to the firstborn sons of Egypt, even taking the life of Pharaoh's own son. Finally, Pharaoh let the children of Israel go. Passover was to be a lasting ordinance for generations to come. In Leviticus, the LORD said that on the fourteenth day of the first month (of the religious new year) the LORD's Passover was to begin at twilight.
UNLEAVENED BREAD (Hag Hamatzot)	**15-21 NISAN** *(MARCH OR APRIL)*	Leviticus 23:6-8 Exodus 12:15-20	In Leviticus 23, *Hag HaMatzot* (Hawg Hah MAHT zot) or *Hag HaMatzah*, also known as the "Feast of Unleavened Bread," is mentioned as a separate feast on the fifteenth day of the same month as Passover. Today, however, the feasts of Pesach, Unleavened Bread, and Firstfruits have all been incorporated into the celebration of Passover, and reference to *Passover* means all three feasts. Passover is celebrated for eight days, Nisan 14-21. The LORD said that for seven days the children of Israel must eat unleavened bread. This bread, made in a hurry without yeast, represents how the LORD brought the Israelites out of Egypt in haste. In Scripture, leaven also represents sin. Orthodox Jews believe that not only is eating bread with leaven unlawful during the Feast of Unleavened Bread, but even having leaven present in one's house or apartment is forbidden. Today, cleansing the house before Passover is often a symbolic search to remove any hypocrisy or wickedness. Unleavened Bread is one of the three pilgrimage feasts when all Jewish males were required to go to Jerusalem to "appear before the LORD." (Deut. 16:16)
FIRSTFRUITS (Yom HaBikkurim)	**16 NISAN** *(MARCH OR APRIL)*	Leviticus 23:9-14	**Firstfruits: Offerings are Given for the Spring Barley Harvest** On *Yom HaBikkurim* (Yome Hah-Bee-koo-REEM) people offered the first ripe sheaf (firstfruits) of barley to the LORD as an act of dedicating the harvest to him. On Passover, a marked sheaf of grain was bundled and left standing in the field. On the next day, the first day of Unleavened Bread, the sheaf was cut and prepared for the offering on the third day. On this third day, Yom HaBikkurim, the priest waved the sheaf before the LORD. Counting the days (*omer*) then begins and continues until the day after the seventh Sabbath, the 50th day, which is called *Shavuot* or Pentecost (the next feast on the calendar). Jewish people rarely celebrate Yom HaBikkurim today, but it has great significance for followers of Jesus as the most important day of the year, the day of Jesus' resurrection.
FEAST OF WEEKS *or* **PENTECOST (Shavnot)**	**6 SIVAN** *(MAY OR JUNE)*	Leviticus 23:15-22	**Feasts of Weeks: Offerings are Given and Commemorates Giving of the Law** Fifty days after Passover, *Shavuot* (Sha-voo-OTE) is celebrated. Also known as Pentecost, Feast of Weeks, the Feast of Harvest, and the Latter Firstfruits, it is the time to present an offering of new grain of the summer wheat harvest to the LORD. It shows joy and thankfulness for the LORD's blessing of harvest. Often called *Matin Torah* (giving of the Law), it is tied to the Ten Commandments because it is believed God gave Moses the Ten Commandments at this time. Historically, children receive treats for memorizing Scripture at Shavuot. The book of Ruth is often read to celebrate the holiday. Pentecost is a popular day for Jewish Confirmation. Shavuot is one of the three pilgrimage feasts when all Jewish males were required to go to Jerusalem to "appear before the LORD." (Deuteronomy 16:16)
FEAST OF TRUMPETS *or* **NEW YEAR (Rosh HaShanah)**	**1 TISHRI** *(SEPTEMBER OR OCTOBER)*	Leviticus 23:23-25	**Feast of Trumpets: The Beginning of the Civil New Year** *Rosh HaShanah* (Rosh Ha-SHA-nah), the Ten Days of Repentance that follow it, and Yom Kippur make up the High Holy Days. Jewish tradition says that God writes every person's words, deeds, and thoughts in the Book of Life, which he opens and examines on this day. If good deeds outnumber sinful ones for the year, that person's name will be inscribed in the book for another year on Yom Kippur. So during Rosh HaShanah and the Ten Days of Repentance, people can repent of their sins and do good deeds to increase their chances of being inscribed in the Book of Life. Prior to Rosh HaShanah, the *shofar* (ram's horn) is blown to call people to repent and remind them that the holy days are arriving. During the Rosh HaShanah synagogue services, the shofar is blown 100 times.

	YESHUA (JESUS)	FASCINATING FACTS
Passover	Jesus ate the Passover with his disciples, saying that he had eagerly desired to eat this Passover with them before he suffered and that he would not eat it again until the kingdom of God comes. (Luke 22:7-16) After the Passover meal, they sang a hymn and went to the Mount of Olives. (Matthew 26:30) The hymn sung during Passover is the *Hallel* which includes Psalm 118:22: "The stone the builders rejected has become the capstone." Jesus is the capstone that the builders rejected. (Matt. 21:42; 1 Pet. 2:7) Jesus was crucified on Passover Day as the "Lamb of God who takes away the sin of the world." (John 1:29) The Lord's Supper is a remembrance of his sacrifice as the perfect Passover Lamb and the fullfilment of the new covenant between God and man. (Luke 22:20; 1 Cor. 5:7; Eph. 2:11-13) Prophecy of this sacrifice is found in Psalm 22. The Hebrew prophet Isaiah also spoke of the sufferings and sacrifice of the Messiah, and how that sacrifice would be the ultimate atonement for the sins of God's people. (Isaiah 53)	• Jesus' parents traveled to Jerusalem yearly to celebrate Passover. At age 12, Jesus went with them. (Luke 2:41-50) • The Passover lamb must be a perfect male with no spot or blemish. (Exodus 12:5) • The cup of the Lord's Supper is the third cup of the Passover *seder*, the cup of redemption. The bread of the Lord's Supper is the *afikomen*. It is the matzah that is broken, hidden, found, bought for a price, and then eaten to end the meal. *Afikomen* means "I came" in Greek. • A hymn is usually sung at the end of the passover service, as was the case with Jesus and his disciples. (Matthew 26:30)
Unleavened Bread	*Matzot* is plural for *matzah*. Unleavened bread (matzah) is a symbol of Passover. Leaven represents sin. (Luke 2:1; 1 Cor. 5:8) Matzah stands for "without sin" and is a picture of Jesus, the only human without sin. Jesus said that the "bread of God is he who comes down from heaven and gives life to the world" and that he (Jesus) is the "bread of life," the "bread that came down from heaven," "the living bread" which a man may eat and not die. (John 6:32, 35, 41, 48) While leaven is a symbol of sin, the Messiah is "unleavened" or sinless. He conquers the grave with his resurrection because he is not a sinner under the curse of death. Jesus was scourged and pierced at his crucifixion. As the prophet Isaiah proclaims, "By his stripes we are healed." (Isaiah 53:5) All of the festivals instituted by God, including Passover and Unleavened Bread, are "shadows of things to come." (Col. 2:17)	• The only type of bread eaten during the eight days of Passover/ Unleavened Bread is matzah. It is made with flour and water only, not any leaven. It is striped and pierced during baking. • The utensils used must never touch leaven. Bakery goods are made with matzah meal. • On the night before Passover, the father does a final search for any remaining leaven in the house. Traditionally, by candlelight, he sweeps any remaining bread crumbs onto a wooden spoon with a goose feather. When finished, the bread crumbs, the feather, and the spoon are placed in a bag and burned the next morning.
Firstfruits	Yom HaBikkurim is a picture of Jesus' resurrection. Jesus rose on the third day of Passover season, Nisan 16, the day of Firstfruits. That event gave new meaning to this agricultural holiday. The apostle Paul, a Jewish believer and rabbi, wrote, "But Christ has indeed been raised from the dead, the firstfruits of those who have fallen asleep. For as in Adam all die, so in Christ all will be made alive. But each in his own turn: Christ, the firstfruits; then, when he comes, those who belong to him." (1 Cor. 15:20, 22, 23, NIV) Jesus' resurrection is the promise of the future resurrection of believers. (John 5:28, 29) Although most believers in Jesus have never heard of Yom HaBikkurim, they celebrate it as Resurrection Day, or Easter.	Biblical events that happened on this day: • The manna, which God provided from heaven as food for the Israelites while they wandered in the wilderness, stopped after they crossed the Jordan River into the Promised Land. (Josh. 5:10-12) • Queen Esther risked her life to save the Jewish people from annihilation. (Esther 3:12-5:7) • Jesus rose from the dead on the third day. (Luke 24:44-47) • Since the Temple was destroyed in AD 70, firstfruits sacrifices and offerings are no longer offered on this day. Today, Jews use this date to begin the counting of the days (omer). On the 33rd day of counting the omer, a minor rabbinical holiday called Lag B'Omer is celebrated where campfires are built and people roast potatoes and sing songs.
Pentecost	Jesus told his disciples to wait in Jerusalem following his crucifixion, resurrection, and ascension. They were all together in the upper room for Shavuot on the 50th day after the Sabbath of Passover week, thus, the first day of the week. The Holy Spirit filled the house, with a sound like a mighty wind and what appeared to be tongues of fire, and filled the disciples. (Acts 2) The apostle Peter referred to the prophet Joel who said that God would "pour out his Spirit on all flesh." (Joel 2:28-32) Peter also said that the risen and exalted Jesus had poured out the Holy Spirit. (Acts 2:32, 33) The people responded to Peter's message with repentance, and more than 3,000 were baptized. (Acts 2:37-40) The new covenant between God and Israel (Jeremiah 31:31; Hebrews 9:14, 15) is initiated on Shavuot, 50 days after the death of Christ.	• Shavuot is celebrated 50 days after Passover, so it became known as *Pentecost*, which means "50" in Greek. The days from Passover to Shavuot are counted at weekly Sabbath services. • Special foods for this holiday are dairy foods, such as cheesecake and cheese blintzes, because the Law is compared to milk and honey. • Homes and synagogues are decorated with flowers and greenery, which represent the harvest and the Torah as a "tree of life." Observant Jews often spend the night reading and studying the Torah.
Feast of Trumpets	*Rosh HaShanah* is sometimes referred to as the Day of Judgment. Jesus said he has the authority to judge people (John 5:24-27) and the apostle Paul referred to him as the judge of "the living and the dead." (2 Tim. 4:1) God does have a book of life; Revelation 21:27 calls it the "Lamb's book of life." The only way to have one's name inscribed in it is through faith in Jesus as Savior from sin, and then it is permanent. (John 10:27-30) Those whose names are not in the book will be judged and sentenced to hell: "If anyone's name was not found written in the book of life, he was thrown into the lake of fire." (Rev. 20:15) Some people believe the four spring holidays (Passover, Unleavened Bread, Firstfruits, and Feast of Weeks) were fulfilled in Messiah's first coming and that the three autumn holidays (Feast of Trumpets, Day of Atonement, and Feast of Booths) will be fulfilled at his second coming.	• Rosh HaShanah is a serious New Year holiday, not a happy one like January 1. A common custom is sending cards to relatives and friends to wish them a happy, healthy, and prosperous new year. The message includes the greeting *L'shanah tovah tikatevoo*, which means "May you be inscribed [in the Book of Life] for a good year." • It is traditional to eat apple slices dipped in honey. The apples represent provision, and the honey represents sweetness for the coming year. • Many Jewish people attend Rosh HaShanah and Yom Kippur services even if they have not attended synagogue services the rest of the year.

HOLIDAY	DATE OBSERVED	SCRIPTURE BASIS	GENERAL INFORMATION
DAY OF ATONEMENT (Yom Kippur)	**10 TISHRI** *(SEPTEMBER OR OCTOBER)*	Leviticus 23:26-32	**Day of Atonement: The Day the High Priest Makes Atonement for Sin** *Yom Kippur* (Yome Ki-POOR), also known as Day of Atonement, is the most solemn holy day of the Jewish people. *Yom* means "day" and *Kippur* means "atonement" or "covering." *Atonement* means the reconciliation of God and man. The ten days between Rosh HaShanah and Yom Kippur are known as the "days of repentance." Yom Kippur is the final day of judgment when God judges the people. In Bible times, the High Priest sacrificed an animal to pay for his sins and the sins of the people. It was a time of fasting and prayer. The shofar (ram's horn) is blown at the end of the evening prayer service for the first time since Rosh HaShanah. When the high priest was finished with the atonement sacrifice, a goat was released into the wilderness. This "scapegoat" carried Israel's sins away, never to return. (Leviticus 16:8-10, 20-22, 29-34)
FEAST OF BOOTHS *or* TABERNACLES (Sukkot)	**15-21 TISHRI** *(SEPTEMBER OR OCTOBER)*	Leviticus 23:33-43	**Feast of Booths: Commemorates the 40-Year Wilderness Journey** *Sukkot* (Soo-KOTE or SOO-kote), also known as "Feast of Tabernacles," is a week-long celebration of the fall harvest and a time to build booths (temporary shelters of branches) to remember how the Hebrew people lived under God's care during their forty years in the wilderness. (Nehemiah 8:14-17) The celebration is a reminder of God's faithfulness and protection. Jews continue to celebrate Sukkot by building and dwelling in temporary booths for eight days. The four special plants used to cover the booths are citron, myrtle, palm, and willow. (Leviticus 39:40) Sukkot is one of the three pilgrimage feasts when all Jewish males were required to go to Jerusalem to "appear before the LORD." (Deuteronomy 16:16)
REJOICING IN THE LAW (Simchat Torah)	**22 or 23 TISHRI** *(SEPTEMBER OR OCTOBER)*	Leviticus 23:36	**Joy of Torah: Celebrates the Completion of Reading the Torah** The eighth and final day of the celebration of Sukkot was appointed by God as a sacred assembly. Today the final day is known as *Simchat Torah* (SIM-khat TOE-rah or SIM-khat Toe-RAH) meaning "Rejoice in the Torah, God's Word." Starting in the Middle Ages, it is a celebration of the giving and receiving of the *Torah* or the *Pentateuch* (the first five books of the Bible) which is the foundation of Jewish belief and faith. Torah also means "Law" or direction. Followers of Jesus accept the Torah and the other books of the Jewish Scriptures. They believe that "Above all, you must understand that no prophecy of Scripture came about by the prophet's own interpretation. For prophecy never had its origin in the will of man, but men spoke from God as they were carried along by the Holy Spirit." (2 Peter 1:20, 21)
FEAST OF DEDICATION (Hanukkah) (Chanukah)	**25 KISLEV-2 TEVET** *(NOVEMBER OR DECEMBER)*	John 10:22 Also Book of Maccabees (Apocrypha)	**Feast of Dedication: Commemorates the Purification of the Temple** *Hanukkah* (KHA-noo-kah), the Feast of Dedication, celebrates the Maccabees' victory over the Greeks and the rededication of the Temple in 165 BC after Seleucid king Antiochus Epiphanes defiled it by sacrificing a pig on the altar and pouring the blood on the Scripture scrolls. The Maccabees' victory, a miracle of God's deliverance, is recorded in the books of Maccabees, which are included in the Apocrypha. Hanukkah is also known as the Feast of Lights because of a legendary miraculous provision of oil for the eternal light in the Temple. After cleansing the Temple, the supply of oil to relight the eternal flame (the symbol of God's presence) was only enough for one day. But God performed a great miracle, and the flame burned for the eight days necessary to purify new oil.
FEAST OF LOTS (Purim)	**14 or 15 ADAR** *(FEBRUARY OR MARCH)*	Book of Esther	**Feast of Lots: Commemorates the Preservation of the Jewish People** *Purim* (POOR-im) marks the deliverance of the Jews through Jewish Queen Esther in Shushan, Persia (Susa, Iran). Esther was her Persian name, meaning "star." Her Hebrew name was *Hadassah*, which means "myrtle." The annual celebration of Purim is a joyous feast remembering the foiled plot of Haman to kill all the Jews living within King Xerxes's (Ahasuerus's) kingdom. Esther's uncle Mordecai uncovered the plot and warned Esther, who then told the King. The King had Haman executed. Adar 14 and 15 became days of joy and feasting. (Esther 9:18-32) Purim is celebrated on Adar 14 in most cities except those cities surrounded by walls since the time of Joshua. Walled cities celebrate Purim on Adar 15 *(Shushan Purim)*. In Jewish leap years, when there is an extra month of Adar, Purim is always celebrated during the second month.

	YESHUA (JESUS)	FASCINATING FACTS
Day of Atonement	The Holy of Holies, in the Temple, was separated from the congregation by a veil from floor to ceiling. It was entered once a year on Yom Kippur, when the High Priest offered the blood sacrifice of atonement on behalf of the people. When Jesus died on the cross, the thick veil was ripped from top to bottom. (Luke 23:44-46) Christ came as high priest and entered the Holy of Holies (heaven itself) once for all, not by the blood of goats and calves but by his own blood, having obtained eternal redemption. (Hebrews 9:11-28) Believers in Jesus accept his sacrifice on the cross as the final atonement for sin, "being justified freely by his grace through the redemption that is in Christ Jesus." (Romans 3:21-25a) When Messiah returns, Israel will look on him, whom they pierced, and repent. (Zechariah 12:10) On this day of repentance, Israel will be forgiven and permanently restored. (Isaiah 66:7-14; Romans 11:26)	• After the Temple was destroyed in AD 70, Jewish people could no longer offer the prescribed sacrifices for atonement from sins. They have substituted prayer, good works, and charitable donations hoping to take away the penalty for their sins. • Yom Kippur is a day of fasting. No work is done on this day, including at home. Many Jewish people spend the day at synagogue, praying for forgiveness of their sins. Immediately after the evening service, they have a "break fast" meal. • The book of Jonah is read during the afternoon service to remind people of God's forgiveness and mercy.
Feast of Booths	Two ceremonies were part of the last day of Sukkot: 1. People carrying torches marched around the Temple, then set these lights around the walls of the Temple, indicating that Messiah would be a light to the Gentiles. (Isaiah 49:6) 2. A priest carried water from the pool of Siloam to the Temple, symbolizing that when Messiah comes the whole earth will know God "as the waters cover the sea." (Isa. 11:9) When Jesus attended the Feast of Tabernacles, on the last day of the feast, he said, "If anyone is thirsty, let him come to me and drink. Whoever believes in me, as the Scripture has said, streams of living water will flow from within him." (John 7:37, 38) The next morning while the torches were still burning, he said, "I am the light of the world." (John 8:12) Sukkot represents the final harvest when all nations will share in the joy and blessings of God's Kingdom. During that time, all believers will celebrate this feast. (Zech. 14:16-19)	• Sukkot is a happy feast when people rejoice in God's forgiveness and material blessings. • The sukkah, or booth, is a temporary structure built of wood or wood and canvas. The roof is made of branches and leaves, with enough open spaces to see the stars. The sukkah is decorated with fall flowers, leaves, fruits, and vegetables. Many Jewish people erect booths on their lawns or balconies and eat at least one meal a day in them. • A *lulav*, made up of willow, palm, and myrtle branches, is waved in all four directions (north, south, east, and west) and up and down to symbolize that God's presence is everywhere.
Rejoicing in Law	John 1:1 reads, "In the beginning was the Word, and the Word was with God and the Word was God." John 1:14 reads, "... and the Word became flesh and dwelt (tabernacled) among us." Jesus is the Word which became flesh (incarnated) and dwelt (tabernacled) among us. The Word of God is a lamp to our feet and a light for our path. (Psalm 119:105) Jesus, the Word made flesh, is also a lamp to our feet and light for our path that leads to salvation. (John 8:12) We rejoice (*simchat*) in the Torah—the written Torah and the *incarnate Torah*—Jesus. Jesus said that he came to fulfill both the Law and the Prophets. (Matthew 5:17) Torah is the written word; Jesus is the living Word.	• In Israel, Simchat Torah is usually celebrated on 22 Tishri. In other places, it is 23 Tishri. • In the synagogue, the Torah is divided into portions and read each week in the worship service. During Simchat Torah, men and women in the congregation receive an *aliyah*, which is a chance to read a portion of the Torah from the pulpit. When finished, the congregation celebrates by marching around the sanctuary, carrying the Torah scrolls, singing, and praising God. Then, the reading of the Torah is completed by reading the last chapter of Deuteronomy. The reading of the Torah begins again with Genesis 1 for the next year.
Dedication	Although the history behind Hanukkah is recorded in books that were written in the time between the Hebrew Scriptures and the New Testament, the book of John tells us that it was celebrated in Jesus' day: "Then came the Feast of Dedication at Jerusalem. It was winter, and Jesus was in the temple area walking in Solomon's Colonnade." (John 10:22, 23) The Feast of Dedication is a reminder of those who courageously remain faithful to God in the face of persecution. One of the major themes throughout the New Testament is remaining faithful to Christ, especially during persecution. (Matt. 5:10-12; 1 Cor. 4:12; 2 Cor. 4:9) The book of Revelation speaks specifically to the persecution believers will face before the return of Christ. (Rev. 2:10; 13:10) Hanukkah is also a reminder that God is faithful and delivers his people not only from the oppression of Antiochus Epiphanes, but also from the oppression of sin and death.	• Hanukkah is primarily a family celebration that centers around the lighting of a nine-candle *menorah*, or candlestick, called a *hanukkiyah*. Each night another candle is lit with the center candle called a *shammash*, or servant candle, until all nine are lit. • Holiday foods include *latkes* (potato pancakes) and donuts fried in oil. The oil is a reminder of the miracle of the oil. • Perhaps because Hanukkah falls close to Christmas, it is now traditional to give presents, often one per night after the candles are lit. • Children play dreydel games with a top that reminds them of the great miracle of God's deliverance from the Greeks. Hanukkah is also called the "Festival of Lights."
Feast of Lots	Purim celebrates the story told in the book of Esther. (Esther 9:18-32) It is a celebration of God's faithful protection of his people. The Jews of Esther's day were delivered from an irrevocable decree of the Persian king Ahasuerus. God also has an irrevocable decree that all people are sinners and deserve death. (Genesis 2:17; Romans 3:23) However, the Messiah delivers all who believe in him from that irrevocable decree as well. (Isaiah 53; Romans 6:23) Many have and may continue to persecute believers in Messiah, but Isaiah's prophecy suggests that they will not prevail because "God is with us," or literally because of *Immanuel*. (Isaiah 8:10)	• The word *purim* means "lots" and refers to the lot Haman cast to decide the day for the destruction of the Jewish people. (Esther 3:7) • God's name is not mentioned in the book of Esther, but his providence and provision are obvious. • Purim is a happy and noisy holiday. To celebrate, the *megillah* (scroll of the book of Esther) is read in the synagogue. Whenever Haman is mentioned, everyone boos, stamps feet, and shakes noisemakers (called *groggers*). Whenever Mordecai is mentioned, everyone cheers. • *Hamantashen* is a three-cornered cookie which represents Haman's hat.

JEWISH FEASTS & HOLIDAYS

Gregorian Year	2005	2006	2007	2008	2009	2010	2011	2012
Holiday	(Starts at sundown the previous day)							
Pesach (Passover)	April 24	April 13	April 3	April 20	April 9	March 30	April 19	April 7
HagHaMatzoh (Unleavened Bread)	April 25	April 14	April 4	April 21	April 10	March 31	April 20	April 8
Yom HaBikkurim (First Fruits)	April 26	April 15	April 5	April 22	April 11	April 1	April 21	April 9
Shavuot (Pentecost)	June 13	June 2	May 23	June 9	May 29	May 19	June 8	May 27
Jewish Year Starts on Rosh HaShanah	5766	5767	5768	5769	5770	5771	5772	5773
Rosh HaShanah (New Year)	Oct. 4	Sept. 23	Sept. 13	Sept. 30	Sept. 19	Sept. 9	Sept. 29	Sept. 17
Yom Kippur (Day of Atonement)	Oct. 13	Oct. 2	Sept. 22	Oct. 9	Sept. 28	Sept. 18	Oct. 8	Sept. 26
Sukkot (Feast of Booths)	Oct. 18	Oct. 7	Sept. 27	Oct. 14	Oct. 3	Sept. 23	Oct. 13	Oct. 1
Simchat Torah	Oct. 26	Oct. 15	Oct. 5	Oct. 22	Oct. 11	Oct. 1	Oct. 21	Oct. 9
Chanukah (Festival of Lights)	Dec. 26	Dec. 16	Dec. 5	Dec. 22	Dec. 12	Dec. 2	Dec. 21	Dec. 9
Purim (Feast of Lots)	March 25 2005	March 14 2006	March 4 2007	March 21 2008	March 10 2009	Feb. 28 2010	March 20 2011	March 8 2012

Week 9

Featured Book: End Leviticus and Begin Numbers

Contents:

Peek at the Week

Lesson	Key Events	Find Jesus
9.1	Census of First Generation Exodus Israelites	Jesus Will Come From Tribe of Judah
9.2	The Encampment of Israel	Levites' Ministry—*A Type of Christ*
9.3	The Tribe of Levi (The Consecrated Tribe)	Age for Levite and Jesus' Public Ministry
9.4	Nazarite Vow; Priestly Blessing; Silver Trumpets	Trumpet Will Sound when Jesus Returns
9.5	Complaints and Rebellion Against God and Moses Led to Destruction	Spirit of Jesus IS for All People
9.6	Israel's Complaints and Rebellion Led to Wanderings in the Wilderness	Accept Jesus as Your Lord Before Too Late
9.7	God Affirms the Leader and Priests He Has Chosen	Jesus, God's Final Chosen High Priest

Chronological Notes

* Timetable	Key Events
At the beginning of the 2nd Year after Exit 1445 (or 1279) BC	- Moses erects the Tabernacle and God's glory fills it - Israel's dedication celebration for the Tabernacle - Israel dedicates the Levi Priests - Moses dedicates and anoints High Priests: Aaron and sons - Israel celebrates the Passover Feast - Israel learns the Holy laws for Priests and People - Israel leaves wilderness of Sinai (Numbers 10:11) - Israelites from Egypt should have entered Promised Land - Unbelieving Israelites begin to wander in wilderness
1445–1405 BC (or 1279–1239 BC)	**Israelite nation wanders in the wilderness a total of 40 years in fulfillment of God's punishment for unbelief**
40 Years after Exodus 1405 (or 1239) BC	Unbelieving Israelites from Egypt die in wilderness Second generation Israel enters Promised Land

**All dates are approximate, with uncertainties from Bible scholars leading to early and late dates for some events.*

Intro to Numbers

Key Word	Key Chapters
Wanderings	14

Title

"Numbers" refers to two "numberings" of the Israelites, which today is called a "census". The Hebrew name for this book is "Bemidbar," *which* means "in the wilderness."

Key word "wanderings" refers to the forty years the Israelites wandered in the wilderness, after being punished by God for their unbelief in His ability to enable them to conquer the Canaanite people and live in the Promised Land

Summary

The first five books of the Old Testament (Genesis, Exodus, Leviticus, Numbers and Deuteronomy) are called the Pentateuch (pronounced "Pen-ta-tuck" or "took").

This word comes from the Greek translation in which "penta" means "five" and "teuch" means "a tool." The Pentateuch is a five-book communication tool from God to man. These five books are called the "Torah" in the Hebrew language, which means "instruction" or "law." Numbers is the fourth book in the Pentateuch (Torah).

The Book of Numbers is a law and history book.

Numbers records the historical account of what happened to the Israelites after they left Mt. Sinai where they made the covenant agreement with God, built the Tabernacle, established the priesthood according to God's pattern, and they received God's laws for holy living.

After conducting the second Passover festival around the newly built Tabernacle at Mount Sinai, the Israelites were led by the angelic cloud to go to the outskirts of the Promised Land.

The Israelites then sent twelve spies to preview the land. After forty days, the spies returned with their report. It was truly a land "flowing with milk and honey" just as God had promised. But ten of the twelve also reported that the people in the land were giants, who were too great for them to conquer.

As a result of the bad report, the nation rebelled against God, in spite of the two faithful spies who had confidence in God's ability to bring them victoriously into the land.

Finally, because of their unbelief and rebellion, God condemned the nation to "wander" in the wilderness for forty years, until the unbelieving exodus adult Israelites would all die in the wilderness. Although this generation would not enter in, their children would along with the two spies who believed God.

In addition to recording Israel's wilderness wanderings experience, Numbers records the two censuses (numberings) taken of the Israelites.

The first census in Numbers 1, records the number of the first-generation exodus Israelites. They should have entered the Promised Land, but instead died in the wilderness because of their unbelief.

The second census in Numbers 26, records the number of the second-generation exodus Israelites. After witnessing their parents die in the wilderness, they were full of faith and ready to enter the Promised Land.

- ❑ **Timetable:** All dates are approximate.

  *(** The dates in parenthesis reflect some Bible scholars understanding that the exodus took place in the 13th century instead of the 15th)*

  - **1445 BC** *(or 1279 BC)*
    One month after Tabernacle completion, census taken of first-generation Israelites who came out of Egypt. At the beginning of Numbers, this generation was originally supposed to enter the Promised Land at this time.

  - **Between 1445–1405 BC** *(or 1279–1239 BC)*
    For approximately thirty-eight years, Numbers records events of the first-generation Israelites, who were condemned by God to wander in the wilderness for a total of forty years, because they did not believe God could give them the Promised Land. Since they did not believe, they did not receive.

  - **1405 BC** *(or 1239 BC)*
    Forty years after the exodus from Egypt, a census was taken of the second-generation Israelites. At the end of Numbers, this generation was ready to enter the Promised Land. The book of Numbers records approximately six months of their activity prior to moving to the Promised Land.

- ❑ **Author:** Most Likely Moses

  - **About the writer:**

    Most Bible scholars believe that Moses wrote the book of Numbers, or priests recorded the events Moses directed them to record.

  - **Date of writing:** ~ 1405 BC

    Most likely written during the life of Moses and possibly edited by priests after his death.

    For more details on differing views for the authorship and dates for the Pentateuch, review the Author section in the Intro to Genesis.

❑ **Major Events in Numbers:**

<u>**First Generation after Exodus (Chapters 1–21)**</u>

- **Chp 1: First numbering (census) of Israel**
- **Chp 2–10: Final days at Mt. Sinai**
- **Chp 10–14: From Sinai to outskirts of Promised Land (Kadesh-Barnea)**
- **Chp 14–19: Punished to wander 40 years, rebellions led to deaths and more laws**
- **Chp 20: Moses and Aaron sin, Aaron dies**
- **Chp 21: Second generation arrive at Moab**

<u>**Second Generation after Exodus (Chapters 22–36)**</u>

- **Chp 22–24: Balaam hired to curse the Israelites**
- **Chp 25: Moabites seduce the Israelites**
- **Chp 26: Second census of the Israelites**
- **Chp 27–30: Worship laws and vows repeated**
- **Chp 31–33: Battle and Review of the Israelites' Journey**
- **Chp 34–36: Boundaries, Inheritances**

❑ **Historical Locations:**

Review key locations on Map "The Exodus," in Week 6.

Reading Assignment:
Leviticus 27:1–34
Numbers 1:1–54

Lesson 9.1

I. Lesson Exercise

Special Dedication Vows to the Lord

A person could make a special vow to dedicate people, animals or property to God.

❒ **People Dedications**

A person was dedicated to the Lord by making a special vow of dedication and paying the Lord's specific value for that person to the priests. (Lev. 27:1–2)

- **Dedication values were:**
  a) Male between age of 20 and 60—50 pieces of silver (Lev. 27:3)
  b) Female between age of 20 and 60—30 pieces of silver (Lev. 27:4)
  c) Boy between 5 and 20—20 pieces of silver (Lev. 27:5)
  d) Girl between 5 and 20—10 pieces of silver (Lev. 27:5)
  e) Boy between 1 month and five years—5 pieces of silver (Lev. 27:6)
  f) Girl between 1 month and five years—3 pieces of silver (Lev. 27:6)
  g) Man older than 60—15 pieces of silver (Lev. 27:7)
  h) Woman older than 60—10 pieces of silver (Lev. 27:7)

❒ **Animal Dedications**

Animals that could not be dedicated to the Lord were:

- The firstborn animals because they already belonged to the Lord. (Lev. 27:26)
- But if it was the firstborn of an unclean animal, then payment could be given for that animal to the priest in place of giving the animal itself. (Lev. 27:27)

❒ **Property Dedications**

- **Property that could be dedicated to the Lord was:**
  a) house (Lev. 27:14)
  b) land of ancestral property (Lev. 27:16)
  c) land or field that was purchased (Lev. 27:22)

- **Paying Tithes**

  The tenth (called "tithe" in KJV) *"belongs to the Lord and must be set apart to him as holy,"* was to be given to the priests.

  a) The people were to bring all their tithes to the Tabernacle, of their produce, such as grain or fruit and every tenth animal. Money could be brought in place of the produce or animals, if they lived far away from the Tabernacle. (Lev. 27:30–33; Deut. 14:22–29)

  b) The priests were also to pay tithes. (Num. 18:25–32)

Census of First-Generation Exodus Israelites

On the first day of the second month (meaning one month after Passover month), in the second year after the exodus out of Egypt, God told Moses to get a count of the community of Israelites, by tribes and families.

In today's language, the official registration of a population— to record names, total number of people by families and obtain other organized information about them—is called a "census."

In the census, only the men who were able to go to war were listed, by:

- name
- tribe they came from
- total number of war-ready men in each tribe

1) At what age did the census for men begin? (Num. 1:3,18,45) _________

2) In America, what modern day registry does this remind you of? _______

3) What was the total of war-ready men from the tribes (Num. 1:46) ______

4) The men in which tribe were not counted and why? (Num. 1:49–51)

   ____

When camped in one location, each tribe of Israel had an assigned position located around the Tabernacle, with the Tabernacle in the center of their encampment.

The Levite tribe also had assigned locations around the Tabernacle.

5) Why did God position the Levites between the Tabernacle and the other tribes? (Num 1:53) ____

II. Find Jesus in the Lesson and III. Closing Thoughts:

Jesus Will Come from the Tribe of Judah

- **Old Testament Records of the Twelve Tribes**

Each of the twelve tribes had a specific area of the camp in which God purposefully assigned them to live.

> When the Israelites' forefathers had moved south to Egypt approximately 400 years earlier, they had done so as a family. of twelve households, each headed by one of the sons of Jacob, who was renamed Israel by God.
>
> While they were slaves in Egypt, the Israelites preserved their family divisions. Over the years, the families of the twelve sons developed into tribal families or tribes.

In the book of Numbers, when God directed Moses to take a census of the Israelites by tribes, as well as by families, they were able to do this without a problem.

Throughout their history,
the Israelite tradition of keeping
accurate family records
will be significant in determining
the family tree of Jesus Christ.

- **New Testament Record of the Tribe of Judah**

From Matthew 1:3, we read that Jesus Christ was a descendant of Jacob's son Judah.

> As a result, the tribe of Judah was always blessed to be a strong group.

Lesson 9.2

Reading Assignment:
Numbers 2:1–3:51

I. Lesson Exercise

The Encampment of Israel[1]

Each tribe will be assigned its own area in the camp, and the various groups will camp beneath their family banners. The Tabernacle will be located at the center of these tribal compounds.
Numbers 2:2

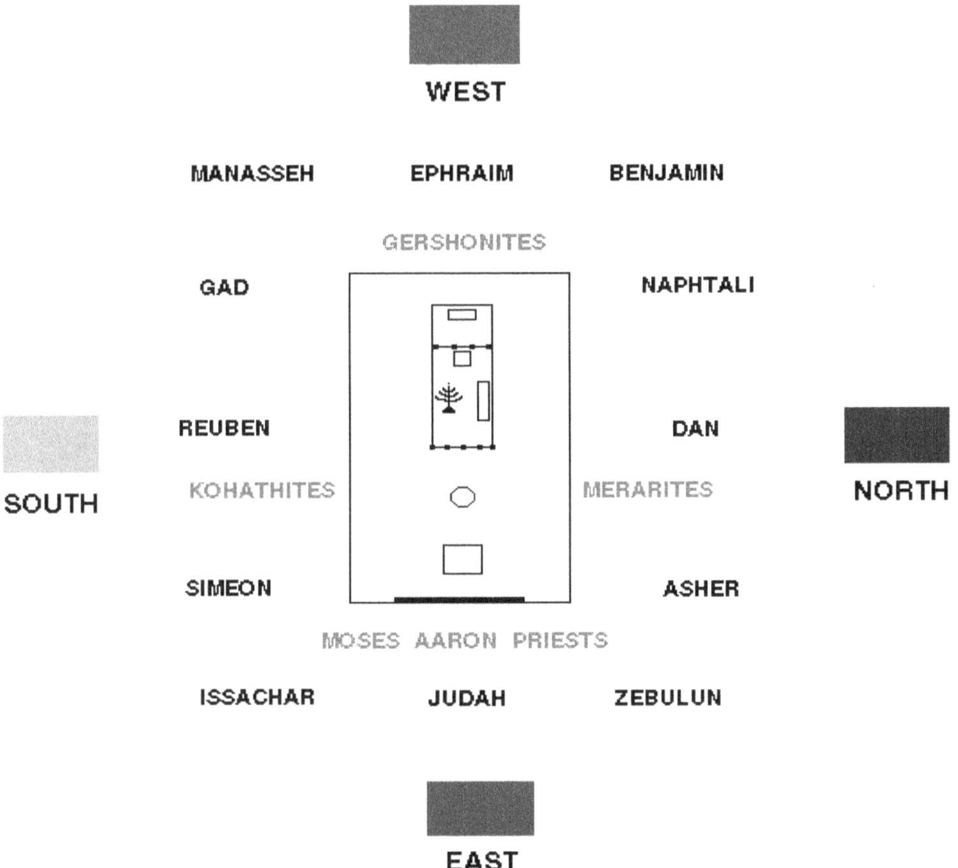

From looking at the diagram, notice how the Tabernacle is located at the center of the tribes of Israel. Let us review the basic make-up of the Tabernacle from Exodus Chapter 40.

6) What two pieces of furniture were in the Tabernacle Courtyard on the east?

   a) ____________________ (Ex. 40:6), b) ____________________ (Ex. 40:7)

7) What three pieces of furniture were in the Holy Place? (Ex. 40:4, 5)

   a) ____________________ , b) ____________________, c) ____________________

8) What is the one piece of furniture in the Most Holy Place? (Ex. 40:3)

   ____

[1]Appendix C

II. Find Jesus in the Lesson and III. Closing Thoughts

The diagram "The Encampment of Israel" and the below text is reprinted by permission of Rusty Russell; 1998 Bible Knowledge Accelerator from the BibleHistory.com website:

Bracketed information has been added by the author of Know His Word Bible Study.

Levites Ministry—*A Type of Christ and His People*[1]

God camps with His people. His plan was always that He would dwell in us and be our God. He leads us, He cares for us and He speaks to us with the soft voice of a husband that is desperately in love with His bride.

The flags of each tribe point to the real banner of God, Jesus Christ. The four faces and the four colors speak of Him. He is our standard. The Lord is called Jehovah Nissi [the Lord our banner].

As the Levite stood between man and God [in the Old Testament], **so Jesus Christ stands between man and a holy God; to be a mediator, and to meet vengeance with mercy.**

Each tribe had a specific banner:

According to Jewish tradition it was believed that the banners of the tribes were as follows:

Judah: **East**

(Lion of gold with a scarlet background).

Reuben: **South**
(Man on gold background).

Ephraim: **West**
(Ox of black on gold background).

Dan: **North**
(Eagle of gold on a blue background)

[1]Appendix C

Lesson 9.3

Reading Assignment:
Numbers 4:1–5:31

I. Lesson Exercise

The below text is reprinted by permission of Rusty Russell; 1998 Bible Knowledge Accelerator from BibleHistoy.com website.

Bracketed information and bold text have been added by the author of Know His Word Bible Study.

Tribe of Levi (The Consecrated Tribe) [1]

Now although there are the twelve tribes of Israel, we notice thirteen names when we identify their places in the encampment.

This is because of the special privilege given to the tribe of Levi when they supported Moses by joining him "on the Lord's side," at the time of Israel's rebellion [Exodus 32:26–29].

From that moment on they were ordained for the service of God and set apart as the priestly tribe.

This would have left only eleven tribes, but the large tribe of Joseph was divided into two, consisting of the descendants of his sons Ephraim and Manasseh.

Each was regarded as an individual tribe [Jacob had adopted Joseph's sons as his own before his death—Genesis 48].

Not only was the loyal tribe of Levi involved in an act of dedication but also in one of substitution.

On that night of terror in Egypt when the firstborn of every Egyptian family had been slain, the Israelite firstborn lived because a lamb had died in substitution for him. As soon as this happened God called on Moses to consecrate all the firstborn, and those who would be born in future, to His service [Exodus 11:5; 12:12; 13:2, 11–15].

They [Israelite firstborn] **had been saved from death while those around them had died. From then on, they were to be set apart for service of God. [God required the firstborn sons to be redeemed**—Ex. 22:29; 34:20].

When the Levites were chosen as the consecrated tribe, in an act of substitution they took the place [for service of God] previously required of the firstborn son in each family [Num. 3:12–13, 40–41].

[1]Appendix C

Moses and his brother Aaron belonged to the tribe of Levi, the third son of Jacob. Levi had three sons: Gershon, Kohath, and Merari.

Moses and his brother sprang from the family of Kohath. Having chosen Moses to be leader of his people, God gave further honor to the family of Kohath by selecting Aaron to be the first of his High Priests, and commanding that only the descendants of Aaron should serve as High Priests, representing the people to God.

The rest of the men of Levi, known as Levites, were charged with the care of the sanctuary (Tabernacle).

This was a holy commission in which no other group of people in Israel was permitted to participate. Only the Levites could handle the Tabernacle and its furnishings when the camp was on the march. When the camp came to rest, the Levites were the ones to erect the Tabernacle, care for it, and assist the High Priests (Aaron and his sons) in their work. "

The Levite Camp[1]

Camped just outside the Tabernacle were the Levite tents. The Levites performed the priestly duties and therefore were mediators between God and the people.

The tribe of Levi was divided into four families. Their tents were pitched between the tabernacle and the people, one family on each side.

- The **Kohathites** on the south numbering 8,600.
- The **Gershonites** on the west numbering 7,500.
- The **Merarites** on the north side numbering 6,200.
- On the eastern side were the tents of **Moses, Aaron the high priest, and Aaron's sons the priests.**

---

9) What was the age of the Levite men who were qualified to work in Tabernacle service? (Num. 4:3, 23, 30) ______________________

[1]Appendix C

Preserving Purity in Israel's Camp

God instructed Moses again to keep the Israelite community pure from defilement. In Numbers Chapter 5, God talked about three specific areas to maintain purity.

To preserve the purity in Israel's camp, God gave specific instructions:

- To protect from defiling the camp with disease, remove anyone from the camp who has a contagious skin disease (leprosy), or a discharge, or who has been defiled by touching a dead person. (Num. 5:1–3)
- To protect from betraying the Lord, the Israelites were not to wrong another person, because God would consider this an act of betraying Him. (Num. 5:6)
- To protect for purity in marriage, review God's instructions for satisfying a jealous husband's suspicions about his wife being unfaithful. (Num. 5:11–31)

<u>II. Find Jesus in the Lesson and III. Closing Thoughts</u>

Age for Public Ministry of Levites and Jesus

"And He said to them, "Why did you seek Me?
Did you not know that I must be about My Father's business?"
Luke 2:49 NKJV

Luke 2:41–52 tells a story from Jesus' boyhood when He was twelve years old. In verse 49, Jesus' words reveal that at twelve, He knew He was the Son of God.

However, in verses 51–52 we read that Jesus continued to live with his parents, where He grew up developing spiritually, physically, intellectually, and socially.

Jesus did not begin His full, public ministry work until a later age.

10) At what age did Jesus begin public ministry, and how did this compare to the age Levite priests began their work? (Numbers 4:3 and Luke 3:23) ____

Lesson 9.4

Reading Assignment:
Numbers 6:1–27
Numbers 10:1–36

I. Lesson Exercise

Special Nazarite Vow to the Lord

A man or woman could take the special "Nazarite vow," in which they set themselves apart to the Lord in a special way, for a period of time.

11) What did a person do as long as the Nazarite vow was in effect in their life?

   a) Num. 6:3—Give up ______________________________
   b) Num. 6:3—Not use ______________________________
   c) Num. 6:3—Not eat ______________________________
   d) Num. 6:5—Never cut ______________________________
   e) Num. 6:6—Never go near __________________________

At the end of the vow period, the Nazarites offered sacrifices at the Tabernacle. In addition to these sacrifices, they gave uncommon offerings.

12) What was the uncommon offering the Nazarites gave to the Lord?

   a) What was put on the fire beneath the peace-offering sacrifice? (Num. 6:18) ____
   b) What else was offered? (Num. 6:21) __________________________

The Priestly Blessing is God's Blessing on Israel

One of the most famous prayers of blessing from the Bible is the one God told the High Priests to speak over the Israelites in Numbers 6:24–26.

Num. 6:24–26 King James Version

The LORD bless thee, and keep thee

The LORD make his face shine upon thee, and be gracious unto thee

The LORD lift up his countenance upon thee, and give thee peace.

✞

Num. 6:24–26 New Living Translation

May the LORD bless you and protect you.

May the LORD smile on you and be gracious to you.

May the LORD show you his favor and give you his peace.

- **The first section of the priestly blessing** gives the idea of being prosperous with health, wealth, and family, with an associated prayer for God to protect one in prosperity.
- **The second section of the priestly blessing** gives the idea of God lighting up one's life, as with giving His wisdom, with a prayer for God's grace to temper the enlightened life.
- **The third section of the priestly blessing** gives the idea of having God's favor from being in God's presence, with an associated prayer for God's peace in all life experiences.[2]

Two Silver Trumpets

God had Israel make two trumpets beaten (shaped) from silver (Num. 10:1–2, 8). Only the high priests, Aaron's descendants, were to blow them. They used them to:

- **Call the people to assemble at the entrance of the Tabernacle (10:3–4, 7)**
    - Blow two trumpets to call all the people to assemble
    - Blow one trumpet to call for only the leaders to assemble
- **Alert the people it was time to break camp and to march forward (10:5–6)**
    - Sound short blasts to give the signal to move
    - For first blow, tribes on east move; second blow, tribes on south move
- **Sound the alarm in times of war (10:9)**
    - So the Lord will remember Israel
    - So the Lord will rescue Israel from their enemies
- **Blow the trumpets in times of gladness (10:10)**
    - Sound them at the annual feasts
    - Sound them at beginning of each month to rejoice over offerings

13) What else did blowing the trumpets remind God of? (Num. 10:10)

____

[2]Appendix C

The Israelites Break Camp and Move Forward

Arise, O Lord, and let your enemies be scattered!
Let them flee before you!
Numbers 10:35

It was the twentieth day of the second month (after Passover month), in the second year after the Israelites left Egypt.

As God had instructed, Moses first led the Israelites to Mt. Sinai to worship Him. This worship included a little over one-year period where they:

- made a covenant agreement with God
- built a Tabernacle
- established the priesthood
- received laws for holy living

All these steps confirmed the Israelite nation as the unique chosen people of God.

When the Israelites left Mt. Sinai, they left in an orderly manner as explained in Numbers 10:11–36.

> Moses invited his brother-in-law Hobab, to travel with them to the Promised Land because of his knowledge of the wilderness.
>
> Moses assured him he would be blessed with Israel (Num. 10:29–32).

Look at the map in Week 6 "The Exodus," to see the travel routes of the Israelites after they left Mt. Sinai (Mt. Horeb).

II. Find Jesus in the Lesson and III. Closing Thoughts

The Trumpet Will Sound with Purpose,
When Jesus Returns to Earth

The trumpets sounded with purpose among the Israelites in the Old Testament as described in Numbers 10:1–10.

When Jesus (Son of Man) returns to earth the second time, He will have His angels sound the trumpet blast to gather an assembly of people. (Matthew 24:29–31)

14) Who will be gathered by the trumpet sound at Jesus' return?

____

Reading Assignment:
Numbers 11:1–13:33

Lesson 9.5

I. Lesson Exercise

Complaints and Rebellion against God and Moses Led to Destruction

By their continued complaining, the first generation of Israelites...

> who God brought out of Egypt with great miracles, and who God fed, clothed, taught and lived among throughout their one-year transformation from slaves to nation in the wilderness

...prove they are ungrateful and unappreciative of all God has done for them and promised them.

So the Israelites find out God is still a consuming fire.

- God sent fire among Israel in judgment for their latest set of complaints. **This place of judgment became known as "Taberah—the place of burning."** (Num. 11:3)

- **The foreigners** began to crave the good things of Egypt. They **influenced the people of Israel to complain** about not having those things. (Num. 11:4–6)

- God sent quail for a month to address Israel's latest food complaints. Then God caused a severe plague to break out among the people while they were still eating the quail meat. **This place of judgment became known as "Kibroth-hattaavah"—"the place of cravings."** (Num. 11:31–34)

- Miriam and Aaron criticized Moses because his wife was a Cushite. **God sent the contagious skin disease "leprosy" on Miriam for seven days**, and she had to live outside the camp during the time of her disease. (Num. 12:1, 9, 14)

- God was always quick to defend Moses when different groups criticized him, because **Moses was meeker than any other person on earth.** (Num. 12:3)

- God communicates with prophets by visions and dreams; but **God spoke to Moses directly and not in riddles.** Moses saw God as He was. (Num. 12:6–8)

Moses Gets Help

But Moses replied, 'Are you jealous for my sake? I wish that all the Lord's people were prophets, and that the Lord would put his Spirit upon them all!' Numbers 11:29

The pressure of listening to Israel's repeated complaints, along with instructing them in God's ways and praying for them every time they angered God, became a burden too heavy for Moses to bear. God had a solution for this, too.

God had Moses gather seventy of Israel's leaders around the Tabernacle. Then He transferred some of the Spirit from Moses on them so they could help bear the burden of the people.

15) For one time only, what did the leaders do after God placed some of the Spirit that was on Moses on them? (Num. 11:25) ____________

Two of the leaders, who were not with the others, began to prophesy in the camp.

Numbers 11:29 above is Moses' response to Joshua who wanted to make them stop prophesying because they had not been with Moses and the seventy around the Tabernacle.

Moses was not jealous or intimidated at hearing others in the camp had prophesied. Furthermore, he desired that everyone was so close to God that all would prophesy. Compare Moses' words in Numbers 11:29 with Paul's words in 1 Corinthians 14:5.

Are We There Yet?

The Israelites finally arrived at the Promised Land. They camped at Kadesh, in the wilderness of Paran. Find this on the "Exodus" map in Week 6.

God told Moses to send a leader from each of the twelve tribes to go into the land of Canaan to check out the land and the people. The twelve spies came back with a good report and a bad report.

16) What good report did all the spies bring back to Israel? (Num. 13: 27) ____

17) What bad report did ten of the twelve spies bring back? (Num. 13:28)

____

18) Which two spies had faith in God and encouraged the people that God would help them conquer the land? (Num. 13:30, 14:6)

_______________________, _______________________

II. Find Jesus in the Lesson

The Spirit of Jesus Is for All People

God anointed Jesus with the Holy Spirit and power to miraculously heal and teach the people, overcome all temptations of satan, and conquer death. (Luke 4:1–15, Acts 10:38, Romans 8:11)

Jesus sent this same Holy Spirit and power for all believers, empowering them to live victorious lives like Jesus. (John 16:7–15, Acts 1:8, Acts 2:17–18, Romans 8:11–14).

By Jesus sending the gift of the Holy Spirit, Moses' wish for all the Lord's people to be filled with the Spirit of God has come true. (Numbers 11:29)

III. Closing Thoughts

Then the LORD said to Moses, "Is there any limit to my power? Now you will see whether or not my word comes true!"
Numbers 11:23

Giants in the Land versus God Almighty

The Anak people were giants. They were so huge, ten spies said Israel was like "grasshoppers" compared to the Anaks.

> At the sight of this giant problem, the ten spies discouraged the whole nation from having faith in God's ability to give them the land by conquering the people. The two spies' faith was not enough to sway mass unbelief.

When God gives a promise to His children, He expects us to exercise faith in Him, believing He is able to bring His promises to pass, even in the face of "giant" problems.

> When Moses questioned God's ability to provide meat every day to Israel for one month in the wilderness, God let Moses know there is no limit to his power (Num 11:23).

As God Almighty,
God is well able to do whatever He promises.

Lesson 9.6

Reading Assignment:
Numbers 14:1–15:41

I. Lesson Exercise

The Israelites' Complaints and Rebellion Led to Wanderings in the Wilderness

The complaints of the adults in the first-generation exodus Israelites, while at the outskirts of the Promised Land, ...

- Israelites said they wish they had died in Egypt, or in wilderness. (Num. 14:2)
- The community of Israel talked about stoning Caleb and Joshua because of their continued words of faith in God. (Num. 14:10)
- God said none of those who treated Him with contempt (the complaining, rebellious unbelievers) would enter the Promised Land. (Num. 14:22–23)
- Because the spies explored the land for forty days, Israel was punished to wander in the wilderness for forty years—a year for each day. (Num. 14:34)
- The ten spies with the bad report were struck dead with a plague. (Num. 14:37)

After Moses told the Israelites God's punishment, they decided to go in and conquer the land, but it was too late.

19) What happened to the Israelite army who tried to go conquer Canaan after God's punishment? (Num. 14:43–44) ______________________

God Moves On…

After pronouncing His punishment on Israel, God moves on to provide additional instruction to this Israelite generation on His laws and holy living.

It is now too late for the Israelites who were over 20 years old to enter into the Promised Land. They missed the opportunity for receiving this blessing in their lifetime.

II. Find Jesus in the Lesson and III. Closing Thoughts

Accept Jesus as Your Lord, Before It Is Too Late

"Don't let it be said, too late, too late, to enter the golden gates."

These words are from an old spiritual song. They utter a warning to all not to wait until it is too late to repent and accept Jesus Christ as the Lord and Savior of your life.

> **If you die without accepting Christ, then it will be too late to confess Him.**
>
> **If Jesus returns to earth for His saints, and you have not accepted Him, it will be too late to confess Him after seeing Him.**

God, who prevented the adults in the exodus Israelites from entering into the earthly Promised Land because of their unbelief, will also prevent unbelievers (meaning all who do not accept Jesus as Lord and Savior of their life by faith) from entering His heavenly Promised Land.

> **Instead of entering the "golden gates" to live in eternal paradise with Christ, any unbeliever who waits too late to accept Christ will be condemned to experience eternal torment away from God's holy presence.**

For God
so loved the world
that he gave his only Son,
so that everyone who believes in him
will not perish but have eternal life.
John 3:16

But cowards who turn away from me,
and unbelievers,
and the corrupt, and murderers, and the immoral,
and those who practice witchcraft,
and idol worshipers,
and all liars—

their doom is in the lake that burns with fire and sulfur.

This is the second death.
Revelation 21:8

Lesson 9.7

Reading Assignment:
Numbers 16:1–18:32

I. Lesson Exercise

God Affirms the Leader and Priests He Has Chosen

Korah influenced Dathan, Abiram, and 250 other prominent leaders in Israel to join in rebellion against Moses. They expressed the people's growing feelings that Moses, Aaron and his sons should not be the only ones allowed to enter God's holy presence.

> They understood that everyone in Israel was holy, set apart by God, so in their minds all should be able to enter the Tabernacle.
>
> Furthermore, Korah, a Levite assistant to priests, wanted to be a priest, although he was not Aaron or Aaron's son.
>
> Finally, the people blamed Moses for not bringing them into the Promised Land. They wondered if Korah or Moses were right.

Proof # 1

When Korah, Dathan and Abiram's arrogance made God and Moses angry, Moses organized a test to prove to everyone God had chosen him as Israel's leader.

- At Moses' word, the Lord made the earth open up and swallow Korah, Dathan and Abiram, everything they owned, and all who followed their wrong teaching. (Num. 16:33-34)
- Fire blazed from the Lord and burned up the 250 prominent men who were burning incense. (Num. 16:35)

20) Who atoned for the people and stopped the plague? (Num. 16:39–40) ____________________

21) What became of the 250 incense burners? (Num. 16:39–40)

____

Proof # 2

God said buds would sprout on the staff of the man He had chosen for High Priest.

- **When Aaron's staff budded, this meant "Aaron was the man."** (Num. 17:5)
- **Aaron's staff with buds was placed in the Ark of the Covenant.** (Num. 17:10)

Provisions for the Priests

The priests were not assigned land as an inheritance, and their only work was caring for and guarding the Tabernacle.

God said He Was the Priests' Inheritance. (Num. 18:8–30)

- All the offerings brought to the Lord were literally given to the priests, to take care of them and their families as their payment for taking care of the Tabernacle.
- The best was given to God, so the best belonged to the priests.
- Also, the Levites gave the tenth of the tithes people gave them to the Lord by giving it to the High Priest.

Priests and Levites were not to treat the holy offerings as common, or they would die.

II. Find Jesus in the Lesson and III. Closing Thoughts

Jesus Christ, God's Final Covenant Chosen High Priest

In Hebrews Chapter 9, the scripture revisits how Aaron's rod that budded was stored in the Ark of the first covenant. God commanded this to remind the children of Israel that God had chosen Aaron and his male descendants as the High Priest of that Covenant. All who were not a part of Aaron's lineage were destroyed when they tried to perform the High Priest duties.

Hebrews Chapter 7, 9 and 10 further explain that for the final Covenant between God and humankind, Jesus Christ, is God's chosen High Priest. His priesthood is not through the lineage of Aaron, but instead through the lineage of Melchizedek, who was a Priest of God prior to Aaron.

If therefore perfection were by the Levitical priesthood, (for under it the people received the law,) what further need was there that another priest should rise after the order of Melchisedec, and not be called after the order of Aaron?...

For it is evident that our Lord sprang out of Juda; of which tribe Moses spake nothing concerning priesthood.

And it is yet far more evident: for that after the similitude of Melchisedec there ariseth another priest,

Who is made, not after the law of a carnal commandment, but after the power of an endless life.

For he testifieth, Thou art a priest for ever after the order of Melchisedec.

Hebrews 7:11-17

"Death of Korah, Dathan, and Abiram" *by Gustave Doré*

Num 16:32 And the earth opened her mouth, and swallowed them up, and their houses, and all the men that *appertained* unto Korah, and all *their* goods.

Bible Tidbits: The Trumpet Sound[3]

The "trumpet sound" has a significant role in getting the attention of God's people for a variety of reasons. In the King James Bible, the common instrument "shofar" or "ram's horn" and the priests' silver trumpets are both translated into the English word "trumpet." Other translations distinguish the instruments.

A few passages introducing the trumpet sound topic from throughout the Bible are presented here, but this topic is worthy of further study.

Voice as a Sound of a Trumpet

Bible passages describing God's Voice speaking from heaven usually associate It with the sound of a trumpet or ram's horn. Review passages which seem to reveal that God's Voice either sounds like a ram's horn or that a trumpet sound occurs as He speaks. This indicates God's Voice is very majestic sounding.

- There was a sound of a trumpet when God spoke at Mt. Sinai with Moses and Israelites brought out of Egypt (Ex. 19:10–20; 20:19–20, Heb. 12:18–26).
- While in the Spirit on the Lord's Day, John heard a Great Voice like a trumpet sound as He received the Revelation of Jesus Christ (Rev. 1:10, 11; 4:1).

First Trump

God's initiation of His covenant with Israel at Mt. Sinai, where he gave the Ten Commandments and Law with the voice of the trumpet, is known as the "First Trump" of God, for summoning His people from Israel and all nations (Ex. 19:6).

Shofar or Ram's Horn Trumpet Sound

The Shofar or Ram's Horn is the most mentioned sacred Jewish biblical instrument of the whole Bible. The ram's "horns" were first introduced as significant when the "ram in the bush" sacrificed on the altar by Abraham in Isaac's place was caught in the thickets by its horns (Genesis 22:13).

Here are examples of how the shofar was used in the Old Testament to…

- Gather God's people at Mt. Sinai (Exodus 19:13, 16, 17)
- Celebrate the annual Festival of Trumpets and proclaim liberty in the year of Jubilee (Leviticus 23:23-25; 25: 9, 10)
- Break down walls and bring defeat to Israel's enemies (Joshua 6:1–5; Judges 6:34, 7:16–21)
- Celebrate the Ark of the Covenant (2 Samuel 6:15, 1 Chronicles 15:28)
- Rally the people for war (Jeremiah 4:5, 6:1, 16–19; 1 Samuel 13:3–4)
- Stop fighting among brethren (2 Samuel 2:26–29, 18:15, 16)
- Warn of judgment for sin (Isaiah 58:1, Ezekiel 33:1–6)
- Announce the establishment of a king (1 Kings 1:33–39, 2 Kings 11:12, 14)
- Gather the people to worship (Isaiah 27:13)
- Praise and Worship God (Psalm 47:5–6, 98:5–6, 150:3)
- Warn of the Day of God's Judgment (Joel 2:1, Zeph. 1:14–17)

[3]Appendix C

Bible Tidbits: The Trumpet Sound[3]

Silver Trumpets

God told Moses to have two silver trumpets made as part of His instructions regarding the Tabernacle (Numbers 10:1–10). They were made from one piece of beaten, hammered silver. Only the priests, who were the sons of Aaron, were allowed to blow the silver trumpets to...

- Call people to gather at the Tabernacle: two trumpets blown for everyone, one trumpet for leaders only.
- Signal to break up camp and move on from a location.
- Sound as an alarm for danger.
- Signal when going to war so the Lord would remember to rescue Israel from their enemies.
- Celebrate in times of gladness, giving praise to God (e.g. 2 Chron. 5:12–14).
- Celebrate daily and monthly ceremonies and annual festivals.

Revelation Trumpets

Seven angels are given seven trumpets to sound for God's judgments on the earth during the Tribulation period. Six trumpets sound to bring six different plagues on the earth, while the seventh trumpet declares the establishment of Christ's kingdom on earth (Revelation 8, 9, 11:15).

Last Trump / Great Trump

Scripture References: Zech. 9:14, Matt. 24:31, 1 Cor. 15:52, 1 Thess. 4:16–18

Some scholars believe the Last Trump will gather the believers (dead and alive) in Christ to meet Him in the air before the Tribulation period, while the Great Trump will be sounded to signify the Second Coming of Christ to the earth with His holy angels to establish His Millennial Kingdom.

Some scholars believe there will be only one Last (Great) Trump sounded at the time of the Second Coming of Christ. They believe this parallels the symbolic message of the two silver trumpets blown by the priests in the Old Testament.

[3]Appendix C

Week 10

Featured Book: Numbers

Contents:

Peek at the Week

Lesson	Key Events	Find Jesus
10.1	Jesus in the Law of Moses	Jesus in Sacrifice, Rock, Bronze Snake
10.2	Balak, Balaam and the Talking Donkey	Jesus—Star, Scepter, Ruler out of Jacob
10.3	Census of Second-Generation Adult Exodus Israelites	Judah is Exalted Because of Jesus
10.4	Dividing the Promised Land Among the Tribes	Christian Meaning of the Jewish Feasts
10.5	Vows and Vengeance	Jesus Made and Fulfilled His Vow
10.6	The New Israel	Jesus in the Wilderness
10.7	Promised Land Boundaries	Jesus Ministered in the Promised Land

Chronological Notes

* Timetable	Key Events
1445–1405 BC (or 1279–1239 BC)	**Israelite nation wanders in the wilderness a total of 40 years in fulfillment of God's punishment for unbelief**
40 Years after Exodus 1405 (or 1239) BC	- Unbelieving Israelites from Egypt die in wilderness - Second generation Israel enters Promised Land

**All dates are approximate.*

Reading Assignment:
Numbers 19:1–21:35

Lesson 10.1

I. Lesson Exercise, II. Find Jesus in the Text and III. Closing Thoughts

Jesus in the Law of Moses

In Luke 24:44 Jesus said that **"all things must be fulfilled, which were written in the law of Moses, and in the prophets, and in the psalms, concerning me."**

To see the imagery of Jesus in the Old Testament, one certainly needs the help of the Holy Spirit as explained in 1 Corinthians 2:11–16.

In today's lesson, there are three strong symbolisms for Jesus Christ that can be seen and are worthy of extra attention.

They are:

- Jesus in the red heifer sacrifice
- Jesus in the rock that Moses struck
- Jesus in the bronze snake

These symbolisms are briefly reviewed here. For more detail see references.

🕮 Jesus in the Red Heifer Sacrifice

> ***The blood of goats and bulls and the ashes of a heifer sprinkled on those who are ceremonially unclean sanctify them so that they are outwardly clean.***
>
> ***How much more, then, will the blood of Christ, who through the eternal Spirit offered himself unblemished to God, cleanse our consciences from acts that lead to death, so that we may serve the living God! Hebrews 9:13–14***

The Old Testament purpose of the red heifer ordinance was to produce purifying ashes[1]. When fresh water was poured over these ashes, the mixture was then used in the ***"water for the purification ceremony...for the removal of sin"*** (Num.19:9).

The mystery of the red heifer sacrifice is that it points to Jesus' death on the cross to produce purifying blood for the removal of sin from humankind, as seen in these symbols:

Bring thee a red heifer without spot, wherein is no blemish, and upon which never came yoke. Numbers 19:2 KJV

[1]Appendix C

- **Red Heifer**:

  A heifer is a female cow. Review Leviticus 27:4 with Matthew 26:14–15 to see how the priest's price of thirty pieces of silver for Jesus was the same price for a female who was dedicated to the Lord.

  So, the female cow symbolized Jesus who would die for us. The heifer's unique red color symbolized the blood Jesus shed as a substitute sacrifice for humankind.

  Like the specially chosen red heifer, Jesus was "born to die." (Hebrews 2:14)

- **Without spot, no blemish**:

  This is the same description for Jesus in 1 Peter 1:19. This symbolized Jesus' sinless nature and life. (Hebrews 4:15)

- **Upon which never came yoke**:

  Yokes were put on animals to force them to do actions. A red heifer who never had a yoke put on it was symbolic of Jesus giving His life willingly on the cross to remove humankind's sin.

  Jesus was not forced. (John 10:17–18; Hebrews 10:5–10)

It will be taken outside the camp and slaughtered
Numbers 19:3

  - This was the only animal completely killed outside the camp in the priest's presence. This symbolized Jesus' death on the cross outside the city on Golgotha's Hill (Calvary) (Luke 23:26–33). It also symbolizes His death on earth, away from the heavenly city and Tabernacle (Rev. 15:5)

- **"Heifer must be burned—its hide, meat, blood and dung… take cedarwood, a hyssop branch, and scarlet thread and throw them into the fire." Numbers 19:5–6**

  - **Burning fire in the Bible symbolizes the fiery wrath of God's judgment!**

    - **The entire heifer was burned**. This represented Jesus giving His life as a sacrificial substitute, taking on God's judgment for humankind sin, by His shameful suffering and crucifixion on the cross. (Heb. 10:11; 2 Cor. 5:21)

    - **Cedarwood thrown in the fire** points to Jesus' excruciating crucifixion on the wooden cross. (Matt. 27:32–25)

- **Hyssop branch thrown in burning fire** points to Jesus, the plant (Isaiah 53:2) and branch (Jer. 23:5) by whose stripes we are healed, because the hyssop plant had purification and healing properties in it. Consider the hyssop offered to Jesus for pain relief. (Psalm 51:7, John 19:29)
- **Scarlet in burning fire** represents judgment for sins (sins are compared to scarlet in Isaiah 1:18), as Jesus carried the sins of the world on the cross (1 Peter 2:23–24). It also points to the scarlet robe the soldiers placed on Jesus in mockery prior to His crucifixion (Matt. 27:28).

🕮 Jesus in the Rock that Moses Struck

And did all drink the same spiritual drink:
for they drank of that spiritual Rock that followed them:
and that Rock was Christ. 1 Cor. 10:4 KJV

First Corinthians 10:1–4 describes the Israelites' exodus and wilderness journey from a spiritual point of view. Verse 4 describes the "Rock" that produced the water:

- The first time God used Moses to bring water from the rock, he directed Moses to "strike" it (Exodus 17:5–6). 1 Cor. 10:4 explains the "rock" symbolized Jesus. Some scholars believe that "striking" the rock symbolized Jesus' crucifixion. And the water that gushed forth symbolized the living water Jesus would supply to humankind after His crucifixion and resurrection. (John 7: 37–39)
- When Moses struck the rock twice, he disobeyed God's direction to "speak" to the rock. God's punishment on Moses was severe as He revealed that Moses acted in unbelief. (Num 20:8–12).

🕮 Jesus in the Bronze Snake

Jesus compared the bronze snake Moses raised on a pole to save people from death by poisonous snakes (Num 21:4–9)...

...to His cross experience to save people from eternal death.

All who look on Jesus in faith will be saved. (John 3:14–15)

Lesson 10.2

Reading Assignment: Numbers 22:1–24:25

I. Lesson Exercise

Balak, Balaam and the Talking Donkey

They have wandered off the right road and followed the way of Balaam son of Beor, who loved to earn money by doing wrong.

But Balaam was stopped from his mad course when his donkey rebuked him with a human voice.
2 Peter 2:15–16

In the New Testament, Apostle Peter describes Old Testament Balaam's motivation behind his ungodly actions. Balaam spoke curses over people for money.

1) What did God promise to do to anyone who cursed Abraham, which also applied to Abraham's covenant descendants (Gen. 12:3, Num. 24:9)? ______________________________

2) Who caused Balaam's donkey to speak? (Num. 22:28) __________

3) Balak, King of Moab, asked Balaam to curse Israel three times. What did God cause Balaam to do instead of cursing them? (Num. 24:10)

   ____

After Balak's attempts to curse Israel failed, Balaam gave Balak advice on how to hurt Israel by using Midianite (Moabite) women to seduce their men. As a result, some 24,000 Israelites were defiled and destroyed. Later Israelite warriors killed Balaam in battle. (Num. 25:1–18, Num. 31:8, 16)

II. Find Jesus in the Lesson

Jesus— a Star, a Scepter, a Ruler out of Jacob (Numbers 24:15–25)

God used Balaam to tell Balak a final prophecy about what the blessed Israelites would do to the Moabites in the future, and to other enemies of Israel. In verse 17, Balaam described someone who would rise from Jacob (out of Israelite people) to be a "star" and a "scepter," which symbolized this person would be a ruler. This ruler would lead Israel in triumph over the Moabites and all their enemies. He said this ruler would not be born in the present time, ***"but far in the distant future."***

Scriptures reveal Jesus, born some 1,500 years after this prophecy, is the ruler Balaam prophesied about. (Matt. 1:2; Luke 1:31–33 and 3:23–38; Rev. 11:15 and 22:16)

Ancient writings by the Rabbis identify Numbers 24:15–25 as a passage that points to the Messiah. [2]

[2]Appendix C

III. Closing Thoughts: God Means What He Says!

God is not a man, that He should lie,
Nor a son of man, that He should repent.
Has He said, and will He not do?
Or has He spoken, and will He not make it good?
Numbers 23:19 New KJV

In the second message God gave Balaam to pass on to Balak, in Numbers 23:19, God reveals that He says what He means, He means what He says, and He will do what He says! Hallelujah!!!

"The Angel Appearing to Balaam" *by Gustave Doré*

Doré Bible Illustrations **• Free to Copy**
www.creationism.org/images/

Num 22:23 And the ass saw the angel of the Lord standing in the way, and his sword drawn in his hand: ... and Balaam smote the ass, to turn her into the way.

Lesson 10.3

Reading Assignment: Numbers 25:1–26:65

I. Lesson Exercise

Census of Second-Generation Adult Exodus Israelites

Not one person that was counted in this census had been among those counted in the previous census taken by Moses and Aaron in the wilderness of Sinai.

For the LORD had said of them, "They will all die in the wilderness." The only exceptions were Caleb son of Jephunneh and Joshua son of Nun.
Numbers 26:64–65

In preparation for going into the Promised Land, conquering it, and dividing the territory among the twelve tribes, a second census of the war-able men over twenty years of age was taken. The total number of people was less than 2000 different from the first census, although all new people were counted.

Reuben, Simeon, Gad, Ephraim, and Naphtali tribes were reduced in numbers, while the others increased. Some Bible teachers believe Simeon's numbers went so low because of God's judgment on that tribe for being seduced by Moabite (Midianite) women to worship gods of Moab. In Numbers 25:14, it was a leader of a Simeon tribe killed for this arrogant sin. He may have led others in the tribe to sin also.

Israelite Tribe	First Census	Second Census
Reuben	**46,500**	**43,730**
Simeon	**59,300**	**22,200**
Gad	**45, 650**	**40, 500**
Judah	**74,600**	**76,500**
Issachar	**54,400**	**64,300**
Zebulun	**57,400**	**60,500**
Ephraim	**40,500**	**32,500**
Manasseh	**32,200**	**52, 700**
Benjamin	**35,400**	**45,600**
Dan	**62,700**	**64,400**
Asher	**41,500**	**53,400**
Naphtali	**53,400**	**45,400**
Total	**603, 550**	**601,730**

II. Find Jesus in the Lesson and III. Closing Thoughts

Judah Is Exalted because of Jesus

Jacob's prophecy to his son Judah in Genesis 49:8–10 gives insight on why Judah continues to be the largest tribe. For one thing, Jacob prophesied that Judah would be praised by his brothers, and he would defeat his enemies.

When you read the prophecy overall, Judah is a recognized leader and victorious ruling nation among the tribes. Judah will continue to be a dominant, successful tribe. Ancient Rabbis recognized Judah as the tribe from which the Messiah would come.[3] It was the tribe in which Jesus Christ was born. (Matt. 1:1–2)

[3]Appendix C

Lesson 10.4

Reading Assignment:
Numbers 27:1–29:40

I. Lesson Exercise:

Dividing the Promised Land among the Tribes

After forty years of wilderness wanderings, the time for the new generation of Israelites to inherit the Promised Land was finally near.

God gave to Moses the instructions on how the land should be divided among the tribes.

- **Land would be divided based on the number of people (population) of each tribe. This means the smaller tribes will get less land than larger tribes.** (Numbers 26:51–56)
- **Determining which specific land area was to be assigned to each tribe was determined by a process of "casting lots."** (Num. 26:55)
    - The practice of "casting lots" to make decisions was only used lawfully in the Old Testament when God specifically directed its use. By no means were the Israelites to go to witches or sorcerers for divination purposes to determine things (Deut. 18:9–11).
    - In the New Testament church, God has given the Holy Spirit to guide Christians in what God has assigned them in life. The last time lots were cast in the Bible is Acts 1:26, prior to the Holy Spirit being poured out. Now, we depend on God's indwelling Spirit to guide us into all truth (John 16:13–15).
- **The Levites were not included in the census. They were not to be given an inheritance of land when it was divided among the Israelites.** (Numbers 26:62)
- **The inheritance is normally given to the sons in a family. But if a man dies and has no sons, then the inheritance was to be given to his daughters.**
    - If he had no daughters, then the inheritance goes to his brothers. If his father had no brothers, then the inheritance went to the nearest relative in his clan.
    - Daughters who inherited land had to marry someone from within their own tribe. This is because inherited land was not to be passed from tribe to tribe. (Numbers 36:5–10)

From Moses to Joshua

Change in Leadership: From Moses to Joshua

After Moses and Aaron sinned by striking the rock twice, God told them they would not lead the people of Israel into the Promised Land.

Sadly, Moses, Aaron, and Miriam suffered the fate of the other "over twenty" first generation exodus Israelites, except for Caleb and Joshua. They too would die in the wilderness.

Miriam died and was buried while they were camped at Kadesh.

At the next camp around Mount Hor, God told Moses and Aaron to bring Aaron's son Eleazar with them to the top of the mountain. There Moses put Aaron's priestly garments on Eleazar who would now replace Aaron as High Priest for Israel. Aaron died on the top of the mountain. Israel mourned for him thirty days. (Num. 20)

God appointed Joshua, son of Nun, to replace Moses as Israel's leader. Joshua served as a prophet, judge and military leader.

Now that Moses would not be leading Israel into the Promised Land, **God selected Joshua** for this purpose. (Numbers 27:18–19)

4) What did God allow Moses to do with the Promised Land before he died? (Numbers 27:12–13) ________________________________

5) What did God tell Moses to transfer to Joshua? (Numbers 27:20)

____

God's Holy Offerings

God instructed Israel to present offerings in a manner that was "very pleasing" to Him. Offerings were presented at "appointed times," which included holy days and holy assemblies of the people on specific days and in specific seasons of the year.

Offerings had three common materials, a) a clean animal with no physical defects, b) a grain offering of choice flour mixed with olive oil, and c) a drink offering.

There were daily offerings in the morning and evening; weekly offerings on the Sabbath, offered in addition to the daily offerings; and monthly offerings on the first day of each month, also offered in addition to the daily offerings.

There were offerings associated with holy celebrations (festivals).

All the above offerings were required all the time. Freewill offerings, special vow offerings, or peace and thanksgiving offerings were offered in addition to the daily, weekly, and monthly offerings.

II. Find Jesus in the Lesson and III. Closing Thoughts

There is a direct link between the Christian faith and the offerings and feasts of Israel. It is impossible to discuss them all in this study.

The below chart, reprinted by permission of David R. Reagan and LambLion Ministries, [4] presents a Christian interpretation of the feasts.

Also, see the chart "Yearly Feasts of the Lord for the Nation of Israel" at the end of this week's daily study pages.

The Christian Meaning Of The Jewish Feasts

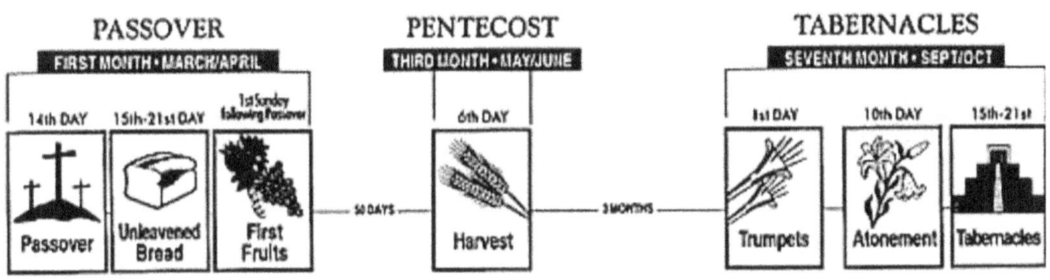

FEAST	CHRISTIAN EVENT	KEY CONCEPT
Passover	*Crucifixion of Jesus*	Justification
Unleavened Bread	*Burial of Jesus*	Sanctification
First Fruits	*Resurrection of Jesus*	Glorification
Harvest	*Descent of Holy Spirit*	Power
Interval of 3 Months	*Current Age of the Church*	Church Kingdom
Trumpets	*Gathering of the Church (?)*	Rapture
Day of Atonement	*Second Coming of Jesus (?)*	Jewish Remnant
Tabernacles	*Inauguration of the Millennium*	Earthly Kingdom

[4]Appendix C

Be Careful in Making Vows to God

Lesson 10.5

Reading Assignment:
Numbers 30:1–31:54

I. Lesson Exercise

I Made a Vow to the Lord, and I Won't Take It Back

There is an old spiritual song with a simple melody, where

Song Leader sings:	***"I made a vow to the Lord"***
Congregation sings in response:	***"And I won't take it back"***
Song Leader sings:	***"It was a holy vow"***
Congregation responds again:	***"And I won't take it back"***

Today's lesson begins with God's laws related to making vows.

- A man who makes a vow to the Lord or pledge must never break it. (Num. 30:2)
- If a young woman makes a vow or pledge under oath, while she is still living in her father's home under his care, then when the father hears of her vow, if he says nothing, then she will have to keep it. But, if he refuses to let her fulfill the vow or pledge on the day he hears of it, then it is invalid. She does not have to keep it. The Lord will forgive her for not fulfilling it. (Num. 30:3–5)
- If a woman makes a rash vow or pledge before she is married, that her husband learns about after she is married, and he does not raise any objections to her keeping the vow, then she will have to keep it. But if he raises an objection on the day he hears it, she will not have to keep the vow or pledge. (Num. 30:6–8)
- A woman who is a widow or divorced must fulfill all her vows and pledges no matter what. (Num. 30:9)

God-Directed Vengeance

In Numbers 25:16–18, God told Moses to have the Israelites destroy the Midianites because of how they tricked them into sinning against God.

In this lesson, the time for vengeance, by God's specific direction, has come.

- God directed Israel to take 1,000 men from each tribe into battle, for a total of 12,000 men. (Num. 31:6)
- Phinehas, son of Eleazar the priest, led Israel into battle. They carried the holy objects of the sanctuary and the trumpets for sounding the charge. (Num. 31:6)

6) Who did Israel's army kill? (Num. 31:7-8) a)_________________,

b) _________________________, c) _________________________

7) Who else did Moses tell the soldiers to kill? (Num. 31:17)
a) _________________________, b) _________________________

After a great victory, the Midianite wealth was transferred to Israel. First, it was purified, then divided among the priests, men in battle and rest of the people according to God's instructions. Finally, thankful soldiers gave an extra offering.

8) What reason did the soldiers give Moses for presenting the items of gold they captured as an offering to the Lord? (Num. 31:48–50)

____

II. Find Jesus in the Lesson and III. Closing Thoughts

Jesus Made and Fulfilled His Vow to God
Jesus Christ, as Son of God and Son of Man, made a holy vow to sacrifice His life for humankind's redemption. When it came time to fulfill that vow, Jesus became weak in His flesh as He approached the time of His severe persecution and crucifixion.

Jesus prayed fervently and received fresh strength from God to help Him fulfill his vow. (Hebrews 10:4-10, Matthew 26:38-44, Luke 22:43-44)

Jesus made a vow to God to sacrifice His life to redeem humankind:

For it is not possible for the blood of
bulls and goats to take away sins.
That is why Christ, when he came into the world, said,

"You did not want animal sacrifices and grain offerings.
But you have given me a body so that I may obey you...

Then I said, `Look, I have come to do your will, O God--
just as it is written about me in the Scriptures.' "

Christ said, "You did not want animal sacrifices or grain offerings or
animals burned on the altar or other offerings for sin,

nor were you pleased with them"
(though they are required by the law of Moses).
Then he added, "Look, I have come to do your will."

He cancels the first covenant in order to establish the second.
And what God wants is for us to be made holy
by the sacrifice of the body of
Jesus Christ once for all time.
Hebrews 10:4–10

Jesus asked God if the need for the vow of suffering could be removed.

*He told them,
"My soul is crushed with grief to the point of death.
Stay here and watch with me."*

*He went on a little farther and
fell face down on the ground, praying,
"My Father! If it is possible,
let this cup of suffering be taken away from me.
Yet I want your will, not mine."*

*Then he returned to the disciples and found them asleep.
He said to Peter,
"Couldn't you stay awake and watch with me even one hour?
Keep alert and pray.
Otherwise temptation will overpower you.
For though the spirit is willing enough, the body is weak!"*

*Again he left them and prayed,
"My Father! If this cup cannot be taken away until I drink it,
your will be done."*

*He returned to them again and found them sleeping,
for they just couldn't keep their eyes open.*

*So he went back to pray a third time, saying the same things again.
Matt. 26:38–44*

✞

Jesus was strengthened to do God's will, to fulfill His vow, even knowing the great suffering, He would have to endure.

*Then an angel from heaven appeared and strengthened him.
Luke 22:43–44*

✞

Just like Jesus, Christians can be strengthened in weak moments to fulfill their vows to God and fulfill God's will for their lives, by fervent prayer and fasting.

Lesson 10.6

Reading Assignment:
Numbers 32:1–33:56

I. Lesson Exercise: The New Israel

The attitude and actions of new generation Israel has improved greatly over the forty years. Consider the more positive, upbeat comments in this week's lessons.

- **Trusting Israel**: when they obeyed God by not fighting Edom their relative (Num. 20:14–21)
- **Singing Israel**: when God supplied them water at Beer (Num. 21:16–18)
- **Informed Israel**: aware of "Book of the Wars of the Lord" (Num. 21:14) and writings of ancient poets (Num. 21:27), but more aware of God's power.
- **Recording Israel**: when keeping accurate records of their census (Num 26:63–64) and of their journey experiences (Num. 33:2)
- **Victorious Israel**: victory over Canaanites in Negev (Num. 21:1–3); victory over King Sihon and Amorites (Num. 21:21–32); victory over King Og and people of Bashan (Num. 21:33–35); victory over Midianites (Num. 31:1–24)
- **Thankful Israel**: in gratitude for safety of all 12,000 men who warred against Midianites, solders gave a special offering to God (Num. 31:48–50)

Special Request for Occupying Newly Conquered Territory

- Look again at the Map in Week 6 "Exodus"
  - Look at the path of Israel's wilderness journeys during their forty-year wandering period, from Kadesh-Barnea to Elath.
- Look at the Map "Holy Land: Then—Twelve Tribes"
  - Look at the land east of Jordan discussed in today's lesson, that was given to Gad, Reuben, and the half-tribe of Manasseh.

9) Why did God tell the Israelites to drive out all the people who lived in the Promised Land? (Num. 33:55–56) ____________________

II. Find Jesus in the Lesson and III. Closing Thoughts

Jesus in the Wilderness

After Israel made their covenant with God, the angelic cloud led them to the Promised Land through the wilderness. After Jesus was anointed by God to begin His public ministry, He was led by the Spirit of God to the same wilderness, where He overcame the devil and wild beasts.

Read about this in Matthew 4:1–11 and Mark 1:12–13. Christians will also have wilderness experiences to strengthen our faith.

Reading Assignment:
Numbers 34:1–36:13

Lesson 10.7

I. Lesson Exercise

Promised Land Boundaries

Look at the Map "Holy Land: Then—Twelve Tribes" for the boundaries of the Promised Land.[5]

- Southernmost boundary = Kadesh-barnea (Num. 34:4)
- Western boundary = Coastline of the Mediterranean Sea (Num. 34:6)
- Northern boundary = begin at Mediterranean Sea, run eastward to Mount Hor, then to Lebo-hamath, on thru Zedad and Ziphron to Hazar-enan. (Num. 34:7–9)
- Eastern boundary waters = Sea of Galilee, Jordan River, Dead Sea (Num. 34:10–12)

Towns and Cities of Refuge

- Israelites were to give the **Levites towns** for their homes and the surrounding lands to provide pasture for their cattle, flocks and other livestock. (Num. 35:2–3)
- The **Cities of Refuge** were a place of protection for someone who killed another person. They were protected from the dead person's relatives who wanted to avenge the death of their loved one before the case was judged as murder or an accident. (Num 35:9–34)
- Murder pollutes the land. There was no atonement for murder except for executing the murderer. But there must be more than one witness to verify if a person performed an act of murder or not. (Num 35:30)
- There were no jails, prisons, detention centers, or penal institutions of any sort, but there were the Cities of Refuge. If one person killed another person, they would be safe in the Cities of Refuge until their case was properly judged. If they were found guilty of murder, then their punishment was death. If innocent, then they must remain in the City of Refuge for their safety until the High Priest dies.

II. Find Jesus in the Lesson

Jesus Ministered in the Promised Land

When God identified the boundaries of the Promised Land He was giving Israel, the areas mentioned included the Jordan river and Sea of Galilee. When Jesus walked the earth, He ministered in these areas.

We find Jesus was baptized and began His public ministry by walking by way of the sea, beyond Jordan, around the Sea of Galilee. Read about this in Matthew 4:12–15 and Mark 1:14–17.

[5]Appendix C

Holy Land: Then—Twelve Tribes

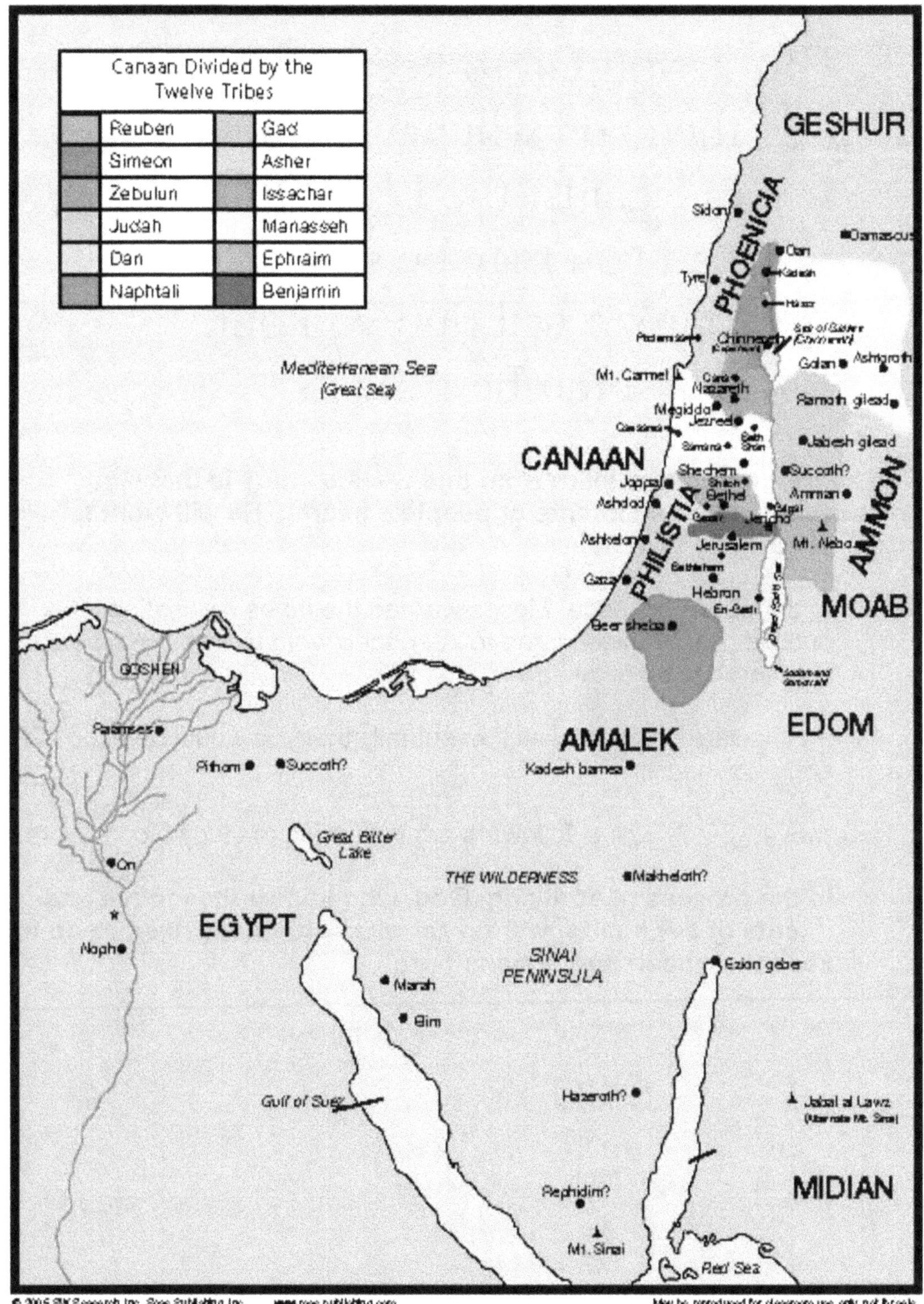

Canaan Divided by the Twelve Tribes
Reuben
Gad
Simeon
Asher
Zebulun
Issachar
Judah
Manasseh
Dan
Ephraim
Naphtali
Benjamin
GESHUR
PHOENICIA
Sidon
Damascus
Dan
Tyre
Mediterranean Sea
(Great Sea)
Mt. Carmel
Golan
Nazareth
Ramoth gilead
Megiddo
Jezreel
Jabesh gilead
CANAAN
Shechem
Succoth?
Joppa
Bethel
Amman
AMMON
Ashdod
Jericho
Mt. Nebo
Ashkelon
Jerusalem
PHILISTIA
Gaza
Hebron
MOAB
Beer sheba
GOSHEN
EDOM
AMALEK
Pithom
Succoth?
Kadesh barnea
Great Bitter Lake
THE WILDERNESS
Makheloth?
On
EGYPT
Noph
SINAI
PENINSULA
Ezion geber
Marah
Elim
Gulf of Suez
Hazeroth?
Jabal al Lawz
Rephidim?
MIDIAN
Mt. Sinai
Red Sea

III. Closing Thoughts

Keep Your Heart and Actions Pure

> "But if you fail to keep your word,
> then you will have sinned
> against the LORD,
> and you may be sure that
> your sin will find you out."
> Numbers 32:23

One important thing to learn from this week's study is that God knows the motive and intents of people's hearts. He will work to purify us to make us holy.

In the above passage, Moses warned the tribes requesting land outside the Promised Land to keep their word to help the others fight for their inheritance.

If they were being deceitful, eventually their sin would be exposed and punished.

In Hebrews 4:12–13, Jesus' followers are instructed to study God's Word.

In the process of studying, God, who knows the motive and intents of our hearts, will reveal what Christians need to do to keep their heart and actions pure.

Yearly Feasts of the Lord for the Nation of Israel

Feast	Old Testament Meaning	Bible Reference	Month of Sacred Year	Day	Corresponding Modern Month	New Testament Meaning *(Already Fulfilled)*
Passover	To remind Israel of how God mightily delivered them out of Egypt. God made the death angel "pass over" Israel when he saw the blood of the lamb on the outside doorposts.	Lev. 23:4–5, Ex. 12:12–14 Ex. 12:21–28	1 (Nisan or Abib)	14	March – April	Jesus became the lamb that was killed for us. His blood is used to remove our sins from God. Death can not keep us when it comes for us and sees the blood of Jesus in our souls. Death must pass over us, letting us go to eternal life with God. John 1:29; 1 Cor. 5:7
Unleavened Bread	To remind Israel of the day that God freed them from being under the bondage (sinful rule) of the Egyptians.	Lev. 23:6–8 Ex. 12:15–17	1 (Nisan or Abib)	15–21	March – April	Leaven symbolizes sin. God wants no sin to be in our lives. This Feast symbolized sinless Jesus, the Bread of Life, being broken for us during his crucifixion and death, to deliver us from sin's ruling presence over our lives. 1 Cor. 5:7–8; Matt. 26:17, 26
Firstfruits	The beginning of harvest was a time of joy, which Israel was to celebrate. They were to present to God the first sheaf of grain as a token of the harvest to come.	Lev. 23:9–14	1 (Nisan or Abib)	16	March – April	This feast symbolized the resurrection of Jesus Christ. When Jesus rose from the dead and ascended to heaven, he represented the first of many who would also be resurrected and join him in heaven. 1 Corinthians 15,20,23
O. T. name is "Weeks" **N. T. name is "Pentecost"**	Celebrate the finished product of the grain, 50 days (7 weeks + 1 day) after seeing a part of it at the feast of firstfruits. Each family brought two loaves of bread made from their harvest of grain.	Lev. 23:15–21, Deut. 16:9–10, Acts 2:1 (also called the Feast of Harvest in Exodus 23:16)	3 (Sivan)	6 (50 days after the sabbath day before the Feast of Firstfruits)	May – June	50 Days after the resurrection of Jesus (spiritual firstfruit), the "Day of Pentecost was Fully Come", when the Holy Spirit came to finish the work Jesus began. By living inside believers, he would make many people the children of God (more spiritual fruit or harvest for God). Matthew 18:18–19; Acts 1:8; Acts 2:1, 4, 15–21

Yearly Feasts of the Lord for the Nation of Israel

Feast	Old Testament Meaning	Bible Reference	Month of Sacred Year	Day	Corresponding Modern Month	New Testament Meaning *(To Be Fulfilled in the Future)*
Trumpets (*Rosh Hashanah*)	To blow trumpet s (Ram's Horn = Shofar) To announce 7th month of the year, which was the month when Day of Atonement took place.	Leviticus 23:23–25	7 (Tishri)	1	September – October	**Symbolism:** It symbolizes the New Testament promise that one day a Divine Trumpet will sound; then all people redeemed by the blood of Jesus will be rise up to meet Him in the air ("the rapture"). When this trumpet sounds, the dead believers will rise first, followed by the living. 1Cor. 15:51–52; 1Thess. 4:16–17
Day of Atonement (*Yom Kippur*)	This was the most sacred day of Israel's year. Atonement means "to cover". Animal sacrifices were made on this day to atone or cover the sins of the people and to obtain God's forgiveness for their sins. The priest took the blood of the animals into the Most Holy Place of the Tabernacle and sprinkled it on the mercy seat before God. They asked God to accept the blood as payment for the sins of the people.	Leviticus 23:26–32	7 (Tishri)	10	September – October	For the Christian church Jesus made atonement for our sins when he was crucified, died and rose from the dead. His one time sacrifice on our behalf put an end to yearly animal sacrifices being needed. He entered into the Most Holy Place on high in heaven and remains there representing us before God. **Symbolism:** Some Christian Bible scholars teach that the Day of Atonement symbolizes the future time when the Jewish nation as a whole will accept Jesus (Yeshua) as their Messiah, repenting of their sins and accepting his atoning blood. This will occur after the rapture of the Christian church. Hebrews 9:11–12; Zechariah12:10
Tabernacles (Booths or Ingathering)	To remind the Israelites of the tabernacles or tents they had lived in for forty years in the wilderness, as they waited to enter the Promised Land.	Leviticus 23:33–44	7 (Tishri)	15–21	September–October	**Symbolism:** This feast symbolizes for us today that this earth is our temporary home. One day all believers in Christ - Jews and Gentiles - will live with God in a new heaven and a new earth forever. Also, scholars believe when Jesus will reign as King on earth during the Millennium, this feast of tabernacles will be reestablished for all people to observe. Zech. 14:16–19

Week 11

Featured Book: Deuteronomy

Contents:

Peek at the Week

Lesson	Key Events	Find Jesus
11.1	Moses' Final Sermon	Joshua is a "type" of Christ
11.2	Do Not Be Afraid; the LORD will Fight for You!	Jesus and the Ten Commandments
11.3	LOVE is the #1 Thing!	Jesus and the "Shema"
11.4	God's Requirements for Israel	Jesus and the Shema Continued
11.5 11.6 11.7	Six Hundred Thirteen (613) Commands to Follow	Jesus Came to Fulfill the Law of Moses, Not to Destroy

Chronological Notes

* Timetable	Key Events
1445–1405 BC (or 1279–1239 BC)	Israelite nation wanders in the wilderness a total of 40 years in fulfillment of God's punishment for unbelief
1405 (or 1239) BC 40 Years after Exodus	- End of Israel's forty-year wilderness wanderings - Moses gives his final words to Israel before Joshua leads - Second generation Israel into the Promised Land

**All dates are approximate, with uncertainties from Bible scholars leading to early and late dates for some events*

Key Word(s)	Key Chapters
Second Law Covenant Love and Law	Deut. 10

Intro to Deuteronomy

Title

"Deuteronomy" means "second law." Deuteronomy summarizes the Covenant agreement between God and Israel, with Moses reviewing and renewing these agreements with the second-generation exodus Israelites.

Key words "Covenant Love and Law" are based on the idea Deuteronomy introduces, that "love" is the basis for the law of covenant agreement between God and Israel.

Summary

In Deuteronomy, Moses and the Israelites are camped on the east side of Canaan. This is the land God promised to give to Abraham, Isaac, and Jacob's descendants. While camped on the plains of Moab, waiting to enter Canaan, Moses gives a long sermon to the Israelites just before he dies.

As a result of his sin near the end of the forty-year wilderness journey, Moses suffers the same fate as the other "over twenty" first generation exodus Israelites. He will not enter the Promised Land. God directs Moses to anoint Joshua to lead the Israelites in his place.

Deuteronomy consists mostly of Moses' final sermon. It can be divided into three sections.

> **In section one**, Moses reviews the Israelite's history. This historical review includes the covenant agreement between God and the first-generation exodus Israelites, their rebellion that prevented them from entering the Promised Land, and their experiences in forty years of wilderness wanderings.
>
> **In section two**, Moses restates the law a second time for the second-generation exodus Israelites. He presents the Ten Commandments; ceremonial worship laws for Tabernacle offerings and feasts; and moral and civil laws for holy living.
>
> **In section three**, Moses foretells of Israel's future triumphs and failures, which includes a prophetic song.

When Moses finishes his sermon, he walks up Mount Nebo, where God attends to his death. The body of Moses is never seen again.

Deuteronomy is an important book for Christians to know. According to Tim LaHaye Prophecy Study Bible's article on Deuteronomy, passages from the book of Deuteronomy are quoted over 200 times in the New Testament. One example of this is when Jesus Christ quotes passages from this book to use in overcoming satan's temptations. Compare Matthew 4:1–11 with Deuteronomy 6:13, 16; 8:3.

- ❒ **Timetable:** *(all dates approximate)* 1405 **or 1239 BC**
    - End of Israel's forty-year wilderness wanderings
    - Moses' final words before Joshua leads Israel into Promised Land
- ❒ **Author: Moses**
    - **About the writer:** The author writes Deuteronomy in the first-person language using words "I" and "me" throughout the book. The strongest evidence for Moses' authorship is his own words in Deuteronomy 31:9–13. After Moses' death, the priests are the ones who likely finalized the writings.
    - **Date of writing**: ~ 1405 BC
      For more details on differing views for the authorship and dating of the Pentateuch, review the Author section in the Intro to Genesis.
- ❒ **Major Events in Deuteronomy:**

Key Events	Deut.
Moses Sermon: Section One	
○ Review of Israel's history	1 – 4
Moses Sermon: Section Two	
○ Second Presentation of Covenant Agreements: Ten Commandments	5
○ Second Giving of Ceremonial, Moral, and Civil Laws	6 - 26
○ Covenant Renewal, Blessings and Curses	27 - 29
○ Final Covenant Instructions	30
Moses Sermon: Section Three	
○ Moses identifies Joshua as God's choice to Israel	31 - 33
○ Moses foretells Israel's future triumphs and failures	
Moses Death	
○ Moses sees Promised Land then dies in mountain with God	34

Historical Locations:

There are two maps in this study you can look at to see the east side of Canaan, which is the plains of Moab, where the Israelites are camped at in Deuteronomy.

- Week 6, look at map "Exodus"
- Week 10, look at map "Holy Land: Then—Twelve Tribes"

Moses Final Sermon

Lesson 11.1

Reading Assignment:
Deut. 1:1–3:20

I. Lesson Exercise

Moses' Final Sermon

The Israelites are camped on the east side of Canaan, in the plains of Moab. They are ready to enter the land God promised to give them, as the descendants of Abraham, Isaac, and Jacob.

By God's original plan, first generation exodus Israelites should have entered Canaan forty years before. However, the rebellion and unbelief of the first group's adults caused a "breach" in God's promise. This means God delayed fulfilling the promise. But now the time is right!

Moses, who also will not enter the Promised Land, because of his own sin, gives one final sermon to the Israelites. In this sermon, Moses reviews Israel's history, their covenant agreement with God, and warns them of pitfalls in their future.

Moses not only speaks these God-inspired words, but he writes them in a book (Deuteronomy), so the Israelites would not forget them in the future.

Review of Israel's History

📖 **Travel-time History**

- Exits Egypt 430 years after entering Egypt (Exodus 12:40–41)
- Arrives at Mt. Sinai two months after exodus from Egypt (Ex. 19:1–2)
- Departed from Mt. Sinai after one year (Num. 10:11)
- Arrived at border of Canaan (Kadesh-barnea) a little over one year after exodus (Numbers 10:33, 12:16) *(second month of second year since the exodus)*
- Forty days at border of Canaan while spies investigated the land (Num. 13:25)
- Remained at border of Canaan a long time after rebellion and punishment (Deuteronomy 1:46)
- Thirty-eight more years of wilderness wanderings (Deuteronomy 2:14)
- Arrived at border of Canaan again after a total of forty years wilderness journey (Numbers 14:34, Deuteronomy 2:7)

1) What was the normal travel time between Mt. Sinai and Kadesh-barnea, which was the border of Canaan? (Deut. 1:2) ____________

🕮 Wilderness Experiences History—Some Highlights

- Israel became "too numerous as the stars" like God said. (Deut. 1:10, Gen. 15:5)
- God approved of wise and respected men from each tribe to be judges, so Moses would only deal with tough people problems and quarrels. (Deut. 1:9–18)
- God, who helped Abraham's grandson Esau's descendants (Edomites) and Abraham's nephew Lot's descendants (Moabites and Ammonites) conquer giants in the land God gave them, also helped Abraham's chosen family the Israelites conquer giants in the extra land God gave to them. (Deut. 2:10–12; 20–21; 3:11)
- God would not let Israel start a war with their relatives, who were the Edomites, Moabites and Ammonites. (Deuteronomy 2:4–5, 9, 18–19)
- The punishment of forty years of wandering was calculated based on wandering one year for each day the spies surveyed the land. Also, God vowed that all the men old enough to fight in battle would die in the wilderness. (Deut. 1:14)
- The wilderness was a great and terrifying place. God used it to test Israel, to see if they would obey him. During forty years of wandering, God met Israel's every need, they lacked nothing. He looked out for the best places for them to camp. God blessed them, caring for them as a father cares for a child.
(Deut. 1:19, 31–32; Deut. 2:7; Deut. 8:2)
- God helped Israel win great battles on the east side of Canaan. They destroyed fortified cities acquiring land and wealth. At their request, the land was given to the tribes of Reuben, Gad and half tribe of Manasseh (Deut. 3:1–20)

2) Why did the spies go explore the land in the first place? Was it God's idea or the people's idea? (Deut. 1:22–23) ______________________

Israel became "too numerous as the stars," just like God had said.

II. Find Jesus in the Lesson and III. Closing Thoughts

Joshua is a "Type" of Christ[1]

> ***Instead, your assistant, Joshua son of Nun,***
> ***will lead the people into the land.***
> ***Encourage him as he prepares to enter it.***
> ***Deuteronomy 1:38***

Joshua, not Moses, will lead the Israelites into the Promised Land.

Joshua is an Old Testament "type" of Jesus Christ

- The name Joshua means "Jehovah Saves" and is translated as "Jesus" in the New Testament passage Hebrews 4:8 KJV.
- Just as Joshua will lead Israel into possessing the Promised Land of God, Jesus is ready to lead New Testament Christians into possessing all the promises of God on earth, and in the world to come. (2 Corinthians 2:19–20)
- Just as the Israelites had to believe God, follow their leader Joshua and fight for what was already given them by God, similarly, Christians must believe God, follow the leading of their Lord and Savior Jesus Christ, and fight for the abundant life that is rightfully already given them by God.

Christians receive eternal life immediately when spiritually reborn. This occurs when a person accepts Jesus as Lord and Savior of their life (John 3:5–16, Romans 10:9–10).

To experience abundant life on earth, which is the inheritance right of every Christian, **requires a good fight of faith during earthly life**. (John 10:10; Mark 10:29–30).

[1]Appendix C

Lesson 11.2

Reading Assignment: Deut. 3:21–5:33

I. Lesson Exercise

Do Not Be Afraid; the Lord Will Fight for You!

What encouraging words from Moses as he reassures Israel. The same way God had helped Israel defeat the two nations on the east side of Canaan, He will lead them in victory on the west side. Israel's secret weapon was to obey God!

- If Israel obeyed God's laws, they would live to enter and occupy the Promised Land. (Deuteronomy 4:1)
- Israel was not to add to or subtract from the commands God had given them through Moses. (Deuteronomy 4:2)
- If Israel kept God's commands, then the other nations would say,

"What other nation is as wise and prudent as this!" Deut. 4:6

Breaking and Keeping Covenant

- One way for Israel to break covenant with God, which would bring God's fiery wrath on them, was to make idols of any shape or form and worship them. This was strictly forbidden by God. (Deut. 4:23–24)
- God would do two things to Israel for breaking covenant with Him. He would cause them to a) quickly disappear from the Promised Land; and b) be scattered among other nations where only a few of them would survive. (Deut. 4:26–27)
- As a faithful keeper of His solemn covenant agreement with Israel's ancestors—Abraham, Isaac, and Jacob—God promised He would never totally abandon Israel or destroy them completely. (Deut. 4:39)

3) How does Moses describe God, who made the Covenant with Israel? (Deut. 4:39) a) The Lord is God in ______________; b) there is no ______________

II. Find Jesus in the Lesson and III. Closing Thoughts

Jesus and the Ten Commandments

Moses repeated the Ten Commandments to second generation exodus Israel. They were children when their parents accepted God's covenant the first time.

In Mark 10:17–31, a rich man ran to Jesus, kneeled and asked what he needed to do to inherit eternal life. Jesus told him to keep the commandments.

The rich man said he had followed these commandments from the time of his youth. Jesus, looking on the man with a deep heart of love, told him two more things he needed to do. These additional requirements caused the man to walk away sad.

4) What were these two additional requirements?

   a) Mark 10:21 a______________________________

   b) Mark 10:21 b______________________________

Lesson 11.3

Reading Assignment:
Deut. 6:1–9:29

I. Lesson Exercise:

Love Is the #1 Thing!

Do not worship any other gods besides me
Deut. 5:7 and Ex. 20:3

As God gave Commandment #1, He was very clear in describing Himself as a jealous God. In Exodus 34:14 King James Version, it says **God's name is "Jealous."**

Today's text begins to emphasize the love relationship God wants with Israel. God does not just want the Israelites' obedience, He wants their love, because He loves them. It is from a heart of love that God pours out blessings on Israel, but only if they love and obey Him alone. God will not share Israel's affection with any other god.

God's Love for Israel

- **"The Lord did not choose you and lavish his love on you because you were larger or greater than other nations … It was simply because the Lord loves you." Deut. 7:7–8**
- **"He is the faithful God who keeps his covenant for a thousand generations and constantly loves those who love him and obey his commands." Deut. 7:9**
- **"If you listen to these regulations and obey them faithfully, the Lord your God will keep his covenant of unfailing love with you, as he solemnly promised your ancestors." Deut. 7:12**
- **"He will love you and bless you and make you into a great nation." Deut. 7:13**
- **"So you should realize that just as a** [loving] **parent disciplines a child, the Lord your God disciplines you to help you." Deut. 8:5**

Israel's Love for God

- **"You must love the Lord your God with all your heart, all your soul and all your strength." Deut. 6:5**
- **"You must not worship any of the gods of the neighboring nations, for the Lord your God, who lives among you, is a jealous God." Deut. 6:14**

Love Is the #1 Thing!

Shema Yisrael

"Hear, O Israel, the Lord our God, the Lord is One"

This phrase is perhaps the most famous of all Jewish sayings. It comes from Deuteronomy 6:4 and is known as "**Shema Yisrael**[2]**.**"

The full "Shema" (famous Jewish prayer)**[1] is based on three paragraphs from the Jewish "Torah,"** which consists of the first five books of the Bible.

Shema's three paragraphs are:

1. Deuteronomy 6:4–9,
2. Deuteronomy 11:13–21
3. Numbers 15:37–41

The first paragraph of the Shema, Deuteronomy 6:4–9, is found in today's lesson.

- **Deut. 6:4**
  - **This first verse emphasizes the God of Israel is one God.** It is very important to realize that Israel (and Christians) do not serve multiple (three) Gods, but "The Lord our God, the Lord is ONE" (King James Version).
- **Deut. 6:5**
  - **This second verse directs Israel in loving this one God with "all."**
- **Deut. 6:6**
  - **The third verse directs Israel to commit to obeying the commands of this one God with their whole heart.**
- **Deut. 6:7**
  - **This fourth verse directs Israel to diligently teach their children love and obedience for Israel's one God.**
- **Deut. 6:8–9**
  - **These last verses direct Israel to diligently learn and remember God's commands.** This was to be done by keeping them on their hands, forehead, doorposts and gates.

[2]Appendix C

God's Plan for Israel's Real Life and Permanent Riches

Deuteronomy 8:3 explains that "real life" comes by feeding on **every word of the Lord** because people need more than physical bread (food) for real life.

God planned to give Israel power to become rich, to fulfill the covenant He made with their ancestors. But God did not want them to become proud, forgetting how God brought them out of Egypt and through the dangerous wilderness. (Deut. 8:17–18)

God directed Israel to destroy the seven powerful nations with His help. He did not want Israel to intermarry with people of these nations. This is because God knew those nations' ungodly influences would lead Israel to worship their false gods. (Deut. 7:2–4)

II. Find Jesus in the Lesson and III. Closing Thoughts

Jesus and the "Shema"

And one of the scribes came,
and having heard them reasoning together,
and perceiving that he had answered them well, asked him,
"Which is the first commandment of all?"

And Jesus answered him,
"The first of all the commandments is,

Hear, O Israel; The Lord our God
is one Lord:

And thou shalt love the Lord thy God with all thy heart,
and with all thy soul, and with all thy mind, and with all thy strength:
this is the first commandment.

[31]And the second is like, namely this,
Thou shalt love thy neighbour as thyself.
There is none other commandment greater than these. "

Mark 12:28–31 KJV

Lesson 11.4

Reading Assignment:
Deut. 10:1–12:32

I. Lesson Exercise

Rewritten Terms of the Covenant

Moses told the story of how God rewrote the terms of the covenant agreement (Ten Commandments) on two tablets of stone Moses took back up the mountain. Moses had crushed the first set in anger, at sight of the exodus Israelites' golden-calf worship, and that so soon after they made the covenant agreement with God.

5) Where did God tell Moses to place the tablets of stone, with the Ten Commandments written on them by the finger of God? (Deut. 10:2)

   ____

✞

God's Requirements for Israel

6) Name seven requirements God placed on Israel as His covenant children?

a) Deut. 10:12 to ____________________ Him

b) Deut. 10:12 to ____________________ to His will

c) Deut .10:12 to ____________________ Him and

d) Deut. 10:12 to ____________________ Him with all your heart and soul

e) Deut .10:13 to ____________________ the Lord's commands and laws

f) Deut. 10:16 cleanse ______________

g) Deut. 10:19 show ________________ to foreigners

✞

Moses explained that God was worthy of Israel's praise. (Deut. 10:21)

God gave Israel a choice between having a blessing or a curse.

He had Israel pronounce blessings on their nation from the top of Mt. Gerizim for keeping covenant with God.

They also pronounced curses on their nation from Mt. Ebal, which would occur if they broke their covenant with God. (Deut. 11:26–30)

When they entered into the Promised Land, Israel was required to:

a) Break down the altars for worship of false gods;

b) Burn the Asherah poles and carved idols used for worship of false gods; and

c) Erase the names of the false gods of the nations they drove out of the land that God had given to Israel. (Deut 12:3)

God also required all of Israel to worship Him at the one location God selected. (Deut 12:5)

II. Find Jesus in the Lesson and III. Closing Thoughts

Jesus and Shema Continued

Today's lesson covers the second paragraph of the Shema, which is Deut. 11:13–21.

In this paragraph of the Shema, Israel is reminded of the blessings for loving and serving God with all their heart and soul and following His commandments. They are also reminded of the consequences for not following God's laws, and finally they are instructed to teach their children God's laws.

In the New Testament, Jesus explained that He came to fulfill the law, not to abolish it…

"Don't misunderstand why I [Jesus] have come.

I did not come to abolish the law of Moses or the writings of the prophets.

No, I came to fulfill them."
Matthew 5:17

Reading Assignment:
Deut. 13:1–16:17
Deut. 16:18–21:9
Deut. 21:10–25:19

Lesson 11.5, 11.6, 11.7

I. Lesson Exercise

Six Hundred Thirteen (613) Commands to Follow

... and obey all his requirements, laws, regulations, and commands. Deut. 11:1

God required the Israelites to obey a whole lot of commands. In the Jewish religion, it was determined God gave 613 commands to follow. According to God's repeated warnings, not even one of the 613 laws was to be broken.

Note: "Jews" are what Israelites are called today. In the Jewish religion, the Torah is the same as the first five books of the Christian Bible. The word "Torah" means the "Teachings" or "Instructions," which are the laws of God through Moses.

The total list of laws has been described as being one of three kinds:

- **Ceremonial laws:** Laws for the Tabernacle, offerings, and worship
- **Moral laws:** Laws that define what is right or wrong
- **Civil laws:** Laws on relations between individuals or between individuals and employers, on property rights, personal dignity and freedom or personal injury

II. Find Jesus in the Lesson and III. Closing Thoughts

Jesus came to fulfill the Law of Moses, not to destroy it!

Don't misunderstand why I** [Jesus] **have come.

I did not come to abolish the law of Moses or the writings of the prophets.

No, I came to fulfill them.

I assure you,
until heaven and earth disappear,
even the smallest detail of God's law
will remain until its purpose is achieved.

So if you break the smallest commandment
and teach others to do the same,
you will be the least in the Kingdom of Heaven.

But anyone who obeys God's laws and
teaches them
will be great in the Kingdom of Heaven.

But I warn you—

unless you obey God better than the teachers of religious law
and the Pharisees do,
you can't enter the Kingdom of Heaven at all.

Matthew 5:17–20

God sent Jesus to establish the "spirit of the law" in Christians' hearts.

This means Christians do not experience immediate destruction for breaking the law.

On the other hand, from the above text, Jesus makes it clear that Christians do value the wisdom found in the law for improving our everyday lives.

Jesus sent His spirit to change men's hearts, which enables Christians to live holy. (Rom. 1:1–17; Gal. 2:20)

The section that follows contains a detailed look at the law. Review its contents carefully to gain insight on:

"The Path You Should Walk"

"The Giving of the Law Upon Mt. Sinai" *by Gustave Doré*

Doré Bible Illustrations **• Free to Copy**
www.creationism.org/images/

Exo 19:18 And mount Sinai was altogether on a smoke, because the Lord descended upon it in fire: and the smoke thereof ascended as the smoke of a furnace, and the whole mount quaked greatly.

The Path You Should Walk

Reference Material

Contents:

The Path You Should Walk[1]

The Bible is God's set of instructions for life. Properly interpreted and applied to one's life, God's instructions describe **the path that one should walk** in order to be safe, in the center of God's will and to experience His bountiful blessings day by day.

> **In the first five books of the Bible** (Torah / Pentateuch / Law books of Moses)**, God provides detailed instructions on what humankind needs to do to live holy** (meaning to live like Him)**.**

Some of the laws from the Bible's law books no longer apply today because of the work of Jesus Christ. For example, laws related to animal sacrifices no longer apply. Also, some of the laws were expanded in the New Testament. Review Jesus' Sermon on the Mount in Matthew Chapters 5–7. As an example, compare Ex. 20:13 with Matt. 5:21–25.

Many of God's instructions in the Law Books are still valid for Christians today in order to travel in God's holy path for our daily walk-through life. Below is a list of the general categories of laws in the Bible's law books. The Ten Commandments provide an overview of the laws. A more detailed listing of all the laws follows in the next chart.

> Meditate on all the laws. Allow the Holy Spirit to help you understand "**The Path You Should Walk**" to please God.

God	**Poor and unfortunate**
Torah (God's Word / Laws)	**Prayer and Blessing**
Agriculture and animal husbandry	**Priests and Levites**
Business practices	**Prophecy**
Clothing	**Punishment and restitution**
Court and judicial procedures	**Ritual purity and impurity**
Criminal laws	**Sabbatical and Jubilee years**
Dietary laws	**Sacrifices and offerings**
Employees, servants, slaves	**Forbidden relations**
Firstborn	**Signs and symbols**
Idolatry and idolatrous practices	**Tabernacle and sacred objects**
Injuries and damages	**The King**
Lepers and leprosy	**Tithes and Taxes**
Love and brotherhood	**Times and seasons**
Marriage, divorce and family	**Vows, oaths and swearing**
Nazarites	**Wars**

[1]Appendix C:

"But, Didn't Jesus Abolish the Law and Those 613 Original Commandments?"[2]

reprinted by permission from "The Refiner's Fire**

In a word: NO!

The 613 Mitzvot (Commandments) were more of a man-made tradition rather than an actual number of commandments sent down by Yahweh (meaning God).

The idea originated in the Talmud* which says there are both "positive" and "negative" mitzvot (do's and don'ts) which can be divided into 365 Negative Mitzvot (to remind us not to do bad things every day of the year) plus 248 Positive Mitzvot—the number of bones in the human body—for a total of 613.

In this way, we are able to obey the mitzvot with our entire body.

Similarly, the *tzitzit* (knotted fringes) of the tallit (prayer shawl) are also connected to the 613 commandments.

Torah commentator Rashi declared that the number of knots on a *tzitzit* (in its Mishnaic spelling) has the value of 600.

When doubled over, each tassel has eight threads and five sets of knots, which totals 13—for a grand total of 613.

This concept reminds *tallit* wearers of all Torah commandments.

The world needs to be made aware of the fact that, while God gave us many commands that He ultimately condensed into just ten, He did not "do away with Torah." [His divine instructions found in the first five books of the Bible]

What Yeshua [Hebrew for Jesus] ***did*** attempt to bring to light was the rabbinical, man-made "stuff" - the opinions and traditions that kept people in bondage.

Paul verified this when he said:

> ***Do we then nullify the Law through faith?***
> ***May it never be! On the contrary, we establish the Law.***
> ***Romans 3:31***

So, what exactly were the original 613 commandments?

YHWH gave us 248 positive Mitzvot/Commandments ("the Do's"), and 365 negative ones ("the Don'ts").

They are as follows *[on the following pages]*:

*[*Note: Talmud is the Jewish sourcebook on the law containing ancient rabbinical teachings on how to interpret and apply the Law]*

[2]Appendix C

"But, Didn't Jesus Abolish the Law and Those 613 Original Commandments?"[2]

reprinted by permission from "The Refiner's Fire**

248 Positive Mitzvot/Commandments:

"The Do's"

RELATIONSHIP TO GOD

- P 1 Ex. 20:2 To believe in God
- P 2 Deut. 6:4 To acknowledge the unity of God
- P 3 Deut. 6:5 To love God
- P 4 Deut. 6:13 To fear God
- P 5 Ex. 23:25; Deut. 11:13; 13:5 To serve God
- P 6 Deut. 10:20 To cleave to God
- P 7 Deut. 10:20 On taking an oath by God's Name
- P 8 Deut. 28:9 On walking in God's ways
- P 9 Lev. 22:32 On sanctifying God's Name

TORAH

- P 10 Deut. 6:7 On reciting the Shema [prayers of faith] each morning and evening
- P 11 Deut. 6:7 On studying and teaching Torah
- P 12 Deut. 6:8 On binding Tefillin [small case containing Hebrew text from the law] on the head
- P 13 Deut. 6:8 On binding Tefillin on the hand
- P 14 Num. 15:38 On making Tzitzit [knotted fringes] with thread of blue, garments corners
- P 15 Deut. 6:9 On affixing a Mezuzah [case with Hebrew text from law] to doorposts and gates
- P 16 Deut. 31:12 On Assembling each 7th year to hear the Torah [Law of God] read
- P 17 Deut. 17:18 On that a king must write a copy of Torah for himself
- P 18 Deut. 31:19 On that everyone should have a Torah scroll
- P 19 Deut. 8:10 On praising God after eating, grace after meals

[2]Appendix C

"But, Didn't Jesus Abolish the Law and Those 613 Original Commandments?"[2]

reprinted by permission from "The Refiner's Fire**

TEMPLE AND THE PRIESTS

- P 20 Ex. 25:8 — On building a sanctuary / (Tabernacle/Temple) for God
- P 21 Lev.19:30 — On respecting the sanctuary
- P 22 Num. 18:4 — On guarding the sanctuary
- P 23 Num.18:23 — On Levitical services in the Tabernacle
- P 24 Ex. 30:19 — On Cohanim [priests] washing hands and feet before entering Temple
- P 25 Ex. 27:21 — On kindling the Menorah [golden lampstand] by the Cohanim
- P 26 Num. 6:23 — On the Cohanim blessing Israel
- P 27 Ex.25:30 — On the Showbread before the Ark
- P 28 Ex. 30:7 — On burning the incense on the Golden Altar twice daily
- P 29 Lev. 6:6 — On the perpetual fire on the altar
- P 30 Lev. 6:3 — On removing the ashes from the altar
- P 31 Num. 5:2 — On removing unclean persons from the camp
- P 32 Lev. 21:8 — On honoring the Cohanim
- P 33 Ex. 28:2 — On the garments of the Cohanim
- P 34 Num. 7:9 — On Cohanim bearing the Ark on their shoulders
- P 35 Ex. 30:31 — On the holy anointing oil
- P 36 Deut. 18:6–8 — On the Cohanim ministering in rotation/watches
- P 37 Lev. 21:2–3 — On the Cohanim being defiled for dead relatives
- P 38 Lev. 21:13 — On that Cohen haGadol [High Priest] may only marry a virgin

[2]Appendix C

"But, Didn't Jesus Abolish the Law and Those 613 Original Commandments?"[2]

reprinted by permission from "The Refiner's Fire**

SACRIFICES

- P 39 Num. 28:3 On the twice daily burnt, tamid, offerings
- P 40 Lev. 6:13 On Cohen haGadol's twice daily meal offering
- P 41 Num. 28:9 On Shabbat [Sabbath] additional offering
- P 42 Num. 28:11 On New Moon, Rosh Chodesh [beginning of new month], additional offering
- P 43 Lev. 23:36 On Pesach [Passover] additional offering
- P 44 Lev. 23:10 On the second day of Pesach meal offering of the Omer
- P 45 Num. 28:26 On Shavuot [Feast of Harvest] additional offering
- P 46 Lev. 23:17 On the two loaves of bread wave offering on Shavuot
- P 47 Num. 29:1–2 On the Rosh HaShannah additional offering
- P 48 Num. 29:7–8 On the Yom Kippur additional offering
- P 49 Lev. 16 On the service of Yom Kippur, Avodah
- P 50 Num. 29:13 On the Sukkot [Feast of Booths] offerings
- P 51 Num. 29:36 On the Shemini Atzeret additional offering
- P 52 Ex. 23:14 On the three annual Festival pilgrimages to the Temple
- P 53 Ex. 34:23 On appearing before YHVH [God] during the Festivals (Deut. 16:16)
- P 54 Deut. 16:14 On rejoicing on the Festivals
- P 55 Ex.12:6 On the 14th of Nisan slaughtering the Pesach lamb
- P 56 Ex.12:8 On eating the roasted Pesach lamb night of Nisan 15
- P 57 Num. 9:11 On slaughtering the Pesach Sheini, Iyyar 14, offering
- P 58 Num. 9:11; On eating Pesach Sheini lamb with Matzah and Maror [unleavened bread, bitter herbs]
- P 59 Num. 10:9-10 Trumpets for Feast sacrifices brought and for tribulation

"But, Didn't Jesus Abolish the Law and Those 613 Original Commandments?"[2]

reprinted by permission from "The Refiner's Fire**

SACRIFICES cont'd...

• P 60	Lev. 22:27	On minimum age of cattle to be offered
• P 61	Lev. 22:21	On offering only unblemished sacrifices
• P 62	Lev. 2:13	On bringing salt with every offering
• P 63	Lev.1:2	On the burnt-offering
• P 64	Lev. 6:18	On the sin-offering
• P 65	Lev. 7:1	On the guilt-offering
• P 66	Lev. 3:1	On the peace-offering
• P 67	Lev. 2:1	On the meal-offering
• P 68	Lev. 4:13	On offerings for a Court (Sanhedrin) that has erred
• P 69	Lev. 4:27	Fixed Sin-Offering, by one unknowingly breaking a karet [sin punishable by death]
• P 70	Lev. 5:17	Suspensive Guilt-Offering if doubt of breaking a karet
• P 71	Lev. 5:15	Unconditional Guilt-Offering, for stealing,etc.
• P 72	Lev. 5:1–11	Offering higher or lower value, according to ones means
• P 73	Num. 5:6–7	To confess one's sins before God and repent from them
• P 74	Lev.15:13	On offering brought by a zav (man with a discharge)
• P 75	Lev.15:28	Offering brought by a zavah (woman with a discharge)
• P 76	Lev.12:6	On offering brought by a woman after childbirth
• P 77	Lev.14:10	On offering brought by a leper after being cleansed
• P 78	Lev. 27:32	On the tithe of one's cattle
• P 79	Ex.13:2	Sacrificing the first-born of clean (permitted) cattle
• P 80	Ex. 22:28	On redeeming the first-born of man,

[2]Appendix C

"But, Didn't Jesus Abolish the Law and Those 613 Original Commandments?"[2]

reprinted by permission from "The Refiner's Fire**

SACRIFICES cont'd...

•	P 81	Ex. 34:20	On redeeming firstling of an ass, if not...
•	P 82	Ex.13:13	...breaking the neck of the firstling of an ass
•	P 83	Deut.12:5–6	On bringing due offerings to Jerusalem without delay
•	P 84	Deut. 12:14	All offerings must be brought only to the Sanctuary
•	P 85	Deut.12:36	On offerings due from outside Israel to the Sanctuary
•	P 86	Deut.12:15	On redeeming blemished sanctified animal offerings
•	P 87	Lev. 27:33	On the holiness of substituted animal offerings
•	P 88	Lev. 6:9	On Cohanim eating the remainder of the meal offerings
•	P 89	Ex. 29:33	On Cohanim eating the meat of Sin and guilt offerings
•	P 90	Lev.7:19	Burn consecrated offerings that've become tameh/unclean
•	P 91	Lev.7:17	Burn remnant of consecrated offerings not eaten in time

VOWS

•	P 92	Num. 6:5	The Nazir [one who has taken the Nazarite Vow] letting his hair grow during his separation
•	P 93	Num. 6:18	Nazir completing vow shaves his head and brings sacrifice
•	P 94	Deut. 23:24	On that a man must honor his oral vows and oaths
•	P 95	Num. 30:3	On that a judge can annul vows, only according to Torah

[2]Appendix C

"But, Didn't Jesus Abolish the Law and Those 613 Original Commandments?"[2]

reprinted by permission from "The Refiner's Fire**

RITUAL PURITY

- P 96 Lev. 11:8 Defilement by touching certain animal carcasses, and...
- P 97 Lev. 11:29 ...by touching carcasses of eight creeping creatures
- P 98 Lev. 11:34 Defilement of food and drink, if contacting unclean thing
- P 99 Lev.15:19 On Tumah [ritual impurity] of a menstruant woman
- P100 Lev.12:2 On Tumah of a woman after childbirth
- P101 Lev.13:3 On Tumah of a leper
- P102 Lev.13:51 On garments contaminated by leprosy
- P103 Lev.14:44 On a leprous house
- P104 Lev.15:2 On Tumah of a zav (man with a running issue)
- P105 Lev.15:6 On Tumah of semen
- P106 Lev.15:19 Tumah of a zavah (woman suffering from a running issue)
- P107 Num.19:14 On Tumah of a human corpse
- P108 Num.19:13 Law of the purification water of sprinkling, mei niddah
- P109 Lev.15:16 On immersing in a mikveh [ritual bath] to become ritually clean
- P110 Lev.14:2 On the specified procedure of cleansing from leprosy
- P111 Lev.14:9 On that a leper must shave his head
- P112 Lev.13:45 On that the leper must be made easily distinguishable
- P113 Num.19:2–9 On ashes of the red heifer, used in ritual purification

[2]Appendix C

"But, Didn't Jesus Abolish the Law and Those 613 Original Commandments?"[2]

reprinted by permission from "The Refiner's Fire**

DONATIONS TO THE TEMPLE

- P114 Lev. 27:2–8 On valuation for a person himself to the Temple
- P115 Lev. 27:11 On the valuation for an unclean beast to the Temple
- P116 Lev. 27:14 On the valuation of a house as a donation to the Temple
- P117 Lev. 27:16 On the valuation of a field as a donation to the Temple
- P118 Lev. 5:16 If benefit from Temple property, restitution plus 1/5th
- P119 Lev. 19:24 On the fruits of the trees fourth year's growth
- P120 Lev. 19:9 On leaving the corners (Peah) of fields for the poor
- P121 Lev. 19:9 On leaving gleanings of the field for the poor
- P122 Deut. 24:19 On leaving the forgotten sheaf for the poor
- P123 Lev. 19:19 On leaving the misformed grape clusters for the poor
- P124 Lev. 19:10 On leaving grape gleanings for the poor
- P125 Ex. 23:19 On separating and bringing First-fruits to the sanctuary
- P126 Deut. 18:4 To separate the great heave-offering (terumah)
- P127 Lev. 27:30 To set aside the first tithe to the Levites
- P128 Deut. 14:22 To set aside the second tithe, eaten only in Jerusalem
- P129 Num. 18:26 On Levites' giving tenth of their tithe to the Cohanim
- P130 Deut. 14:28 To set aside the poor-man's tithe in third and sixth year
- P131 Deut. 26:13 A declaration made when separating the various tithes
- P132 Deut. 26:5 A declaration made bringing first-fruits to the Temple
- P133 Num. 15:20 On the first portion of the Challah [bread] given to the Cohen [family of the priest]

[2]Appendix C

"But, Didn't Jesus Abolish the Law and Those 613 Original Commandments?"[2]

reprinted by permission from "The Refiner's Fire**

THE SABBATICAL YEAR

- P134 Ex. 23:11 On ownerless produce of the Sabbatical year (shemittah)
- P135 Ex. 34:21 On resting the land on the Sabbatical year
- P136 Lev. 25:10 On sanctifying the Jubilee (50th) year
- P137 Lev. 25:9 Blow Shofar on Yom Kippur in the Jubilee and slaves freed
- P138 Lev. 25:24 Reversion of the land to ancestral owners in Jubilee year
- P139 Lev. 25:24 On the redemption of a house within a year of the sale
- P140 Lev. 25:8 Counting and announcing the years till the Jubilee year
- P141 Deut. 15:3 All debts are annulled in the Sabbatical year, but...
- P142 Deut. 15:3 ...one may exact a debt owed by a foreigner

CONCERNING ANIMALS FOR CONSUMPTION

- P143 Deut. 18:3 Cohen's due in slaughter of every clean animal
- P144 Deut. 18:4 On first of the fleece to be given to the Cohen
- P145 Lev. 27:21 (Cherem vow) one devoted thing to God, other to Cohanim [priests]
- P146 Deut. 12:21 Slaughtering animals, according to Torah, before eating
- P147 Lev.17:13 Covering with earth the blood of slain fowl and beast
- P148 Deut. 22:7 On setting free parent bird when taking the nest
- P149 Lev.11:2 Searching for prescribed signs in beasts, for eating
- P150 Deut.14:11 Searching for the prescribed signs in birds, for eating
- P151 Lev. 11:21 Searching for prescribed signs in locusts, for eating
- P152 Lev. 11:9 Searching for prescribed signs in fish, for eating

[2]Appendix C

"But, Didn't Jesus Abolish the Law and Those 613 Original Commandments?"[2]

reprinted by permission from "The Refiner's Fire**

FESTIVALS

- P153 Ex.12:2; Deut.16:1 Sanhedrin to sanctify new moon, & and reckon years & seasons
- P154 Ex.23:12 On resting on the Shabbat
- P155 Ex.20:8 On declaring Shabbat holy at its onset and termination
- P156 Ex.12:15 On removal of chametz, leaven (yeast) on (Nisan 14) Pesach
- P157 Ex.13:8 Tell of Exodus from Egypt first night Pesach (Nisan 15)
- P158 Ex.12:18 On eating Matzah [unleavened bread] the first night of Pesach, (Nisan 15)
- P159 Ex.12:16 On resting on the first day of Pesach
- P160 Ex.12:16 On resting on the seventh day of Pesach
- P161 Lev. 23:35 Count the Omer 49 days from day of first sheaf (Nisan 16)
- P162 Lev. 23 On resting on Shavuot
- P163 Lev. 23:24 On resting on Rosh HaShannah
- P164 Lev.16:29 On fasting on Yom Kippur
- P165 Lev.16:29 On resting on Yom Kippur
- P166 Lev. 23:35 On resting on the first day of Sukkot
- P167 Lev. 23:36 On resting on (the 8th day) Shemini Atzeret
- P168 Lev. 23:42 On dwelling in a Sukkah (booth) for seven days
- P169 Lev. 23:40 On taking a Lulav (the four species) on Sukkot
- P170 Num. 29:1 On hearing the sound of the Shofar [ram's horn] on Rosh HaShannah

[2]Appendix C

"But, Didn't Jesus Abolish the Law and Those 613 Original Commandments?"[2]

reprinted by permission from "The Refiner's Fire**

COMMUNITY

- P171 Ex. 30:12 On every male giving half a shekel annually to Temple
- P172 Deut. 18:15 On heeding the Prophets
- P173 Deut. 17:15 On appointing a king
- P174 Deut. 17:11 On obeying the Great Court (Sanhedrin)
- P175 Ex.23:2 On in case of division, abiding by a majority decision
- P176 Deut. 16:18 Appointing judges & officers of the court in every town
- P177 Lev. 19:15 Treating litigants equally/impartially before the law
- P178 Lev. 5:1 Anyone aware of evidence must come to court to testify
- P179 Deut. 13:15 The testimony of witnesses shall be examined thoroughly
- P180 Deut. 19:19 On condemning witnesses who testify falsely
- P180 Deut. 19:19 False witnesses punished, as they intended upon accused
- P181 Deut. 21:4 On Eglah Arufah, on the heifer when murderer unknown
- P182 Deut. 19:3 On establishing Six Cities of Refuge
- P183 Num. 35:2 Give cities to Levites—who've no ancestral land share
- P184 Deut. 22:8 Build fence on roof, remove potential hazards from home

IDOLATRY

- P185 Deut. 12:2 On destroying all idolatry and its appurtenances
- P186 Deut. 13:17 The law about a city that has become apostate/perverted
- P187 Deut. 20:17 On the law about destroying the seven Canaanite nations
- P188 Deut. 25:19 On the extinction of the seed of Amalek
- P189 Deut. 25:17 On remembering the nefarious deeds of Amalek to Israel

[2]Appendix C

"But, Didn't Jesus Abolish the Law and Those 613 Original Commandments?"[2]

reprinted by permission from "The Refiner's Fire**

WAR

•	P190	Deut. 20:11	Regulations for wars other than ones commanded in Torah
•	P191	Deut. 20:2	Cohen for special duties in war; also men unfit return
•	P192	Deut.23:14	Prepare place beyond the camp, so to keep sanitary and...
•	P193	Deut.23:15	...so include a digging tool among war implements

SOCIAL

•	P194	Lev.5:23	On a robber to restore the stolen article to its owner
•	P195	Deut.15:8;	On to give charity to the poor (Lev.25:35-36)
•	P196	Deut.15:14	On giving gifts to a Hebrew bondman upon his freedom
•	P197	Ex.22:24	On lending money to the poor without interest
•	P198	Deut.23:21	On lending money to the foreigner with interest
•	P199	Deut.24:13; Ex.22:25	On restoring a pledge to its owner if he needs it
•	P200	Deut.24:15	On paying the worker his wages on time
•	P201	Deut.23:25	Employee is allowed to eat the produce he's working in
•	P202	Ex.23:5	On helping unload when necessary a tired animal
•	P203	Deut.22:4	On assisting a man loading his beast with its burden
•	P204	Deut.22:1, Ex.23:4	On that lost property must be returned to its owner
•	P205	Lev.19:17	On being required to reprove the sinner
•	P206	Lev.19:18	On love your neighbor as yourself
•	P207	Deut.10:19	On being commanded to love the convert / proselyte
•	P208	Lev.19:36	On the law of accurate weights and measures

[2]Appendix C

"But, Didn't Jesus Abolish the Law and Those 613 Original Commandments?"[2]

reprinted by permission from "The Refiner's Fire**

FAMILY

- P209 Lev. 19:32 On honoring the old (and wise)
- P210 Ex. 20:12 On honoring parents
- P211 Lev.19:3 On fearing parents
- P212 Gen.1:28 On being fruitful and multiplying
- P213 Deut. 24:1 On the law of marriage
- P214 Deut. 24:5 On bridegroom devoting himself to his wife for one year
- P215 Gen.17:10; Lev.12:3 On circumcising one's son
- P216 Deut. 25:5 If a man dies childless his brother marries widow, or...
- P217 Deut. 25:9 ...release her/the-widow (Chalitzah)
- P218 Deut. 22:29 A violator must marry the virgin/maiden he has violated
- P219 Deut. 22:18 The defamer of his bride is flogged & may never divorce
- P220 Ex. 22:15 On the seducer must be punished according to the law
- P221 Deut. 21:11 Captive women treated according to special regulations
- P222 Deut. 24:1 The law of divorce, only be means of written document
- P223 Num. 5:15 Suspected adulteress has to submit to the required test

JUDICIAL

- P224 Deut. 25:2 On whipping transgressors of certain commandments
- P225 Num. 35:25 On exile to city of refuge for unintentional homicide
- P226 Ex. 21:20 On beheading transgressors of certain commandments
- P227 Ex. 21:16 On strangling transgressors of certain commandments

[2]Appendix C

"But, Didn't Jesus Abolish the Law and Those 613 Original Commandments?"[2]

reprinted by permission from "The Refiner's Fire**

- P228 Lev. 20:14 On burning transgressors of certain commandments
- P229 Deut. 22:24 On stoning transgressors of certain commandments
- P230 Deut. 21:22 Hang after execution, violators of certain commandments
- P231 Deut. 21:23 On burial on the same day of execution

SLAVES

- P232 Ex.21:2 On special laws for treating Hebrew bondman
- P233 Ex.21:8 Hebrew bondmaid married to her master or his son, or...
- P234 Ex.21:8 ...allow the redemption to the Hebrew bondmaid
- P235 Lev.25:46 On the laws for treating an alien bondman

TORTS

- P236 Ex.21:18 On the penalty for a person inflicting injury
- P237 Ex.21:28 On the law of injuries caused by an animal
- P238 Ex.21:33 On the law of injuries caused by an pit
- P239 Ex.21:37 On the law of punishment of thieves
- P240 Ex.22:4 On the law of a judgment for damage caused by a beast
- P241 Ex.22:5 On the law of a judgment for damage caused by a fire
- P242 Ex.22:6 On the law of an unpaid guardian
- P243 Ex.22:9 On the law of a paid guardian
- P244 Ex.22:13 On the law of a borrower
- P245 Lev.25:14 On the law of buying and selling
- P246 Ex.22:8 On the law of litigants
- P247 Deut.25:12 Save life of one pursued, even if need—kill oppressor
- P248 Num.27:8 On the law of inheritance

[2]Appendix C

"But, Didn't Jesus Abolish the Law and Those 613 Original Commandments?"[2]

reprinted by permission from "The Refiner's Fire**

365 Negative Mitzvot/Commandments:

"The Don'ts"

IDOLATRY AND RELATED PRACTICES

- N 1 Ex.20:3 Not believing in any other god except the one God.
- N 2 Ex.20:4 Not to make images for the purpose of worship
- N 3 Lev.19:4 Not to make an idol (even for others) to worship
- N 4 Ex.20:20 Not to make figures of human beings
- N 5 Ex.20:5 Not to bow down to an idol
- N 6 Ex.20:5 Not to worship idols
- N 7 Lev.18:21 Not to hand over any children to Moloch
- N 8 Lev.19:31 Not to practice sorcery of the ov, necromancy
- N 9 Lev.19:31 Not to practice sorcery… or familiar spirits
- N 10 Lev.19:4 Not to study idolatrous practices
- N 11 Deut.16:22 Not to erect a pillar that people assemble to honor
- N 12 Lev.20:1 No figured stones (dias) to lay prostrate on
- N 13 Deut.16:21 Not to plant trees in the Sanctuary/Temple
- N 14 Ex.23:13 Swear not by an idol nor instigate an idolater to do so
- N 15 Ex.23:13 Not to divert any non-Jew to idolatry
- N 16 Deut.13:12 Not to try to persuade a Jew to worship idols
- N 17 Deut.13:9 Not to love someone who seeks to mislead you to idols
- N 18 Deut.13:9 Not to relax one's aversion to misleader to idols
- N 19 Deut.13:9 Not to save the life of a misleader to idols
- N 20 Deut.13:9 Not to plead for (defend) the misleader to idols
- N 21 Deut.13:9 Not to oppress evidence unfavorable to the misleader

[2]Appendix C

"But, Didn't Jesus Abolish the Law and Those 613 Original Commandments?"[2]

reprinted by permission from "The Refiner's Fire**

IDOLATRY AND RELATED PRACTICES continued...

- N 22 | Deut.7:25 | No benefit from ornaments which have adorned an idol
- N 23 | Deut.13:17 | Rebuild not a city destroyed as punishment for idolatry
- N 24 | Deut.13:18 | Not deriving benefit from property of an apostate city
- N 25 | Deut.7:26 | Do not use anything connected with idols or idolatry
- N 26 | Deut.18:20 | Not prophesying in the name of idols
- N 27 | Deut.18:20 | Not prophesying falsely in the name of God
- N 28 | Deut.13:3-4 | Listen not to one who prophesies in the name of idols
- N 29 | Deut.18:22 | Not fearing or refraining from killing a false prophet
- N 30 | Lev.20:23 | Imitate not the ways nor practice customs of idolaters
- N 31 | Lev.19:26; Deut.18:10 | Not practicing divination
- N 32 | Deut.18:10 | Not practicing soothsaying
- N 33 | Deut.18:10 | Not practicing enchanting
- N 34 | Deut.18:10 | Not practicing sorcery
- N 35 | Deut.18:10 | Not practicing the art of the charmer
- N 36 | Deut.18:10 | Not consulting a necromancer who uses the ov
- N 37 | Deut.18:10 | Not consulting a sorcerer who uses the ydo'a
- N 38 | Deut.18:10 | Not to seek information from dead, necromancy
- N 39 | Deut.22:5 | Women not to wear men's clothes or adornments
- N 40 | Deut.22:5 | Men not wearing women's clothes or adornments
- N 41 | Lev.19:28 | Not tattoo yourself, as is manner of the idolaters
- N 42 | Deut.22:11 | Not wearing a mixture of wool and linen...
- N 43 | Lev.19:27 | Not shaving the temples/sides of your head
- N 44 | Lev.19:27 | Not shaving your beard
- N 45 | Deut.16:1 | Not making cuttings in your flesh over your dead

[2]Appendix C

"But, Didn't Jesus Abolish the Law and Those 613 Original Commandments?"[2]

reprinted by permission from "The Refiner's Fire**

PROHIBITIONS RESULTING FROM HISTORICAL EVENTS

- N 46 Deut.17:16 Not returning to Egypt to dwell there permanently
- N 47 Num.15:39 Not to follow one's heart or eyes, straying to impurity
- N 48 Ex.23:32; Deut.7:2 Not to make a pact with the seven Canaanite nations
- N 49 Deut.20:16 Not to spare the life of the seven Canaanite nations
- N 50 Deut.7:2 Not to show mercy to idolaters
- N 51 Ex.23:33 No one serving false gods to settle in Eretz-Israel [land of Israel]
- N 52 Deut.7:3 Not to intermarry with one serving false gods
- N 53 Deut.23:4 Not to intermarry at all with a male from Ammon or Moav
- N 54 Deut.23:8 Exclude not marrying a descendant Esau if a proselyte
- N 55 Deut.23:8 Not to exclude marrying an Egyptian who is a proselyte
- N 56 Deut.23:7 Not permitted to make peace with Ammon and Moav nations
- N 57 Deut.20:19 Not destroying fruit trees, even in time of war
- N 59 Deut.25:19 Not forgetting the evil which Amalek did to us

BLASPHEMY

- N 60 Lev.24:16; Ex.22:27 Not blaspheming the Holy Name of God [rather]:
- N 61 Lev.19:12 Not violating an oath by the Holy Name...
- N 62 Ex.20:7 Not taking the Holy Name in vain...
- N 63 Lev.22:32 Not profaning the Holy Name of God
- N 64 Deut.6:16 Not testing/trying His (YHVH God) promises and warnings
- N 65 Deut.12:4 Do not destroy houses of worship or holy books
- N 66 Deut.21:23 Leave not body of executed criminal hanging overnight

[2]Appendix C

"But, Didn't Jesus Abolish the Law and Those 613 Original Commandments?"[2]

reprinted by permission from "The Refiner's Fire**

TEMPLE

•	N 67	Num.18:5	Be not lax in guarding the Sanctuary/Temple
•	N 68	Lev.16:2	Cohen haGadol enter sanctuary only at prescribed times
•	N 69	Lev.21:23	Cohen with blemish enter not Temple, from altar inwards
•	N 70	Lev.21:17	Cohen with a blemish not to minister in sanctuary
•	N 71	Lev.21:18	Cohen with temporary blemish minister not in sanctuary
•	N 72	Num.18:3	Levites & Cohanim not to interchange functions
•	N 73	Lev.10:9	Drunk persons may not enter sanctuary or teach Torah
•	N 74	Num.18:4	A Zar (non-Cohen) not to minister in sanctuary
•	N 75	Lev.22:2	Tameh (unclean) Cohen not to minister in sanctuary
•	N 76	Lev.21:6	Cohen who is tevul yom, not to minister in sanctuary
•	N 77	Num.5:3	Tameh (unclean) person not to enter any part of Temple
•	N 78	Deut.23:11	Tameh person enter not camp of Levites (Temple mount)
•	N 79	Ex.20:25	Build not an Altar of stones that were touched by iron
•	N 80	Ex.20:26	Not to have an ascent to the altar by steps
•	N 81	Lev.6:6	Not to extinguish the altar fire
•	N 82	Ex.30:9	Offer nothing, but specified incense, on Golden Altar
•	N 83	Ex.30:32	Not to make any oil same as the Oil of Anointment
•	N 84	Ex.30:32	Anoint none with special oil except Cohen Gadol and King
•	N 85	Ex.30:37	Not to make incense same as burnt on altar in sanctuary
•	N 86	Ex.25:15	Not to remove staves from their rings in the Ark
•	N 87	Ex.28:28	Not to remove the Breastplate from the Ephod
•	N 88	Ex.28:32	Make not any incision in Cohen haGadol's upper garment

[2]Appendix C

"But, Didn't Jesus Abolish the Law and Those 613 Original Commandments?"[2]

reprinted by permission from "The Refiner's Fire**

SACRIFICES

•	N 89	Deut.12:13	Offer not sacrifices outside Sanctuary/(Temple) Court
•	N 91	Lev.22:20	Dedicate not a blemished animal to be offered on altar
•	N 92	Lev.22:22	Not to slaughter a blemished animal as a korban
•	N 93	Lev.22:24	Not to dash the blood of a blemished beast on the Altar
•	N 94	Lev.22:22	Not to burn the inner parts of blemished beast on altar
•	N 95	Deut.17:1	Not to sacrifice a beast with a temporary blemish
•	N 96	Lev.22:25	Not to offer a blemished sacrifice of a gentile
•	N 97	Lev.22:21	Not to cause a consecrated offering to become blemished
•	N 98	Lev.2:11	Not to offer leaven or honey upon the Altar
•	N 99	Lev.2:13	Not to offer a sacrifice without salt
•	N100	Deut.23:19	Offer not on altar: "hire of harlot" or "price of dog"
•	N101	Lev.22:28	Not to slaughter an animal & its young on the same day
•	N102	Lev.5:11	Not to put olive oil on the sin meal-offering
•	N103	Lev.5:11	Not to put frankincense on the sin meal-offering
•	N104	Num.5:15	Not to put olive oil on the jealousy offering, sotah
•	N105	Num.5:15	Not to put frankincense on the jealousy offering
•	N106	Lev.27:10	Not to substitute sacrifices
•	N107	Lev.27:26	Not to change sacrifices from one category to the other
•	N108	Num.18:17	Redeem not the firstborn of permitted (clean) animals
•	N109	Lev.27:33	Not to sell the tithe of the herd of cattle
•	N110	Lev.27:28	Not to sell a devoted (by the Cherem vow) field
•	N111	Lev.27:28	Not to redeem a devoted field
•	N112	Lev.5:8	Not to split head of bird slaughtered for sin-offering

[2]Appendix C

"But, Didn't Jesus Abolish the Law and Those 613 Original Commandments?"[2]

reprinted by permission from "The Refiner's Fire**

SACRIFICES continued...

- N113 Deut.15:19 Not to do any work with a dedicated beast
- N114 Deut.15:19 Not to shear a dedicated beast
- N115 Ex.34:25 Slaughter not Pesach/Passover lamb if chametz is about
- N116 Ex.23:10 Leave not sacrificial portions of Pesach lamb overnight
- N117 Ex.12:10 Allow not meat of Pesach lamb to remain till morning
- N118 Deut.16:4 No meat of Nisan 14 festive offering remain till day 3
- N119 Num.9:13 No meat of 2nd Pesach lamb offering remain till morning
- N120 Lev.22:30 No meat of thanksgiving offering to remain till morning
- N121 Ex.12:46 Not to break any bones of Pesach lamb offering
- N122 Num.9:12 Not to break any bones of 2nd Pesach lamb offering
- N123 Ex.12:46 Not to remove Pesach offering from where it is eaten
- N124 Lev.6:10 Not to bake the residue of a meal offering with leaven
- N125 Ex.12:9 Not to eat the Pesach offering boiled or raw
- N126 Ex.12:45 Not to allow an alien resident to eat Pesach offering
- N127 Ex.12:48 An uncircumcised person may not eat the Pesach offering
- N128 Ex.12:43 Not to allow an apostate to eat the Pesach offering
- N129 Lev.12:4 Tameh (ritually unclean) person may not eat holy things
- N130 Lev.7:19 Eat not meat of consecrated things that've become tameh
- N131 Lev.19:6-8 Not to eat sacrificial meat beyond the allotted time
- N132 Lev.7:18 Eat not sacrificial meat slaughtered in wrong intention
- N133 Lev.22:10 A zar/non-Cohen may not eat terumah / (heave offering)
- N134 Lev.22:10 A Cohen's sojourner or hired worker may not eat terumah
- N135 Lev.22:10 An uncircumcised person may not eat terumah
- N136 Lev.22:4 Tameh (ritually unclean) Cohen may not eat terumah

[2]Appendix C

"But, Didn't Jesus Abolish the Law and Those 613 Original Commandments?"[2]

reprinted by permission from “The Refiner’s Fire**

SACRIFICES continued...

- N137 Lev.22:12 Bat-Cohen [daughter of a priest] if married to non-Cohen not to eat holy food
- N138 Lev.6:16 Not to eat the meal-offering of a Cohen
- N139 Lev.6:23 Eat not sin-offering meat sacrificed within Sanctuary
- N140 Deut.14:3 Not to eat consecrated animals that have become blemished
- N141 Deut.12:17 Eat not unredeemed 2nd corn tithe outside Yerushalayim [God’s chosen place for His presence to be for worship]
- N142 Deut.12:17 Consume not unredeemed 2nd wine tithe outside Jerusalem
- N143 Deut.12:17 Consume not unredeemed 2nd oil tithe outside Jerusalem
- N144 Deut.12:17 Eat not an unblemished firstling outside Yerushalayim
- N145 Deut.12:17 Eat not sin or guilt offerings outside Sanctuary court
- N146 Deut.12:17 Not to eat the meat of the burnt offering at all
- N147 Deut.12:17 Eat not lesser sacrifices before blood dashed on altar
- N148 Deut.12:17 A zar/non-Cohen is not to eat the most holy offerings
- N149 Ex.29:33 A Cohen not to eat first fruits outside Temple courts
- N150 Deut.26:14 Eat not unredeemed 2nd tithe while in state of impurity
- N151 Deut.26:14 Not eating the 2nd tithe while in mourning
- N152 Deut.26:14 On 2nd tithe redemption money (only for food and drink)
- N153 Lev.22:15 Not eating untithed produce, tevel
- N154 Ex.22:28 Not changing the order of separating the various tithes
- N155 Deut.23:22 Delay not payment of offerings, freewill or obligatory
- N156 Ex.23:15 Go not to Temple on pilgrim festivals without offering
- N157 Num.30:3 Not to break your word, even if without an oath

[2]Appendix C

"But, Didn't Jesus Abolish the Law and Those 613 Original Commandments?"[2]

reprinted by permission from "The Refiner's Fire**

PRIESTS

- N158 Lev.21:7 A Cohen may not marry a harlot, zonah
- N159 Lev.21:7 A Cohen marry not a woman profaned from the priesthood
- N160 Lev.21:7 A Cohen may not marry a divorcee
- N161 Lev.21:14 Cohen haGadol may not marry a widow
- N162 Lev.21:15 Cohen haGadol may not take a widow as a concubine
- N163 Lev.10:6 Cohen with disheveled hair may not enter the sanctuary
- N164 Lev.10:6 Cohen wearing rent garments may not enter sanctuary
- N165 Lev.10:7 Cohanim leave not Temple courtyard during the service
- N166 Lev.21:1 Common Cohen must not be defiled for dead, except some
- N167 Lev.21:11 Cohen haGadol may not be under one roof with dead body
- N168 Lev.21:11 Cohen haGadol must not be defiled for any dead person
- N169 Deut.18:1 Levites have not part in the division of Israel's land
- N170 Deut.18:1 Levites share not in the spoils of war
- N171 Deut.14:1 Not to tear out hair for the dead

[2]Appendix C

"But, Didn't Jesus Abolish the Law and Those 613 Original Commandments?"[2]

reprinted by permission from "The Refiner's Fire**

DIETARY LAWS

- N172 Deut.14:7 Not to eat any unclean animal
- N173 Lev.11:11 Not to eat any unclean fish
- N174 Lev.11:13 Not to eat any unclean fowl
- N175 Deut.14:19 Not to eat any creeping winged insect
- N176 Lev.11:41 Not to eat anything that creeps on the earth
- N177 Lev.11:44 Not to eat creeping thing that breeds in decayed matter
- N178 Lev.11:42 Not to eat living creatures that breed in seeds / fruit
- N179 Lev.11:43 Not to eat any detestable creature
- N180 Deut.14:21 Not to eat any animal that died naturally
- N181 Ex.22:30 Not to eat an animal that is torn or mauled
- N182 Deut.12:23 Not to eat any limb taken from a living animal
- N183 Ge.32:33 Not to eat the sinew of the thigh-vein
- N184 Lev.7:24 Not to eat blood
- N185 Lev.7:23 Not to eat certain types of fat of clean animal
- N186 Ex.23:19 Not to boil young male goat (meat) in its mother's milk
- N187 Ex.34:26 Not to eat young male goat cooked in its mother's milk
- N188 Ex.21:28 Not to eat the flesh of a condemned and To be stoned ox
- N189 Lev.23:14 Eat not bread made from grain of new crop, before Omer [special offering]
- N190 Lev.23:14 Eat not roasted grain of new crop, before Omer offering
- N191 Lev.23:14 Eat not green ears of new crop, before Omer (Nisan 16)
- N192 Lev.19:23 Not to eat orlah
- N193 Deut.22:9 Eat not growth of mixed vineyard planting,kilai hakerem

[2]Appendix C

"But, Didn't Jesus Abolish the Law and Those 613 Original Commandments?"[2]

reprinted by permission from "The Refiner's Fire**

DIETARY LAWS

- N194 Deut.32:38 Not to use wine libations for idols, yayin nesech
- N195 Lev.19:26; Deut.21:20 No eating or drinking to excess, gluttony and drunkenness
- N196 Lev.23:29 Not to eat anything on Yom Kippur / Day of Atonement
- N197 Ex.13:3 Not to eat chametz, leaven(ed), on Pesach
- N198 Ex.13:7 Not to eat an admixture of chametz/leaven(ed) on Pesach
- N199 Deut.16:3 Not to eat chametz, leaven(ed), after noon of 14 Nisan
- N200 Ex.13:7 No chametz may be seen in our homes during Pesach
- N201 Ex.12:19 Not to possess chametz, leaven(ed), during Pesach

NAZIRITES

- N202 Num.6:3 A A Nazir may not drink wine or any beverage from grapes
- N203 Num.6:3 A Nazir may not eat fresh grapes
- N204 Num.6:3 A Nazir may not eat dried grapes
- N205 Num.6:4 A Nazir may not eat grape seeds/kernels
- N206 Num.6:4 A Nazir may not eat grape peels/husks
- N207 Num.6:7 Nazir may not rend himself tameh (unclean) for the dead
- N208 Lev.21:11 Nazir must not become tameh entering house with corpse
- N209 Num.6:5 A Nazir must not shave his hair

[2]Appendix C

"But, Didn't Jesus Abolish the Law and Those 613 Original Commandments?"[2]

reprinted by permission from "The Refiner's Fire**

AGRICULTURE

•	N210	Lev.23:22	Reap not a whole field without leaving corners for poor
•	N211	Lev.19:9	Not to gather ears of grain that fell during harvesting
•	N212	Lev.19:10	Not to gather the misformed clusters of grapes
•	N213	Lev.19:10	Not to gather single fallen grapes during the vintage
•	N214	Deut.24:19	Not to return for a forgotten sheaf
•	N215	Lev.19:19	Not to sow diverse kinds of seed in one field, kalayim
•	N216	Deut.22:9	Not to sow grain or vegetables in a vineyard
•	N217	Lev.19:19	Not to crossbreed animals of different species
•	N218	Deut.22:10	Work not with two different kinds of animals together
•	N219	Deut.25:4	Muzzle not animal working field to prevent from eating
•	N220	Lev.25:4	Not to cultivate the soil in the 7th year, shemittah
•	N221	Lev.25:4	Not to prune the trees in the 7th year
•	N222	Lev.25:5	Reap not self-grown plant in 7th year as ordinary year
•	N223	Lev.25:5	Gather not self-grown fruit in 7th yr. as ordinary year
•	N224	Lev.25:11	Not to till the earth or prune trees in Jubilee year
•	N225	Lev.25:11	Reap not aftergrowths of Jubilee year as ordinary year
•	N226	Lev.25:11	Not to gather fruit in Jubilee year as in ordinary year
•	N227	Lev.25:23	Sell not one's Eretz Yisrael land holdings permanently
•	N228	Lev.25:33	Not to sell/change the open lands of the Levites
•	N229	Deut.12:19	Not to leave the Levites without support

[2]Appendix C

"But, Didn't Jesus Abolish the Law and Those 613 Original Commandments?"[2]

reprinted by permission from "The Refiner's Fire**

LOANS, BUSINESS, AND THE TREATMENT OF SLAVES

- N230 Deut.15:2 Not to demand payment of debts after (7th) Shmitah year
- N231 Deut.15:9 Not to refuse loan to poor because Shmitah year is near
- N232 Deut.15:7 Not to deny charity to the poor
- N233 Deut.15:13 Not sending a Hebrew bondman away empty handed
- N234 Ex.22:24 Not demanding payment from a debtor known unable to pay
- N235 Lev.25:37 Not lending to another Jew at interest
- N236 Deut.23:20 Not borrowing from another Jew at interest
- N237 Ex.22:24 Not participating in an agreement involving interest
- N238 Lev.19:13 Oppress not an employee by delaying paying his wages
- N239 Deut.24:10 Not taking a pledge from a debtor by force
- N240 Deut.24:12 Not keeping a poor man's pledge when he needs it
- N241 Deut.24:17 Not taking any pledge from a widow
- N242 Deut.24:6 Not taking one's business (or food) utensils in pledge
- N243 Ex.20:13 Not abducting an Israelite
- N244 Lev.19:11 Not stealing
- N245 Lev.19:13 Not robbing
- N246 Deut.19:14 Not fraudulently altering land boundaries / landmarker
- N247 Lev.19:13 Not usurping our debts / do not defraud
- N248 Lev.19:11 Not repudiating debts, denying receipt of loan/deposit
- N249 Lev.19:11 Not to swear falsely regarding another man's property
- N250 Lev.25:14 Not wronging/deceiving one another in business
- N251 Lev.25:17 Not wronging/misleading one another even verbally

[2]Appendix C

"But, Didn't Jesus Abolish the Law and Those 613 Original Commandments?"[2]

reprinted by permission from "The Refiner's Fire**

)ANS, BUSINESS, AND THE TREATMENT OF SLAVES

- N252 Ex.22:20 Not harming the stranger among you verbally
- N253 Ex.22:20 Not injuring the stranger among you in business/trade
- N254 Deut.23:16 Not handing over a slave who's fled to Israel
- N255 Deut.23:17 Take no advantage of a slave who's fled to Israel
- N256 Ex.22:21 Not afflicting the orphans and widows
- N257 Lev.25:39 Not employing a Hebrew bondman in degrading tasks
- N258 Lev.25:42 Not selling a Hebrew bondman
- N259 Lev.25:43 Not treating a Hebrew bondman cruelly
- N260 Lev.25:53 Not allowing a heathen to mistreat a Hebrew bondman
- N261 Ex.21:8 Not selling a Hebrew maidservant. and if you marry her...
- N262 Ex.21:10 ...withhold not: food, raiment, or conjugal rights
- N263 Deut.21:14 Not selling a captive woman
- N264 Deut.21:14 Not treating a captive woman as a slave
- N265 Ex.20:17 Not coveting another man's possessions/property...
- N266 Deut.5:18 Covet not one's possessions, even the desire forbidden
- N267 Deut.23:26 A worker is not to cut down standing grain during work
- N268 Deut.23:24 A hired laborer not to take more fruit than he can eat
- N269 Deut.22:3 Not ignoring lost property to be returned to its owner
- N270 Ex.23:5 Refuse not to help man or animal collapsing with burden
- N271 Lev.19:35 Not cheating/defrauding with measurements and weights
- N272 Deut.25:13 Not to possess false/inaccurate weights and measures

[2]Appendix C

"But, Didn't Jesus Abolish the Law and Those 613 Original Commandments?"[2]

reprinted by permission from "The Refiner's Fire**

JUSTICE Continued...

- N273 Lev.19:15 — A Judge is not to commit unrighteousness
- N274 Ex.23:8 — A Judge is not to accept bribes/gifts from litigants
- N275 Lev.19:15 — A Judge is not to favor (be partial to) a litigant
- N276 Deut.1:17 — Judge not avoid justice being in fear of wicked person
- N277 Lev.19:15 Ex. 23:3 — A Judge not to decide in favor of poor man, out of pity [rather]:
- N278 Ex.23:6 — A Judge is not to discriminate against the wicked
- N279 Deut.19:13 — Judge not to pity one who killed or caused loss of limb
- N280 Deut.24:17 — A Judge not perverting justice due strangers or orphans
- N281 Ex.23:1 — Judge not to hear one litigant in absence of the other
- N282 Ex.23:2 — Court may not convict by majority of one in capital case
- N283 Ex.23:2 — Judge accept not colleague's opinion, unless sure right
- N284 Deut.1:17 — Not appointing an unlearned judge ignorant of the Torah
- N285 Ex.20:16 — Not bearing false witness
- N286 Ex.23:1 — A Judge is not to receive a wicked man's testimony
- N287 Deut.24:16 — A Judge receive not testimony from litigant's relatives
- N288 Deut.19:15 — Not convicting on the testimony of a single witness
- N289 Ex.20:13 — Not murdering a human being
- N290 Ex.23:7 — No conviction based on circumstantial evidence alone
- N291 Num.35:30 — A witness must not sit as a Judge in capital cases

[2]Appendix C

"But, Didn't Jesus Abolish the Law and Those 613 Original Commandments?"[2]

reprinted by permission from "The Refiner's Fire**

JUSTICE Continued...

- N292 Num.35:12 Not killing a murderer without trial and conviction
- N293 Deut.25:12 Not to pity or spare the life of a pursuer
- N294 Deut.22:26 Not punishing a person for a sin committed under duress
- N295 Num.35:31 Not accepting ransom from an unwitting murderer
- N296 Num.35:32 Not accepting a ransom from a willful murderer
- N297 Lev.19:16 Hesitate not to save life of another person in danger
- N298 Deut.22:8 Not leaving obstacles on public or private domain
- N299 Lev.19:14 Not misleading another by giving wrong advice
- N300 Deut.25:2–3 Inflict not more than assigned number lashes to guilty
- N301 Lev.19:16 Not to tell tales
- N302 Lev.19:17 Not to bear hatred in your heart toward your brethren
- N303 Lev.19:17 Not to put one another to shame
- N304 Lev.19:18 Not to take vengeance on another
- N305 Lev.19:18 Not to bear a grudge
- N306 Deut.22:6 Not to take entire bird's nest, mother and her young
- N307 Lev.13:33 Not to shave a leprous scall
- N308 Deut.24:8 Not to cut or cauterize (remove) other signs of leprosy
- N309 Deut.21:4 Plow not a valley where slain body found
- N310 Ex.22:17 Not permitting a witch/sorcerer to live
- N311 Deut.24:5 Take not bridegroom from home in first year of marriage
- N312 Deut.17:11 Not to differ from or disobey the Cohanim and the Judge

[2]Appendix C

"But, Didn't Jesus Abolish the Law and Those 613 Original Commandments?"[2]

reprinted by permission from "The Refiner's Fire**

JUSTICE Continued...

- N313 Deut.13:1 Not to add to the Mitzvot/commandments of Torah
- N314 Deut.13:1 Not to detract from the Mitzvot/commandments of Torah
- N315 Ex.22:27 Not to curse a judge
- N316 Ex.22:27 Not to curse a ruler
- N317 Lev.19:14 Not to curse any Jew
- N318 Ex.21:17 Not cursing parents
- N319 Ex.21:15 Not to strike parents
- N320 Ex.20:10 Not to work on Shabbat
- N321 Ex.16:29 Not to walk beyond permitted limits, eruv, on Shabbat
- N322 Ex.35:3 Not to inflict punishment on the Shabbat
- N323 Ex.12:16 Not to work on the first day of Pesach
- N324 Ex.12:16 Not to work on the seventh day of Pesach
- N325 Lev.23:21 Not to work on Shavuot
- N326 Lev.23:25 Not to work on Rosh HaShannah
- N327 Lev.23:35 Not to work on the first day of Sukkot
- N328 Lev.23:36 Work not 8th-day/Shemini-Atzeret, (after Hoshana Rabba)
- N329 Lev.23:28 Not to work on Yom Kippur / the Day of Atonement

[2]Appendix C

"But, Didn't Jesus Abolish the Law and Those 613 Original Commandments?"[2]

reprinted by permission from "The Refiner's Fire**

INCEST AND OTHER FORBIDDEN RELATIONSHIPS

- N330 Lev.18:7 No relations with one's mother
- N331 Lev.18:8 No relations with one's father's wife
- N332 Lev.18:9 No relations with one's sister
- N333 Lev.18:11 No relations with step-sister
- N334 Lev.18:10 No relations with one's son's daughter
- N335 Lev.18:10 No relations with one's daughter's daughter
- N336 Lev.18:10 No relations with one's daughter
- N337 Lev.18:17 No relations with a woman and her daughter
- N338 Lev.18:17 No relations with a woman and her son's daughter
- N339 Lev.18:17 No relations with a woman and her daughter's daughter
- N340 Lev.18:12 No relations with one's father's sister
- N341 Lev.18:13 No relations with one's mother's sister
- N342 Lev.18:14 No relations with wife of father's brother
- N343 Lev.18:15 No relations with one's son's wife
- N344 Lev.18:16 No relations with brother's wife
- N345 Lev.18:18 No relations with sister of wife, during wife's life
- N346 Lev.18:19 No relations with a menstruant
- N347 Lev.18:20 No relations with another man's wife
- N348 Lev.18:23 Men may not lie with beasts
- N349 Lev.18:23 Women may not lie with beasts
- N350 Lev.18:22 A man may not lie carnally with another man
- N351 Lev.18:7 A man may not lie carnally with his father
- N352 Lev.18:14 A man may not lie carnally with his father's brother

[2]Appendix C

"But, Didn't Jesus Abolish the Law and Those 613 Original Commandments?"[2]

reprinted by permission from "The Refiner's Fire**

INCEST AND OTHER FORBIDDEN RELATIONSHIPS

- N353 Lev.18:6 Not to be intimate with a kinswoman
- N354 Deut.23:3 A mamzer may not have relations with a Jewess
- N355 Deut.23:18 No relations (harlotry) with a woman outside marriage
- N356 Deut.24:4 Remarry not your divorced wife after she has remarried
- N357 Deut.25:5 Childless widow marry none except late Husband's brother
- N358 Deut.22:29 Divorce not wife, who he has to marry after raping her
- N359 Deut.22:19 Divorce not wife, after falsely slandering her
- N360 Deut.23:2 Man unable of procreation (eunuch) not to marry Jewess
- N361 Lev.22:24 Not to castrate a man or beast

THE MONARCHY

- N362 Deut.17:15 Not appointing a king who is not of the seed of Israel
- N363 Deut.17:16 A king not to accumulate an excess number of horses
- N364 Deut.17:17 A king not taking many wives
- N365 Deut.17:17 A king not amassing great personal wealth

[2]Appendix C

How Will You Answer These Questions?
The answers from God's Holy Word, the Bible
From "Hebrew-English New Covenant: Prophecy Edition[3]

Q: Am I promised salvation by following the law to the best of my ability?

A1: **For whosoever shall keep the whole law, and yet offend in one point, he is guilty of all.** *James 2:10*

A2: **Cursed be he that confirmeth not all the words of this law to do them. And all the people shall say, Amen.** *Deut. 27:26*

Q: Is there anyone without sin?

A: **For there is not a just man upon earth, that doeth good, and sinneth not.** *Ecclesiastes 7:20*

Q: What is sin?

A: **Whosoever committeth sin transgresseth also the law: for sin is the transgression of the law.** *1 John 3:4*

Sin is committed when any one of God's commandments is not fully kept.

Q: What is the penalty of sin under the law?

A: **The LORD said, Behold, all souls are mine; as the soul of the father, so also the soul of the son is mine: the soul that sinneth, it shall die.** *Ezekiel 18:4*

Q: According to the law, what will atone for your sins?

A: **For the life of the flesh is in the blood: and I have given it to you upon the altar to make an atonement for your souls: for it is the blood that maketh an atonement for the soul.** *Leviticus 17:11*

Q: Is God satisfied with the blood of animal sacrifices?

A1: **To what purpose is the multitude of your sacrifices unto me? saith the LORD: I am full of the burnt offerings of rams, and the fat of fed beasts; and I delight not in the blood of bullocks, or of lambs, or of he goats.** *Isaiah 1:11*

A2: **Neither by the blood of goats and calves, but by his own blood he [Jesus] entered in once into the holy place, having obtained eternal redemption for us.** *Hebrews 9:12*

Q: Who has provided eternal Salvation for us?

A. **But God who commendeth his love toward us, in that, while we were yet sinners, Christ died for us. Much more then, being now justified by his blood, we shall be saved from wrath through him.** *Romans 5:8–9*

[3]Appendix C

How Will You Answer These Questions?
The answers from God's Holy Word, the Bible
From "Hebrew-English New Covenant: Prophecy Edition[3]

Q: Is there any other Messiah besides Jesus Christ?

A1: **Jesus said, "... for if ye believe not that I am he, ye shall die in your sins."** *John 8:24*

A2: **I, even I, am the LORD; and beside me there is no saviour.** *Isaiah 43:11*

Q: Do you know how to be saved?

A1. **Believe on the Lord Jesus Christ, and thou shalt be saved.** Acts 16:31

A2: **Seek ye the LORD while he may be found, call ye upon him while he is near: Let the wicked forsake his way, and the unrighteous man his thoughts: and let him return unto the LORD, and he will have mercy upon him; and to our God, for he will abundantly pardon.** *Isaiah 55:6*

So the trouble is not with the law, for it is spiritual and good. The trouble is with me, for I am all too human, a slave to sin.

Romans 7:14

✞

So now there is no condemnation for those who belong to Christ Jesus.

And because you belong to him, the power of the life-giving Spirit has freed you from the power of sin that leads to death.

The law of Moses was unable to save us because of the weakness of our sinful nature. So God did what the law could not do. He sent his own Son in a body like the bodies we sinners have.

And in that body God declared an end to sin's control over us by giving his Son as a sacrifice for our sins.

He did this so that the just requirement of the law would be fully satisfied for us, who no longer follow our sinful nature but instead follow the Spirit.

Romans 8: 1–4

[3]Appendix C

Week 12

Featured Books:

End **Deuteronomy**, Begin **Joshua, and**
One passage from Psalms and 1 Chronicles

Contents:

Peek at the Week

Lesson	Key Events	Find Jesus
12.1	Covenant Blessings and Curses	Jesus Christ Came to Redeem Us From the Curse of the Law
12.2	Covenant Renewal	It's Your Choice (Accepting Jesus as Your Lord and Be Blessed)
12.3	Prophetic Song and Psalm of Moses	Jesus Tells How Israel Rejects God
12.4	Moses Blesses Israel Smooth Transition from Moses to Joshua	Rahab's Destiny is Saved
12.5	Preparation for Conquest of Canaan	Jesus and the Jordan River
12.6	Israel Begins Conquest of Canaan	Grace Thru Jesus
12.7	Israel Conquers the Southern and Northern Areas of Canaan	Christians are More Than Conquerors Thru Jesus Christ

Chronological Notes

* Timetable	Key Events
1405 (or 1239) BC 40 Years after Exodus	End of Israel's forty-year wilderness wanderings; Moses gives his final words to Israel and dies at 120 years Joshua leads second generation Israel into Promised Land
1398 (or 1232) BC	Israel conquers major areas of Canaan in 7 years
1375 (or 1210) BC	Joshua dies at 110 years of age

**All dates are approximate.*

Lesson 12.1

Reading Assignment:
Deuteronomy 26:1–29:1

I. Lesson Exercise

***You have declared today that the LORD is your God.
You have promised to obey his laws, commands, and regulations
by walking in his ways
and doing everything he tells you.***

***The LORD has declared today that you are his people,
his own special treasure, just as he promised,
and you must obey all his commands.***

***And if you do, he will make you greater than any other nation.
Then you will receive praise, honor, and renown.
You will be a nation that is holy to the LORD your God,
just as he promised."
Deut. 26:17–19***

Covenant Blessings and Curses

In today's lesson, Israel and God renewed their covenant relationship, with Israel's promise to follow God and God's promise to make Israel greater than any other nation.

This was a life-or-death agreement.

Israel would experience many blessings for keeping covenant with God, but there were also many curses if they broke covenant.

As a visual reminder of this truth, Moses told the tribes to do something unique after they conquered the Canaan area.

Israel was to divide into two groups with one gathered around a barren-looking mountain (Mt. Ebal) to shout out the covenant curses, and the other gathered around a lushy-green looking mountain (Mt. Gerizim) to shout out the covenant blessings.

In this way, the mountains became their witnesses before God.

1) Which tribes were to stand on Mt. Gerizim, to proclaim a blessing over Israel? (Deut. 27:12) ______________, ______________, ______________,

______________, ______________, ______________

2) Which tribes were to stand on Mt. Ebal to proclaim a curse? (Deut..27:13) ______________, ______________, ______________,

______________, ______________, ______________

Curses: Yesterday and Today, but They Don't Have To Be Forever

Deut. 27:11–26 lists the categories of things a person could be cursed for.
Deut. 28:15–68 lists what a cursed person actually experiences in life.

Based on a study of these passages as well as others in the Bible, Derek Prince Ministries summarizes the cursed person's experiences as taking on seven forms[1]:

- humiliation
- barrenness
- sickness of all kinds
- poverty or failure
- defeat
- helplessness (the tail)
- weaknesses (beneath)

Derek Prince Ministries goes on to describe the seven marks of a curse as follows:

- mental or emotional breakdown
- repeated or chronic sickness
- female problems
- breakdown of marriage or family alienation
- continued financial insufficiency
- being accident-prone
- history of suicide or unnatural deaths[1]

But thank God Jesus Christ came to redeem humankind from the curses pronounced on us by the law!

<u>II. Find Jesus in the Lesson</u>

Jesus Christ Came to Redeem Us from the Curse of the Law! (KJV)

But Christ has rescued us from the curse pronounced by the law.

When he was hung on the cross,
he took upon himself the curse for our wrongdoing.
For it is written in the Scriptures,

"Cursed is everyone who is hung on a tree."
Galatians 3:13

[1]Appendix C

Through the power and purpose of Jesus Christ's redemption ministry, the effects of curses can be broken.

III. Closing Thoughts

Blessings: Yesterday, Today, and They Can Be Forever!

Deuteronomy 28:1–14 lists the blessings from God, which are directly opposite to the curses.

As Derek Prince Ministries[1] points out, from the blessings of God in Christ:

- instead of humiliation, you have exaltation
- instead of barrenness, you have reproductive-ness
- instead of sickness of all kinds, you have health
- instead of poverty and failure, you have prosperity and success
- instead of defeat, you have victory
- instead of helplessness, you have authority (you are the head)
- instead of weaknesses, you have strength (you are above only)

In the New Testament, God describes blessings for followers of Christ in this way,

All praise to God, the Father of our Lord Jesus Christ,
who has blessed us with every spiritual blessing
in the heavenly realms because we are united with Christ.

He has showered his kindness on us,
along with all wisdom and understanding.
Ephesians 1:3, 8

[1]Appendix C

Lesson 12.2

Reading Assignment: Deuteronomy 29:2–31:29

I. Lesson Exercise:

Covenant Renewal

All Israel stood together in the plains of Moab, with Moses mediating the Covenant renewal between them and God. The terms of the covenant applied to Israel's:

- Tribal leaders, judges, all officers, all men of Israel, their little ones, wives, and the foreigners living among them, who were present (Deut. 29:9)
- Besides those who were present, Moses explained God was making that day's covenant with all future generations of Israel (Deut. 29:14)

When God said all, He really expected everyone in Israel to keep covenant.

- God did not want anyone who heard the covenant to think they were exempt from keeping it.
    - This is because anyone who mistakenly thought they did not have to keep it, would then break the covenant, and bring ruin to themselves and hurt the nation. (Deut. 29:19-20)
- From Deuteronomy 29:29, we learn that there are secret things that belong to God that He would not reveal to humankind (all the "why's" and "what for's" of every activity).
    - On the other hand, what God does reveal in the form of laws, commands and instructions were for Israel and descendants to use forever, to help them obey and live.

3) Describe all the things God was willing to do to restore Israel, after they broke covenant and suffered curses, but then turned back to him. (Deut. 30:2–5)

   a) Restore ______________________________

   b) Gather ______________________________

   c) Return ______________________________

   d) Make more __________-______________

God's Covenant Is for Everyone…

II. Find Jesus in the Lesson

It's Your Choice

God gave the Israelites a clear, near, and understandable choice to make between:

prosperity and disaster,

life and death,

blessings and curses,

by accepting or rejecting His covenant terms. (Deut. 30:11–14, 19)

God presents New Testament covenant terms to all humankind today to accept or reject.

Instead of 613 commands, laws and regulations, God's terms require acceptance of Jesus as Lord and Savior of our lives.

Then this is the beginning for one to experience a blessed life (abundant and eternal).

Without Christ, a person is cursed and has eternal death.

… But, It's Your Choice!

(John 3:16, 10:10, 14:6; Rom. 3:23–26, 6:23; 1 John 5:1–12)

III. Closing Thoughts

Public Reading of the Law

Moses wrote down the laws of the Covenant.

He told the priests to read it to Israel and the foreigners living among them every seventh year.

This would keep every generation knowledgeable of the laws they were expected to keep. (Deut. 31:9–13)

Reading Assignment:
Deuteronomy 31:30–32:52
Psalm 90

Lesson 12.3

I. Lesson Exercise

Prophetic Song

Moses and Joshua went to the Tabernacle where God formerly commissioned Joshua to replace Moses.

While there, God revealed to Moses Israel's future.

Israel was going to abandon the true God for false gods, breaking the covenant agreement it had just renewed with Him.

God explained that because of this, terrible trouble would come down on Israel.

Yet, out of a true heart of loving, commitment for Israel, God told Moses to teach the Israelite people a special song now.

The song was special because it prophesied about Israel's future blessings and curses, but it also spoke of the Israelite people's return to God's favor after their time of trouble.

The song is in Deuteronomy 32:

- 32:1–4 God, the Rock, does everything just and fair
- 32:5–9 Israel, God's special possession, is deceitful and twisted
- 32:10–14 God guarded Israel as His most precious possession
- 32:15–20 Israel soon became fat and unruly, offering sacrifices to demons, non-gods; neglecting God, the Rock, who fathered them
- 32:21–27 God roused Israel's jealousy by blessing other nations
- 32:28–34 God planned for one person in Israel to chase a thousand of its enemies; two persons to put ten thousand enemies on the run
- 32:35–38 Israel's day of disaster arrives and cursed destiny overtakes the nation
- 32:39–42 False gods do not save Israel, for Israel's God is the only true and living God; He wounds and heals
- 32:43 God avenges blood of His servants; cleanses His land and Israel

III. Find Jesus in the Lesson

Jesus Tells How Israel Rejects God

Jesus explained how God wanted to gather Israel to Him like a hen gathers her chickens under her wings, but Israel rejected God. (Matthew 23:37)

This is similar wording to Moses' description of God, who cared for Israel like an eagle cares for her chicks, but Israel would abandon God in the future. (Deut. 32:10–18)

Like an Eagle Cares for Her Chicks,

God Cared for Israel

As a Hen Protects Her Chicks

Beneath Her Wings,

God Wanted to Gather Israel

III. Closing Thoughts

Psalm 90: A Prayer of Moses

Before Moses died, he left this beautiful song-like prayer on record.

Psalm 90 begins by describing God as an eternal being, which is contrasted with man's limited life span of hopefully seventy or eighty years. One important request in the prayer is for God to "teach us to make the most of our time." This includes experiencing God's joy, goodness, miracles and glory to make man's life's work successful.

Reading Assignment:
Deuteronomy 33:1–34:12
Joshua 1:1–2:24

Lesson 12.4

I. Lesson Exercise

Moses Blesses Israel

Just before the Israelite's ancestor Jacob (Israel) died, he spoke prophetic blessings over each one of his sons, whose descendants became twelve tribes, which formed the nation of Israel. (Genesis 49)

Similarly, just before Moses died, he spoke prophetic blessings over each of the twelve tribes of Israel. They are recorded in Deuteronomy 33.

The first part of his blessing identified all the parties involved, who are:

Verse 2—The LORD

Verse 3—the people, all your holy ones

Verse 4—Moses, who charged them to keep the law

Verse 4—Israel, God's special possession

Verse 5—The LORD, who became king in Israel

Verse 5—the leaders and tribes of Israel, who gathered together in holy assembly around their king.

4) Trivia Question: Which one of the twelve tribes of Israel is not mentioned in Moses' Blessing of Deuteronomy 33? ______________

5) Thought Question: Why do you think the mention of this tribe is missing? Consider Genesis 49:7 for one possible answer.

____

Smooth Transition

At the ripe age of 120 years old, Moses died with this excellent testimony,

"his eyesight was clear, and he was as strong as ever" (Deut. 34:7)

Moses climbed up to Mount Nebo to look out over the Promised Land that he would not enter but could see from the mountain side.

Then, according to Deut. 34:5–6 Moses died in the land of Moab, where the Lord buried him. No one knows the exact place where Moses' body was buried as God took care of that.

After thirty days of mourning, God began to speak to Joshua, the new leader in Israel.

There is a special phrase God spoke to Joshua that has been mentioned several times now.

Moses said it to the Israelite people (Deut. 31:6);

Moses said it to Joshua (Deut. 31:7);

God commissioned Joshua with the words (Deut. 31:23);

God spoke them to Joshua three more times (Joshua 1:6,7,9);

Finally, the people said it to Joshua (Joshua 1:18).

6) What special phrase was spoken seven times as described above?

____

II. Find Jesus in the Lesson and III. Closing Thoughts

Rahab Saves the Spies ➲

The Spies Save Rahab ➲

Rahab's Destiny Is Saved!

Rahab was a harlot. This means she slept around with many men performing ungodly deeds for money. Sadly, she considered this her job.

But, in today's lesson, Rahab invited two men to spend the night at her house who represented God, and the fear of their God put the fear and faith of God in her. (Reference James 2:25, 26 and Hebrews 11:31)

Rahab made a decision that not only saved her and her family's life, but it changed her destiny.

- Rahab chose to live among the Israelites.
- Rahab married an Israelite man. This means she accepted the Israelite's pathway of life as instructed by God according to God's instructions in Numbers 15:14–15 and Leviticus 19:33–34. Ruth 4:21 with Matthew 1:5.

7) In whose family tree is Rahab found? (Matt. 1:5) __________

Rahab changed from a harlot

to a blessed woman of God!

Key Word(s)	Key Chapter(s)
Victory	6

Intro to Joshua

Title

"Joshua" means "Jehovah saves" or "Jehovah is salvation." In the Greek language, Joshua is translated to the word "Jesus," as in Hebrews 4:8.

Key word "victory" describes this book's theme of Israel's victory in conquering the Promised Land.

Summary

Joshua is the first of twelve Old Testament history books.

It is named after Joshua, son of Nun, who replaced Moses after his death. Joshua leads Israel in conquering all the powerful cities and strongholds in the Promised Land. This included conquering thirty-one kings and their kingdoms.

God enabled Israel to do this in fulfillment of His promise to Abraham, Isaac, and Jacob, to give their descendants the land of Canaan *(the Promised Land).*

Joshua then divided the entire Promised Land among the tribes of Israel. At the end of Joshua's leadership, God gave "the people of Israel rest from all their enemies." He explained, "For the Lord has driven out great and powerful nations for you." (Joshua 23:1, 9a)

Not one of God's promises He made to the Israelites failed, as long as their leader Joshua led the nation in obediently following God's commands.

Born in slavery in Egypt, Joshua's many experiences during Israel's forty years of wilderness wandering had well prepared him for this moment in Israel's history.

Joshua was one of the two only remaining first generation exodus Israelites. He assisted Moses, which included leading the newly formed Israelite warriors in victory over the Amalekites.

Joshua was one of the original twelve spies that surveyed Canaan for the first time. Only he and Caleb spoke confidently about God's ability to enable Israel to overcome the mighty nations already in the land.

God rewards Joshua and Caleb with conquering and living in the Promised Land after all the unbelieving adults of their generation died off in the wilderness.

Officially commissioned by God to be the military general for the Israelite army who will conquer the land of Canaan, Joshua leads Israel in victory after victory over their enemies.

The Joshua-generation Israelites are marked by their obedience and faith in God. Joshua leads them in strict adherence to the commands of God.

This included following Moses' final instructions.

There are several notable miracles in the book, such as:

- Overflowing Jordan River parted so Israel could cross on dry land
- Seven-day march and final shout caused Jericho's walls to fall
- Sun stayed up well past its normal setting time, which gave Israel extra daylight to finish defeating their enemies

There are also memorable stories, such as:

- Captain of God's army showed himself to Joshua
- Harlot Rahab helped the spies and saved her family
- Achan's sin caused the Israelite army to experience defeat

These miraculous and memorable acts reminded Israel that their victory is assured only by strict obedience to God.

❒ **Timetable** (approximate)	**Key Events**
1405 (or 1239) BC	End of Israelite forty-year wilderness wandering; Moses dies at 120 years; Joshua leads Israel
1398 (or 1232) BC	Israel conquers major areas of Canaan in seven years
1375 (or 1210) BC	Joshua dies at 110 years of age

❒ **Author:** Most Likely Joshua, with final editing by someone else such as the priests

- **About the writer:** Joshua was a writer, as indicated in Joshua 8:32, 24:26.
- **Date of writing:** Some Bible scholars believe the level of detail used to describe the battles indicates Joshua wrote about the conquests of Canaan lands near the time the events occurred.

  The conclusion of the book, which talks about the death of Joshua and High Priest Eleazar, had to be written by someone else, which could have been the priests. In general, the priests, as keepers of the law, are thought to have provided editing services as needed.

❒ Major Events in Joshua:

Conquest of Canaan (Chapters 1 – 12)

- **Preparation for Conquests**
    - **Prep of Commander Joshua (1)**
    - **Prep of Israelite people (2–6)**
- **Warfare**
    - **Conquering the Central lands (6–8)**
    - **Conquering the Southern lands (9–10)**
    - **Conquering the Northern lands (11)**
    - **Review of lands Conquered (12)**

Settlement of Canaan (Chapters 13–24)

- **Review of lands to be Conquered (13)**
- **Land assigned to tribes on East (13)**
- **Lands already conquered assigned to some tribes on West (14–17)**
- **Towns assigned for Cities of Refuge and Levites (20–21)**
- **Eastern Tribes return home (22)**
- **Joshua's Final Words (23–24)**
- **Joshua and Eleazar's death (24)**

Historical Locations:

The land of Canaan was taken over by the Israelite nation as Israel conquered the people and settled into the Canaanite lands.

Lesson 12.5

Reading Assignment:
Joshua 3:1–6:27

I. Lesson Exercise

Preparation for Conquest of Canaan

God commanded Joshua, Joshua commanded the leaders, the leaders commanded the people saying something like, "Get ready, get ready, get ready," because:

> ***In three days you will cross the Jordan River and***
> ***take possession of the land the Lord your God has given you.***
> ***Joshua 1:11b***

Two spies Joshua sent to secretly checkout the land learned that the nations in Canaan were all afraid of Israel, in terror of Israel's coming. (Joshua 2:9)

Follow Israelite activities from the east side of the Jordan River to the west.

- The Israelite masses were to follow the Levitical priests for the march across the Jordan. (Joshua 3:2)
- Levitical priests carried the Ark of the Covenant across the Jordan. (Joshua 3:2)
- It was the harvest season at the time of Israel's crossing, and the Jordan was overflowing its banks. (Joshua 3:15)
- Joshua told the priests to take a few steps into the river and stop. (Joshua 1:8)
- When the feet of the priests touched the water at the river's edge, then the water began piling up at a town upstream. The water below that point flowed on to the Dead Sea until the riverbed was dry. (Joshua 3:16)
- It's a miracle! Although the river had been overflowing, shortly after the priests' feet touched the water, then between one and three million people were able to walk on a riverbed that was now dry ground. (Joshua 3:17)
- Joshua directed Israel to build two memorials to remind them of the great miracle God performed to bring them across the Jordan River.
    - One of the memorials was in the middle of the riverbed.
    - The other was at the Israelites' first campsite they made after the miracle using stones from the middle of the riverbed. (Joshua 4:3–9).

Covenant Ceremonies continued

8) Prior to entering Canaan, what did the entire male population of Israel do as part of their covenant agreement with God? (Joshua 5:3–4)

   ____

9) Prior to entering Canaan, what required annual feasts did Israel celebrate beginning the fourteenth day of the first month? (Joshua 5:10–11)

   ____

Israel's Commander to God's Commander (Joshua 5:13–15)

Joshua:	**"Are you friend or foe?"**
Man with sword in hand:	**"Neither one, I am commander of the Lord's army."**

This is what the mysterious man facing Joshua as he approached Jericho said. He was the commander of God's spiritual army, who was present to function at God's command in the conduct of the upcoming earthly battles.

> If Joshua, commander of Israel's earthly army, followed God's commands, then the commander of God's spiritual army would fight in the invisible, spiritual world for Israel.

And the Walls Came Tumbling Down— Victory at Jericho

A totally radical success, Israel won their first Canaanite battle with a most unusual battle strategy from God.

10) How many times was the entire Israelite army to march around Jericho city once, outside its walls? (Joshua 6:3) _______________

11) Briefly describe what Israel's army did on the seventh day? (Joshua 6:15–24) ____

II. Find Jesus in the Lesson

Jesus and the Jordan River

12) In the New Testament, Jesus had an experience with the same Jordan River Joshua and Israel miraculously crossed over.

Read Matthew 3:13–17 to find out what this experience was:

____

III. Closing Thoughts: Jericho Curse

We have already seen that when God's holy men speak curses or blessings, God honors their words as if He had spoken them Himself.

The curse spoken by Joshua in Joshua 6:26 will be honored over 500 years after this time, when it is still in affect during the days of King Ahab of Israel.

We will revisit this curse and its fulfillment at that time. (1 Kings 16:33–34)

Reading Assignment:
Joshua 7:1
I Chronicles 2:7
Joshua 7:2–9:27

Lesson 12.6

I. Lesson Exercise

Israel Begins Conquest of Canaan by Conquering Central Areas

The cities of Jericho, Ai, Bethel, and Gilgal were Israel's first areas of conquest. God's strategy of having Israel start in the middle of Canaan created a quick disconnect between the northern and southern cities.

> This prevented kings from the north and south from coming together in a large mass to fight against Israel.

Battlefield Lessons, Learned the Hard Way

Israel's second battle in Canaan ended in sad defeat but with valuable lessons learned. Let us review some of these lessons.

❒ **Israel's spies decided the first battle strategy against Ai.** (Joshua 7:2–3)

- The spies' strategy did not work. Israel was soundly defeated. (Joshua 7:4–5)
- At first Joshua's reaction seemed to blame God for the defeat. (Joshua 7:6–9)
- God let Israel lose the battle because of the sinful actions of the one man, Achan. He stole and hid some treasures that God told them not to take. (Joshua 7:1)
- When Joshua learned the real cause of their defeat, God instructed Israel to remove the sin from within their camp by taking Achan, his whole family, everything he stole, and all that he owned out to the Valley of Trouble (Achor). There they stoned Achan and his family, burned their bodies, and piled a heap of stones on top of them all. (Joshua 7:15, 24–26)

❒ **God decided Israel's second battle strategy against Ai.** (Joshua 8:1–8)

13) Did God's battle strategy work? (Josh. 8:25) ____________________

14) In addition to Ai, what other city was destroyed? (Josh. 8:17) ______

15) What did the Lord allow the Israelites to do with the cattle and treasures from the city of Ai? (Josh. 8:27) ______________________

16) What did Joshua do to the king of Ai? (Josh. 8:29) _______________

Moses Is Gone, But His Instructions Are Not Forgotten

Moses' final instructions to Israel before his death are fulfilled in today's lesson.

- Review Deut. 11:29–32, Deut. 27:11–14.
- Then read Joshua 8:33–35 to see which instructions from Moses were fulfilled.

II. Find Jesus in the Lesson and III. Closing Thoughts

A Little Sin Always Brings Great Destruction, Except for God's Grace through Jesus

Deuteronomy 29:29 explains how God keeps secret things to Himself. This means He does not reveal all things so that man can understand them. **What God does reveal to us is ours to use to be successful in life.** This happens as we act upon what He has revealed.

- For example, who can satisfactorily answer the question as to why Achan's taking some of the treasures from Jericho was a sin worthy of his and his family's death, when God gave Israel permission to enjoy the treasures from Ai? God does not reveal the "why" to satisfy our understanding of this.

The one thing we learn about God from these stories, is that our success or failure is strictly determined by obeying God's exact instructions, whatever they are, whether they make sense to our human minds or not.

- From Achan's way of looking at things, he was just taking a little of the great treasures God said not to touch. But from God's way of looking at things, Achan sinned against Him by disobeying His commands, which is the definition of sin (disobedience to God's commands).

Whether the action of sin is great or small, it is the attitude of sin, meaning the willingness to disobey God, which is always a big deal in God's view. At any time, we are subject to experiencing great destruction in our lives for just a little sin, except for God's grace, which we have access to through Jesus Christ our Lord.

Sin Destroys You

For the wages of sin is death,
but the free gift of God is eternal life
through Christ Jesus our Lord. Romans 6:23

But Jesus Frees You!

The Extermination of the Canaanites

reprinted by permission [2]

In Israel's first battle inside the boundaries of the Promised Land, they killed every human being except for Rahab and her family (Josh 6:21). This total extermination of everyone in the city of Jericho was simply in obedience to a command of the Lord.

> The Lord had commanded that all Canaanites living within the designated land boundaries given to Israel were to be exterminated. ("Canaanite" is a general term used for the several different peoples who lived in that land.)
>
> No mercy was to be shown to them, and no treaties of any kind were to be made with them (Ex. 23:31–33; 34:11–17; Lev. 18:24–25; Deut. 7:1–2; 20:16–18). All of their religious images and artifacts were to be destroyed also.
>
> These people had been set apart for complete and utter destruction. Joshua and the Israelites were to carry out the Lord's command.

Some people have questioned the morality of God's command to exterminate the Canaanites. But the Scriptures and archaeology justify this command.

> The Canaanite society had become terribly degenerate. Their perverted religious practices had so polluted them that their iniquity was as great as it could be (cf. Gen. 15:16). They worshiped a large number of deities who were characterized by wicked behavior that in turn dictated the behavior of the Canaanites…

Leviticus 18 is a key chapter in understanding the character of the Canaanites. This chapter details those forbidden practices that were abhorrent to God, including those related to forbidden relationships.

> These practices characterized the people of Canaan (Lev. 18:3, 24–28). Other evils, such as child sacrifice, were part of Canaanite life as well.
>
> The nations that inhabited the Promised Land were just as evil as the residents of Sodom and Gomorrah (Gen. 18, 19) or those people who lived in the days of Noah (Gen. 6:5,11).

[2]Appendix C

The Extermination of the Canaanites

reprinted by permission [2]

It was clear that Israel could have absolutely no contact with these people, or else Israel would become infected with the same moral and spiritual sickness. Israel was called repeatedly to be a holy people, different from the peoples who inhabited Canaan (Deut. 7:1–4).

There was no room for compromise or coexistence.

The Canaanites had evidently come to the place spiritually where they would never turn to the true God (like those mentioned in Rom. 1:24–28).

A few, like Rahab of Jericho (Josh. 6:17), may have come to the God of Israel, but they were rare exceptions. And too, it should be noted that any Canaanite wishing to avoid death could have easily fled outside the borders of the Promised Land and been safe.

The taking of the land under Joshua lasted about six years. A person could flee outside of the boundaries from anywhere in the land in two or three days.

It must also be remembered that God is sovereign.

He is the great Creator and can do what He wishes with His creation. He has the right and the power to deal with those who violate His holy laws.

✞

And the LORD passed by before him *[Moses],*
and proclaimed,

The LORD! The LORD!

A God merciful and gracious, slow to anger, and abundant in loving-kindness and truth,

Keeping mercy and loving-kindness for thousands, forgiving iniquity and transgression and sin,

but , Who will by no means clear the guilty,
visiting the iniquity of the fathers

upon the children and children's children,
to the third and fourth generation.

Exodus 34:6 – 7 AMP

[2]Appendix C

Lesson 12.7

Reading Assignment: Joshua 10:1–12:6

I. Lesson Exercise

Israel Conquers the Southern Areas of Canaan

The Gibeonites deceived Joshua and Israel's leaders into making a peace treaty with them by pretending to be from a faraway country. By making a binding oath, the peace treaty was a covenant agreement between Israel and Gibeon.

> God would be angry if Israel did not honor their covenant (Joshua 9:1–27). After learning they had made an oath with a Canaanite city nearby, since they could not kill them, they made the Gibeonites chop wood and carry water for the Tabernacle.

The city of Gibeon is located just northwest of Jerusalem. When the southern king of Jerusalem heard Gibeon had made a peace treaty with Israel, he asked four other kings to join him in destroying Gibeon. This forced Israel to turn its attention to fighting the southern areas ruled by these kings.

17) What five kingdoms did Israel destroy in the south Canaan battle? (Josh 10:3)

   a) ______________
   b) ______________
   c) ______________
   d) ______________
   e) ______________

18) What two miracles (supernatural acts) did God perform to help Israel win?

   a) Joshua 10:11 ________________________
   b) Joshua 10:12—13 _____________________

Israel Conquers the Northern Areas of Canaan

The northern city of Hazor had at one time been the capital of the large federation of kingdoms listed in Joshua 11:1–3, 10. At the king of Hazor's request, they all mobilized in war against Israel. Israel totally defeated these kingdoms, killing all the people, destroying all the cities, until

Joshua took control of the entire land,
just as the Lord had instructed Moses. Josh. 11:23

All the giants that had lived in the area were destroyed. The only people who still lived were the Gibeonites (also called Hivites), because of the treaty they had made.

II. Find Jesus in the Lesson and III. Closing Thoughts

Christians Are More Than Conquerors

"If God is for us, who can ever be against us?"

He that spared not his own Son,
but delivered him up for us all,
how shall he not with him also
freely give us all things?...

Nay, in all these things
we are more than conquerors
through him that loved us.

Romans 8:31, 32, 37 (KJV)

From a human viewpoint, Joshua and the Israelite army were no match for the mighty nations God instructed them to conquer.

But for God's people, the number of warriors or weapons is not what will make the difference in conquering enemies or not.

Instead, what really matters is if God is on your side.

In the New Testament, God has given His Son Jesus Christ to be our Savior. Along with Jesus Christ, God also willingly gives us His supernatural blessings, so we can experience overwhelming victory in every area of our lives.

However,

in order to win,

You may have to fight!

"Joshua Committing the Town of Ai to the Flames" *by Gustave Doré*

Doré Bible Illustrations • Free to Copy
www.creationism.org/images/

Jos 8:20 And when the men of Ai looked behind them, they saw, and, behold, the smoke of the city ascended up to heaven, and they had no power to flee this way or that way: ....

"Destruction of the Army of the Amorites" *by Gustave Doré*

Doré Bible Illustrations • Free to Copy
www.creationism.org/images/

Jos 10:11 ...the Lord cast down great stones from heaven upon them unto Azekah, and they died: *they were* more which died with hailstones than *they* whom the children of Israel slew with the sword.

"Joshua Commanding the Sun to Stand Still" *by Gustave Doré*

Doré Bible Illustrations **• Free to Copy**
www.creationism.org/images/

Jos 10:13 And the sun stood still, and the moon stayed, until the people had avenged themselves upon their enemies. *Is* not this written in the book of Jasher? So the sun stood still in the midst of heaven, ...

The Kingdom of God on Earth and the Role of The Servant of God in Establishing It

Excerpt from “Prophecy and History in Relation to the Messiah”[1]
by Alfred Edersheim 1880–1884

Alfred Edersheim (1825–1889)

Born in the early 1800s in Vienna, Austria to Jewish parents, Edersheim was well educated both in secular subjects of the day and in Talmudic traditions of his family's Jewish faith.

As a young man he converted to Christianity, as he came to believe Jesus Christ is the Jewish Messiah. He went on to become a Presbyterian minister and eventually a vicar in Church of England.

His unique position as a scholar trained him in both Jewish and Christian traditions, including:

> All the Biblical languages;
>
> Extensive knowledge and understanding of the culture and religious beliefs in early first century Roman-ruled Judea.
>
> This makes him quite an authority on all things Biblical.

He wrote several books. Four of them are still available for purchase:

- ***Bible History—Old Testament***
- ***Prophecy and History in Relation to the Messiah: The Barburton Lectures for 1880–1884***
- ***The Life and Times of Jesus the Messiah***
- ***The Temple—It's Ministry and Services***

The pages that follow reprint an excerpt from Edersheim's book:

Prophecy and History in Relation to the Messiah,
Lecture II, p. 44 – 46

This writing gives an overview of the concept of the Kingdom of God on earth and how Israel was sent as the first servant of God to establish it; while Jesus of Nazareth was sent as the final.

Enjoy!

[1]Appendix C

Excerpt from "Prophecy and History in Relation to the Messiah"[1]
by Alfred Edersheim 1880–1884

The ideal object of Israel's calling, and hence of their history and institutions, seems expressed in the first promise to their father Abraham:

"In thee and in thy seed shall all the families of the earth be blessed."

This promise is so fundamental as to be thrice repeated to Abraham (Gen. 12:3, 18:18, 22:18); it is renewed to Isaac (Gen. 24:4); and reiterated to Jacob (Gen. 28:14).

If this promise had any real divine meaning, it must have been intended to mark, as it were, the planting-ground for the Kingdom of God, whence in the fullness of time and of preparation it would be transplanted into the heathen world; **in other words, the blessings of that kingdom were to be imparted trough Israel to the world at large.**

There is nothing narrow or particularistic, but a grand universalism, even about this earliest presentation of the promise in a concrete form.

And that such was the object and mission of Israel, is clearly indicated on the eve of the Sinaitic legislation:

"Ye shall be My property from among all nations, for all the earth is mine; ye shall be unto Me a kingdom of priests and a holy nation."
(Ex. 19:5)

As Israel was ideally, so all nations were through their ministry to become really the possession of God: a kingdom of priests, a holy people; for all the earth, as well as Israel, was God's.

And the realization of this would be the kingdom of God on earth.

All the institutions of Israel were in strict accordance with this ideal destiny. Alike the laws, the worship, the institutions, and the mission of Israel were intended to express these two things: acknowledgment of God and dependence upon God.

Thus viewed, the whole might be summed up in this one term, which runs through the whole Old Testament: "The Servant of Jehovah."

The patriarchs were the Servants of the LORD;

Israel was the Servant of the LORD; and their

threefold representative institutions expressed the same idea.

[1]Appendix C

Excerpt from "Prophecy and History in Relation to the Messiah"[1]
by Alfred Edersheim 1880–1884

The ***Priest*** **was to be wholly the Servant of the LORD.** Hence the smallest transgression of the ordinances of his calling involved his destruction or removal.

The *King* was not to bear rule in the manner of heathen princes, but **to be the Servant of the LORD**, in strictest subordination to Jehovah. Hence Saul, despite his nobler qualities was really the Antichrist; and David, despite his grievous faults, the typical Christ of Israel's royalty, because of his constant acknowledgement of God's kingship.

And the ***Prophet*** was **simply the Servant of the LORD**, telling naught but God's Word, in such strict adherence to the letter of his commission, that its slightest breach brought immediate punishment.

And the **Messiah**, as summing up in Himself ideal Israel—its history, institutions, mission, and promise—**was to be the Servant of the LORD.**

Hence the prophecies which most clearly portray Him— those of Isaiah—might be headed by this title: The Book of the Servant of Jehovah;

the idea rising, through people, prophet, king, even through a foreign instrumental doer of His behest, up to Him as *the* Servant of the LORD,

the ideal Sufferer by and for the unrighteousness of man,

the ideal Sacrifice and Priest for his sins,

the ideal Teacher in his ignorance,

Comforter in his sorrow,

Restorer in his decay and

Dispenser of all blessing to the world at large—

the Spirit-anointed One, out of Whose fullness all were to receive, and Who would fulfill all that Israel had meant and prepared.

Or, going backwards,

He was to be the Son of Man,

the Second Adam, whose victory would restore what sin had lost: the true Son of God, God manifest in the flesh.

This, we believe, the Old Testament meant, and Jesus of Nazareth came to fulfill.

[1]Appendix C

Answers: 1st Quarter Weeks 1–12

Appendix A: Answers

Week 1

Lesson 1.1

1) God told Adam and Eve to multiply and fill the earth; subdue the earth; be masters over fish, birds and all animals. This instruction was given to both the male and female as God's original earthly work plan for them together.

2) From Gen. 3:16–17, Eve's role changed, as now a) she would have intense pain in order to have children, and b) her husband would be the head in their relationship. Adam's role changed as now it would take hard labor for him to eat any food, working hard until the day he dies and his body returns to the ground from which he came.

   Before the curse, Adam and Eve's blessing was to rule the earth, being its lord, master and caretaker. After the curse, they had to work hard with great pain, sorrow, and anguish, just to do the basics of having children, living, and eating.

3) According to Colossians 1:15–17, Jesus Christ "is the one through whom God created everything in heaven and earth. He made the things we can see and the things we can't see.. Everything has been created through Him and for Him. He existed before everything else began, and He holds all creation together."

Lesson 1.2

4) a) Cain founded a city.
   b) Jabal became the first herdsman who lived in tents.
   c) Jubal was the first musician— the inventor of the harp and flute;
   d) Tubal-cain was first to do metalwork, making instruments of bronze and iron.

5) During Seth's lifetime, people first began to worship the Lord

6) Enoch suddenly disappeared when God took him because of their close relationship

7) God told Noah that He had decided to destroy all living creatures, wiping them all from the face of the earth. He would do this by covering the earth with a flood that would destroy every living thing.

Lesson 1.3

8) God said there had to be a male and a female of every living creature so that each species would survive the flood. With the male and female they would be able to reproduce more of their kind by mating. If there were two males or two females, then they could not reproduce and that species would not continue.

9) Noah and his wife, Noah's son Shem and his wife; Noah's son Ham and his wife; Noah's son Japheth and his wife

10) God said He would never again curse the earth, destroying all living things again as he had done. Read Gen. 8:21 in KJV.

11) The rainbow

12) a) Peleg's name means "division," b) his name represented the fact that during his lifetime the earth was divided.

Lesson 1.4

13) No, the Tower of Babel project was not God's will. God wanted the people to spread out and fill the whole earth. But with the Tower of Babel, they were planning to stay in one place and not scatter abroad to fill the whole earth.

14) With different languages, the people would not be able to understand each other. Then they would scatter over the whole earth as God wanted.

15) God Most High helped Abram conquer his enemies

Lesson 1.5

16) God was going to wait until the sin of the Amorites had run its course before returning Abraham's descendants to replace them in the land of Canaan, which God promised Abraham to give them because of their covenant agreement

Lesson 1.6

17) God singled Abraham out because He knew He could trust Abraham to direct his sons and families to keep the way of the Lord and do what is right and just, which would allow God to keep His promise to Abraham.

18) The angels of God forewarned Lot, his wife and his daughters to flee and not look back at the cities that were being destroyed. If they looked back they would die. Lot's wife unbelievingly and disobediently looked back. She died instantly by being turned into a pillar of salt.

19) A prophet

20) Isaac's birth caused Sarah to laugh

Lesson 1.7

21) God heard the boy Ishmael crying

22) Yes

Week 2

Lesson 2.1

1) Jacob

Lesson 2.2

2) Isaac sent Jacob back to their relatives in Abraham's father's family (Terah) who were living in Haran in the territory of Paddan-Aram. On Abraham's family tree with father and brothers, look for Bethuel and Laban mentioned in Gen. 28:2

3) Jacob

Lesson 2.3

4) Esau finally realized marrying the Canaanite women did not please his father. When Esau found out Isaac sent Jacob to Abraham's homeland for a wife, then he assumed marrying a descendant of Abraham's family is the type of wife who would please his father. Since Ishmael was Abraham's son by Hagar, he thought marrying a daughter of Ishmael would please his father. But this did not really make sense considering Abraham had sent Ishmael away from Isaac. So Esau's marrying Ishmael's daughter to connect with Isaac's family seems out of order.

5) He named the place Bethel—"house of God"

6) Jacob offered to work for Rachel's father seven years in return for marrying Rachel

7) Jacob worked a total of fourteen years in payment for Rachel

8) Judah's name means "praise," because Leah said the following as a result of bearing another boy, "Now I will praise the Lord!"

Lesson 2.4

9) In Jacob's dream, God let Jacob know that He had seen all Laban had done to him, which is why God had blessed him to become wealthy at Laban's expense. God reminded Jacob of his vow to serve Him. He told Jacob it was time for him to return to his homeland in order to fulfill that vow.

10) God caused whatever flock Laban said Jacob could have (such as streaked or speckled or spotted males), to begin producing more of than any other kind.

11) "Rachel stole her father's household gods and took them with her"

12) John said Jesus was the "Lamb of God who takes away the sin of the world!"

Lesson 2.5

13) Jacob's new name is Israel. Based on Gen. 32:28, "Israel" means Jacob had struggled with God and man and won.

14) Peniel means "face of God"

15) Dinah's brothers told the men of Shechem that in order for the prince to be approved by them to marry their sister Dinah, they had to be circumcised. But, the real reason was because Simeon and Levi had planned to kill them all, when they were too weak to walk from the circumcision. And this they did.

16) Jesus was born in Bethlehen-Ephrathah, in the land of Judah

Lesson 2.6

(No questions to be answered)

Lesson 2.7

17) The Lord was with Joseph and blessed him greatly

18) Joseph was a very handsome and well-built man, and he was a blessed, smart business man

19) God was with Joseph in prison, blessing him there also.

Week 3

Lesson 3.1

1) 30 years old
2) 30 years old
3) about 30 years old

Lesson 3.2

4) The brothers believed God was punishing them for their sins from what they had done to their brother Joseph years before
5) Reuben and Judah

Lesson 3.3

6) Esrom = Hezron in KJV

Lesson 3.4

7) Jacob was buried with his father Isaac and his grandfather Abraham in the cave Abraham had purchased from the Hittites. In the cave Abraham and his wife were buried; Isaac and Rebekah were buried; and Leah was buried there.
8) Joseph was buried—embalmed and placed in a coffin—in Egypt
9) Joseph told the Israelites to take his bones with them back to the land of Canaan when God leads the nation back to live there.

Lesson 3.5

10) In Job's first test, Job lost all his children and all his riches
11) In Job's second test, Job lost his health

Lesson 3.6

12) Job said he hated his life, and he did not want to go on living.
13) No, Job did not understand God's point of view, because God thought the highest of Job and bragged on him to satan. But Job thought he was a "target" for God to test or punish for some sin Job was unaware he had committed.

Lesson 3.7

14) Jesus' name of Emmanuel (Immanuel) means "God is with us." This means when Jesus walked and talked the earth in the flesh, He was God on earth living among the world and people He created.

Week 4

Lesson 4.1

(No questions to be answered)

Lesson 4.2

1) Miserable comforters

2) Job says he would speak to a hurting friend in such a way to help them and to take away the hurting person's grief.

3) We should "trust God" even in the most tragic of situations. This does not mean a person will not question what God allows; but it does mean that the person will not sin against God. Also, they will continue to pray and seek God to soothe their broken hearts.

Lesson 4.3

4) Job warned his friends that they were in danger of punishment for their negative, fault-finding attitude concerning Job's pain

5) Zophar asked God to give the wicked a "bellyful of trouble"

6) Job told his friends that all their explanations were wrong

Lesson 4.4

7) Eliphaz said Job could have committed these sins:
   vs. 6) must have lent money to his friend and retained the clothing his friend gave him for a pledge, instead of returning it as he was supposed to do
   vs. 7) must have refused to give water to the thirsty and food to the hungry
   vs. 9) must have sent widows away without helping them and
   vs. 9) must have crushed the strength of orphans

Lesson 4.5

8) The people were looking for "ore," silver, gold and copper from stone

9) To find sapphires, gold dust, uncover other precious stones and hidden treasures

10) Wisdom

Lesson 4.6

11) Job thought he would surely die surrounded by his family after a long, good life

12) Job said his heart was broken

Lesson 4.7

13) Elihu believed man was formed from the clay. This belief lines up with the Genesis story of how man's body was formed

14) God speaks in dreams and visions

Week 5

Lesson 5.1

1) Elihu called himself a man of well-rounded knowledge (another "know-it-all"?)

Lesson 5.2

2) Job basically became speechless before God as he could not answer God

Lesson 5.3

3) After Job prayed for his friends, the Lord restored Job's fortunes

4) "The Lord blessed Job in the second half of his life even more than in the beginning." This included double riches, and 7 more sons, 3 more super-beautiful daughters. He also lived 140 more years, seeing his descendants to four generations.

Lesson 5.4

5) Moses was a beautiful baby whose very appearance impressed not only his parents, but also made an impression on one of Pharaoh's daughters. God protected him in the Nile River and guided his basket boat straight to Pharaoh's daughter in the river. From there Moses was raised in the palace of Egypt

6) The Midianites were descendants of Abraham and Keturah.

7) "God replied, 'I AM THE ONE WHO ALWAYS IS.' Just tell them, 'I AM has sent me to you.'" God also said, "Tell them, 'The LORD, the God of your ancestors Abraham, the God of Isaac, and the God of Jacob—has sent me to you.' This will be my name forever; it has always been my name, and it will be used throughout all generations."

Lesson 5.5

8) Moses would be as a "God" to Aaron his brother

9) Aaron would be Moses' "spokesman"

10) God said Moses would seem like a "god" to Pharaoh

11) Aaron would be like Moses' prophet, speaking Moses words from God

Lesson 5.6

(No questions to be answered)

Lesson 5.7

12) The death angel of the Lord passed over the Israelites homes when he saw the blood of the lambs over the doorposts of their homes, so that none of their firstborn were killed. But the firstborn of Egypt were killed, including animals

Week 6

Lesson 6.1

1) God did not lead Israel to the Promised Land by the shortest route in order to avoid going through Philistine territory. God knew the Philistines would have wanted to fight the Israelites who were not ready to engage in fighting yet.
2) So Pharaoh would think the Israelites were confused and trapped. God had always planned to perform the Red Sea miracle.
3) The Israelites foolishly said that their Egyptian slavery was far better than dying out in the wilderness."
4) God opened the Red Sea waters to allow over one million Israelites to walk safely across on dry ground. Once Israel had crossed, God closed the waters back to drown all the Egyptian warriors who followed Israel under the sea.
5) Just before drowning, the Egyptian warriors shouted "The Lord is fighting for Israel against us."

Lesson 6.2

6) Jethro told Moses to choose capable men from all over Israel to be judges over the people, in groups of 1,000, 100, 50, and 10. Moses still judged the hard cases.
7) The people prepared for hearing God per God's instructions to: a) Wash their clothing; b) Set boundary lines around the mountain that the people were not to cross; c) Abstain from intimate relations
8) There was a powerful thunder and lightning storm, a dense cloud came, a long, loud blast from a ram's horn was heard, heavy smoke hovered over the top of the mountain, and then the whole mountain shook with a violent earthquake.

Lesson 6.3

(No questions to be answered)

Lesson 6.4

9) They saw the God of Israel

Lesson 6.5

(No questions to be answered)

Lesson 6.6

10) Nadab, Abihu, Eleazar, Ithamar

11) God gave Moses the two stone tablets inscribed with the terms of the covenant written by the finger of God. These were the "Ten Commandments" on two stone tablets.

12) All men 20 years old and up

13) They were to pay a ransom amount of one-fifth of an ounce of silver

14) a) Bezalel son of Uri, grandson of Hur, of the tribe of Judah; and
b) Oholiab son of Ahisamach, of the tribe of Dan

Lesson 6.7

15) 40 days and 40 nights, and in all that time he did not eat or drink

16) God wrote the terms of the covenant—the Ten Commandments —on the stone tablets that Moses had cut in the similar shape of the first ones God had provided (Exodus 34:4)

Week 7

Lesson 7.1 (No questions to be answered)

Lesson 7.2 (No questions to be answered)

Lesson 7.3

1) a) Set up the Tabernacle on the first day of the new year, b) Take the anointing oil and sprinkle it on the Tabernacle and on all its furnishings to make everything "holy."

2) a) At entrance of Tabernacle wash Aaron and his sons with water; b) Clothe Aaron with holy garments and anoint with oil to serve as High Priest; c) Dress Aaron's sons in holy tunics; d) Anoint sons just like Aaron to serve as High Priests. In this way Aaron's male descendants were set apart to serve as the High Priests, from generation to generation.

3) God's glorious presence filled the tabernacle; Moses could not enter for God's glory

4) When the cloud lifted from the Tabernacle, then the Israelite camp moved. When the cloud rested back on the Tabernacle, the people stayed in that location, until it lifted again. At night fire was in the cloud, providing light for the camp.

Lesson 7.4

5) Day 3— Zebulun; Day 4— Reuben;

6) Day 7— Ephraim; ; Day 8— Manasseh

7) Day 10— Dan

8) God spoke to Moses from between the two cherubim above the Ark's cover

Lesson 7.5

9) The Levites substituted for all the firstborn sons of the Israelites

10) The Israelites began serving at the age of 25, and must retire at age of 50.

11) Passover celebration exception: If any Israelite was ceremonially unclean at Passover time, or if they were on a journey and could not celebrate Passover with everyone else, then they must keep the Passover one month later, at twilight on the appointed day.

Lesson 7.6

(No questions to be answered)

Lesson 7.7

12) Moses applied some of the second ram's blood (ram of ordination) to Aaron and his sons' a) right ear; b) thumb on right hand; and c) big toe on right foot

13) Author's answer to the Thought Question: To anoint the High Priests to hear the "right" things from God, to do the "right" work of God with their hands; and to walk in the "right" places as directed by God

Week 8

Lesson 8.1

1) God's fire enveloping the offerings on the altar was a good thing for all, because it meant God took out His judgment on the animals that were sacrificed on the altar. This made the people acceptable to Him, so they were joyous.

2) a) God's consuming fire burned up Nadab and Abihu in judgment, and b) this was a bad thing for them.

Lesson 8.2

3) The High Priests examined a person to officially declare if they were ceremonially clean or unclean.

4) Definition of "contagious" means "spread by direct or indirect contact. So the purpose of having someone with a contagious skin disease live in isolation is so they would not give the disease to others while it can be transferred to others.

5) "The priest must burn the linen or wool clothing or the piece of leather because it has been contaminated by an infectious mildew. It must be completely destroyed by fire."

6) Mary and Joseph brought two turtledoves or two pigeons because they were poor

7) Jesus told them to go show themselves to the priests. According to the Law of Moses, although Jesus had healed them, only the priests could pronounce them clean so they could rejoin the main community of Israel

Lesson 8.3

8) The house must be torn down, and all its stones, timbers, and plaster carried out of town to the place designated as ceremonially unclean. (Today we might think of this place as a large garbage dump area on the outskirts of a city.)

9) a) Most Holy Place, b) Tabernacle, c) altar, d) priests, e) all Israel's community

Lesson 8.4

10) The sins of unlawful relations caused the entire land to be defiled

11) The land would soon vomit the Canaanites out of it

Lesson 8.5

12) Psychic and mediums were to be stoned to death

13) Do not treat God's name as common or ordinary

Lesson 8.6

14) Eat the produce that grows naturally during the Sabbath year

15) God was going to order His blessing so that the land will produce a tremendous enough crop to support them for three years

Lesson 8.7

16) Yes, the foreigner must treat the Israelites slaves as servants hired on a yearly basis. Foreigners also had to abide by God's rules for Israel.

Week 9

Lesson 9.1

1) Twenty years old was the youngest age for war-able men to be included in the census

2) Draft for men to go into the army, but in America the age is now 18 years old

3) 603,550 (over half a million war-ready men)

4) Men from the Levite tribe were not counted in census, because they were set apart to be in charge of the Tabernacle

5) The position of the Levite priestly tribes in the camp— which was between the Tabernacle and other tribes—served to protect the people of Israel from God's fierce anger.

Lesson 9.2

6) Tabernacle Courtyard: a) Brass Altar (for sacrifices); b) Brass Laver (for washing)

7) Holy Place: a) Golden Lampstand on southside; b) Altar of Incense on westside;
c) Table of Shewbread (Bread of Presence) on northside

8) Ark of the Covenant was the one piece of furniture in the Most Holy Place. But it included the cover which was also called "Mercy Seat" or "Atonement Cover"

Lesson 9.3

9) Age of Levite men for service in Tabernacle, between 30 and 50 years old

10) Jesus began public ministry at 30 years of age, which is the earliest age the Levite priests began service in the Tabernacle.

Lesson 9.4

11) a) give up wine and other alcoholic drinks; b) not use vinegar made from wine, not drink fermented drinks or fresh grape juice; c) not eat grapes or raisins;
d) never cut their hair throughout the time of their vow; e) never go near a dead body during the period of their vow, even if it was their close family.

12) a) the uncommon offering at the end of the vow, was to put the hair they shaved at entrance of the Tabernacle on the fire beneath the peace offering; b) any special vow made in addition to the regular vow requirements

13) Blowing the trumpets also reminded God of His covenant with Israel

14) chosen people of Jesus will be gathered from farthest ends of heaven and earth

Lesson 9.5

15) The seventy men prophesied after the Spirit of God came upon them

16) Good Report: The land was a magnificent country, flowing with milk and honey, which meant it would abundantly provide for Israel's many needs

17) Bad Report: The people living there, who the Israelites would have to conquer, were big, powerful and lived in fortified cities and towns. They saw giants there also (descendants of Anak). They said they felt like and were grasshoppers compared to the people they had to fight. So they did not believe Israel could conquer them.

18) Caleb and Joshua

Lesson 9.6

19) They were attacked by the Amalekites and Canaanites who chased them away

Lesson 9.7

20) Aaron

21) Eliezar the priest (Aaron's son) collected the 250 bronze incense burners, that had been used by the men who were burned in the fire, then the burners were hammered out into a sheet of metal to cover the brazen altar

Week 10

Lesson 10.1

(No questions to be answered)

Lesson 10.2

1) Cursed is everyone who curses Israel

2) The Lord caused the donkey to speak.

3) Instead of cursing Israel, God caused Balaam to bless Israel three times

Lesson 10.3

(No questions to be answered)

Lesson 10.4

4) Moses climbed to top of Mt. Nebo east of the river and looked over at the Promised Land

5) Transfer Moses authority to Lead Israel to Joshua

Lesson 10.5

6) a) Killed all men; b) killed all five Midianite kings; c) Killed Balaam, son of Beor

7) a) Kill all the boys; b) Kill all the women who have slept with a man

8) Because all Israel's men who went into the battle were saved; not one was killed

Lesson 10.6

9) They needed to drive out all the people in the land, so those people would not harass the Israelites. God did not want to have to do to Israel what Israel was supposed to do in driving the current peoples out of the land

Lesson 10.7

(No questions to be answered)

Week 11

Lesson 11.1

1) Eleven days if you went by the way of Mount Seir

2) The people decided to first send out scouts (spies) to advise them on the best route to take and decide which towns to capture. God did support this plan. (Num. 13:1–3)

Lesson 11.2

3) a) both in heaven and on earth; b) there is no other god besides Israel's God

4) a) Go and sell all you have; b) give the money to the poor

Lesson 11.3 (No questions to be answered)

Lesson 11.4

5) Place the two stones with the Ten Commandments written on them in the Ark of the Covenant.

6) Seven requirements God placed on Israel were
a) to fear Him;
b) to live according to His will;
c) to love Him;
d) and to worship Him with all your heart and soul;
e) to obey the Lord's commands;
f) cleanse your sinful hearts;
g) show love to foreigners

Lesson 11.5, Lesson 11.6, Lesson 11.7 (No questions to be answered)

Week 12

Lesson 12.1

1) Simeon, Levi, Judah, Issachar, Joseph, Benjamin

2) Reuben, Gad, Asher, Zebulun, Dan, Naphtali

Lesson 12.2

3) a) Restore their fortunes;
b) Gather them back from all nations where they were scattered;
c) Return them to the land that belonged to their ancestors;
d) Make them even more prosperous and numerous than their ancestors

Lesson 12.3

(No questions to be answered)

Lesson 12.4

4) Simeon

5) In Genesis 49:7, Jacob, the father of Simeon, spoke a prophetic prayer over him. In this prayer he said of Simeon and Levi that their descendants would be scattered throughout the nation of Israel. Perhaps, Moses prayer does not mention Simeon separately because Simeon is mingled in with the other tribes. Also, note how Levi has been scattered among the nations also. In the book of Judges we will see how the Levites, who are not given an inheritance of land, are assigned towns throughout Israel. Also, you will see how Simeon's land is combined in Judah's areas.

6) "Be strong and courageous!"

7) Rahab is found in Jesus' family tree as one of his earthly ancestors

Lesson 12.5

8) They were all circumcised, which means they had to wait there until all healed

9) Passover, Firstfruits and Unleavened Bread, the three required spring festivals

10) Six times, one time each for six days and the people were to march silently
(no talking, no shouting)

11) Got up early and marched around the city seven times, with the priests blowing their horns. But at the end of the seventh time around, the priests blew one long horn blast. At Joshua's command, the people shouted as loud as they could. Suddenly, the walls of Jericho collapsed, and the Israelites charged the city

12) Jesus was baptized by John the Baptist in the Jordan River

Lesson 12.6

13) Yes, because Israel destroyed the entire city and all the people of Ai

14) Bethel was also destroyed.

15) God allowed Israel to keep the cattle and the treasures of Ai for themselves

16) Joshua hung the king of Ai on a tree and left him there until evening. Then at sunset Israel took the body down, threw it in front of the city gate. Next they piled a great heap of stones over the dead body.

Lesson 12.7

17) a) Jerusalem; b) Hebron; c) Jarmuth; d) Lachish; e) Eglon

18) a) The Lord destroyed the Amorites with a hailstorm that killed more of them than the Israelites killed with the sword;
b) In answer to Joshua's prayer to let the sun and moon stand still; the sun and moon did indeed stand still until the Israelites had defeated their enemies. This means that physical day had longer daylight than in normal days.

Test Ideas

Test Ideas

Any test given over First Quarter Bible reading needs to be simple.

This is so the test will leave the students with a positive feeling of accomplishment. There is a lot of material in the Bible that has been covered during these first twelve weeks, and no one should be expected to retain all that detail.

Test Purpose

- **Is:**
  To confirm the students understand “big picture” concepts from their reading,

- **Is Not:**
  To verify if students remember a lot of detail

The test should not be given as “Pass” or “Fail” or “Graded” at all.

Instead this test should be an opportunity for the students to reflect back on the material from a big picture point of view.

After the test has been given, have a group discussion to go over the answers.

Test Example— First Quarter Big Picture

Attached are the Test Questions the author gave to students after they participated in the Bible Study Sunday School Pilot program in 2006..

The answers are included immediately following the test.

Test # 1 Idea

Question # 1:

Why are sickness, disease, poverty, and death in the world today?

Question #2:

Who are the chosen (covenant) people of God, and why?

Question #3:

What is the Promised Land God gave to His chosen people?

Question # 1:
Why are sickness, disease, poverty and death in the world today?

Short Answer:
Adam and Eve's sin in the Garden of Eden brought the curses of sickness, disease, poverty, and death on all humankind, which is still in the world today.

Long Answer:
Genesis Chapters 1 and 2 speak clearly of God's perfect design in creating the earth for humankind to multiply in, replenish and dominate. The very breath of our eternal and holy creator was the source of the first man and woman's life. Adam and Eve and their offspring were destined to live in paradise conditions forever. Everyone born to Adam and Eve would have the same breath of life from God, which would bless and nourish them, spiritually and naturally.

By **Genesis Chapter 3**, we learn of the sad turn of events that caused "sure death" to come on Adam and Eve and all their offspring. Deceived by God's adversary the devil who used the crafty serpent as his spokesman, Eve disobeyed God first, then she convinced her husband to disobey God's one and only "do not" command. The curse of sure death that fell upon Adam and Eve was immediate separation from God's life-giving nature. God also pronounced curses on humankind as a result of their sin, such as pain in child-birth, challenges in relationships, and hardships in producing food to eat. **Romans 5:12** explains how these curses applied to all of Adam's offspring, who were to share in the death curse, from the one-man Adam.

As the one who plants the seed to produce humankind in the woman's body, Adam's new sinful nature was transported to all who are born from the seed of a man. Jesus, on the other hand, who was not born of an earthly father, did not have sin in his nature, because Mary conceived Jesus by the impartation of the Holy Spirit in her womb (not by having relations with a man). **Matthew 1:18–25**

Through the redemptive work of God's only begotten Son, Jesus Christ—by his death on the cross, burial and resurrection—all who believe on the living Jesus and His work to restore humankind to life in God can have access to health, wealth, and abundant life in the world today, along with eternal life in the world to come. But this requires an active fight of faith to experience.

Mark 10:29–30, John 10:10, Rom 5:17–21, Eph 6:10–18, I Peter 2:21–24

Question #2:
Who are the chosen (covenant) people of God, and why?

Short answer:

Who: Chosen people of God are descendants of Abraham, Isaac and Jacob (Israel) who became known as the nation of Israel after Jacob's new name from God.

Why: The reason they were chosen by God to be His special nation of people is because of the covenant agreement God made to Abraham in Genesis Chapters 12, 15, and 17. God intended to bless the whole world through Abraham's seed.

Long answer:

Who: Chosen people of God are descendants of Abraham, Isaac and Jacob. Abraham's other children through his concubines were not considered the chosen people. Also, the children of Isaac's other son Esau, were not considered a part of the chosen people. God blessed all the seed of Abraham, but only his descendants through his son Isaac and his grandson Jacob formed the chosen nation.

Why: The reason is God made an eternal covenant agreement with Abraham to bless his "seed," not seeds, and the seed would come through one specific pathway from the nation of Israel formed by Jacob's twelve sons.

God made the agreement in **Genesis Chapters 12, 15, and 17** initially with Abraham. He confirmed the covenant agreement with Isaac in **Genesis 26:24**; and God confirmed the covenant agreement again with Jacob in **Genesis 46:3.**

In addition, the entire nation of Israel entered into their own covenant agreements with God. Israel renewed their covenant relationship with God at different points in their history, which preserved their status as God's chosen (meaning covenant) people. God intended the Israelites to be His kings and priests representing God's holy ways to the world, which was to draw the world to God. God agreed to make Israel a great nation as long as they would keep His covenant agreements.

From this Know His Word Bible Study – 1st Quarter, read Genesis 12:1–3, Exodus Chapter 24, Deuteronomy Chapter 26.

Question #3: What is the Promised Land God gave to his chosen people?

Short answer:
The land God promised to give Abraham and his descendants. God also showed the same land to Moses before his death as confirmation of the promise. Read Gen. 13:12, 14–15; Gen. 15:18–21; Deut. 34:1–4

Long answer:

In addition to the above, consider these points about the "Promised Land":

God told Abraham he was taking the land away from the Canaanites (Amorites) because of their sin. He said the land was vomiting out the current residents. God warned the Israelites that the land could vomit them out too if they chose to sin like the current inhabitants, but he would never give it away forever. Gen. 15:16; Lev. 18: 24-28

God assigned land to other nations that He did not give to Israel. Deut. 2:9, 12, 19

Also, the inheritance of land God assigned to individual tribes could not be transferred between tribes, because each inheritance was to remain with each tribe (Num. 36:7). When we began our study of this land, we called it the land of Canaan, which included many nation-states of people. But after Israel occupies the land, it will become known as the land of Israel and later it will also be called the land of Judah.

In modern times, the area of the Bible referred to as the "Promised Land" is generally known as Palestine.

Endnotes and References

I. **General List of References for 1st–4th Quarter Books:** Basis for scripture interpretations, including development of Bible Book Summaries, Bible Book Introductions and Chronological Dates

II. **Endnotes and References for 1st Quarter by Sections**

III. **Art Credits**

I. General List of References for 1st–4th Quarter Books

❒ Bibles

- ***Holy Bible, Sword Study Bible,*** **King James Easy Read Bible (KJVER)** (New Kensington, PA: Whitaker House, 2001, 2015)
- ***The One Year Chronological Bible,*** **New Living Translation (NLT)** (Wheaton, IL: Tyndale House Publishers, Inc., 2000)
- ***Messianic Jewish Family Bible,*** **Tree of Life Version (TLV)** (Syracuse, NY: Messianic Jewish Family Bible Society, 2018)
- Tim LaHaye, general ed., et al. ***Tim LaHaye Prophecy Study Bible,*** **King James Version (KJV)** (AMG Publishers, 2000)
- ***NIV Archaeological Study Bible: An Illustrated Walk through Biblical History and Culture*** (Grand Rapids, MI: The Zondervan Corporation, 2005)
- David H. Stern, ***Complete Jewish Bible*** **(CJB)** (Clarksville, MD: Jewish New Testament Publications, Inc., 1998)
- Dr. K. Daniel, Fried, Ed., ***The Hebrew-English New Covenant (New Testament)*** (Powder Springs, GA: Hope of Israel Publications, 2003)
- **The Chronological Study Bible** (Thomas Nelson, Inc., 2008)
- Sol Scharfstein, ***Torah and Commentary – The Five Books of Moses: Translation Rabbinic and Contemporary Commentary*** (Jersey City, NJ: KTAV Publishing House, Inc., 2008)
- ***The Amplified Bible (AMP)*** (La Habra, CA: The Lockman Foundation and The Zondervan Corporation, 1987)
- ***The International Inductive Study Bible*****, New American Standard Bible (NASB)** (Chattanooga, TN: Harvest House Publishers, 1992, 1993 Precept Ministries)
- Finis Jennings Dake, ***Dake's Annotated Reference Bible,*** **The Holy Bible King James Version Text** (Lawrenceville, GA: Dake Bible Sales, Inc., 1963)
- Martin Abegg Jr., Peter Flint, & Eugene Ulrich, ***The Dead Sea Scrolls Bible: The Oldest Known Bible Translated for the First Time into English*** (New York, NY: Harper Collins Publisher, 1999)

❒ Bible Study Reference Books and Resources

- Nelson's Pocket Reference Series, ***The Bible Handbook*** (Nashville, TN: Thomas Nelson, Inc. Publishers, 1993, 1995)
- Lawrence O. Richards, ***The Bible Reader's Companion: Your Guide to Every Chapter of the Bible*** (Owings Mills, MD: Halo Press is a trademark of Ottenheimer Publishers, Inc., 1991)

- Paul N. Benware, ***Survey of the New Testament: The Essential Bible*** (Chicago, IL: First Published by Moody Publishers in the US, Text 1990, 2003 by Benware; Worldwide co-edition organized and produced by Angus Hudson Ltd./Tim Dowley & Peter Wyatt trading as Three's Company, 2003)
- ***Bible Book Surveys***, Got Questions.org–Bible Questions Answered (Got Questions Ministries, 2002–2007)
- ***New American Bible (NAB): Bible Book Introductions***, USCCB, The New American Bible (United States Conference of Catholic Bishops, November 11, 2002)
- Andrew E. Hill, John H. Walton, ***A Survey of the Old Testament,*** **Second Edition** (Grand Rapids, MI: Zondervan, 1991, 2000)
- Robert H. Gundry, ***A Survey of the New Testament*, Second Edition** (Grand Rapids, MI: Zondervan, 2003)
- John H. Walton, ***Chronological and Background Charts of the Old Testament: Revised and Expanded*** (Grand Rapids, MI: Zondervan, 1978, 1994)
- H. Wayne House, ***Chronological and Background Charts of the New Testament*** (Grand Rapids, MI: Zondervan, 1981)
- Trent C. Butler, PhD., general ed., ***Holman Bible Dictionary*** (Nashville, TN: Holman Bible Publishers, 1991)
- Paul N. Benware, ***Understanding End Times Prophecy: A Comprehensive Approach,*** **Revised and Expanded** (Chicago, IL: Moody Publishers, 1995, 2006)
- James Strong, LL.D., S.T.D. ***The New Strong's Expanded Exhaustive Concordance of the Bible Red-Letter Edition.*** Dictionaries include contributions by John R. Kohlenberger, III (Nashville, TN: Thomas Nelson Publishers, 2001)
- Kevin J. Conner, Ken Malmin, ***Interpreting the Scriptures: A Textbook on How To Interpret the Bible*** (Portland, Oregon: City Bible Publishing, 1993)
- Discovery Series Bible Study, ***How Can I Understand the Bible*** (Grand Rapids, MI: RBC Ministries–Discovery House Publishers, 2003, 2006)
- Alfred Thompson Eade, S.T.D., ***The Expanded Panorama Bible Study Course*** (Fleming H. Revell Company, MCMLxl *(1961))*

- Josh McDowell, ***The New Evidence That Demands a Verdict*** (Nashville, TN: Thomas Nelson Publishers, 1999)
- ***Rose Book of Bible Charts, Maps & Time Lines*** (Torrance, CA: Rose Publishing, Inc. RW Research, Inc., 2005)
- Thomas V. Briscoe, ***Holman Bible Atlas*** (Nashville, TN: Broadman & Holman Publishers, 1998)
- Alfred Edersheim, ***Bible History: Old Testament***, New Updated Edition (Peabody, MA, Hendrickson Publishers, Inc., 1995); Originally published1876 –1887 in seven volumes; This one-volume edition is a complete, unabridged reproduction of the 1890 seven-volume edition.
- Alfred Edersheim, ***Prophecy and History in Relation to the Messiah: The Barburton Lectures for 1880–1884*** (Eugene, OR, Wipf & Stock Publishers, 2005); Originally published by Longmans, 1901
- Alfred Edersheim, ***The Life and Times of Jesus the Messiah*****:** New Updated Edition, Complete and Unabridged in One Volume (Peabody, MA, Hendrickson Publishers, Inc., 1993)
- Alfred Edershiem, ***The Temple: Its Ministry and Services***, Undated Edition (Peabody, MA, Hendrickson Publishers, Inc., 1994)
- Rachmiel Frydland, ***What the Rabbis Know About the Messiah: A Study of Genealogy and Prophecy***, Third Edition (Columbus, OH, Messianic Publishing Company, 2002)
- David H. Stern, ***Jewish New Testament Commentary*** (Clarksville, MD: Jewish New Testament Publications, Inc., 1992)
- David H. Stern, ***Restoring the Jewishness of the Gospel: A Message for Christians*** (Clarksville, MD: JNT, Inc., 1990)
- Howard F. Vos, ***Nelson's New Illustrated Bible Manners & Customs: How the People of the Bible Really Lived*** (Nashville, TN: Thomas Nelson, Inc., 1999)
- John F. Walvoord, ***Every Prophecy of the Bible: Clear Explanations for Uncertain Times by One of Today's Premier Prophecy Scholars*** (Colorado Springs, CO: Victor an imprint of Cook Communications Ministries, 1999)
- Flavius Josephus, ***The Complete Works of Josephus*****, Translated by William Whiston** (Edinburgh, Scotland: William P. Nimmo; Philadelphia, Pennsylvania: Porter and Coates; Kregel Publications, a division of Kregel, Inc., 1960, 1978, 1981), "Antiquities of the Jews" and "Wars of the Jews"
- Wayne Blank, ***Daily Bible Study: Church of God***, (The Church of God Daily Bible Study: A Ministry of God's Word: 2007)

II. Endnotes and References for 1st Quarter by Sections

❒ Author's Introduction and Notes

1. ***Messianic Jewish Family Bible,*** **Tree of Life Version (TLV)** (Syracuse, NY: Messianic Jewish Family Bible Society, 2018)

2. Challenges in Understanding the Bible:

   - ***Interpreting the Scriptures: A Textbook on How to Interpret the Bible***; by Kevin J. Conner and Ken Malmin; 1993 by City Bible Publishing
   - ***How Can I Understand the Bible***; by Discovery Series Bible Study Discovery House Publishers, 2003, 2006 RBC Ministries

3. Principles for Interpreting Bible Scriptures and Prophecy:

   References:

   - ***Interpreting the Scriptures: A Textbook on How to Interpret the Bible***; by Kevin J. Conner and Ken Malmin; City Bible Publishing; 1983; p. 15–16
   - ***Understanding End Times Prophecy: A Comprehensive Approach***; by Paul N. Benware; Moody Publishers; 2006; Chapter 1 - p. 21–33

4. Calendar Notes: Jewish, Julian and Gregorian Calendars

   References:

   – ***The Biblical Feast Days: God's Calendar***, Michael Scheifler's Bible Light Homepage (biblelightinfo.com)
   – ***Judaism 101: Jewish Calendar***, Tracey R. Rich (jewfaq.org)

❒ Bible Facts, Construction, Book Summaries, Layout Charts

1. Bible Facts: Evidence for Integrity of the Bible and Bible Canon–References

- ***How We Got the Bible: Ten Key Points, Rose Book of Bible Charts, Maps & Time Lines*** (Torrance, CA: Rose Publishing, Inc. RW Research, Inc., 2005), p. 25, used by permission
- Josh McDowell, ***The New Evidence That Demands a Verdict*** (Nashville, TN: Thomas Nelson Publishers, 1999), Chapter 1–The Uniqueness of the Bible, pages 3–7
- Martin Abegg Jr., Peter Flint, & Eugene Ulrich, ***The Dead Sea Scrolls Bible: The Oldest Known Bible Translated for the First Time into English*** (New York, NY: Harper Collins Publisher, 1999)

- Pamphlets, **Rose Publishing, Inc (**Torrance, CA: Rose Publishing, Inc, Bristol Works, Inc., 2008)
    - ***Bible Translations Comparison: Compare Twenty Popular Versions of the Bible*** **Pamphlet**
    - ***The Gospels: "Lost and found"*** **Pamphlet**

2. Comparison Chart: Old Testament Books in Hebrew (Jewish), Protestant and Catholic Bibles–References:

- Jewish and Christian Bibles: A Comparison chart by Felix Just, S.J., Ph.D. (catholic-resources.org/Bible/Heb-Xn-Bibles.htm), based on last updated Feb. 26, 2007
- "An article from *Funk & Wagnalls® New Encyclopedia:* The Bible – Order of Books" (The History Channel website, 2006)

3. Hulitt Gloer, **"Old Testament Quotations in the New Testament,"** ***Holman Bible Dictionary*** (Nashville, TN: Holman Bible Publishers, 1991), p. 1045, Article reprinted by permission
4. Testament Means Covenant: Reference

- # **Saint Jerome**, BELIEVE—Religious Information Source Website, (This subject presentation updated on 09/03/2007)

5. Bible Construction Timeline – References:

- Pamphlets, **Rose Publishing, Inc** (Torrance, CA: Rose Publishing, Inc, Bristol Works, Inc., 2008)
    a. ***How We Got The Bible*** – *A Time Line of Key Events in the History of the Bible*
    b. ***Bible Time Line:*** *300 Key People & Events in the Bible*
- David H. Stern, ***Complete Jewish Bible*** **(CJB) –** Introduction: Other Features of the Bible (Clarksville, MD: Jewish New Testament Publications, Inc., 1998)

6. **Bible Bookcase:** ***Rose Book of Bible Charts, Maps & Time Lines*** (Torrance, CA: Rose Publishing, Inc. RW Research, Inc., 2005), p. 14, used by permission
7. ***The One-Year Chronological Bible*****, New Living Translation (NLT)** (Wheaton, IL: Tyndale House Publishers, Inc., 2000)
8. Books of the Old Testament Chart ***"Chronological Layout of Old Testament Books"*** based on General Order Events Occurred – References

- Chart reprinted by permission of Paul N. Benware, *Survey of the Old Testament: The Essential Bible* (Chicago, IL: First Published by

Moody Publishers in the US, Text 1988, 1993 by Benware; Worldwide co-edition organized and produced by Angus Hudson Ltd./Tim Dowley & Peter Wyatt trading as Three's Company, 2003), p. 18-19

9. **Chronological Summary of the Old Testament** – Reference

- ***Part 2: The Foundational Books–Survey of the Old Testament: The Essential Bible*** (Chicago, IL: First Published by Moody Publishers in the US, Text 1988, 1993 by Benware; Worldwide co-edition organized and produced by Angus Hudson Ltd./Tim Dowley & Peter Wyatt trading as Three's Company, 2003), 24-159
- Special Thanks to N. Walker of Williams Temple COGIC, Houston, TX for formatting the table using the data provided by J. Price

10. Comparison Chart: Chronology of Old Testament 17 Prophetic Books - Five Major Prophets and Twelve Minor Prophets – References: Bible Book Introduction sections for the Prophetic books as seen in the below Bibles

- ***Survey of the Old Testament: The Essential Bible*** (Chicago, IL: First Published by Moody Publishers in the US, Text 1988, 1993 by Benware; Worldwide co-edition organized and produced by Angus Hudson Ltd./Tim Dowley & Peter Wyatt trading as Three's Company, 2003)
- Tim LaHaye, general ed., et al. ***Tim LaHaye Prophecy Study Bible*, King James Version (KJV)** (AMG Publishers, 2000)
- ***The One Year Chronological Bible,* New Living Translation (NLT)** (Wheaton, IL: Tyndale House Publishers, Inc., 2000)

❒ **Apologetics: Bible and Christian Pages 26 - 40**

1. **References: Definition of Apologetics**
   - **Multiple Authors, What is Apologetics, Bible.org, 2013, (bible.org)**
   - **Apologetics 101, Dead Theologians Society, 2013, (deadtheologianssociety)**
2. **King James Version versus Non-KJV**
   - David W. Daniels**, Look What's Missing** (Chick Publications, 2017)
3. **Messianic Bible**
   - Cooper, David L., **Messiah: His Historical Appearance** (Biblical Research Society, 1958)
   - Rydelnik, Michael, **The Messianic Hope: Is the Hebrew Bible Really Messianic?** (Nashville, TN: B&H Publishing Group, 2010)

4. **Christian and Christendom**

   - Geisler, Dr. Norman, Essential Doctrine Made Easy, Key Christian Beliefs, Rose Publishing, Inc., 2007
   - The Trinity, What is the Trinity and What do Christians Believe?, Rose Publishing, Inc., 1999
   - *What is Christendom?, Got Questions.org, 2013

5. **Jesus' Divinity**

   - Komoszewski, Sawyer, and Wallace, **Reinventing Jesus—How Contemporary Skeptics Miss the Real Jesus and Mislead Popular Culture** (Kregel Publications, 2006)
   - Bible Study Tools.com, 2013, history/early-church-fathers

6. **Israelology, Vital Part of Systematic Theology**

   - Arnold G. Fruchtenbaum, Th.M., Ph.D. ***Israelology: The Missing Link in Systematic Theology*** (Ariel Ministries, 1989, revised 1992, 1993, 1994, 1996, 2001, 2016, 2018, 2020)

7. **Extra-Biblical Evidence**

   - David L. Cooper, **Messiah: His Historical Appearance**, 1958 (Los Angeles, CA: Biblical Research Society)
   - Josh McDowell, **The New Evidence That Demands A Verdict**, 1999, (Nashville, TN: Thomas Nelson Publishers)
   - NIV **Archaeological Study Bible**, 2005, (Grand Rapids, MI: Zondervan)
   - John Urquhart, **The Inspiration and Accuracy of the Holy Scriptures** (1895), Kessinger Publishing's Rare Reprints

8. Septuagint FAQ's

   - Flavius Josephus, **Appendix Dissertation IV, The Complete Works of Josephus,** (Grand Rapids, Michigan: Kregel Publications, 1960, 1978, 1981), p. 662 - 677
     i) "The copy of the books of the Old Testament used by Josephus in his Antiquities was the ancient collection or library made by Nehemiah, and was free from the additions and alterations made afterwards in the other copies which still exist"
   - Alfred Edersheim, **The Life and Times of Jesus the Messiah: New Updated Edition, Complete and Unabridged in One Volume** (1993: Hendrickson Publishers, Inc.), pages 15 – 22

- David W. Daniels, **Did Jesus Use the Septuagint?** (Ontario, CA: Chick Publications, 2017)
- **Which Old Testament text did Jesus prefer and quote from? Septuagint or Hebrew Tanakh?** (bible.ca)
  - How Jesus quoted the Old Testament Septuagint or Hebrew Tanakh; A conservative, bible believing perspective!
  - Lee Martin McDonald, James A. Sanders, Editors: **The Canon Debate**
  - Craig A. Evans, **The Scriptures of Jesus and His Earliest Followers**, p 191-194, 2002
  - Septuagint Online 2024
  - **Septuagint Bible w/Apocrypha**, (biblestudytools.com), lxx
  - **Elpenor's Bilingual (Greek / English) Old Testament** (ellopos.net/elpenor/greek-texts), Septuagint

9. **BibleStudyTools.com, 2013, history early church fathers**

❒ **Old Testament: Weekly Study Intro Pages**

1. Overview of the Old Testament – Reference:

- Paul N. Benware, ***Survey of the Old Testament***, p. an adaptation of the text on pages 15 – 22 is used by permission

2. Hebrew Bible / Old Testament - References:

- Rabbi Barry Dov Lerner, **"Torah, Hebrew Bible"**, About.com – Judaism : Rabbi Lerner answers the question "Is the Old Testament the same as the Torah?"
- Lisa Katz, **"What is the Torah?,"** About.com - Judaism : Description of Written Torah and Oral Torah
- Dennis Prager, **"What Does 'Judeo-Christian' Mean?"** (jewishworldreview.com)
- **The Pontifical Biblical Commission: The Jewish People and their Sacred Scriptures in the Christian Bible** 2001 :
  This article provides a thorough discussion on this subject matter in three sections –
  a) I. The Sacred Scriptures of the Jewish people are a fundamental part of the Christian Bible; II. Fundamental themes in the Jewish Scriptures and their reception into faith in Christ and III. The Jews in the New Testament.
- **Judaism**, (hopeofisrael.net, 2007)
  This article provides an excellent discussion on "Jews Entrusted With

Scripture"; "The Role of the Scribes"; and "The Oldest Biblical Manuscripts & Inscription"

3. Glossary of Some Hebrew Words – References: glossary and definition of terms collected from several resources:

– David H. Stern, Complete Jewish Bible; Glossary

– Sol Scharfstein, Chronicle of Jewish History from the Patriarchs to the 21st Century (Hoboken, N.J., KTAV Publishing House, Inc.), p. 68, 92, 106, 111, 112

4. The Messiah, Our Savior – Revealed from the Beginning – Reference:

– Dr. K. Daniel, Fried, Inset of the front cover, ***Hebrew-English New Covenant (New Testament)*** (Powder Springs, GA: Hope of Israel Publications, 2003)

5. Jewish Scholars Used as Resources for "Find Jesus in the Lesson" – References – Google Web page references for additional background information for Alfred Edersheim, Rachmiel Frydland, David H Stern.

6. Find Jesus in the Lesson - References:

Internet Resources, as available in 2007

- Jerome Dominguez, M.D., **The Jerome Bible Commentary: Jesus Christ and His Church in Every Book of the Bible** (jesus/bible/index.html, 2007)
- **324 Messianic Prophecies,** (hopeofisrael.net , 2007)
- **Over 300 Prophecies Jesus Fulfilled Amazing**! (bibleprobe.com, 2007)
- **Ten Prophecies Fulfilled by Yeshua; Ten More Prophecies Fulfilled by Yeshua;** The Refiner's Fire, (therefinersfire.org, 2007)
- **Jews For Jesus Website** (2007) : Does the New Testament mistranslate and misuse the Hebrew Bible when it quotes the prophecies?, and other such questions are addressed.
- **Response to… "The Fabulous Prophecies of the Messiah**," (christian-thinktank.com, 2007)
- **Clarifying Christianity, Messianic Prophecies** (clarifyingchristianity.com, 2007)

Books, Booklets, Pamphlets

- John F. Walvoord, ***Every Prophecy of the Bible: Clear Explanations for Uncertain Times by One of Today's Premier***

Prophecy Scholars (Colorado Springs, CO: Victor an imprint of Cook Communications Ministries, 1999)

- Josh McDowell, "Support of Deity: Old Testament Prophecies Fulfilled in Jesus Christ", ***The New Evidence That Demands a Verdict*** (Nashville, TN: Thomas Nelson Publishers, 1999), Chapter 8
- Discovery Series, Questions Skeptics Ask About Messianic Prophecy, Managing Editor: David Sper, 1997 RBC Ministries--Grand Rapids, MI 49555, "I hope that by the time you have read this booklet you will realize that messianic prophecy is not easy to understand, but it is legitimately fulfilled in Jesus Christ--contrary to the arguments of skeptics."
- "100 Prophecies Fulfilled by Jesus," ***Rose Book of Bible Charts, Maps & Time Lines*** (Torrance, CA: Rose Publishing, Inc. RW Research, Inc., 2005), p. 81-86; also can be purchased as a Pamphlet

❒ **The Book of Genesis Preparatory Study Material – References:**

1. Paul N. Benware, ***Various Views on Origins***, *Survey of the Old Testament: The Essential Bible, p. 30*, 31

"Various Views on Origins" - **References:**

- ***Original Article "Various Views on Origins"**
  Paul N. Benware, *Survey of the Old Testament* (Chicago, First published in the USA by Moody Publishers, 1988, 1993, Angus Hudson Ltd/Tim Dowley & Peter Wyart trading as Three's Company, 2003), p. 30 - 31
- ****The Day-Age View** (Old Earth)
  Davis A. Young, *Christianity and the Age of the Earth* (Grand Rapids: Zondervan, 1982).
- *****The Ruin-Reconstruction View** (Gap Theory)
  Arthur Custance, *Without Form and Void* (Brockville, Ont.: Arthur Custance, 1970).
- ******Young Earth View** (Young Earth)
  John C. Whitcomb, *The Early Earth*, rev. ed. (Grand Rapids: Baker, 1986); Henry Morris, *Scientific Creationism* (San Diego; Creation-Life, 1981).

2. Rev. Clarence Larkin, **Dispensational Truth, Second Work** Gen. 1:26-28 (Rev. Clarence Larkin Est, 1920), p. 28 - 29
   Dispensational Truth by Rev. Clarence Larkin. Used by permission of Rev. Clarence Larkin Est., P.O. Box 334, Glenside, PA 19036, U.S.A.

❒ Week 1

Lesson 1.1

1. **References for "Chronological Notes' Timetable Dates"**:
   Dates in all Chronological Notes charts are derived from the One Year Chronological New Living Translation Bible by Tyndale Publishing and Tim LaHaye's Bible Prophecy Bible by AMG Publishers, as well as from Old Testament and New Testament Survey books and other Bible Study reference books identified in the General List of References for 1st–4th Quarter Books.
2. References for discussion on Moses' Authorship and dating of Pentateuch
   - Alfred Edersheim, **Prophecy and History in Relation to the Messiah: The Barburton Lectures For 1880 – 1884** (Eugene, OR, Wipf & Stock Publishers, 2005); Originally published by Longmans, 1901; Chapters VII and VII
   - **Chronological Study Bible** (Thomas Nelson, Inc. 2008), p. 3
3. Rachmiel Frydland, Chapter 3, ***What the Rabbis Know About the Messiah – A Study of Genealogy and Prophecy***, pages 11 – 13
4. Dr. K. Daniel, Fried, Ed., ***Prophecy, The Hebrew-English New Covenant (New Testament***), page 1 includes quote from Midrash
5. Alfred Edersheim, ***The Life and Times of Jesus the Messiah*****:** New Updated Edition, Appendix 9

Lesson 1.3

6. Rachmiel Frydland, Chapter 4, ***What the Rabbis Know About the Messiah – A Study of Genealogy and Prophecy***, pages 15 – 17

Lesson 1.5

7. References for circumcision as physical sign – Tim LaHaye Bible Prophecy book notes on Gen. 17; and Holman Bible Dictionary

8. Read about ancient custom of using a slave girl to birth the family heir when the wife could not in "***New Illustrated Bible Manner & Customs***", p. 17, 39-40 and in Archeological Study Bible, p. 30

9. Read about Israel's restoration to the Promised Land in "***Tim LaHaye Prophecy Bible - Israel in Two Centuries***", p. 874

10. Bible Tidbits – Oldest Language

    – **Sumerian-language** (britannica.com, 2024)

    – **What's the World's Oldest Language?** (scientificiamerican.com, 2024)

11. Flavius Josephus, ***The Complete Works of Josephus*: Translated by William Whiston** (Edinburgh, Scotland: William P. Nimmo; Philadelphia, PA: Porter and Coates; Kregel Publications, a division of Kregel, Inc., 1960, 1978, 1981), p. 379, 423, public domain text

12. G.J. Goldberg, **Flavius Josephus Home Page**, 1998–2005, (josephus.org), includes a special section on "Josephus' Account of Jesus: The Testimonium Flavianum," which addresses concerns with the authenticity of Josephus' testimony of Christ

❒ **13. Week 1 Maps**

- World Map, public domain site
- Middle East: Then and Middle East Now maps, **Rose Book of Charts, Maps & Time Lines;** (Torrance, CA: Rose Publishing, 2005 RW Research, Inc.), 120, 121
- Thomas V. Briscoe, ***Holman Bible Atlas Maps*** 16, 3, 20, 21, 22, 23 used by permission (Nashville, TN: Broadman & Holman Publishers, 1998), pages 4, 36, 46 – 48, 50

❒ **Week 2**

Lesson 2.1

1. Charts on Abraham's Family Tree – **Abraham's Father's Family Tree and Abraham, Isaac and Jacob's Family Tree**, copyright by Jennifer B. Price, June 2008. Special thanks to Cosette Nazon and Yisrael Communications, Park Forest, IL

Lesson 2.2

2. Read about ancient customs of birthright and blessings in ***"Nelson's Illustrated Bible Manners and Customs***", p. 40-41 and Archeological Study Bible, p. 36 and 43

Lesson 2.3

3. Read about ancient customs on marriage arrangements in "Nelson's Illustrated Bible Manners and Customs", p. 38-39
4. Read about ancient custom of using handmaids to birth family heirs in "***New Illustrated Bible Manner and Customs***", p. 40

Lesson 2.4 – Bible Tidbits

5. Sol Scharfstein, Commentary on Gen. 28:22, ***Torah and Commentary – The Five Books of Moses,*** p. 97

Lesson 2.6

6. Adapted from **"Some Ancient Civilizations"** (infoplease.com/ipa, as it appeared on March 25, 2008, Information Please Database© 2007, Pearson Education, Inc.) Reproduced by permission of Pearson Education, Inc. publishing as InfoPlease. All rights reserved.

Lesson 2.7

7. Read how Pharaoh is a title ***in "Nelson's Illustrated Bible Manners and Customs***", p. 52-53

❒ **Week 3**

Lesson 3.3

1. Alfred Edersheim, Chapter 19, **Bible History: Old Testament**, New Updated Edition, p. 100 - 101
2. ***Historical Timeline of Ancient Egypt*** - This page is researcher Dr. Joel A. Freeman's understanding of which Egyptian dynasties were in power during the time of Biblical stories, as it appeared October 2007, The Historical Timeline of Egypt – courtesy of Return to Glory, (freemaninstitute.com). Reprinted by permission.

❒ **Week 4**

Lesson 4.2

1. Retribution principle and Job's suffering discussed in "A Survey of the Old Testament" by Andrew Hill and John Walton, p. 324, 338

❒ **Week 5**

Intro to Exodus: Background

References for Israel in Egypt Until the Fourth Generation / 400 – 430 Years

1. Paul N. Benware, Survey of the Old Testament: The Essential Bible, p. 48
2. “How Long Was the Israelites’ Egyptian Bondage”, by Bible Apologists Alden Bass, Bert Thompson, Ph.D., and Kyle Butt, M.A. (ApologeticsPress.Org, as of Feb. 2008)
3. Map (4): Egypt Land of Bondage, Thomas V. Briscoe, Holman Bible Atlas, used by permission (Nashville, TN: Broadman & Holman Publishers, 1998), page 6

Lesson 5.4

4. For additional reading on the results of Moses’ anger, that led to his killing the Egyptian, read the following booklet - ***Moses: His Anger and What It Cost Him***, 2002, 2204, 2006 RBC Ministries

Lesson 5.5

5. Read how the word “Eber” leads to the named “Hebrews” at these links

- Eber, Wikipedia, the free encyclopedia, as of Jan 2007
- Wayne Blank, ***The Church of God Daily Bible Study - Hebrew***; A Ministry of God’s Word, as of Jan 2007

6. Sol Scharfstein, ***Torah and Commentary – The Five Books of Moses***
7. Definitions of Monotheism and Polytheism, from Polytheism, Wikipedia, the free encyclopedia
8. Chart – “Names of God (54, 55); Jesus and the Names of God (56)” – Rose Book of Bible Maps, Charts and Time Lines, by Rose Publishing, Inc., p. 130

Lesson 5.6

9. “Pharaoh’s hard heart”, Lawrence O. Richards, ***The Bible Reader's Companion: Your Guide to Every Chapter of the Bible*** (Owings Mills, MD: Halo Press is a trademark of Ottenheimer Publishers, Inc., 1991), p. 56

Lesson 5.7

10. Passover, Passover Celebration and Pesach Seder – References:

- ***Passover on the NET – The Story of Passover (Pesach),*** (holidays.net, 2007)
- ***How to Conduct a Passover Seder,*** (ehow.com, 2007)
- Tracey R. Rich, ***Judaism 101: Pesach: Passover,*** (jewfaq.org)
- Richard Bank, Chapter 14, ***The Everything Judaism Book*** (Avon, MA, Adams Media Publication, 2002),

11. References for the Chart "Moses Ten Plagues: True God of Israel against False gods of Egypt

- ***Against All the Gods of Egypt*** by David Padfield; Padfield.com The Church of Christ in Zion, Illinois, 2002 , (padfield.com, 2007)
- "Against All Gods: Purpose of the Ten Plagues," by Timothy Sliedrecht; Tyndale Theological Seminary Old Testament Survey – 7 March 2005

12. NIV Archaeological Study Bible: An Illustrated Walk through Biblical History and Culture (Grand Rapids, MI: The Zondervan Corporation, 2005), book of Exodus articles on "Archaeological Sites," "Ancient Texts and Artifacts," "Cultural and Historical Notes," "Ancient Peoples, Lands and Rulers," pages 84 – 154

❑ **Week 6**

Lesson 6.1

1. Name of first month in Hebrew or Jewish Calendar is Abib or Nisan, reference ***The International Inductive Study Bible***, 1992, 1993 Precept Ministries, Harvest House Publishers, Chart on "The Jewish Calendar", p. 200

Lesson 6.2

2. Map "The Exodus," adapted from Tear Off Bible Maps series (c)1991 by Abingdon Press Used by permission
3. Bible Tidbits – Reference

- John F. Walvoord, Roy Zuck, The Bible Knowledge Commentary: Old Testament (David c. Cook, 1985), p. 307

Lesson 6.3

4. Chart – "The Ten Commandments and You" – ***Rose Book of Bible Maps, Charts and Time Lines***, by Rose Publishing, Inc., p. 57
5. The below references are helpful in understanding how the Tabernacle of Moses showed so many references to the ministry of Jesus Christ.

- "The Tabernacle" pamphlet by Rose Publishing, Inc., Torrance, California
- Images of the Tabernacle of Moses: ***God's Prophetic Pattern Study Material, Pictures, Drawings***; copyright 2005 by John Robert Lucas
- ***The Tabernacle of Moses Is the Body of Christ Jesus***; Chapter 1 by Lionel Cabral Ministries (tabernacleofmoses.org , 2007)

- The Tabernacle of Moses: A Dwelling Place for God; A Study of the Redemptive Plan of God in the Tabernacle in the Wilderness; based on Kevin J. Conner's book (web-based study and images, 2007)

6. "Shadows of Messiah in the Tabernacle in the Old Covenant" is reprinted by permission of Bruce Hart, (preceptaustin.org, Covenant: Abrahamic versus Mosaic, 2007)

❒ **Week 7**

1. Holy Anointing Oil - References:

– David Stewart, ***Healing Oils of the Bible*** (Marble Hill, MO, Care Publications, 1937), Chapter 4 pages 64 47

– Heart to Heart: Holy Anointing Oil, parsontoperson.blogspot.com, Friday, September 07, 2007

– Walter Beuttler, Peter Macinta, The Holy Anointing Oil Ex. 30:22 33 , pastorpete.tripod.com/HA.html

– Gleanings in Exodus, 56. The Anointing Oil, www.pbministries.org/books/pink/Gleanings_Exodus/exodus_56.htm

2. Fragrant Incense – References::

– Dr. Mark Hanby, ***Anointing the Unsanctified – An Unveiled Revelation in Spiritual Authority*** (Shippensburg, PA, Destiny Image Publishers, Inc., 1993, 1998), Chapter 1

– David Stewart, ***Healing Oils of the Bible***, Chapter 4

– Incense, The Good Shepherd Orthodox Mission, (thegoodshepherd.org.au, 2007)

3. Atonement Procedures Result in Forgiveness of Sin – References:

– Alfred Edersheim, ***The Temple – Its Ministry and Services*** (Peabody, MA, Hendrickson Publishers, Inc., 1994), Chapter 5 Sacrifices: Their Order and Their Meaning

4. Set Apart to Serve, Dressed to Serve and Consecrated to Serve - References

– David M. Levy, ***The Tabernacle: Shadows of the Messiah – Its Sacrifices, Services, and Priesthood*** (Bellmawr, NJ, Friends of Israel Gospel Ministry, Inc.), Part III: The Priesthood

– ***The High Priest and His Garments*** (Exodus chapters 28 and 39)

❒ **Jesus in the Tabernacle Reference Material**

1. The below references were used in developing the charts:

   - Jesus in the Tabernacle—Introduction.
   - Table 1. Jesus in the Tabernacle—Materials
   - Chart 2 Jesus in the Tabernacle—Furniture

- ***The Tabernacle: Shadows of the Messiah*** by David M. Levy; 1993 by The Friends of Israel Gospel Ministry, Inc.; ninth printing 2005

- ***The Tabernacle of Moses: The Riches of Redemption's Story as Revealed in the Tabernacle*** by Kevin J. Conner; 1976 by City Bible Publishing

2. The below references were used in developing the chart:

   - Table 3. Jesus in the Sacrifice Offerings—Materials
   - Table 4. Jesus in the Sacrifice Offerings— Special Offerings
   - Tables 5. Jesus in the Sacrifice Offerings— Animals

- ***The Tabernacle: Shadows of the Messiah*** by David M. Levy; 1993 by The Friends of Israel Gospel Ministry, Inc.; ninth printing 2005

- ***Tim LaHaye Prophecy Study Bible***; 2000 by AMG Publishers; Chart on "The Sacrifices of Israel" by Arnold Fruchtenbaum, p. 123

- ***Chronological and Background Charts of the Old Testament*** by John H. Walton; 1978, 1994; Zondervan Publishers; Chart on Sacrificial System, p. 22

❒ **Week 8**

Lesson 8.1

1. References for Chart - "The Four Blood Sacrifices in the Old Testament", reprinted by permission, New Life Community Church, Feb 20, 2008

Lesson 8.2

2. References:

- ***None of These Diseases: The Bible's Health Secrets for the 21st Century***, by S.I. McMillen, M.D. and David E. Stern, M.D. ; Millennimum Three Edition; 1963, 1984, 2005 fifth printing; Published by Feliming H. Revell

- ***The Maker's Diet: The 40-day health experience that will change your life forever***, by Jordan S. Rubin; 2004; The Berkley Publishing Group

Lesson 8.7

3. Chart – "Feasts & Holidays of the Bible" and "Jewish Feasts & Holidays" – ***Rose Book of Bible Maps, Charts and Time Lines***, by Rose Publishing, Inc., p. 58–62

❒ Week 9

Lesson 9.2, Lesson 9.3

1. "The Encampment", "Levites' Ministry", and "The Tribe of Levi (The Consecrated Tribe)", "The Levite Camp" by Rusty Russell; 1998 ***The Bible Knowledge Accelerator***, reprinted by general permission granted to all, (biblehistory.com, 2007)

Lesson 9.4

2. Reference for further background reading on the prayer of blessing's meaning:

- **A Taste of Torah in Honor of Shabbat,** by Rabbi Avi Weiss; Parashat Naso – June 5-6, 1998. Sivan 12, 5758; Shabbat Forshpeis; © 5758/1998. All rights reserved. Rabbi Avi Weiss, Hebrew Institute o Riverdale

3. Bible Tidbits: The Trumpet Sound

- Richard Aaron Honorof, ***Biblical Uses of Jewish Trumpets (Shofars and Silver Trumpets),*** © 2002, revised © 2005,

- Richard Aaron Honorof, ***The Mystery of the Shofar of God!,*** © 11/98, updated © May/2004,

- Rick Kurnow, The Biblical Use of The Shofar, © 2005,

- Dominick Zangla, ***The Shofar (Ram's Horn)***, Teaching Article of Prepare the Way Ministries

❑ Week 10

Lesson 10.1

1. Reference: ***The Red Heifer*** by Rabbi Chaim Richman with picture of Red Heifer; (templemount.org; July 7, 1997, July 10, 1997. July 7, 1998)

Lesson 10.2

2. Numbers 24:17 – 19 – References

– Alfred Edersheim, ***Appendix 9, The Life and Times of Jesus the Messiah,*** p. 984

– Sol Scharfstein, ***Torah and Commentary***, p. 404

Lesson 10.3

3. Rachmiel Frydland, ***What the Rabbis Know About the Messiah,*** Chapter 6

Lesson 10.4

4. ***The Christian Meaning of the Jewish Feasts***, David R. Reagan of LambLionMinistries, Home of Christ in Prophecy; Copyright MMVI; (lamblion.org , 2007), image reprinted by permission of David R. Reagan

Lesson 10.7

5. Map – "Holy Land: Then – Twelve Tribes"; ***Rose Book of Bible Maps, Charts and Time Lines***, by Rose Publishing, Inc., p. 128
6. Table 3-1 reprinted by permission from the book, ***Now is the Time for God's Children to be Filled with His Holy Spirit*** by Jennifer Price, 1998; republished as "Now is the Time for God's Children to Know His Spirit" (Know His Spirit Workbook), 2008

❑ Week 11

Lesson 11.1

1. Alfred Edersheim, ***Bible History*** – Old Testament, 339

Lesson 11.3

2. "Shema Yisrael" article by Rabbi Shraga Simmons, linked from Jewish Literacy Homepage (aish.com, 2007), Site contents copyright © 1995 - 2007 Aish HaTorah

The Path You Should Walk

1. Richard Bank, ***The Everything Judaism Book*** (Avon, MA, Adams Media Publications, 2002), Chapter 6, Living in Accordance with the Law
2. ***But, Didn't Jesus Abolish the Law and Those 613 Original Commandments***, reprinted by permission of The Refiner's Fire, Sep 2007, (therefinersfire.org)
3. Dr. K. Daniel Fried, ***Hebrew –English New Covenant***, Page 9–10

❑ Week 12

Lesson 12.1

1. Derek Prince, ***"Blessing or Curse – You Can Choose: Freedom from Pressures You Thought You Had to Live With***" (Grand Rapids, MI: Chosen Books, a division of Baker Book House Company, 1990)
2. "The Extermination of the Canaanites," excerpt reprinted by permission, Paul N. Benware, ***Survey of the Old Testament: The Essential Bible***, p. 89-90

❑ The Kingdom of God and the Role of the Servant of God in Establishing It

1. Alfred Edersheim, excerpt from Lecture II, ***Prophecy and History in Relation to the Messiah,*** pages 44 - 46

III. Art Credits

- ❒ **Public Domain Religious Clip Art: Breadsite.org**

  - **Page #'s**: 7-19, 7-22

- ❒ **World Missions Collection Clip Art Graphics**
  Thanks to the World Missions Collection Clip Art Graphics for granting me permission to use clip art from their Volume 1 and Volume 2 collections and providing the high-quality digital images to use in this work.

  - **Page #'s** : 1-6, 1-11, 1-15, 1-23, 1-28, 2-11, 2-15, 2-24, 3-3, 5-24, 6-4, 6-13, 6-25, 7-9, Tab-3, Tab-12, 10-5, 12-16

- ❒ **The Bible in Pictures**
  Thanks to the Administrator of the creationism.org Website for making the Bible in Pictures and Dore' Bible Illustrations woodcut drawings available to the general public, and for providing high quality digital images for use in this work.

  - **Page #'s**: 9-24, 10-7, 11-16, 12-23, 12-24

The daily reading assignments in ***Know His Word Bible Study*** correlate to the organization of the daily scripture readings in the ***New Living Translation One-Year Chronological Bible.*** This chart correlates the lessons in this Bible Study to the dates of the year in that Bible.

Bible Study	Lesson Numbers	One-Year Chronological Bible Date
	1st Quarter	
• Week 1	Lessons 1.1–1.7	January 1–January 7
• Week 2	Lessons 2.1–2.7	January 8–January 14
• Week 3	Lessons 3.1–3.7	January 15–January 21
• Week 4	Lessons 4.1–4.7	January 22–January 28
• Week 5	Lessons 5.1–5.7	January 29–February 4
• Week 6	Lessons 6.1–6.7	February 5–February 11
• Week 7	Lessons 7.1–7.7	February 12–February 18
• Week 8	Lessons 8.1–8.7	February 19–February 25
• Week 9	Lessons 9.1–9.7	February 26–March 4
• Week 10	Lessons 10.1–10.7	March 5–March 11
• Week 11	Lessons 11.1–11.7	March 12–March 18
• Week 12	Lessons 12.1–12.7	March 19–March 25
	2nd Quarter	
• Week 13	Lessons 13.1–13.7	March 26–April 1
• Week 14	Lessons 14.1–14.7	April 2–April 8
• Week 15	Lessons 15.1–15.7	April 9–April 15
• Week 16	Lessons 16.1–16.7	April 16–April 22
• Week 17	Lessons 17.1–17.7	April 23–April 29
• Week 18	Lessons 18.1–18.7	April 30–May 6
• Week 19	Lessons 19.1–19.7	May 7–May 13
• Week 20	Lessons 20.1–20.7	May 14–May 20
• Week 21	Lessons 21.1–21.7	May 21–May 27
• Week 22	Lessons 22.1–22.7	May 28–June 3
• Week 23	Lessons 23.1–23.7	June 4–June 10
• Week 24	Lessons 24.1–24.7	June 11–June 17
• Week 25	Lessons 25.1–25.7	June 18–June 24

3rd Quarter

- Week 26 Lessons 26.1–26.7 June 25–July 1
- Week 27 Lessons 27.1–27.7 July 2–July 8
- Week 28 Lessons 28.1–28.7 July 9–July 15
- Week 29 Lessons 29.1–29.7 July 16–July 22
- Week 30 Lessons 30.1–30.7 July 23–July 29
- Week 31 Lessons 31.1–31.7 July 30–August 5
- Week 32 Lessons 32.1–32.7 August 6–August 12
- Week 33 Lessons 33.1–33.7 August 13–August 19
- Week 34 Lessons 34.1–34.7 August 20–August 26
- Week 35 Lessons 35.1–35.7 August 27–September 2
- Week 36 Lessons 36.1–36.7 September 3–September 9
- Week 37 Lessons 37.1–37.7 September 10–September 16
- Week 38 Lessons 38.1–38.7 September 17–September 23

4th Quarter

- Week 39 Lessons 39.1–39.7 September 24–September 30
- Week 40 Lessons 40.1–40.7 October 1–October 7
- Week 41 Lessons 41.1–41.7 October 8–October 14
- Week 42 Lessons 42.1–42.7 October 15–October 21
- Week 43 Lessons 43.1–43.7 October 22–October 28
- Week 44 Lessons 44.1–44.7 October 29–November 4
- Week 45 Lessons 45.1–45.7 November 5–November 11
- Week 46 Lessons 46.1–46.7 November 12–November 18
- Week 47 Lessons 47.1–47.7 November 19–November 25
- Week 48 Lessons 48.1–48.7 November 26–December 2
- Week 49 Lessons 49.1–49.7 December 3–December 9
- Week 50 Lessons 50.1–50.7 December 10–December 16
- Week 51 Lessons 51.1–51.7 December 17–December 23
- Week 52 Lessons 52.1–52.8 December 24–December 31

Appendix E: Daily Reading Study Guide

Week 1		
Lesson	Scriptures	Page
1.1	Gen 1:1 – 3:24	1-5 –1-8
1.2	Gen 4:1-5:32; 1 Chron 1:1-4; Gen 6:1-22	1-9 – 1-11
1.3	Gen 7:1 – 10:5; 1 Chron 1:5-7; Gen 10:6-20; 1 Chron 1:8-16; Gen 10:21-30; 1 Chron 1:17-23; Gen 10:31-32	1-12 – 1-14
1.4	Gen 11:1-26; 1 Chron 1:24-27; Gen 11:27 – 14:24	1-15– 1-17
1.5	Gen 15:1 – 17:27	1-18– 1-20
1.6	Gen 18:1 – 21:7	1-22– 1-25
1.7	Gen 21:8 – 23:20; Gen 11:32; Gen 24:1-67	1-26– 1-28

Week 2		
Lesson	Scriptures	Page
2.1	Gen 25:1-4; 1 Chron 1:32-33; Gen 25:5-6, 12-18; 1 Chron 1:28-31, 34; Gen 25:19-26, 7-11	2-3– 2-5
2.2	Gen 25:27 – 28:5	2-8– 2-10
2.3	Gen 28:6 – 30:24	2-11– 2-13
2.4	Gen 30:25 – 31:55	2-14– 2-16
2.5	Gen 32:1 – 35:27	2-18 –2-20
2.6	Gen 36:1-19; 1 Chron 1:35-37; Gen 36:20-30; 1 Chron 1:38 – 42; Gen 36:31-43; 1 Chron 1:43 – 2:2	2-21– 2-22
2.7	Gen 37:1 – 38:30; 1 Chron 2:3-6, 8; Gen 39:1-23	2-24– 2-26

Week 3		
Lesson	Scriptures	Page
3.1	Gen 40:1-23; Gen 35:28-29; Gen 41:1-57	3-3 – 3-5
3.2	Gen 42:1 – 45:15	3-6 – 3-8
3.3	Gen 45:16 – 47:27	3-9
3.4	Gen 47:28 – 50:26	3-11– 3-13
3.5	Job 1:1 – 4:21	3-16 –3-18
3.6	Job 5:1 – 7:21	3-19– 3-20
3.7	Job 8:1 – 11:20	3-21– 3-22

Appendix E: Daily Reading Study Guide

Week 4		
Lesson	Scriptures	Page
4.1	Job 12:1 – 14:22	4-3 – 4-5
4.2	Job 15:1 – 18:21	4-6 – 4-8
4.3	Job 19:1 – 21:34	4-9
4.4	Job 22:1 – 25:6	4-10 – 4-11
4.5	Job 26:1 – 29:25	4-12 – 4-14
4.6	Job 30:1 -31:40	4-15 – 4-16
4.7	Job 32:1 – 34:37	4-17 – 4-18

Week 5		
Lesson	Scriptures	Page
5.1	Job 35:1 – 37:24	5-3
5.2	Job 38:1 – 40:5	5-4
5.3	Job 40:6 – 42:17	5-5 – 5-6
5.4	Exodus 1:1 – 2:25; 1 Chron 6:1 – 3a; Exodus 3:1 – 4:17	5-14 – 5-16
5.5	Exodus 4:18 – 7:13	5-17 – 5-20
5.6	Exodus 7:14 – 9:35	5-24 – 5-25
5.7	Exodus 10:1 – 12:51	5-26

Week 6		
Lesson	Scriptures	Page
6.1	Exodus 13:1 – 15:27	6-3 – 6-5
6.2	Exodus 16:1 – 19:25	6-6 – 6-7
6.3	Exodus 20:1 – 22:15	6-11 – 6-14
6.4	Exodus 22:16 – 24:18	6-15 – 6-17
6.5	Exodus 25:1 – 28:43	6-18 – 6-21
6.6	Exodus 29:1 – 31:18	6-22 – 6-23
6.7	Exodus 32:1 – 34:35	6-24 – 6-26

Week 7		
Lesson	Scriptures	Page
7.1	Exodus 35:1 – 36:38	7-3
7.2	Exodus 37:1 – 39:31	7-4 – 7-8
7.3	Exodus 39:32 – 40:38; Numbers 9:15-23	7-9 – 7-10
7.4	Numbers 7:1-89	7-11 – 7-12
7.5	Numbers 8:1 – 9:14; Leviticus 1:1 – 3:17	7-16
7.6	Leviticus 4:1 – 6:30	7-17 – 7-18
7.7	Leviticus 7:1 – 8:36	7-20 - 7-28

Week 8		
Lesson	Scriptures	Page
8.1	Leviticus 9:1 – 11:47	8-3 – 8-5
8.2	Leviticus 12:1 – 14:32	8-9 – 8-11
8.3	Leviticus 14:33 – 16:34	8-12 – 8-14
8.4	Leviticus 17:1 – 19:37	8-15 – 8-17
8.5	Leviticus 20:1 – 22:33	8-18 – 8-19
8.6	Leviticus 23:1 – 25:23	8-20
8.7	Leviticus 25:24 – 26:46	8-21

Week 9		
Lesson	Scriptures	Page
9.1	Leviticus 27:1 – 34; Numbers 1:1-54	9-6 – 9-8
9.2	Numbers 2:1 – 3:51	9-9 – 9-10
9.3	Numbers 4:1 – 5:31	9-11 – 9-13
9.4	Numbers 6:1-27, Numbers 10:1–36	9-14 – 9-16
9.5	Numbers 11:1 – 13:33	9-17 – 9-19
9.6	Numbers 14:1 – 15:41	9-20 – 9-21
9.7	Numbers 16:1 – 18:32	9-22 – 9-23

Appendix E: Daily Reading Study Guide

Week 10		
Lesson	Scriptures	Page
10.1	Numbers 19:1 – 21:35	10-3 – 10-5
10.2	Numbers 22:1 – 24:25	10-6 – 10-7
10.3	Numbers 25:1 – 26:65	10-8
10.4	Numbers 27:1 – 29:40	10-9 – 10-11
10.5	Numbers 30:1 – 31:54	10-12 – 10-14
10.6	Numbers 32:1 – 33:56	10-15
10.7	Numbers 34:1 – 36:13	10-16 – 10-18

Week 11		
Lesson	Scriptures	Page
11.1	Deuteronomy 1:1 – 3:20	11-5 – 11-7
11.2	Deuteronomy 3:21 – 5:33	11-8
11.3	Deut 6:1 – 9:29	11-9 – 11-11
11.4	Deut 10:1 – 12:32	11-12 – 11-13
11.5	Deut 13:1 – 16:17	11-14 – 11-15
11.6	Deut 16:18 – 21:9	
11.7	Deut 21:10 – 25:19	

Week 12		
Lesson	Scriptures	Page
12.1	Deut 26:1 – 29:1	12-3 – 12-5
12.2	Deut 29:2 – 31:29	12-6 – 12-7
12.3	Deut 31:30 – 32:52; Psalm 90	12-8 – 12-9
12.4	Deut 33:1 – 34:12, Joshua 1:1 – 2:24	12-10 – 12-11
12.5	Joshua 3:1 – 6:27	12-15 – 12-16
12.6	Joshua 7:1; 1 Chronicles 2:7; Joshua 7:2 – 9:27	12-17 – 12-18
12.7	Joshua 10:1 – 12:6	12-21 – 12-22

Appendix F: Scripture Index Table

This index table identifies where the daily study lessons for all Bible scriptures are located in each of the Bible Study Quarters. If a Bible book's scriptures are all or mostly covered within the same Quarter, then the book is listed as a whole. If some passages from a Bible book are in a different Quarter from the rest of the book, then the individual passages are listed under the applicable quarter, with the parenthesis also identifying the day of year.

Although an entire book's contents may be studied in one quarter, the scriptures are not always presented in sequential order because they are studied in chronological order. You can find the day each scripture is studied by looking at each quarter's Daily Reading Study Guide, which precedes this table.

1st Quarter	2nd Quarter	3rd Quarter	4th Quarter
Genesis	Joshua 12:7–24:33 (Week 13)	Remaining 2 Kings	Entire New Testament
Job	Judges	2 Chronicles 28:16–36:23	
Exodus	Ruth	Isaiah 1–5; 12–66	
Leviticus	1 Samuel	Jeremiah	
Numbers	2 Samuel	Hosea	
Deuteronomy	1 Kings	Micah	
1 Chron. 1:1–4 (Week 1)	1 Chron. 6:54–81 (Week 13)	Proverbs 25–31	
1 Chron. 1:5—23 (Week 1)	1 Chron. 2:9–55 and 4:1–23 (Week 14)	Remaining Psalms	
1 Chron. 1:24–27 (Week 1)	1 Chron. 9:35–39 (Week 15)	Nahum	
1 Chron. 28–34 (Week 2)	Psalm 59 (Week 15)	Habakkuk	
1 Chron. 1:35–2:2 (Week 2)	Psalm 34 (Week 15)	Zephaniah	
1 Chron. 2:3–6, 8 (Week 2)	Psalms 57, 142, 52 (Week 16)	Daniel	
1 Chron. 6:1–3a (Week 5)	Psalm 54 (Week 16)	Ezekiel	
Psalm 90 (Week 12)	1 Chron. 12:1–7, 19; Psalm 56 (Week 16)	Lamentations	
Joshua 1–12:6 (Week 12)	1 Chron.12:20–22 and 10:1–14 and 9:40–44 (Week 16)	Obadiah	
1 Chronicles 2:7 (Week 12)	1 Chron. 3:1–4a and 11:10–47 (Week 16)	Ezra	
	1 Chron. 11 – 19 (Weeks 16 and 17)	Haggai	

Appendix F: Scripture Index Table

1st Quarter	2nd Quarter cont'd	3rd Quarter cont'd	4th Quarter
	Psalm 51; 1 Chronicles 20:1 and 14:3–7 and 3:5–9 (Week 17)	Zechariah	Entire New Testament
	1 Chronicles 20:2–3 (Week 17)	Esther	
	Psalms 3 and 63 (Week 17)	Nehemiah	
	Psalm 7; 1 Chronicles 20:4–8 (Week 18)	Malachi	
	Psalm 18 (Week 18)	Joel	
	1 Chronicles 21–29 (Week 18)		
	Psalms 4–6, 8–9, and 11 (Week 18)		
	Psalms 12–17; 19–21 (Week 19)		
	Psalms 22–32 (Week 19)		
	Psalms 35–41, 53, 55, 58 (Week 19)		
	Psalms 61–62, 64–67 (Week 19)		
	Psalms 68–70, 86, 101 (Week 19)		
	Psalms 103, 108–110, 122, 124 (Week 20)		
	Psalms 131, 133, 138–141, 143 (Week 20)		
	Psalms 144–145, Psalms 88–89 (Week 20)		
	Psalms 50, 73–73 (Weel 20)		
	Psalms 75–78 (Week 20)		
	Psalms 79–82 (Week 20)		
	Psalms 72, 127 (Week 21)		
	2 Chron. 2–28:15 (Week 21–Week 25)		
	Proverbs 1–24 (Week 21–Week 22)		
	Song of Songs (Song of Solomon)		
	Ecclesiastes		
	Jonah		
	Amos		
	2 Kings 1–16:9 (Week 24-Week 25)		
	Micah 1:1-16, Isaiah 6–11 (Week 25)		

Jennifer B. Price is the Ministry Head of KnowBibleStudies

Find out more:

www.knowbiblestudies.com ; youtube.com/@KnowBibleStudies

All of Jennifer's works are designed with youth and adults in mind to inspire all ages to take a fresh look at God's Word.

Find direct links to her works on the website:

- Know Bible Studies book series
- Holy Writ Tales book series
- Bible Story Drama Videos
- Featured Music
- Promo Videos

Know His Word Bible Study is organized into four "Quarter" books designed to provide an inductive study of the entire Bible in the chronological order events occurred. Therefore, the books are not always studied in the same order as the traditional Bible books layout. Each Quarter book contains most of the daily study lessons for the Bible books as listed below. However, some passages from a Bible book may be found in a different Quarter book.

Consult **Appendix F: Scripture Index Table** for details on where all the scriptures can be found. **Know His Word Bible Study**—

1st Quarter:

Genesis, Job, Exodus, Leviticus, Numbers, Deuteronomy, Half of Joshua

2nd Quarter:

End of Joshua, Judges, Ruth, 1 and 2 Samuel, 1 Chronicles, Psalms, 1 Kings, Proverbs, Song of Songs, Ecclesiastes, 2 Chronicles, 2 Kings, Jonah, Amos (small portion of Isaiah & Micah)

3rd Quarter:

Hosea, Isaiah, Micah, Jeremiah, Nahum, Habakkuk, Zephaniah, Ezekiel, Lamentations, Obadiah, Daniel, Ezra, Haggai, Zechariah, Esther, Nehemiah, Malachi, Joel

4th Quarter:

Intertestamental History and New Testament

www.ingramcontent.com/pod-product-compliance
Lightning Source LLC
Chambersburg PA
CBHW082006140626
46553CB00020B/2432

* 9 7 9 8 8 9 3 9 1 0 2 4 7 *